Economics, Ethics and Power

Economic theory in its neoclassical form is sometimes regarded as free from values; it is simply the theory of economic exchange. This can only hold true if we accept the idea of "Homo Economicus" and the equilibrium economy. But in the real world, away from neoclassical models, there is no intrinsic stability as such. Instead, stability is created by the surrounding social, cultural and political structures. Clearly, it is imperative that ethics features in the analysis of these economic and socio-political structures.

Drawing on Aristotle, Kant, Hume and others, this book conceptualizes the analysis of ethics and economic and social structures. It first considers the key philosophical underpinnings and categories which frame the discussion of ethics in economic theory and then considers individual ethics, social action, financial structures and war. Throughout, ethics are examined in a multicultural context with structural complexities, and the difficulties in finding a coherent set of ethics which provides social cohesion and an open society are considered. A key part of this is the comparison of two ethical principles which can be adopted by societies: *ius soli* or loyalty to constitution, and *ius sanguinis* or loyalty to "Blood and Soil". The latter is argued to lead to problems of Us and the Other.

Introducing the possibility of integrating microscopic ethics into socio-political structures and proposing the eventual existence of a global ethics, this volume is a significant contribution to the emerging literature on economics, social structures and ethics. It will be of particular interest to those working in business and public administration and who have an education in socio-economic areas, but it also has a broad appeal to students and academics in the social sciences.

Hasse Ekstedt is a Senior Researcher at the School of Public Administration at the University of Gothenburg, Sweden.

Routledge Frontiers of Political Economy

For a full list of titles in this series, please visit www.routledge.com/books/series/SE0345

Economics, Ethics and Power

From Behavioural Rules to Global Structures

Hasse Ekstedt

Routledge
Taylor & Francis Group

LONDON AND NEW YORK

First published 2019
by Routledge
2 Park Square, Milton Park, Abingdon, Oxon OX14 4RN

and by Routledge
52 Vanderbilt Avenue, New York, NY 10017

First issued in paperback 2020

Routledge is an imprint of the Taylor & Francis Group, an informa business

© 2019 Hasse Ekstedt

The right of Hasse Ekstedt to be identified as author of this work has been
asserted by him in accordance with sections 77 and 78 of the Copyright,
Designs and Patents Act 1988.

British Library Cataloguing-in-Publication Data
A catalogue record for this book is available from the British Library

Library of Congress Cataloging-in-Publication Data
Names: Ekstedt, Hasse, author.
Title: Economics, ethics and power : from behavioural rules to global
    structures / Hasse Ekstedt.
Description: Abingdon, Oxon; New York, NY : Routledge, 2019. | Series:
    Routledge frontiers of political economy | Includes bibliographical
    references and index.
Identifiers: LCCN 2018013215 (print) | LCCN 2018013627 (ebook) |

    ISBN 9781315271392 (Ebook) | ISBN 9781138281028
    (hardback : alk. paper)
Subjects: LCSH: Economics—Moral and ethical aspects. | Economics—
    Political aspects.
Classification: LCC HB72 (ebook) | LCC HB72 .E425 2019 (print) |
    DDC 174/.4—dc23
LC record available at https://lccn.loc.gov/2018013215

ISBN 13: 978-0-367-58877-9 (pbk)
ISBN 13: 978-1-138-28102-8 (hbk)

Typeset in Bembo
by Apex CoVantage, LLC

Contents

Illustrations

Figures

Pictures

Diagrams

Tables

Acknowledgements

Much of this book has its origin in more general conversations about recent problems that have had a large impact on the world. It has not so much been a matter of seminars and that kind of activities; it has more been quiet talks over a glass of wine. Of course, I must as in earlier books pay my deep respect to my teacher and very good friend, the late Professor Lars Westberg. He was never under the illusion that the social sciences could be separated more than occasionally, and he realized also that human beings are part of physics; so, as does Aristotle, he could write both of physics and the soul.

In Lund I had a very inspiring conversation with Professor Johan Asplund quite some years ago, but together with his writings, it has meant much to me.

I am also very grateful to Professor Björn Rombach, at the School of Public Administration, for good discussions on Kant in general and particularly Kant's paper *"Beantworten der Frage: Was ist Aufklärung?"*, which appears in Chapter 4. Since I read the German original, I discovered differences in different English translations. Björn, who is bilingual in Swedish and German, helped me solve the linguistic fox traps.

I also participate every year in the International Conference on Developments in Economic Theory and Policy in Bilbao, Spain. These conferences are excellent with respect to both intellectual standards and social standards. There is a conscious ambition among the organizing group to contrast perspectives and to introduce new ones. I have presented some parts of this book in the two latest conferences and received very fruitful discussions and good suggestions.

Most important, however, has been my family. In particular, I have discussed many things in this book with my daughter, Dr. Anna Ekstedt, who works as a psychiatrist for children and adolescents, and we have had many discussions about the problem of intellect and emotion and to what extent humans are rational. She has provided me with background material of great value.

Most of all, my beloved wife, Barbro Ekstedt, former interpreter at the European Council, has supported me by reading outlines of ideas, checking my logic as well as my language, and helping me in conceptualizations of aspects which have been strange.

Introduction

"What is truth?"[1]

"What then is truth?" – From Pilate came the question:
Echo replied: From those sealed lips came forth
No word; but with the answer to the Riddle
The Nazarene went down beneath the earth.

But, God be praised, we have with us professors
To whom all knowledge of the truth is clear;
Legion their name – so many are their answers
Have reached by now the doubting Roman's ear.

Strange, though, that Truth, the one and undivided,
So marvellously doth vary hue and shape,
That what is truth in Berlin or in Jena
at Heidelberg is but an idle jape.

It reminds me of Prince Hamlet and Polonious,
And that chameleon cloud – you know the tale;
"Do you see yonder cloud so like a weasel?
– So like a camel? – Very like a whale!"

It is 20 December 2017. I am looking out of the window; the day is indeed gloomy. I happened to read during my morning coffee an article from *The Guardian* a couple of days ago (Sunday, the 17th), which I saved. It was about the linguistic cleaning in the US health system ordered by the current president of the USA. *The Guardian* referred to a report published in *The Washington Post* on the 15th. The top leaders of the US public health agency, the Centers for Disease Control and Prevention, were told not to use seven specific English words in public documents: *diversity, entitlement, fetus, transgender, vulnerable, evidence-based,* and *science-based.* After I read the article, the day turned definitively and most probably irrevocably gloomy.

I went to my bookshelf and looked for a book written by Victor Klemperer in 1946. It was first published in 1957, under the title *Lingua Tertii Imperii: A Philologist Notebook*, and was translated to English in 2000, with the title *The Language of the Third Reich.*

I read in the introduction (p. 2):

> And this too will be the fate of that most serious and decisive of words of our own epoch of transition: one day the word *Entnazifizierung* will have faded away because the situation it was intended to end will no longer exist.
>
> But that won't be for some time yet, because it isn't only Nazi actions that have to vanish, but also the Nazi cast of mind, the typical Nazi way of thinking and its breeding ground: the language of Nazism.

A bit further in the book (pp. 13–14), Klemperer discusses Nazi propaganda and the powerful speeches of Hitler and Goebbels and their influence, but he concludes:

> No, the most powerful influence was exerted neither by individual speeches nor by articles and flyers, posters and flags; it was not achieved by things which one had to absorb by conscious thought or conscious emotions.
>
> Instead Nazism permeated the flesh and blood of the people through single words, idioms and sentence structures which were imposed on them in a million repetitions and taken on board mechanically and unconsciously.
> . . .
>
> But language does not simply write and think for me, it also increasingly dictates my feelings and governs my entire spiritual being the more unquestioningly and unconsciously I abandon myself to it. And what happens if the cultivated language is made up of poisonous elements or has been made the bearer of poisons?

Thus, when the central power starts to change the language either by preferring words or abandoning words, we can draw two conclusions: first, that the central power is in for a very deep-going structural change of the ruling culture, and second, that the systematic changing of words is not an occasional whim but a thoroughly premeditated action.

This is a book on ethics in relation to individuals and macroscopic structures, so why bother about language? Why not tell how to behave as an ethical creature? There is a huge variety of courses and consultants to explain how to apply ethics to different areas. Many of them are probably valuable and some are probably of less value. We have, however, no intention to discuss practical applications of a concept called *ethics*, which appears to be a basic concept to social life and consequently of the highest possible complexity. Aristotle treats it as a basic tool to reach the highest good for the individual as for the society. A course on ethics may need to be lifelong in order to cover some of the more essential aspects of ethics.

Thus, ethics concerns every single aspect of human life, both for individuals and for social creatures affecting the collective structures. It is not something we learn but something we live. Therefore, we also have to analyze different structures affecting our lives and setting the boundaries of our behaviour. It also concerns the difficult question of how the interrelation between microscopic levels and macroscopic structures are created and developed. Since language is the prime means of communication among individuals and between individuals and collective bodies, language is certainly as important from an ethical point of view as actions. But what happens, then, with the freedom to express oneself in a democracy? Another good question is from the poem by Gustav Fröding that began this introduction: What is Truth? If we should have some sort of ethical standard, it is indeed practical to ask that question.

Currently we are in the middle of the worldwide #MeToo movement against sexual harassment, which has had a particular impact in Western Europe and the USA. The movement started in the US with the revelation that a powerful film producer was using his power to force women to submit to his sexual desires. In Sweden it has had an enormous effect and shaken the most prestigious institution in the country, the Swedish Academy, which selects the Laureates for the Nobel Prize in Literature. The #MeToo movement has not only shaken society with respect to sexual harassment; it has also been enlarged to other kinds of abuse of formal power in order to force other people to submit to private pleasures or inappropriate professional behaviour. From an ethical point of view, the campaign should be unnecessary, since the behaviour it focuses on is not any form of acceptable behaviour in Europe or the USA. That also explains why the effects have become so strong, why people in powerful positions in each society have resigned and some organizations have run into a state of confusion regarding what is going on. The campaign has occurred within ethical areas where codes of behaviour have been pretty clear and consequently the breaking of these codes are regarded as completely inappropriate by most people brought up in Western civilization.

The ethics of a society are a mixture of explicit and implicit rules of behaviour. Aristotle defined ethics as a form of tool to achieve the highest good, since no individual in a society can achieve the highest good for himself without the assistance of other members of the society. This implies that human beings are not to be regarded as independent atoms, which is at variance with the neoclassical foundations of economic theory; rather, they need collectively accepted rules of behaviour, some codified and some implicit, both belonging to an ethical superstructure which is an integral part of culturally dependent socialization.

In this book, we will not analyze the different contents of ethical systems but rather discuss the structures and particularly structural conflicts intrinsic to any form of ethical system or between different forms of ethical systems. An example of intrinsic conflicts are the two bases of any ethical system, the principle of "thou shalt" and "thou shalt not", where we will have conflicts between doing good to other people even if we break the law. This was actually raised to the highest level during the Nuremberg trials after WWII, when people were sentenced to death because they obeyed the explicit and/or implicit wishes of Hitler. Their defence was that if they had not obeyed, they would have been killed, but that was not a relevant enough defence. We have many examples of clashes between conscious human considerations and explicit law. Later in the book, we will discuss two important events: Kant's small paper from 1784 on "*Beantworten der Frage: Was ist Aufklärung?*", and Herodotus' summary of a discussion of different forms of government from 486 BC, which exactly analyze this problem from different views.

With respect to clashes between ethical systems, we will discuss the classical problem of *Fides Punica* initiated by Romans, first in relation to Carthage, then to all societies not aligning to the principles of Roman culture and laws. This is the problem of the Other and is of utmost importance in a globalized world.

Two fundamental concepts with respect to ethics are power and war. The power structure of a society fundamentally affects the ethical structure, and consequently, we have the problem of how to judge between ethical approaches or systems. The American political scientist Robert Kaplan wrote a book on intrinsic ethics and ethics towards the environment, where the survival of the intrinsic ethics of a society, in his case the USA, considered a pagan ethos suitable in relation to the rest of the world necessary. We will compare and partly contrast this view with the approach by Carl von Clausewitz with respect to war as the continuation of politics by other means. War is the ultimate violence between two countries, but what happens if the concept of a nation loses its relevance and is replaced by other lines of demarcation? Clausewitz presumed that the continuation of politics into war by other means was followed by a reversal movement back to politics. Will such reversibility be possible?

From a scientific point of view, we may ask if it is possible to give a precise definition of the concept of ethics. Unfortunately, we have to answer: probably not.

That is due to the intrinsic contradictions of the concept which are implicit in the distinction between the principles "thou shalt" and "thou shalt not".

However, not to be totally bewildered, we can continue Aristotle's thoughts on humans as subjects and local and temporal final causes: *A necessary, but most probably not a sufficient, condition for an ethical principle is that all humans must be regarded as subjects and thus a final cause.*

Consequently, we expect as human beings that our free will is somehow recognized.

For those who have the opinion that free will does not exist, I would expect a refutation of our basic principle without assuming that any human being has better contacts with some sort of god than other human beings do. Or, to use George Orwell's words in *Animal Farm*: "All animals are equal, but some animals are more equal than others". Thus ethics as well as causality, alluding to Hume's distinctions, contradicts determinism, the need for ethical behaviour to appear as some form of ordering life in an uncertain environment, where the human being is the main source of uncertainty. It is, given that the humans are subjects and thus final causes.

Although the general principle is probably incomplete, since it is basically an abstract formulation of a part of "thou shalt not", it is of such a generality that it comprises both physical and mental assault, which should ideally be regarded as equally serious.

Going back to the #MeToo movement, a significant feature is that those who are exposed to sexual harassment explicitly or implicitly tell us about their feelings of being utilized as sheer objects for the perpetrators' own pleasure; thus they have been denied their humanity. The physical harassment per se implied also a mental assault.

We will discuss the principle of subordination, and there are three principles which we particularly want to investigate. The first one is, as mentioned above, "King by the Providence of God". It may take several forms, such as "To the ones who are given responsibility, God will also give wisdom", which indicates that responsibility fosters particular wisdom per se. Another variant is "Those who succeed in the competition of the highest posts of the society are also those who are the most fitted".

The second principle is a bit more difficult to analyze and that is claimed by Adam Smith, that the degree of subordination increases when private and common wealth increases.

The third principle is pursued by Otanes, one of the Persians in Herodotus' debate discussing different forms of government in 486 BC. Otanes preferred democracy since all men in a democracy were equal and thus open to information; anybody and everybody could control the rulers. Consequently, democracy was the only system where control of the rulers was held by those who were ruled. Kant's paper from 1784 could be seen as some type of necessary individual characteristics which must be present in order to fulfil Otanes' condition.

This book is written from an economic perspective. Ethics per se belongs to philosophy, but the economic perspective is generally important and of specific methodological interest.

The basic codified economic theory, the neoclassical theory, is void of any needs of ethical complements. It is strictly deterministic. We can see some parallel to Kant's categorical imperative, yet the parallel is illusive since the neoclassical general equilibrium theory is based on pure mathematical axioms, which might be subject to bold interpretations. The parallel helps us illuminate the character of Kant's imperative.

The axiomatic structure of the neoclassical theory has, however, provoked an interesting paradox, Arrow's Impossibility Theorem. It is not particularly remarkable as a logical paradox, as we will explain later, but it is interesting since economic scientists and many political scientists have interpreted it as having something to do with reality, which logical paradoxes never have. It deals with the very axiomatic structure and its limitations, often with the problem of interpreting complex variables to atomic variables and vice versa. But the lack of understanding of its nature shows the difference between intra-axiomatic explanations and axiomatic analysis per se from an exogenous perspective, as such a good illustration of Gödel's Incompleteness Theorem.

However, the economic perspective also enforces structures on different aggregate levels seemingly separate from other social structures. The economic structures are sometimes fairly consonant to social, political and cultural structures and sometimes clearly at variance. Consequently, the economic perspective lays bare contradictive ethical structures in space-time.

As seen from the preceding, we deal with structures a great deal. There is a methodological movement called structuralism; without explaining the concept further, we can say that this book has nothing to do with structuralism per se. Already, the approach that humans are subjects and thus final causes excludes structuralism, to my understanding. The reason why we focus a bit on structures of different kinds is actually our economic theoretical viewpoint. The neoclassical axioms transform agents and commodities to atomic variables and thus empty them of all content; this is, by the way, the same as Kant does when he defines the concept "Das Ding an Sich", which we will carefully discuss later. This implies formally from a mathematical or logical point of view that variables are transformed to equivalents of numbers. Unfortunately, this implies that when we make a logical or mathematical analysis, we have to translate variables from a context-dependent meaning to an atomic variable empty of any meaning except its name. This is basically why some logical paradoxes appear, among them Arrow's paradox, when the variables are used without a precise definition. We will discuss this more principally. Obviously, this is also the basis for Gödel's paradox, where the ultimate interpretation is that logic or mathematics per se has no empirical meaning whatsoever.

Ethics as a concept for scientific study is not an empirical subject such as natural or social sciences and history; it is more like anthropology, where we study faith, social norm systems, cultural patterns and their effects on behaviour and furthermore their aggregate superstructures. A natural question, then, is what happens when we have clashes between different structures. At any rate, we have to start with the question of how humans regard themselves and their abilities. It is obvious that if we believe that there exists an ideal reality, we will have different ethical codes than if we do not. If we believe that there exists an objective reality which everybody perceives in the same way, or if we reject this, we will have differences in our approach to ethics.

Consequently, studies of the concept of ethics require that we have some opinion of the abilities and contexts of the human being. We will therefore start discussing how philosophers have seen humans throughout history, and we will also examine what happens when the approach to space-time and the basic conditions of life have been changed during the last 150 years due to revolutionary scientific revelations. The very time when this book is written is also somewhat revolutionary with respect to Western society; the fear of financial breakdown, the occurrence of isolationistic tendencies, new elites knocking at the door to power, national states no longer evident and so on. The tendencies have always been there, but never in history has a 16-year-old boy with an old computer been able to shake the whole banking system of a nation.[2] New technologies have changed the prospects of life in dimensions we have not foreseen.

Thus we meet new challenges, but the ethical codes do not necessarily have to change. However, their applications do need to be changed, and we do not know the consequences. Obviously we cannot give any answers to such a question, but we must try to reveal sensitive dimensions in human life and particularly the relations between the individual and the aggregate structures.

Structure of the book

The book begins with a prologue which motivates it, dealing with most of all ethics and power in relation to earlier books on the anomalies of economic theory. The basic results of the earlier work were that we could derive a proposition which implied a logical rift between the macroscopic and the microscopic levels of the society; furthermore, we derived another proposition which implied that using money values as representatives of real commodities had no logical implication per se on the real economy. The implications for using money as a political measure are to a large extent that we hide real contradictions and structural anomalies. These findings motivate us to regard economics as a social subsystem, the stability of which is due to the larger social and cultural stability, and that economic structures are imbedded in broader social structures. Consequently, the question of ethics and power must be relevant for economists to consider.

Chapters 1 and 2 deal with the concept of ethics from a philosophical point of view. While Chapter 1 deals with classical philosophy, starting with Aristotle and focussing on the difference between empiricist philosophy à la Hume and more ideological philosophy à la Kant, Chapter 2 deals primarily with the philosophical and scientific developments of the 19th and 20th centuries and their importance to our comprehension of the world and of logic and mathematics. We show in these chapters that mainstream economic theory is based on the mathematics and physics of Descartes and Newton, which imply a belief in general modelling and the existence of general equilibrium. The later scientific and philosophical development implies a new understanding of space-time, where time is related to change and the direction of time is universally implied by the discovery of entropy, but at the same time, the latter concept implies that time at the microscopic level is depending on causal structures and thus has no decisive direction. Consequently, we are able to derive a sort of social time concept.

In Chapter 3 we discuss the implication of our philosophical discussions with respect to economics. Since we dismiss general modelling and general equilibrium, we must direct our analysis towards structural compositions of the economy and structural stability. We will discuss necessities and choice possibilities of the consumer with respect to the concept of lexicographic preferences; with respect to production, we will show the necessity of underpinning the macroscopic analysis with a structural analysis of the microscopic structures. This will lead to the potential ethical conflict between human inventive and innovative skills and the desire for stability. Basic to our discussion is our derived proposition in earlier books:

Proposition 1

Assume a system $A^\star$ consisting of a finite number of subsystems, which are to be regarded as proper classes, $s_1 \ldots s_n$. If then we have a measure allowing us to define an optimizing rule both on $A^\star$ as well as $s_1 \ldots s_n$, optimization of the global system $A^\star$ must imply that at least one of the subsystems s_i must sub-optimize.

>   If on the other hand all the subsystems $s_1 \ldots s_n$ are optimized according
>   to the same optimizing process, the global system $A^\star$ must sub-optimize.
>
>   (Ekstedt 2013:83)

Thus there is no logical link per se between the microscopic and the macroscopic levels.

Chapter 4 deals with the analytical conditions for scientific analysis in social sciences. Physical sciences have the great benefit of analyzing objects which might be dissipative as single objects, but normally the physical structures are stable. However, in social sciences we have two problems: basically our object of investigation is a subject and thus a final cause, which means that humans themselves are the most prominent source of uncertainty. Basically, we form our decisions on a believed axiomatic structure, or we can call it more simply faith.

We discuss the conflicting approaches of Hume and Kant, where the latter presumed that the intellect was the important director of decisions and actions for a rational being. Hume however saw the intellect as the humble servant of passion. Kant's attitude is to a large extent expressed in the neoclassical axiomatic structure and prescribes that rationality is an independent concept from the context. Thus, all persons in the same context would act in the same way, if they were to be rational in the Kantian way. Earlier chapters describe how Hume's approach implies that emotions are due to the current apprehension and that earlier experiences together with more basic memories and social patterns mould the perception and apprehension, which makes rationality a complex cobweb of logical analysis and emotional reactions. Hume's and, to a large extent, Aristotle's views seem to be in line with current psychiatric, neurological and brain research; thus, we may still claim that the individual is rational in a sense, but the general norm for what should be regarded as rationality depends on local social and cultural structures. Furthermore, action follows from an intellectual analysis founded in an emotional state which is itself based on a mixture of perceived microscopic events and observations given a macroscopic apprehension; in other words, it is a mixture of atomistic analysis and holistic beliefs. Thus we discuss more closely the interaction between so-called atomism and holism and come to the conclusion that these approaches to society are interrelated in a combined emotional and intellectual comprehension of the context. Individuals' actions within the collective, particularly in a democracy, are indeed dependent on the individuals' combined intellectual and emotional maturity, which leads us to an analysis of Kant's famous paper from 1784 where he discusses the necessity for the individual to rise from self-imposed immaturity and trust his/her own ability and the necessity of playing a role in collective affairs.

The chapter ends in a discussion of the two ethical forms which sometimes appear as contradictive, "thou shalt" and "thou shalt not".

In Chapter 5 we discuss collective ethics and different forms of government/governance. We start by discussing the market decision/action in relation to the collective decision/action. Furthermore, we discuss the collective decisions in relation to cultural and social homogeneity and asymmetric distribution of knowledge and information. We analyze the role of the complexification of the society in creating structural rifts in the society.

With respect to such questions, we discuss the forms of government based on a debate in 486 BC refereed by Herodotus between three Persians who were forming a new government after having overthrown the tyrant Cambyses. Otanes, Megabyzos and Darios discussed the three classical forms of government: monarchy, oligarchy and democracy. The difference between Otanes and the other two is that Otanes argues for ordinary people ruling their own affairs according to a system of transparency and free speech where the ruled are able to control the rulers. The other two argue that in rule by one person or by a few, it is easier to find the worthy kind of persons. We also relate this discussion to Kant's paper maturity and self- induced immaturity.

We also discuss processes, saturation, anomie and alienation, which creates exclusion of individuals and groups which might evolve into subcultures, threatening the coherence of the collective.

In Chapter 6 we come back to the concept of money and financial aspects. The very basic point of departure is the Roman emperor Vespasianus' claim *"Pecunia non olet"* ["Money does not smell"], which is theoretically correct in the sense that money per se has nothing to do with the measurement of individual and social valuation, as it is linked to the immediate situation of supply and demand. We have so far related our discussion to the neoclassical theory of barter and our Proposition 1, where we claim a logical rift between the macroscopic and the microscopic levels. When we use money as a measure of value, those earlier discussions are irrelevant and we can derive a proposition which says:

Proposition 2

With respect to a real analysis equivalent to barter, Proposition 2 holds.

When we pass over to a non-equilibrium analysis where goals and restrictions are formulated in monetary terms, we lose all logical relations to the real economy and consequently Proposition 1 has no meaning.

This implies that collective policy based on the belief that money values reflect the real economy will in the end have asymmetric results. That is particularly clear when we use austerity policy to curb inflation in order to save the values of assets and liabilities. But this also has negative effects on growth and welfare. Thus, saving an alleged money value which has no links other than being defined in the current commodity basket in the society should be implemented by curbing the growth of the very commodity production which defines the amount of wealth, but through asymmetric effects, it may create gains at the expense of others in the society.

We also discuss the present development from a regulated monetarist system where money as such was controlled to a system of securitizing reminiscent of the Real Bill system which Adam Smith advocated.

Chapter 7 deals with the Other, with respect to individuals as well as nations. The basic question is how the collective chooses to define itself, either according to the principle of *ius soli*, which means that the collective is defined by the geographical area under a certain constitution/legislation and that cultural, ethnical, racial and other differentiating dimensions are not important, or the principle of *ius sanguinis*, which means that the collective is the bearer of some mystic spirit, often summarized under Blood and Soil. We discuss historical experiences where we also show that the *ius soli* principle might lead to extreme variants of social engineering where humans lose their value as a goal per se and become only means in the development of an optimal efficiency of the actions of the collective. We also discuss how both approaches affect the "society of nations" with respect to cooperation and aggressiveness.

In Chapter 8 we end with war. We start from the "rational" war of Clausewitz and show how technical and global development changes both the aims of war and the complexity of consequential effects, leading to increasing difficulties to realize the 'rational' war. Our conclusion is that for those who realize the complexities of the world, a traditional war between states is an anomaly since that is also self-destruction, but at the same time, we realize the increasing gaps in understanding of this. Persons who desire power per se—that is, more the insignia of power than the responsibilities of power—may rise to power by painting a rosy picture of the future and/or riding on waves of fear and hatred, and they may become an enormous threat to the whole world. There is no defence against this except what we earlier discussed: enlightenment and personal maturity, combined with a living and active democracy of full transparency and freedom of speech.

Notes

1 *The Evening Post*. Saturday. August 22, 1925.
   Songs of a Swedish Singer: 'Guitar and Concertina'. By Gustav Froding. Trans. C.D. Locock), George Allen and Unwin Ltd, London.
2 A 16-year-old boy is in court in Sweden for having caused chaos for several days in the computer system of the main banks in spring 2017.

Bibliography

Ekstedt, H., (2013). *Money in Economic Theory*, Routledge, London and New York.

Prologue

Introduction

The Danish existentialist philosopher Sören Kierkegaard once said that faith in its deepest meaning was a preparedness to venture a step out over a depth of 70,000 yards. The author feels a bit like this when entering the issue of ethics. Although touching the issue in earlier books, these have been well within the frames of central economic theory, this new venture is for the author leading into new unexplored areas. In the book *Money, Valuation and Growth: Conceptualization and Contradictions of the Money Economy* (2015:287), we ended the book:

> Thus the two "cousins" the neoclassical theory and Marxian economics lead in fact to the same kind of mechanics/engineering so when Friedman says that free markets are a necessary condition for democracy he cannot possibly mean that free markets have anything to do with the neoclassical theory. Both the neoclassical and the Marxist variants of explaining the economy dismiss the free will and are purely deterministic.
>
> To consciously introduce the free will is indeed difficult and our earlier discussed humbleness with respect to this problem in its full depth requires a metaphysical analysis sooner than a physical analysis.
>
> We have used the word subject and regarded it as a final cause. That means that we stop the analysis so to speak when we stand in front of the interior of the human mind. Thus we define the concept of epistemic cycles but that only tells us that the individual has purposes which are subject to the apprehension of the relevant context. This actually means that St. Thomas' as well as Locke's attitudes can be covered and also behaviouristic attitude.

The quote shows that we were at the end of a road. To enter the question of an eventual economic theory for a democracy requires other intellectual tools and other types of methodological analysis. To the author, it seemed rather obvious that the question of ethics was a necessary concept to investigate. Arrow's paradox is a full stop for economic analysis of the mainstream character. This paradox shows an economy with everyday people able to negotiate, are affected in their actions by aggregate events and are affected by social processes and structures, to mention a few complexities of daily life. This implies that economics has to digest fully that the individual and groups of individuals are social actors of many different dimensions. Thus we get an interaction between the macroscopic and the microscopic levels, which the neoclassical theory not only neglects but postulates against. In the real world this requires rules and regulations, but before that comes some basic ethical principles.

Thus this book should be seen as a successor of the author's earlier research which forced us out of the box of mainstream economic theory and which led to areas in the neighbourhood of metaphysics, although we try to stay out of a direct metaphysical analysis. However, we discuss the role of metaphysical aspects governing behaviour of individuals and collective bodies.

Thus it is necessary to start with a small retrospective glance at the main problems which were discussed in earlier books and also the two suggested propositions which directly contradict the smooth transformation of individual actions into aggregate wholes, which in fact is the very start of entering the problem of ethics.

Economic theory

The so-called mainstream economic theory is not a particularly consistent theory but a mixture between elements from different theories or approaches where the microscopic theory is more or less based on the neoclassical consumption theory and the theory of firm completed with a diversity of elements from property rights/contract theory, market structure analysis, transaction costs theory and household production theory. These elements are not necessarily consistent with each other but are used ad hoc. Basically, however, we may say that microscopic theory has a neoclassical foundation. The lack of a coherent theoretical foundation is not something particularly strange per se in empirical sciences. What is called the central theory was often developed many years ago and new empirical information has been collected since then, which is difficult to handle by the 'central' theory. This of course could mean that the central theory is wrong, but not necessarily, since the new information might involve structures earlier unknown or at least disregarded but which have to be handled systematically in order to relate them to the existent theory. We will later in the book discuss the classical example of the Australian platypus, which took some 80 years to classify scientifically. But the economic mainstream theory, intrinsically contradictive as it is, is used to legitimize political decisions which affect millions if not billions of people in their daily life. Economic theory has merged with ideological considerations which are clearly asymmetric with respect to different individuals and classes of individuals. This is basically the ethical motivation for discussing economic theory and policy in the realm of ethics.

The macroscopic theory is mainly some sort of mixture between neoclassical elements and some elements from so-called Keynesianism, based on Hicks' famous 1937 interpretation of Keynes' *General Theory*. But to this is added theorizing on particular observations like the Phillips curve, Verdoorn's Law, Okun's

Law, rational expectations and stagflation. Such observations are seldom included in some of the basic theoretical approaches but are described and explained in different ways.

When we come to discussions of individual and general welfare, the borders are clearer. Either the analysis is based on neoclassical theory in a rather pure form or others pursue that the market is asymmetric and unstable and needs corrections.

It is, however, fascinating from a theoretical point of view that most analysts, irrespective of approach, seems to be convinced that aggregation from micro-scopic to macroscopic levels is additive in money terms.

The present book has emerged out of four preceding books on anomalies in economic theory in general and of the neoclassical theory in particular. The ethical aspects have more or less arisen, as a necessity, when we have showed the fundamental disequilibrium character of the monetary economy. Thus, we will start with a short overview of our basic critique of economic theory and also highlight some fundamental propositions concerning the problem of aggrega-tion in economic theory. Our basic criticism is directed towards the neoclassical theory since that is the only systematic theoretical structure in economic theory. It is based on an axiomatic structure which we will examine. The so-called Keynesian theory is not a consistent theory which links the individual to the society but a set of relations between macroscopic variables assumed and/or based on econometric findings. There are certain fundamental concepts from Keynes' writings, like liquidity/liquidity preference and marginal propensity to consume given no a priori equality of saving and real investment. However, the Keynesian modelling is sometimes rather similar to neoclassical modelling due to an insufficient dividing line between neoclassical equilibrium and temporary equilibrium in a Keynesian way which is generally poorly defined.

The reason why it is poorly defined is that the neoclassical theory works with additive aggregation which falls out from the very axiomatic structure. Any form of serious criticism of the axiomatic structure basically destroys the ability to aggregate additively. The reason for this is that agents and commodities, con-trary to the neoclassical axiomatic structure, are linked to each other in different kinds of structural relationships. Consequently the commodities are defined by their structural relationships; they are context-dependent. That means that prices depend on the structural composition of the market and consequently exogenous price changes will have structural effects.

Thus when we enter a so-called Keynesian model, this very problem of addi-tive aggregation disappears, and if we shall be able to reintroduce the problem of non-additive aggregation, we must enter rather advanced structural information of distributional and allocative matters. The critique of the Keynesian modelling in the beginning of the 1970s that it lacked a microeconomic foundation was thus perfectly correct; it indeed did. The problem was that leading economists claimed that the neoclassical modelling should replace it completely with some Philips curve reasoning ending up in natural unemployment and furthermore some almost metaphysical theory of rational expectations, which may work on well-defined markets but hardly at the macroscopic level. The problem of addi-tive aggregation was not even mentioned among neoclassical economists or even less among Keynesians.

Neoclassical axiomatic structure

The neoclassical theory has its roots in utility theory. It is instructive to read the early discussions in the late 19th century. There are two particularly clarifying works: J.S. Mill (1990[1863]), "Utilitarianism", and Jevons (1888[1871]) *The Theory of Political Economy* (chapter 3). We can see the full utilitarian approach to the individual and the society in Mill, and in Jevons we meet the necessary omissions and simplifications which make it possible to form a mathematical model.[1] It is interesting that the most devastating critique of a mathematical formulation of a *money economy* appeared in 1803, when Jean-Baptiste Say (1834[1803]:246–247] ruled out money as a measure other than local and temporal and in fact ruled out any form of general equilibrium for the money economy. The so-called Say's Law is a misunderstanding, and reading it in the proper context indicates reasoning similar to Keynes' when he discusses marginal propensity to consume.

Anyway, the modern formulation of the neoclassical theory builds on Jevons' analysis completed with the discussions of the existence of general equilibrium by Pareto/Walras in the end of the 19th century. The modern axiomatic struc-ture was developed by Arrow/Debreu, particularly Debreu (1987[1959]), and was finally completed when Debreu (1982) showed the equivalence between general equilibrium and Nash equilibrium.

The axioms

The neoclassical general equilibrium theory is based on six axioms. All six axioms are necessary to show the *existence* of general equilibrium; thus, the axioms do not tell anything about how to get to general equilibrium from a non-equilibrium starting point. But more than that: if the axioms hold, the mar-ket exchange economy must be in equilibrium and there cannot be a position outside general equilibrium. The reason is that the axioms are supposed to hold for the individuals of the economy; thus, if the individuals are influenced by each other or by the aggregate result, as is the case in the Arrow's paradox, the general equilibrium will not be attained. Actually, it is wrong to use the verb *attain*, since the axioms do not deal with some form of dynamic process but define a *state*.

In technical language the general equilibrium is *nowhere dense*; there exists no environment to the general equilibrium. We may sum up: if general equilibrium, defined by the six axioms in Table P.1, exists, then there is no non-equilibrium. A correlate is that if we are not in general equilibrium, as defined by the axi-oms, then no general equilibrium exists, since the axioms concerning the agents obviously do not hold.

The principles of the proof of the general equilibrium are illustrated in Figure P.1.

Table P.1 The neoclassical axioms of Arrow/Debreu

Economic Rationality	Properties of the Preference Ordering
1 Axiom of Completeness	4 Axiom of Continuity
All commodities in the commodity space are known to everybody	
2 Axiom of Reflexivity	5 Axiom of Convexity
All commodities are identical to themselves	
3 Axiom of Transitivity	6 Axiom of Local Non-satiation
For any three commodities, holds that if $xRy \wedge yRz \Rightarrow xRz$	*For any commodity basket A, there exists at least one commodity x_i such that* $A(x_1, \ldots, x_i + \varepsilon, \ldots, x_n) \geq A(x_1, \ldots, x_i, \ldots, x_n)$

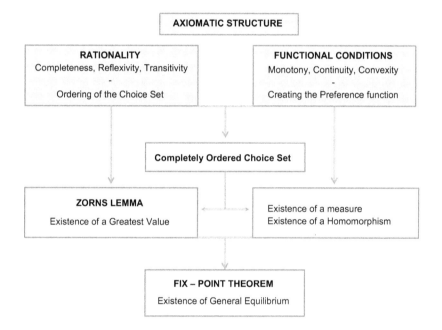

Figure P.1 A sketch of the proof of the existence of general equilibrium

One remarkable thing is that the axioms are void of any a priori economic meaning; they have no economic content per se, and eventual links to economics depend on secondary interpretations. It is also here where the axioms are particularly deceitful.

The mathematical meaning of the Arrow/Debreu axioms is that we actually define an ordered Euclidian space, and we all know that a Euclidian (or sometimes it is called Cartesian) space is a veritable dream for the theoretical analyst because we can actually define our variables in numerical terms, and more than that, we can use as representatives real numbers. From a mathematical point of view this is of outmost importance. However, when we are outside the realm of the axiomatic structure, concerning the character of the agents, we also leave the possibility of representing the economic goods and agents as real numbers. That is why we can say that if we are in general equilibrium, we are in a separate universe which has no neighbourhood. Thus if we are thrown out of general equilibrium, we implicitly say that we are in a space where we cannot represent goods and agents by numbers; consequently there most probably does not exist a general theory of disequilibrium, as opposed to general equilibrium in the neoclassical sense.

The first three axioms, which by all means are said to define rationality, which is true in a very limited meaning, define an equivalence relation, together with the presumption of symmetry: $A = B \Rightarrow B = A$. The equivalence relation implies that if we have two sets X and Y, then to each X_i there exists one and only one Y_j.

Thus:

P1: Let X represent a preference set and Y a choice set. We can then define a function P on X and a function C on Y such that for any two x: $x_i \, P \, x_j$, there exist two y: $y_k \, C \, y_l$.

P2: If now the preference set and the choice set are defined on the same set X of elements, we will have a preference relation between two elements: $x_i \, P \, x_j \Leftrightarrow x_i \, C \, x_j$.

In Figure P.1 we sketch the skeleton of the proof of the existence of general equilibrium. It is important to note that the fundamental mathematical issue underlying the proof is to show that both the preference space and the choice space belong to the same Euclidian space. That means that some of the axioms may look redundant from an economic point of view, as Hausman (2012:13, footnote 1) writes:

Reflexivity is trivial and arguably a consequence of completeness, whereas continuity, which is automatically satisfied for any finite set of alternatives, is needed to prove that preferences can be represented by a continuous utility function.

The point, however, is that the proof of general equilibrium is purely mathematical and that none of the axioms are redundant.

The last three axioms imply together with the equivalence relation that we define an ordered Euclidian (Cartesian) space.

Important correlates to this exercise are:

Corr. 1: P2 is independent of any x_k in X where $k \neq x_i$ and $k \neq x_j$.

This correlate is called *Independence of Irrelevant Alternatives*.

Corr. 2: For any i and j for a preference function P_a and a choice function C_a holds that $x_i \, P_a \, x_j \Rightarrow x_i \, C_a \, x_j$ and conversely $x_i \, C_a \, x_j \Rightarrow x_i \, P_a \, x_j$.

This correlate is often referred to as the *Principle of Revealed Preference*. Corr. 2 is not an empirical principle to be proved but just a rewriting of P2.

The axioms and aggregation

The axioms define the link between the interior preferences (utilities) and the market action (choice). This is what we may call rational. We *prefer* something, R, for some reason before something else, S; consequently we *choose* R before S, which sounds convincing. From this principle, however, we shall extend the analysis to a group of people, market agents. As we see, the axiom does not contain anything about prices, so we have to stick to a barter process. To get the gist of the proof of general equilibrium, we may imagine a flea market.

A number of people come to the flea market and bring different things from their cupboards, wardrobes and sheds. We may call this their initial endowments, and the totality of initial endowments is the entire set of marketable commodities. To illustrate the exchange principle between two agents, we may think of one who brings ice hockey equipment for a kid who has grown out of it and another agent who brings slalom skis and boots. These two decide to make an exchange, provided that the one with the hockey equipment also adds a computer game which was brought. Thus the respective equipment lying unused and worthless in the original wardrobe and shed becomes useful. Consequently, the market exchange increased the utility value for both the agents.

We may now aggregate this simple market exchange to all agents who walk around at the flea market in order to get an overview and make a personal judgement of the different items, and they start to make exchanges until nobody is prepared to make any exchange. Then we implicitly have a relative price vector for all the commodities, which would be upset by any more exchange. Thus we can say that to each distribution of initial endowments, there exists one and only one optimal relative price vector. We define this state as a general equilibrium so that nobody can improve his or her individual satisfaction without someone else's satisfaction being worsened. This is called Pareto optimality. When all individuals are satisfied and we have reached a Pareto optimal situation among the market agents, then we have also brought the society to its maximal welfare. Thus the aggregation is simply the summation of the individual personal satisfaction of all agents.

This implies, however, that the barter per se is the only relevant relation and completely independent of all other relations. Furthermore, a commodity is completely unrelated to all other commodities. Thus, commodities are void of any structural relations, which is also the case for the agents. This is in fact the basic problem which provokes Arrow's Impossibility Theorem.

Barter and production

The pure barter economy which is the basis of the Arrow/Debreu axioms can be modified to include production by attaching production activities to each commodity, and given technology, we can attach qualities of skills to labour and then from the price vector derive labour demand and a price vector for different labour. The problem is that production and consumption decisions must be simultaneous, since if the production decision takes place before the consumption decision, we lack an appropriate price vector and consequently need an invisible hand. The two Russian economists/mathematicians Makarov and Rubinov (1977) investigated this and came to the conclusion that the only difference between the capitalistic market and the communist command economy, which now is outside the market exchange, was that in the capitalistic market the price vector was decided by the capital owners, while in the command economy it was decided by the central authorities. Thus the market exchange principle per se could not discriminate between the capitalistic economy and the command economy (Makarov and Rubinov 1977:202–233).

If we want to make a correction for this in our example from the flea market where the agents want to have newly produced commodities, we may think that they have a bunch of money bills of different size and they negotiate consumption contracts, given volume of maximal production and technology. General equilibrium will then appear with respect to the future contracts. We can of course think of some kind of Ali Baba ghost who brings the goods immediately after the contracts are signed (simultaneously). But introducing time will imply that we slide over to expected utilities, which is rather complicated and outside our scope here.

Homo Œconomicus, rationality and equilibrium

The axioms of the general equilibrium theory are, as we mentioned, defining a Euclidian space which per se has nothing to do with economics. The real purpose of the axioms is to underscore exactly which kind of restrictions must be obeyed in order to create a logical link between the interior mind of the agent and the outer commodity space.

This is indeed a problem, and Wittgenstein addresses it in *Tractatus Logico-Philosophicus* (1974[1921]: Prop. 6.211), where he says:

> Indeed in real life a mathematical proposition is never what we want. Rather, we make use of mathematical propositions *only* in inferences from propositions that do not belong to mathematics to others that likewise do not belong to mathematics. (In philosophy the question, "What do we actually use this word or this proposition for?" repeatedly leads to valuable insights.)

Thus, transforming a problem from a real-world problem to a mathematical/logical problem has certain consequences for the character of the problem. The most apparent problem is that all variables of the real world are complex variables; that is, their interpretation depends and varies with the structural context, either with respect to language or with respect to the physical world. In mathematics however we can only handle atomic variables, which mean that the variables are independent of any physical, social, ethical and linguistic structures.

This very aspect is taken into account by axiom 2 in Table P.1, the Axiom of Reflexivity, which in principle tells us that an item is identical to itself, which does not seem to be one of the more profound truths in the world. Many economists, like Varian (2006) and Hausman (2012), claim that this axiom is trivial, but it is not. In fact it is the most important axiom of the six in transforming the real world to a logical world. Remember that our scope with the axioms was to create equivalence between the preferences and the factual choice, furthermore that we are aiming at a unique relative price vector in general equilibrium. That means that both commodities and agents have to be defined in atomistic terms; that is, they must not be affected by structural matters and contextual changes.

To grasp the problem, we need to use Debreu's (1982) definition of the i:th agent as $(\preccurlyeq_i, e_i)$, a preference relation and an endowment vector. Furthermore, we must see the agents as vectors in a space spanned by the commodity. Consequently all agents must regard the commodities exactly in the same way.

The Axiom of Reflexivity gives rise to Corr. 2 above, Independence of Irrelevant Alternatives, which tells us that any binary ranking is independent of the rest of the commodities in the basket. This is indeed a strong assumption.

Gerard Debreu is one of the few ranking economists who have explicitly noted this, and he does it already in Theory of Value (1987[1959]:28–32) when he states that commodities at different times and different places are different commodities. Thus, given the spatial indexes s and t, spatial and temporal respectively, for a certain commodity $C^\star$ we will have $C^\star_{s0} \neq C^\star_{s1}$ as well as $C^{\star t0} \neq C^{\star t1}$.

We will later follow this track.

Our example from the flea market also highlights a very important condition. Let us start with a hypothetical general equilibrium. If we then add one agent and/or one commodity, we will obviously have to go for another round of relative price negotiations, which will end up in a different equilibrium from the hypothetical one we had at the start. Thus when we above claimed that a general equilibrium is nowhere dense, it means that there cannot be a growth of an economy which changes the dimensionality of the commodity space, and we must have some convergence process where the new dimensions are adapted to the original equilibrium, which by all means also holds if the economy by some kind of shock is thrown out of equilibrium and the agents make exchanges at non-equilibrium prices.

The three first axioms normally are seen as defining rationality, and in some sense that is true, but if we in ordinary language define rationality as *purposeful action*, it opens up other aspects which are not covered by the axioms. When we act at the market, we want to maximize the utility we get from the commodities. The three first axioms, particularly that of reflexivity, then tells us that the utility we get from each of the commodities is independent of any structures of the society and any kind of temporal and spatial context. In fact, the reason why we prefer an item before another is its physical appearance, nothing more, because then our preferences will directly link our utilities to the actual supply or production. With respect to supply/production, only the physical appearance of an item or a process is relevant.

One may think that this is relevant at the very moment of choice when all other considerations concerning the purchases are done, and that is also the implication of Debreu's temporal and spatial specification of a commodity.

It is instructive to look at the early evolution of the neoclassical theory as in Mill and Jevons.[2] In the earlier works by Mill and Jevons, it is exactly here we have the deviation between them. In Mill's philosophical discussion it is included in the agent's utilities, relations to other agents, and so is also the structure of moral aspects of the society as a whole. Jevons also discusses similar aspects but has to admit that they are too complicated to be accounted for, so he dismisses them. In his defence, we may say that he only discusses individual behaviour and never takes the step into aggregating individuals to a society.

However, such an interpretation of the rationality of the consumption decision as follows from the axioms is contrary to modern consumption theory as it appears in household production approach and the characteristics approach, and it is contrary to the everyday experience of most people, probably even the most obedient neoclassical worshippers.

Purposeful action must concern not only preference and budgetary consideration but also structural and contextual consideration, since commodities in real life are not atomic variables but complex variables; that is, they are partly structurally defined, and households create their welfare with the commodities as structural elements.

Arrow's Impossibility Theorem

These kinds of considerations we have mentioned above "explode" in Arrow's Impossibility Theorem. Since it appeared in the beginning of the 1950s, it has caused much discussion and much confusion. In Ekstedt and Fusari (2010:59–62) and Ekstedt (2013:70–74), there are extensive discussions on the implications of Arrow's Impossibility Theorem. A good overview of the Theorem and the standard interpretations are also found on the internet version of the Stanford Encyclopædia of Philosophy; we will here just give a short summary of our findings.

First, it is important to realize that logical paradoxes occur when we have exhausted a set of axioms in the sense that we confront the axiomatic structure with an intrinsic conflict in a used concept. As we have mentioned, and developed in (Ekstedt and Fusari 2010: chapter 2), a mathematical treatment of a problem requires that we transform variables from complex to atomistic. This implies that we force everyday language into precise definitions. In natural science, most of the experiments serve to make the definitions of variables and the contextual conditions of the analysis precise. As scientists we actually violate the natural language. But if we do so and make our mathematical/logical analysis, we also bring into the analysis mathematical garbage which is unnatural to the everyday language. The quote from Wittgenstein is to be understood in this way. Thus, Jevons had to cut out certain dimensions of the analysis vis-à-vis Mill in order to make the problem treatable.

In Arrow's Impossibility Theorem, as in the entire proof of general equilibrium, additive aggregation is fundamental, not as an economic or social assumption but as a necessary consequence of the axiomatic structure. It particularly follows from the Axiom of Reflexivity which, as we have mentioned, also produces the correlate on Independence of Irrelevant Alternatives. Additive aggregation is something which is automatically achieved when we define a Euclidian space, and it is desirable from a calculation point of view. But in reality, additive aggregation is far from universally prevailing. When a bunch of people take an elevator, their respective weights are added to each other so the total sum must not exceed a certain weight. But when we make a good meal, we have the saying "Too many cooks spoil the broth". Irrespective of whether the latter is true, it displays the non-additive principle of aggregation. To be clear, the additive aggregation is valid when we just look at one measurable dimension, like weight. For merging structures and complexes, non-additivity is normally the case.

The practical consequence in the proof of general equilibrium is that we are assured of the possibility of adding agents defined as ordinary commodity vectors into a social optimum, as Figure P.2 exemplifies. A and B are two individual indifferent curves while W is the obtained social welfare function.

The social welfare function possesses the same characteristics as the individual indifference curves; that is why we get the Pareto optimum when we reach a social optima at the same price vector as the individual optima.

However, additive aggregation is indeed a very strong restriction implying that we violate the reality. But let us look a bit more closely at Jevons' analysis, which we have mentioned above.[3]

Mill, in his essay "Utilitarianism", tries to keep his discussion as close to the real world as possible, while Jevons makes logical atomism his analytical basis,

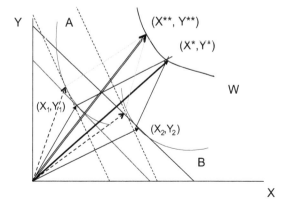

Figure P.2 Additive aggregation

which is natural since his purpose is to develop a mathematical setting of the problem. He only considers the individual as an atom independent of any structural limitations or links. He quotes Bentham on the aspects affecting the valuation of pleasure and pain of an action or choice, which are:

1   its intensity
2   its duration
3   its certainty or uncertainty
4   its propinquity or remoteness

These factors are, according to Jevons, suitable to bring into an economic analysis, which is more limited than the Mill's philosophical analysis. However, Jevons quotes Bentham on three other factors:

5   fecundity, or the chance a feeling has to be followed by feelings of the same kind: that is, pleasure if it be pleasure; pain if it be pain
6   purity, or the chance it has of not being followed by feelings of an opposite kind
7   extent, or the number of persons to whom it extends and who are affected by it

The last three aspects Jevons dismisses for the simplicity of analysis, which is understandable. He limits the utility/preferences to exactly the moment of factual choice, and we exclude all kind of interaction of effects between agents. It is easy to see the similarity of Jevons' limitation and Debreu's temporal and spatial specification of commodities.

When we look at those four aspects which Jevons takes into consideration, they are in fact much broader than the Arrow/Debreu axiomatic structure. The first two are possible to assume within the realm of preferences, but the third aspect requires an expected utility analysis with the following discussions of Allais' paradox. The fourth aspect requires a discussion of transaction costs.

Thus Jevons' analysis is a fairly rich analysis, but he avoids temporal extension and aggregation.

Arrow discusses the very aggregate, although it is not quite clear whether he extends the analysis temporally. In order to introduce the use of concepts like coalitions, we must have an implicit time concept somewhere in mind, since a meaningful coalition must concern a future (potential) action. If he does not, it is a bit hard to see the whole point of the analysis. Thus we think that the commodity concept used in Arrow's Impossibility Theorem does not concern Debreu's temporal and spatial specifications; however, there is no sign of that in the analysis. Then the additive aggregation implies that the agents are not involved and/or affected by the aggregation into a social welfare function. Furthermore, the agents and commodities are void of any structural links whatsoever. Arrow's social welfare function is an aggregate reformulation of the axioms of general equilibrium with exactly the same mathematical substance. Thus

Homo Œconomicus of the general equilibrium is of the same kind as Homo Œconomicus of Arrow's Impossibility Theorem.

Now Arrow defines another type of agent, which may be called Homo Politicus. This agent has the ability to rank commodities but may also be affected by the rankings of other agents. Furthermore, this Homo Politicus is aware that the aggregate outcome may affect individuals and is also aware that it is possible to affect the aggregation by coalitions.

Arrow's conclusion is that the general equilibrium solution which is Pareto efficient and unique can only be obtained in a society populated with Homo Œconomicus. If we have a society populated by agents of the type Homo Politicus, then we cannot obtain general equilibrium and the specific economic interpretation of Pareto efficiency.

The reason why we described Jevons' analysis at such length is that Jevons and Arrow work in opposite ways. If we take into account that the mathematical analysis is a bit different, we see that Jevons realize that if he does not make limitations in the description of the individuals, he will never be able to show any productive mathematical conclusions. Arrow shows that if we add limitations which we have to make in the axiomatic structure in order to achieve productive mathematical results, then we cannot achieve these results.

Thus, Arrow's theorem has provoked much discussion of the conditions of efficiency, democracy and similar stuff, which probably has had some positive results. But these discussions have little to do with the very core of Arrow's Impossibility Theorem. One has the feeling that the lack of understanding of the very anatomy of the paradox has also given rise to many misunderstandings and political conclusions which have been directly counterproductive to the society.

Concerning the very concept of efficiency, we must be aware of the fact that commodities are complex, implying on one hand that they are structurally defined and on the other hand that they are context-dependent in space-time. In such a world, there could hardly be any well-defined efficiency concepts other than locally and temporally.

Thus if we look at the most general efficiency Pareto optimum, this concept falls out very elegantly in the neoclassical equilibrium, but in fact it is a social concept. Let us define it:

Definition: Pareto optimum

In a closed society, a Pareto optimum, given a preference structure and an initial distribution of initial endowments, implies that the allocation of production resources and the distribution of the production results are such that no agent can achieve an improved state without another agent's situation being worsened.

As we see, the fly in the ointment is that preferences are given, as are the initial endowments. That means that we have a complete static situation and that the endowments are atomic items with no structural bindings.

When we pass over to complex commodities and agents which are aware of structural compositions of local and temporal character, the Pareto optimum and principle are still valid as a social concept but are not related to an axiomatic structure, and thus we are in difficulties with respect to valuations.

The mathematical manipulations of the neoclassical theory lead us to believe that prices (relative) should be some sort of measure in scientific meaning. That is correct *if and only if we are in a prevailing general equilibrium and no non-equilibrium ever exists.*

Thus relative prices, of a particular general equilibrium, possess the conditions of a mathematical measure, but they do not possess the conditions of a measure in physical meaning because apart from the very particular general equilibrium there is no unique price vector. Jean-Baptiste Say expresses this very elegantly:

> When I am told that the great pyramid of Ghaize is 656 feet square at the base, I can measure a space of 656 feet square at Paris or elsewhere, and form an exact notion of the space the pyramid will cover; but when I am told that a camel is at Cairo worth 50 *sequins*, that is to say, about 90 ounces of silver, or 100 dollars in coin, I can form no precise notion of the value of the camel; because, although I may have every reason to believe that 100 dollars are worth less at Paris than at Cairo, I can not tell what may be the difference of value.
>
> Say (1834[1803]:247)

Thus with respect to the neoclassical claim that relative prices are a measure of the same kind as the SI system in physics, we can lean back and wait for the ultimate proof that we live in an intertemporal general equilibrium. Until such a proof is produced, the neoclassical analysis of the aggregate level has no social or economic relevance, which is also, partly, proved in Arrow's Impossibility Theorem. Arrow tells us:

> If, on the contrary, the actual market differs significantly from the competitive model, or if the assumptions of the two optimality theorems are not fulfilled, the separation of allocative and distributional procedures becomes, in most cases, impossible.
>
> (Arrow 1963:943)

As mentioned above, we will discuss Arrow's Impossibility Theorem more closely together with some more philosophical and technical aspects, but we may mention here that the American philosopher Howard DeLong (1991) refuted Arrow's theorem on grounds similar to ours. The difference, however, is that DeLong more refutes the interpretations of Arrow's theorem by rejecting Arrow's axioms concerning the social welfare functions which are based on the neoclassical axioms for the individual, and that is obviously a possible way of analysis.[4] The problem with DeLong's analysis is that Arrow's paradox must be traced back to the fundamental axiomatic reasons why the paradox can arise. Thus DeLong's proofs, although correct, create a further question, namely, How can the paradox arise?

Answering that question, we meet the more fundamental problems of aggregation and the distinction between atomic and complex facts, which lead us into the problem of structural complexity. Thus I repeat that logical paradoxes shall not be seen as something that concerns reality per se; it shows that we have some intrinsic problems with our conceptualizations.

We accept Arrow's Impossibility Theorem as a correctly stated logical paradox; we will later in the book explain the general structure of logical paradoxes. But since Arrow's axioms for the social welfare functions are developments of the neoclassical axioms concerning individuals, we start by explaining the problems of the neoclassical axiomatic structure and refute the Axiom of Reflexivity on the grounds of refuting that commodities and agents can be transformed to atomic variables, and thereby we obtain a refutation of additive aggregation. This then leads to a paradox since Arrow's "trick" is to populate his world with people who are not defined by the neoclassical aggregations. This means of course that any conclusions of Arrow's paradox except the purely logical are basically without any meaning. Thus, all kinds of discussions based on allusions to Arrow's paradox may of course be interesting but have no logical substance with respect to Arrow's Impossibility Theorem.

Methodological aspects

There has been much fuss about the use of mathematics in social sciences. We have in the above presentation come down pretty hard on the use of mathematics and logic, so it may seem like we are at variance with the use of mathematics and logic. This is not the case. We have been criticizing a particular axiomatic structure. With respect to logic and mathematics, these are tools, perhaps the only tools, which science has, with respect to systematic handling of observations, which is possible to communicate objectively. Thus, given a proper conceptualization, we always must use logic and mathematics to reach some form of conclusion. The point where social sciences are at variance with natural sciences is the very precision of the concepts. In natural sciences, experiments can be used to increase the precision of the concepts approaching atomic conceptualization, given proper limitations. This is to a small extent possible in microscopic studies where the markets are well defined, but in macroscopic studies it is virtually impossible.

These matters of methodological character are of utmost importance, and it is interesting that Keynes took a very active part in such philosophical discussions which resulted in what may be his most appreciated book from a scientific point of view, *Treatise on Probability*, which appeared in 1921. But already at the age of 20, Keynes held a speech in 1903 where he criticized the naïve use of additive aggregation. In an unpublished paper, "Ethics in Relation to Conduct", read to the Apostles on 23 January 1903, Keynes says the following:

> [T]he unpopularity of the principle of organic unities shows very clearly how great is the danger of the assumption of unproved additive formulas.

The fallacy, of which ignorance of organic unity is a particular instance, may perhaps be mathematically represented thus: suppose f(x) is the goodness of x and f(y). It is then assumed that the goodness of x and y together is f(x) + f(y) when it is clearly f(x+y) and only in special cases will it be true that f(x+y) = f(x) + f(y). It is plain that it is never legitimate to assume this property in the case of any given function without proof.[5]

We also quoted Wittgenstein's Proposition 6.211 above. We can illustrate that quote as a methodological norm for working with mathematics as a tool of analysis.

The logical analysis is trivial. It is the translation arrows which are the essential scientific problem. This is difficult in natural sciences, although they have the great benefit of being able to do controlled experiments. For social sciences the problems are huge, and when we work with a priori axiomatic structures, extreme cautiousness is imperative.

With respect to this, Keynes made a very interesting statement in a letter to Roy Harrod, 10 July 1938 (Keynes' Collected Works):

My point against Tinbergen is a different one. In chemistry and physics and other natural sciences the object of experiment is to fill in the actual values of the various quantities and factors appearing in an equation or a formula; and the work when done is once and for all. In economics that is not the case, and to convert a model into a quantitative formula is to destroy its usefulness as an instrument of thought. Tinbergen endeavours to work

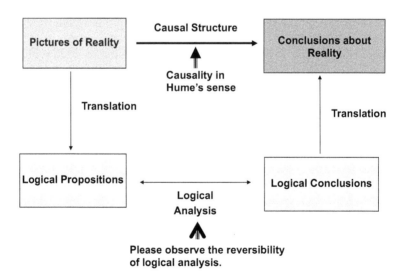

Figure P.3 Mathematics and causality

Source: Ekstedt and Fusari (2010:48)

out the variable quantities in a particular case, or perhaps in the average of several particular cases, and he then suggests that the quantitative formula so obtained has general validity. Yet in fact, by filling in figures, which one can be quite sure will not apply next time, so far from increasing the value of his instrument, he has destroyed it. All the statisticians tend that way. Colin, for example, has recently persuaded himself that the propensity to consume in terms of money is constant at all phases of the credit cycle. He works out a figure for it and proposes to predict by using the result, regardless of the fact that his own investigations clearly show that it is not constant, in addition to the strong a priori reasons for regarding it as most unlikely that it can be so.

The fundamental reason why these problems appear in economics and in all of the social sciences is that while the natural sciences deal with objects, the social sciences deal with subjects who, following Aristotle, are final causes. Thus we can observe inert individual patterns and inert social structures, but these are not intrinsic to the human beings. That also means that aggregate structures are not additive as a rule, but there is a most probable a mixture of additive and non-additive aggregate structures.

A simple example: The simplest form of aggregation is the additive; a set of individuals forms a group given a specific context. Those who are watching a football match at a specific arena are interesting just as an additive assembly from many aspects: as security/fire aspects, income aspects given the price of tickets, the number of hot dogs consumed and so on. However, if we allow for differences in the features between possible subgroups, for example hooligans, young men, young men with fiancées and families, things become more difficult since that will possibly affect the behaviour of and between the subgroups relative to each other and thus the behaviour of the whole group. Thus in the latter case, the additive aggregation will convey information that is rather incomplete, which probably calls for somewhat deeper, sometimes even scientific, investigations and which brings in structural aspects.

Assuming that mathematical a priori axiom systems focus on one detail, as in the case of the neoclassical theory that focuses on the very act of economic exchange, and from that constructing the aggregate behaviour in economic matters for the whole society, is perhaps interesting from a technical and philosophical point of view but has nothing whatsoever to do with empirical sciences. We cannot expand the example of the flea market, even if it is in an impressive mathematical form, to represent the full complexity of society. We cannot discuss the difference in behaviour between Homo Œconomicus and Homo Politicus since the former cannot even choose at the market, since his preference function is assumed on the basis of the existence of no individual structures, no social structures and commodities which are all chosen by everybody for exactly the same reason, namely physical appearance, independent of any social or individual structures and independent of any differences in contexts.

Disequilibrium

In disequilibrium we have nothing but temporal and local equilibria. Jean-Baptiste Say expresses it:

> Nor is the position of Montesquieu, that money-price depends upon the relative quantity of the total commodities to that of the total money of the nation at all better founded. What do sellers and buyers know of the existence of any other commodities, but those that are the objects of their dealing? And what difference could such knowledge make in the demand and supply in respect to those particular commodities? These opinions have originated in the ignorance at once of fact and of principle . . . .
>   Money or specie has with more plausibility, but in reality with no better ground of truth, been pronounced to be a *measure* of value. Value may be estimated in the way of price; but it cannot be measured, that is to say, compared with a known and invariable measure of intensity, for no such measure has yet been discovered.
>
> Say (1834[1803]:246)

As we see, Say does not aggregate the simple example of a flea market into a full-fledged money economy where agents are anonymous to each other. Furthermore we see that he does not, when he discusses measures, discuss a priori mathematical measures but the eventual existence of a physical measure, and we also then refer to the earlier quote from Say. The reason why we lean on Say is that many economists regard him as the (neo-)classical economist par preference, Say's Law for example, where Keynes also went astray.

Thus the temporal and local equilibria in disequilibrium are nothing more than the actual fulfilments of business agreements irrespective of the global uniqueness of a general price vector. Eventual price stability is not created by the market process but by the socio-political and socio-economic environment. The market process has no intrinsic stability per se.

Well, we may then ask if there are any general economic conclusions we can draw in this situation. The answer is yes, but the conclusions are on the negative side though still intriguing, and they trigger another approach to economic research which gives fewer immediate answers to current problems but which is most probably more productive in the longer run and also takes economics fully into the "club" of empirical sciences.

Let us go back to the state before we transformed the agents and commodities to atomistic variables, before Jevons, so to speak. We however save Debreu's definition of an agent and see what we can do with that.

We had said that the effects of transforming agents and commodities to atomic variables are to deprive them of any structural and contextual relations, so that is what we have to put back again, and to do so we may make use of a concept developed by the mathematician/physicist Thomas Brody (1994), *epistemic/*

epistemological cycles. Debreu's definition of an agent including his temporal and spatial distinction should be like:

$$\text{D 1}: \quad \left({}^{t}_{s}\succsim_i, \, {}^{t}_{s}e_i \right)$$

where t and s represent the time and spatial indexes and i the ith individual. This definition tells us that the preference relations as well as the endowment structures are temporal and local. So, we can now illustrate the individual agent's full problem when it concerns rational choice.

Thus the rational choice has two stages. The first step for the individual is to perceive and comprehend the environmental and contextual characteristics of the choice. The second step is then to apply the simple logical principles as described by the so-called axioms of choice in the neoclassical general equilibrium analysis. Then we choose, but our choice is located in time and space and therefore we have to expect "reactions" of some kind *ex post*, which either fulfil our purposes and the epistemic cycle is closed or our choice is a failure.

If it is a failure, then the individual normally revises purposes and/or contextual apprehensions, which for the future lead to changed market behaviour. As a matter of fact, this is the biggest reason for uncertainty in the real world.

Thus we might change Debreu's definition of an agent to

$$\text{D 2}: \quad \left(C^{t}_{i}, \succsim^{t}_{i}, e^{t}_{i} \right)$$

where C denotes Circumstantial and Contextual conditions.

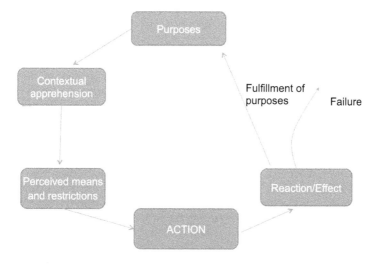

Figure P.4 Epistemic cycle

Source: Ekstedt and Fusari (2010:70)

Going back to the general equilibrium theory, the Axiom of Reflexivity rules our circumstantial and contextual differences. Debreu, through his temporal and spatial limitations of the definition of commodities, on one hand hints that we need to take these matters into consideration but on the other hand, inserting his commodities into the general equilibrium analysis, makes any general equilibrium only temporal and local, and we are back to Say's analysis.

Now we have to look at the concept of disequilibrium in order to see whether we may formulate some general theorems whatsoever.

Our introduction of epistemic cycles is not very promising for formulating some general theory in mathematical forms since by necessity we exclude that the epistemic cycles are uniform in time and space. Even for a single agent, they vary with respect to the kind of decision which is taking place; buying a car has one type of epistemic cycle while buying food for a party has another, so the different choices of the agents are affected by structural and contextual matters and consequently commodities, and other types of choice alternatives are not atomic but complex.

There is in this case one question of overall importance, and that concerns aggregation. We can formulate a proposition concerning this.

Proposition 1

Assume a system $A^\star$ consisting of a finite number of subsystems, which are to be regarded as proper classes, $s_1 \ldots s_n$. If then we have a measure allowing us to define an optimizing rule both on $A^\star$ as well as $s_1 \ldots s_n$, optimization of the global system $A^\star$ must imply that at least one of the subsystems s_i must sub-optimize.

If on the other hand all the subsystems $s_1 \ldots s_n$ are optimized according to the same optimizing process, the global system $A^\star$ must sub-optimize.

(Ekstedt 2013:83)

To prove this, we utilize Russell's paradox and implicitly Cantor's Unaccountability Theorem (Ekstedt 2013:78–80).

It all starts from the difference between atomic variables and complex variables. For atomic variables, it holds generally that the universal set of all sets of atomically defined items belongs to itself. Thus the universal set of real numbers is a set of sets of real numbers.

We may call this kind of items/classes for non-proper classes.

For complex variables, we have however that the universal set of sets of complex items does not belong to itself; Volvo and Citroën are two brands of cars, but lumping them together and calling them for example European cars does not imply that European Cars is a brand of cars. Thus the universal class does not belong to itself; we may call these kinds of classes proper classes.

Consequently we have that if all commodities and agents are stripped of all structural and contextual relations, they and classes of agents or commodities are to be seen as non-proper classes. If however we define individuals in relation to epistemic cycles which are not the same, it implies that the universal class of agents does not belong to itself.

Thus the aggregate behaviour does not belong to the same class of classes of individual behaviour. Consequently the optimization process of the individuals and the aggregate of individuals are based on different conditions.

In Chapter 1 we will see that Russell's concept of non-proper classes/sets is equivalent to the very intricate Kantian concept "Das Ding an Sich" while proper classes/sets are in Kant's terminology equivalent to "Das Ding für Sich", and this will quite naturally lead to the fundamental difference between Immanuel Kant and David Hume, where the latter claims that reason obeys passion while Kant claims that reason is the sole judge of human affairs. We will come back to this.

Proposition 1 is, as a matter of fact, to be seen as a correlate to Arrow's paradox; furthermore, this is precisely what Arrow's paradox shows and nothing else with respect to reality. Any kind of associations to the real world are built on false interpretations of Arrow's Impossibility Theorem.

Finally, we must add that Arrow's Impossibility Theorem necessitates that economic analysis at the macroscopic level cannot be designed without analyzing the role of social structures. When it comes to valuation and particular relative valuations, these are to a high degree dependent on social stratifications, and the fact that we have liquidity and budgetary restrictions doesn't change this. Thus, when entering into a state of disequilibrium, money as a concept enters the analysis in its full complexity.

Money

We have so far discussed something similar to a barter economy. Concerning Arrow's paradox, there is in the original discussion implicitly a sort of enlargement of the concept of commodities to something we may call social states. However, since the defined social welfare function is derived from the six Arrow/Debreu axioms, these "social states" behave like commodities and relative prices can be attached to them, and there is no reason to make some particular comments to them, since we may also work with implicit relative prices.[6] We must make these comments as we now advance to the money economy and there prices are expressed in money terms, although we can also derive implicit relative prices, which in that case will be expressed in money terms. But since money prices can theoretically be used for disequilibrium as well for equilibrium, we must assume that Arrow's Impossibility Theorem deals with the neoclassical equilibrium theory. An application of the theorem to a disequilibrium economy would be nonsense.

Money as we think in ordinary daily terms does not exist in the neoclassical general equilibrium theory. Money as we think of it has three important characteristics: medium of exchange, liquidity and an accounting unit for historical, current and eventual future values. However, in the neoclassical world none of these characteristics are relevant since all relative prices are given in equilibrium and there is no need for liquidity. The most adequate example of what kind of money is needed is by Keynes, who in the first chapter of *Treatise on Money* takes white flat stones as sufficient representative items. Introducing money in the neoclassical theory as a medium of exchange will imply a lot of fuss with neutrality of money, money demand, inflation and growth. Paul Samuelson (1969) wrote an amusing paper on this matter, *What Classical and Neoclassical Monetary Theory Was*, where he points out that accepting the monetary theory as well as the neoclassical axiomatic structure implies that we will have money as a commodity and as such a part of the utility function, and because of this, inflation will implicitly have a positive utility value. It is an interesting hypothesis but may be a little too radical for everybody's taste.

Anyway, many economists believe that they can transpose the results vis-à-vis barter economy to a monetary economy without any trouble. Furthermore, and perhaps worse, economic modelling, irrespective of whether it is neoclassical or Keynesian or something else, uses money values and aggregates in money values as if that is bona fide. Money as we know it in everyday business is a disequilibrium variable. The neoclassical equilibrium theory does not need money; neither does it need monetary policy or any other type of policy. Thus, to assume for example a sort of Friedman's Quantitative Theory of Money as a theoretical addendum to enlarge the barter economy into a money economy is completely meaningless in general equilibrium. It might be OK for a disequilibrium money economy, but it has nothing to do with a neoclassical general equilibrium theory.

Our comments on Arrow's Impossibility Theorem and the subsequent Proposition 1 indicate a theoretical scepticism of the neoclassical theory, and the thought that we should live in a prevailing general equilibrium falls if we look around in the real world. The thought of a convergent process from where we are to some kind of equilibrium is contradictive in terms vis-à-vis the neoclassical axioms which form a structure which is nowhere dense.

However, in disequilibrium, money is an adequate measure for local and temporal business deals by its very acceptance as the highest form of liquidity and medium of exchange. The current values of the agents' incomes and wealth are defined in money with respect to the currently produced commodity basket which has to be sold by the producers and consumed by the consumer. The neoclassical market principle is OK with respect to the microscopic level. However, we have no unique price vector, and the aggregate level is affected by the individuals but not logically dependent in an additive way of the ongoing market transactions. Eventual stability of the market economy depends on the socio-economic and political environment.

One of the friars of Salamanca, Luís Saravia de la Calle, is very outspoken on the matter of what is to be regarded as a just price.

> Excluding all deceit and malice, the just price of a thing is the price which is commonly fetched at the time and place of the deal, in cash, and bearing in mind the particular circumstances and manner of sale, the abundance of goods and money, the number of buyers and sellers, the difficulty of

procuring the goods, and the benefit to be enjoyed by their use, according to an honest man.

(Grice-Hutchinson 1952:79)

The price is clearly, in de la Calle's mind, defined locally and temporally. This means that at the microscopic level there might be a sufficient socio-economic inertia, with respect to single markets, which makes the market in question seemingly stable.

But as well as money adapts to such a state of disequilibrium, it also creates difficulties for the analysts. How shall we treat an aggregate as GDP, for example? Since we have no unique price vectors, such an aggregate must be treated as a measure of volume of transactions made in money during a certain period. If we can assume social inertia and stability of prices, GDP growth in money terms may be interpreted with some confidence as growth of production. However, employment development is rather independent of production changes. The point is that we now discuss relative inertia and stability. Stability of prices is however a problem of itself. How do we measure inflation, how is it created and why is inflation a problem?[7]

If we look at the earlier mention of three intrinsic characteristics of money, medium of exchange, liquidity and medium of contractual relations in space-time, we can see that these are in no way consistent with each other in their appearance in daily economic transactions.

Hume, who was a predecessor of Adam Smith, affected Say a great deal. Hume claimed that for the prospects of growth, the lack of the medium of exchange was most devastating. He also claimed that the money supply should always be in excess of the actual need since that would have a positive effect on the entrepreneurial mind.[8]

It is interesting to listen to public debates on inflation. When discussing the problems of inflation, almost always the risk of hyper-inflation is mentioned. Perhaps this is a sign of the loss of historical knowledge in economics as a science because hyper-inflation historically has occurred in socially deeply unbalanced situations.

First of all we have the case of hyper-inflation like in Germany after WWI, which was deliberately created by the authorities as a consequence of the harsh conditions of the peace treaty.[9] In Argentina at the end of the 1970s and in Russia during the 1990s, the inflation had primarily nothing to do with the market economy but was a sign of fundamental social and political instability and expressed doubts about the institutions of the respective countries.

During "normal" periods inflation, or rather changes of inflation, has mainly three measurable effects: (1) it affects foreign trade, particularly during fixed or semi-fixed currency regimes; (2) it changes the relations between creditors and debtors and lenders and borrowers due to affecting nominally defined assets and liabilities; (3) it changes the income distribution between those who have market-set salaries and those who do not and furthermore the wealth distribution. Often other effects are mentioned, but these are difficult to measure since the effects are intertwined with other contrary effects.

When it comes to money characteristics like liquidity and medium of contractual relations, these contradict the characteristic of medium of exchange. The contractual aspect is particularly unpleasant since a sum of money now represents some medium type of commodity basket of a given dimensionality. Paying a debt at another date than when the debt was incurred implies most probably that the underlying commodity basket for the money economy is different both with respect to dimensionality and quality aspects. That means that strictly we pay back a debt in a different kind of money compared to the one in which we defined the debt. If we politically pursue an austerity policy, the characteristics of medium of exchange and contractual medium will negatively affect growth, and then we must ask about what the nominal valuation really means with respect to distributional and allocation matters, not to mention social stability.

But how is it that we have inflation? During the early 19th century, there was a rather intensive debate about the monetary system between the so-called bullionists (Currency School) and the Real Bill (Banking School) protagonists. The latter was the prevailing approach since Adam Smith, and central to this approach is that its advocators saw no relation between the money supply, which was regulated by the banks themselves according to their position in gold and partly also other securities, and inflation, while the bullionists, particularly the more orthodox, saw money supply as the main root of inflation. In the very situation England was in at that time during the Napoleonic wars, the money supply increased to unprecedented levels, so even bankers such as Henry Thornton who theoretically took a more balanced view between the two approaches were very concerned with the current money supply. However, David Ricardo became the leading figure and wrote the so-called INGOT plan, published posthumously in 1826, which led to the Bank Charter Act of 1844, which in principle institutionalized the Quantity Theory. It is very interesting to see that from the 1980s the Banking School, although not theoretically as much as practically, steadily increased as a structural element in global finance. That means that banks and the financial system base their circulation on securities. The breakdown in 2008 due to over-securitization was much of the same kind as Thornton (1939[1802]) discusses and which was the focus of the bullionist debate in the early 19th century.[10] Theoretically Sargent and Wallace (1982) initiated a discussion on Banking and Currency schools which received a rather harsh answer from Laidler (1984), who pointed out some historical and logical mistakes in the paper. However, apart from Sproul (2000), nobody really engaged in the discussion, which was a bit disappointing since the structural change on the global financial markets was exactly in the direction from the Currency School to the Banking School principle with a declining importance of the Quantity Theory.

Thus with respect to money supply, it most probably has an effect on inflation in the sense of and to the extent which is discussed by the friars of Salamanca during the 16th–17th centuries and Hume (1770[1752]) in his essays on money and other economic matters. However, the Quantity Theory has gravely exaggerated this aspect, which has led to a distorted discussion of monetary matters.

Another important question of inflation when it concerns effects of abundant money supply is whether it is symmetric or asymmetric. If it is asymmetric, it will tend to have structural effects, particularly on consumption but perhaps also, if it is of some duration, on production.

This question of symmetry or asymmetry is of utmost importance when we deal with other causes of inflation.

The reasons for inflation, except money supply, are due to either excess demand/insufficient supply of particularly basic commodities of production or structural inefficiencies of the organization of the production/distribution system. Certainly public fees and taxes play their role, but these fall under the heading of Arrow's paradox, so there is not much to do about them except in political negotiation and persuasion.

Insufficient supply and increasing prices of energy is typically an event which will have strong effects on overall inflation but will also have strong structural effects. Thus we will have a negative income effect and strong structural allocation effects due to differences in substitution possibilities. Mixing up such kind of inflation with money supply inflation is indeed devastating since most people active in industry know that the most efficient way of upholding structural reorganization is to create low consumer demand. However, there is a third effect, and it concerns the more subtle aspect of uncertainty. Structural uncertainty in production with respect to fundamental issues such as energy, infrastructure and eventual introduction of laws are indeed affecting investments severely and will particularly uphold structural reorganization.

When we come to costs and perceived inefficiency caused by regulations and laws within the production system as in the society as a whole, these are without any doubt increasing costs and prices. To live in a civilized and ordered society is costly. The fundamental problem is based upon the fact that the human being, while being the ultimate goal of society and the production process, is also the most important production factor. This creates a double perspective, one from a technical efficiency point of view and the other from an ethical point of view. Ultimately this creates a span from the most possible asymmetric income and wealth distribution combined with slavery to a fairly equal distribution where incomes and wealth are created on mass consumption. In the latter case, we have some sort of optimal distribution of wealth and incomes providing sufficient risk capital together with a sufficient average propensity to consume.

Anyway, these matters create difficulties when societies of different economic and social levels are competing in the world market. Some people in Western countries have some idea that breaking down society is the most efficient way to stimulate investment and growth. The author made in the beginning of the 1970s a small seminar study in economics, where the classical Heckscher-Ohlin approach was compared to Tinbergen's distance model. In the latter approach, the concept of distance was multidimensional in the sense that it contained both geographical distance and economic distance. Lacking computer resources, the investigation had to be limited, but the result was striking: When we compared three groups of countries, industrial countries, (IC), semi-industrial countries

(SIC) and third world countries (TWC), we found that IC traded with IC, SIC traded with IC and TWC traded with IC. The results are of course trivial; it all depends on where market prices are determined.

The production efficiency and the spread of new technologies currently increase at such a speed that an average Western European commodity basket can be produced for the whole world with less than 15% of the world population employed. Consequently, the global employment problem cannot be solved in terms of growth and higher production efficiency. Thus, the world faces a gigantic distribution problem which is not possible to solve within the frames of the current form of market economy.

The fundamental contradiction intrinsic to money

The matters we have discussed above concerning money seem to be completely apart from the barter analysis, and it would indeed be surprising if analytical conclusions could a priori be supposed to hold when we pass over from a neoclassical analysis to an analysis of a money economy. Pro primo, money is meaningless in the neoclassical axiomatic structure. Pro secondo, money prices work and are meaningful in a disequilibrium economy.

However, we can say more. When we prove Proposition 1 above, we must use Russell's paradox (antimony) and his distinction between proper and non-proper sets. Roughly speaking, we can say that all real commodities per se belong to proper sets, where the universal set does not belong to itself, which excludes additive aggregation. Money/money values however belong to non-proper sets, similar to numbers in meaning that the universal set belongs to itself, and that allows additive aggregation.

This will lead us to a second proposition:

Proposition 2

With respect to a real analysis equivalent to barter, Proposition 2 holds.

When we pass over to a non-equilibrium analysis where goals and restrictions are formulated in monetary terms, we lose all logical relations to the real economy and consequently Proposition 1 has no meaning.

The two propositions 1 and 2 are sufficient to show that economic theory built on the principles of the neoclassical theory, which says that the economic sphere in society is in itself enough to analyze and receive results which are consistent with the economic and social reality, is dubious, not to say completely wrong.

The breach between the microscopic level and the macroscopic level as of Proposition 1 implies that the individuals have two levels of decisions which are intertwined; the one concerning themselves and their private conditions and the one concerning the working of the aggregate level. The latter thus implies valuations of the collective development and structures, which only indirectly concerns the individual conditions. This requires social and ethical structures apart from the economic ones, if it is even possible to distinguish clearly between economic, social and ethical structures.

Nevertheless, this is the basic foundation for this book, *Economics, Power and Ethics: From Individual Behavioural Rules to Global Structures*.

Notes

1 In Ekstedt (2015:27–35) there is an analysis of Mill's and Jevons' respective work. There is also a discussion of Jean-Baptiste Say's rejection of general equilibrium in the same context.

2 See a more comprehensive discussion in Ekstedt (2015:27–35).

3 All references to Jevons are taken from chapters 2 and 3 in: Jevons, William Stanley, (1888). The Theory of Political Economy. *Library of Economics and Liberty*, 3 September 2014, www.econlib.org/library/YPDBooks/Jevons/jvnPE2.html

4 DeLong, Howard, (1991). *A Refutation of Arrow's Theorem*. University Press of America, Lanham, New York, and London.

5 Mail from Professor Robert Skidelsky, July 2013. I am grateful to Lord Skidelsky, who called my attention to Keynes' very early awareness of the problems of aggregation and kindly sent me this quote in July 2013.

6 If we shall make a difference between "social states" and commodities, we are definitively leaving the realm of mathematics and Arrow's exercise is redundant.

7 These questions are thoroughly discussed in Ekstedt (2015: chapters 3 and 4).

8 Although Say was very appreciative of Adam Smith, many of his ideas were already contemplated by Hume and Smith learnt much from his correspondence with Hume (Say (1834[1803]:xlii). Interesting also is that Say's grandson Jean-Baptiste Léon Say edited Hume's economic writings "Oeuvre économique de David Hume", 1852, and he claims in the introduction that Hume's publication of his Essays "à une époque où l'économie politique ne formait pas encore une science, mais où elle sortait déjà de son berceau. Adam Smith est son élève" (Diemer 2005:14n).

9 Keynes discusses the WWI peace treaty thoroughly in *The Economic Consequences of the Peace*, and his analysis was unfortunately quite right.

10 This development is discussed in Ekstedt (2015:146–168).

Bibliography

Arrow, K. J., (1963). Uncertainty and the Welfare Economics of Medical Care, *The American Economic Review*, Vol. 53, No. 5.

Brody, T., (1994). *The Philosophy Behind Physics*, Springer Verlag, Berlin, Heidelberg, and New York.

Debreu, G., (1982). Existence of general equilibrium. In K. J. Arrow and M.D. Intrilligator (eds.), *Handbook in Mathematical Economics* (Vol. 2, p. 697), North-Holland Publishing Company, Amsterdam and New York.

Debreu, G., (1987[1959]). *Theory of Value*, Wiley, New York.

DeLong, H., (1991). *A Refutation of Arrow's Theorem*, University Press of America, Lanham, New York, and London.

Diemer, A., (2005, May). *David Hume et les économistes français*, Hermès, Université de Reims, pp. 1–21.

Ekstedt, H., (2013). *Money in Economic Theory*, Routledge, London and New York.

Ekstedt, H., (2015). *Money, Valuation and Growth*, Routledge, London and New York.

Ekstedt, H. and Fusari, A., (2010). *Economic Theory and Social Change Problems and Revisions*, Routledge, London and New York.

Grice-Hutchinson, M., (1952). *The School of Salamanca*, Clarendon Press, Oxford.

Hausman, D.M., (2012). *Preference, Value, Choice, and Welfare*, Cambridge University Press, Cambridge and New York.

Hume, D.A., (1770[1752]). *Essays and Treatises on Several Subjects, Vol. II: Containing Essays, Moral, Political, and Literary*, Printed for T. Cadell (successor of Mr. Millar) in the Strand; and A. Kincaid and A. Donaldson, at Edinburgh.

Jevons, W.S., (1888[1871]). *The Theory of Political Economy*, Macmillan & Co., London, available at internet www.econlib.org/library/YPDBooks/Jevons/jvnPE3.html#

Keynes, J.M., (1938). Letter to Roy Harrod 10th of July, Collected Works of Keynes, available at internet http://economia.unipv.it/harrod/edition/editionstuff/rfh.34a.htm

Laidler, D., (1984). Misconceptions about the Real-Bills Doctrine: A Comment [The Real-Bills Doctrine versus the Quantity Theory: A Reconsideration], *The Journal of Political Economy*, Vol. 92, No. 1, February, pp. 149–155.

Makarov, V.L. and Rubinov, A.M., (1977). *Economic Dynamics and Equilibria*, Springer Verlag, Heidelberg and Berlin.

Mill, J.S., (1990[1863]). Utilitarianism. In *Great Books of the Western World No. 40*, Encyclopædia Britannica, Inc., Chicago, London, New Delhi, Paris, Seoul, Taipei, and Tokyo.

Samuelson, A.P., (1969). What Classical and Neoclassical Monetary Theory Really Was, *Canadian Journal of Economics*, Vol. 1, No. 1, pp. 1–15, and *Collected Scientific Papers*, 1972, Vol. 3, pp. 529–543.

Sargent, T.J. and Wallace, N., (1982). The Real-Bills Doctrine versus the Quantity Theory: A Reconsideration, *The Journal of Political Economy*, Vol. 90, No. 6, pp. 1212–1236.

Say, J.B., (1834[1803]). *A Treatise on Political Economy; or the Production, Distribution, and Consumption of Wealth*, Grigg & Elliot, 9, North Fourth Street, Philadelphia.

Sproul, M.F., (2000). *Three False Critiques of the Real Bills Doctrine*, Department of Economics, California State University, Northridge. http://www.csun.edu/~hceco008/critique.htm

Thornton, H., (1939[1802]). *An Enquiry into the Nature and Effects of the Paper Credit of Great Britain*, George Allen & Unwin, London, available at internet http://oll.libertyfund.org/index.php?option=com_staticxt&staticfile=show.php%3Ftitle=2204&layout=html

Varian, H., (2006). *Intermediate Microeconomics: A Modern Approach*, International Student Edition, W.W. Norton, New York and London.

Wittgenstein, L., (1974[1921]). *Tractatus Logico-Philosophicus*, Routledge and Kegan Paul, London.

1 Ethics in philosophy

The myth[1]

The first Eve, in the Garden of Eden, tempted Adam to eat from the tree of knowledge of good and evil. This mortal sin, beside its deadliness, brought the reflexive intellect to humans. The reflexive intellect is a most dangerous gift. It is like a poison, since it implies that humans also discover the self and otherness and can calculate primary, secondary, tertiary effects and so on and their consequences for self vis-à-vis the other. But all these calculations are uncertain and foggy, due to the deadliness, which leaves the humanity in lifelong doubts of the underlying purposes of words and actions and force mankind into paranoia.

Having received the gift of reflexive intellect, the paradise is lost and closed eternally. An angel guards the paradise with a drawn sword of fire, and will reject any return. The reflexive intellect will hunt and mortify the human mind into loneliness and misery.

God in his mercy, however, sent the second Eve, Saint Mary, who gave birth to Christ, which brought the creative intellect into the world.

The creative intellect is a gift to humans to see beyond the vicious circles created by pure reflexive reasoning, realizing new possibilities of cooperation and collective actions which break the seemingly ironclad conditions of the static reflexive intellect and find ways to happiness in unity with fellow humans as well as rise above the narrow individualism. The humans find ways into new worlds and new heavens, cooperating with each other and God in accomplishing creation according to God's plans.

The myth is nice and appealing and productive for our purposes; we will find traces of it in Aristotle's discussion, although he had nothing to do with the Christian tradition at the time when the myth appeared. It is easy to think of a more general myth which has been adapted into many environments. Basically, it confronts the conflict of passion and intellect and why the beast called human beings can distinguish between and consciously act in relation to ethical categories of good and evil. One of Aristotle's questions is, "Is happiness acquired by learning or habituation, or sent by God or by chance?" This is certainly a valid question, and during history, different answers have been produced. It concerns whether humans are machines/automata or subjects and thereby final causes. The myth obviously aims towards a transformation from automata to subjects by introducing creativity.

Technically speaking we can allude to mathematics or logic when humans obey a certain axiomatic structure but are given the gift to change the axiomatic structure, obtaining different conditions for the social behaviour. Such a leap is outside the realm of the logical "machinery" and we may attach it to faith, creativity, intuition, passion or whatever.

Thus the myth is interesting from the point of view that it separates two types of intellect; the *reflexive* and the *creative*, a distinction which has bearing on the fundamental separation between ethics based on a priori principles à la Kant, ethics based on the assumption of a mutual creation of an organization of society and ethics based on benevolent attitudes and passions for a good life both for self and fellow humans; this is also, at least partly, the distinction underlying Aristotle's question and is expressed in full by David Hume. We will discuss this in depth later.

This distinction does however show up in many ways in philosophical thinking. We may of course think of the famous distinction by Blaise Pascal between *l'esprit de finesse* and *l'esprit de géométrie*, where the latter concerns the deterministic logical calculus while the former concerns the interpretations of the logical results, thus similar to Wittgenstein's analysis. *L'esprit de finesse* is using intuitive thinking, associations and so on.

Furthermore Hans Reichenbach (1938:382) separates *context of discovery* and *context of justification*. Thus, the conviction that there exist two kinds of thinking which are of different qualities but which need to complete each other. Traditionally *l'esprit de géométrie/context of justification* is linked to science, which is natural since we in science actually have to prove or at least disprove a proposition, but the invention/construction of the proposition by itself is an act of *l'esprit de finesse/context of discovery*. Of course, this is further supported by the mathematical development during the 20th century when mathematics and logic was found to be empty of any relations to reality.

The step from the reflective intellect to the creative belongs, according to the myth, to the metaphysical spheres and presupposes a faith based on a general principle to distinguish between faith and reason: "*assensus intellectus veritati*".[2] This principle is in line with Hume's claim:

> Reason is the discovery of truth or falsehood. Truth or falsehood consists in an agreement either to the *real* relations of ideas or to *real* existence or matter of fact. Whatever, therefore, is not susceptible of this agreement or disagreement, is incapable of being true or false, and can never be an object of our reason.
>
> (Hume 2002[1740]:295)

Thus a central question in ethical analysis is whether ethics and moral sentiments are attached to certain aims, such as an ordered life and society, security for the future in the meaning that human actions are foreseeable to a certain degree, or of it is a separate dimension of human nature which is a goal by itself, independent of other dimensions.

Do we act morally to achieve something for ourselves, or do we act morally because we are moral creatures? The above myth suggests the latter, but then we must ask how we achieve such a moral sentiment.

If the first variant is true, then the moral sentiment is subordinated to the contextual situation.

A correlate to this whether we see human beings as subjects or not. If humans are subjects, they cannot be treated as pure means but they are also ultimate goals per se. If this is questioned, we cross the borders of Leviathan before the existence of eventual contracts.

Unfortunately, however, as we discussed in the prologue, analyzing these kinds of things in a scientific way, keeping in mind the two types of thinking above, is difficult since logic and mathematics presume that we have exact definitions, invariant with respect to context and atomic variables. The simplest possible example is two persons who individually are not able to move a big stone but can if they cooperate. Here we have an example where the use of simple predicate calculus, given the axiomatic structure of economic general equilibrium theory, will fail due to an atomic definition of agents in its formulation of additive aggregation.

Thus the scientific analysis of ethics requires the usual *esprit de géométrie* in those parts where logic is required, but to grasp the problem of the complex variables of the real world and to make judgements with respect to contextual dependencies and their effects on individuals and groups of individuals, we need the ability of realizing structural dependences.

Thus the two ways of thinking are and must be integrated when we deal with social sciences in general and ethical analysis in particular.

Ethics and epistemic cycles

In the prologue we discussed briefly the concept of *epistemic cycles*. As we saw, the neoclassical concept of rationality is purely based on a mathematical definition of logical consistence. This is of course a necessary ingredient in the concept but only the last step. In order to act we must base our action on an apprehension and comprehension of the relevant context. The question is then how we arrive at such an apprehension/comprehension. Furthermore, human decisions and actions are part of larger social, economic and ethical structures which govern decisions and actions to a large extent, while structural differences will generally affect the concept of rationality. Thus it is hard to see an immediate ethical attitude with respect to the actual actions even if such an attitude exists on a macroscopic level. Ethics deals with the actions of people in relation to others in a broad sense: short run and long run, born or unborn, earthly living conditions and so on. However, since humans are not gods or demons in the La Place sense, our ethical actions are governed by our feeble knowledge and understanding. In the general equilibrium theory, of the neoclassical approach, only the last step, apprehension/comprehension of the adequate context, is achieved and we just have to make the very action/choice. This was Debreu's interpretation, and it appears even clearer in analyzing Arrow's paradox.

We are reminded of the concept of rationality which, if we use it as purposeful action, can be interpreted as some kind of optimization process. Rationality is consequently a name of a particular logical form, and we saw in the prologue that those axioms (1–3) underlying its technical definition were purely mathematical and are normally used to define an equivalence relation.

Consequently, the ethical principle both on the microscopic and the macroscopic level irrespective of the very content is obviously affected by the *individual's contextual understanding* in that accomplishing an action defines the ethical interpretation. Furthermore, we saw that the way the agents and commodities as well are defined in the neoclassical axiomatic structure, they are void of any structural relationships, since at the very base of any individual epistemic cycle lies the social, economic and ethical structures which we subsequently cannot disregard.

This will affect our choice of philosophical approaches. We are less interested in philosophers who build ethical systems and investigate relations between different ethical systems. Those who interest us are those who discuss the general characteristics of individual understanding and its role for social interaction. We have no interest in presenting a full overview, and the key philosophers will be Aristotle, Hobbes, Hume, Kant and the 20th century logical empiricists, particularly G.E. Moore, Bertrand Russell and Ludwig Wittgenstein. We will not discuss Plato, but concentrate on Kant and to some extent Heidegger. We will also eventually discuss Keynes more as a philosopher than an economist.

A philosopher like Nietzsche would of course be a suitable complement to Hobbes in looking for someone who could restore law and order in Leviathan, but that would take us too far from the main track.

Hegel and followers like Marx could certainly be relevant, but since he and his followers are building societal systems, they are also outside the main track of the chapter. We will however come back to Hegel when we later attack the concept of *otherness*, and Marx in his wide embracing of history and society will often be present as a kind of reference.

Ethics and its connotations

Ethics is indeed a complex concept. From a simple point of view, it can be reduced to a set of implicit behavioural rules which are generic to a certain society. They are generic in the way that they must be an underlying part of an inert civilization. We have to separate the explicit rules which we call laws, regulations and similar and which can be imposed instantly by a ruler, who controls the physical power. Since ethics concerns the implicit behavioural individual rules, they must also be self-imposed by the individual. Mostly this happens by passing on patterns of life in an individual's upbringing and also through socialization in schools and daily interpersonal friction. But this also implies that contrary to law systems, the ethical structure of a society is not codified and therefore it develops over time in an organic way, which is very difficult to analyze.

A central question, with respect to all kinds of ethical courses for business people and consultants on ethical dimensions in business, is whether ethics can be used for other purposes than being a norm for persons adopting a certain ethical structure of behaviour. Thus is ethics or morality something which can be used for achieving different kinds of economic or social benefits.

In philosophy, particularly following an Aristotelian tradition, ethics is an independent aspect in achieving happiness and well-being; if so, we might expect ethical conflicts vis-à-vis other goals. Thus ethical behaviour according to a norm is a means to achieve ultimate human well-being and is not subordinated to any other goals attached to other means. There is a Platonic tradition pursued by Kant and Heidegger claiming an a priori basis for ethics. This is a consequence of the claim that all true understanding of the space is founded in an intuited precondition of the mind, not with respect to the very things and events but of the wholeness, which means that there exists an a priori structure which is true for all humans. We will come back to these differences. However, even an a priori attitude cannot escape the question of how sensual impressions are perceived and apprehended, although we can regard the sensual impression as confusing and misleading sometimes.

However this creates a potential conflict. The society changes socially, structurally and technologically, and laws and regulations become obsolete and have to be changed in conjunction with new societal structures of different kinds. Internally accepted ethical structures are to a great extent a part of the individual's personality and are only linked to external laws and regulations in a very complex way. This leads to the saying: creating a new law takes two months, passing the new law in parliament takes two years, accepting it by the general public takes two generations. Consequently we have all reasons to believe that while a collective body/government has to take into account the different turns on the macroscopic level, the individuals who do not see the totality of the macroscopic level but only those aspects linked to self react in a seemingly irrational way, but given the individuals' apprehension of the macroscopic processes, it might be rational. As we discussed in the prologue, such contradictions will not appear given the agents obeying the neoclassical axiomatic structure. Arrow's paradox was a first, rather rudimentary discussion of the disequilibrium problem, but much more is to come. It is not only the aggregate bodies that change conditions but the individuals themselves in their inventions, innovations and entrepreneurship, and these forces also aggregate bodies to act somehow. Luigi Amoroso (1938:1–21) has a very elegant discussion of the problems:

> It is at this point that the crux of Pareto's system becomes apparent. The internal forces of the economic system are not susceptible of a theoretical representation as simple, elegant, and universal as is the case for the applied forces. They are not only, as for the material macrocosmic systems, forces of conservation, by which – to express it elegantly – the dead city dominates through inertia the living city; they are also directed forces or forces of impulsion, through which the living city forms or attempts to form the city of the future. The internal forces, therefore, are History, they are even Ethics and Politics, something powerful, but vague and indistinct, which is

not susceptible of mathematical representation; an expression of the freedom of the will, which does not allow itself to be enclosed in the meshes of a mechanical representation, and, because it is mechanical, determinist.

Creativity with respect to inventions, innovations and entrepreneurship is not neutral with respect to individuals or to socio-economic structures, and consequently it also has an ethical loading which from the beginning is rather unknown and even unimaginable.

Consequently as we regularly see in politics of different countries, there are so-called "populistic" reactions, which are vague and turned against globalization, internationalization, and often developing into xenophobia. Intellectuals often condemn such "populistic" movements in ethical terms and of course judge them as anti-progressive. The intellectuals are the judges in the power of their skill of verbalization, but they are also the most efficient group to defend their own interests, which not seldom are as conservative and backward-striving as those of ordinary people. The conflict is real and we have to take it seriously: Who will pay for progress? Who will pay for freedom? Who will pay for the open society? If we are not able to answer such difficult ethical questions, we abdicate our responsibility and leave the floor to those who utilize fear, helplessness and segregation for their own power, and this is indeed scary.

We know that to keep a system of laws and regulations which is purely exogenous to the individuals incurs immense costs of enforcement and control. An internalization of an ethical system in line with the collective will is the cheapest possible way of creating a stable society. This was what the Chinese Cultural Revolution was about, and also how the leaders of the French revolution tried to accomplish. This is also what we are doing in Western countries when public media are supposed to defend democratic and liberal values.

Do human beings have an intrinsic ethical compass, as Aristotle thought, or is the human being just a beast with a reflecting intellect, something like what Hobbes proposes, and which can be led to any cruelty or any nobility by a random leader and/or environment?

An ethical system, which we may call a set of implicit rules, is specific for a society, which does not necessarily follow the borders between countries, and has grown out of a history of socio-economic, cultural, political and religious conditions. Thus humans are born into a culture and into an ethical system. Individual questioning of the ethical system is a conscious intellectual act based on observations/education/experience concerning other forms of ethical systems. Thus generally the very discussion of ethical systems often results in a clash between traditional living and intellectual analysis, which often leads to social conflicts, particularly if these are accompanied by class/economic/educational differences. As we are currently experiencing in 2017, such conflicts have the potential of imposing social instability.

Ethics does not primarily concern metaphysics. Metaphysics is often *used* to firmly establish an ethical system in faith and emotions. In fact it can be seen as a set of axioms which are impossible to prove, but by faith one can make them true and a basis for life and the daily social intercourse. Consequently ethical debates based on intellectual discussions are indeed difficult; we may say that people look upon these matters from different perspectives, but it is deeper than that. In the prologue we claimed that the neoclassical axioms created a world which was nowhere dense because it had no environment. Thus there is no way to reach to equilibrium without actually being in it. We may apply the same thinking with respect to ethical systems. They are generally based on traditions, faith, social patterns of living, social relations and so on. An intellectual debate of these things between persons of different ethical opinions is probably ephemeral in its effects and mostly results in harsh voices and stirred emotions. Those factors which have the power to change ethical structures are continuous cultural influences, education and more and more apparent social and economic rifts in the society. But prior to that is how individuals perceive, apprehend and comprehend the socio-economic and cultural environment. Central concepts for all our understanding of our environment is that of time, causality, structure, inertia and reversibility/irreversibility.

Ethics concerns the social relations between individuals as agents and as a collective but not only the momentary behaviour but in a temporal meaning. In fact ethics is the prime glue to link time moments in a society and to make consistent behaviour possible.

Adam Smith links the necessity of consistency and stability of behaviour in relation to the acquisition of valuable property, a discussion which we may easily transfer to the working of the market, investment level and growth.

> Civil government supposes a certain subordination. But as the necessity of civil government gradually grows up with the acquisition of valuable property, so principal causes which naturally introduce subordination gradually grow up with the growth of that valuable property.
>
> (Smith 1952[1776]:309)

We have already mentioned Leviathan, and we will later discuss Hobbes more carefully. However, in the quote there is a dynamic dependency between acquisition of valuable property and the degree of subordination in the civil society.

In the Nordic Sagas, there are a couple of events which could be seen as the first steps from Hobbes' Leviathan to the civil society.

In Snorre Sturlasson's saga of *Egil Skallagrimsson*, which took place in 980–985, we are told that Egil came to his friend's farm, but his friend was in England with the Norwegian king. During Egil's stay at the farm, Ljot, an ill-reputed Swedish fighter, challenged the friend's oldest son about the property. At that time there was a law, *Holmgångslag*, such that a man could challenge anyone about anything and everything, and if he won, he took the property the challenge concerned. Ljot had gained much land that way since he was a mighty fighter. Gyda, the wife of Egil's friend, then asked Egil to fight instead of her son, with the obvious result that Ljot was killed. In Sturlasson's saga of *Grette Asmundsen*, circa 1020–1025, we are told that Eirik Jarl, the representative of the king, gathered prominent men and farmers in Norway to discuss this law, *Holmgångslag*, and they were concerned about the great number of skilled farmers who had been killed in such challenges. Those who won were not able to develop the farms, but let them be destroyed. A new law was decided which abolished *Holmgångslag* and which also made these professional fighters outlaws.

The existence of such a law from the very beginning was not particularly strange. People were searching for new land, and in such a search there were many reasons for conflicts. The areas were often frugal and outside any legislation. Furthermore, the economic conditions of those who searched for new land were more or less similar. A challenge was often a fair way to settle things. From what I learnt from Western movies and Western books, there was a similar situation during the search for new land westwards in the present US.

However when we come to Grette Asmundsen's saga, around forty years after most disputes were settled and cultivation of land was the medium of economic growth, the old law was not only obsolete but counterproductive in the current society, preventing further investments in cultivation.

From a temporal point of view, the *Holmgångslag* concerned a very moment of dispute, mainly on acquisition of new land, while Eirik Jarl's prohibition of such challenges merely concerned the intertemporal conditions for cultivation and for the security of farmers and their investments.

As we understand it, there was nothing particularly moral about the new law, but it made skills with respect to cultivation and cattle breeding more important than physical strength. Thus the individuals had to subordinate to an imposed law which changed the valuation of individual abilities.

This is a very important aspect which Smith raises, also when looking at it from a more principle point of view than Smith does.[3]

Any type of society with a law system requires subordination to the law and a class of persons who uphold the law system, but it is also implicit in the very structure of the law system that it imposes an implicit measure of valuation of human abilities. This is not only present with respect to the law system but also in moral sentiments, customs, fashion. Thus, looking at a society from an abstract point of view, there are almost always explicit or implicit revaluations going on. Some explicitly expressed in prices, laws and regulations, but some less obvious, like obsolescence in patterns of life in a broad sense; more serious is structural unemployment because certain abilities are not demanded or obsolescence of capital stock, implying the fall of even big industries. A rather obvious change which we see in the so-called post-post-industrial society is that the control of production processes, both in the traditional industry as well as in the traditional service sector, is computerized and human beings are used for tasks requiring a higher degree of social interaction than was seen thirty or forty years ago. That means that labour demand nowadays is completed with aspects of social behaviour, appearance, communication abilities and so on. All these aspects lead to revaluations and in the end structural/permanent unemployment. As we mention in the footnote, Smith is aware of such things, but nowadays the scale of processes is made larger.

This chapter was written in 2017, and we have seen the so-called populist movement develop in most of the OECD countries at the same time that revolutionary movements are created in traditional/old-fashioned countries, with respect to religion and customs. These are two sides of the same valuation dynamics. In the OECD countries, people are sorted out from the labour market due to structural changes in technology, world demand, fashion and many other factors.

In the traditional countries, particularly young people see themselves robbed of their abilities due to old-fashioned structures and religious conservatism.

In the rather stable and hierarchical society of Adam Smith, he could look upon the factors of subordination as more or less constant and eternal. This has perhaps changed.

Eirik Jarl did not care a great deal about these men, "bärsärkar", professional fighters; in fact he made them outlaws. Has this changed completely?

The question is who shall subordinate to whom, and in which respect? Furthermore we may ask, if valuations change, does the society have any responsibility for those who are *losers*, and what do we mean by the concept of losers? If we look at these changes as more or less random, it would of course be easy to set up a sort of insurance system.

A central factor which influences any form of ethical system or moral sentiment is how we imagine what we perceive and how we apprehend and comprehend it. It is linked to deep-going ontological and epistemological idiosyncrasies. Roughly we have two ways of imagining the universe: the Platonic/Kantian and the Aristotelian/Humean approaches. There are many different variations of these and sometimes they overlap each other, but it is a simple method of classification. Both approaches claim that humans have mental abilities of different kinds which are unique for human beings. But the fundamental difference is that while Aristotle and most of all Hume claim that our impressions through the senses are the only basis for knowledge, ideas and action, Plato and Kant claim that there exists some a priori knowledge or understanding independent of the sensible impressions. This difference will of course affect the ethical discussions, as we will see.

But first it is of importance to clarify the thoughts about how humans acquire knowledge of the surrounding world.

We will limit our discussion to four main philosophers: Aristotle, Hobbes, Hume and Kant.[4] It might be surprising that we include Hobbes, since he is not one of the more important philosophers, but he is the initiator of contract theory, which is developed in economic theory. However, when we look at these four philosophers, we will use the analytical filter of the mathematical logic and analytical philosophy during the 20th century.

Another of the basic problems at which we aim is the classical conflict between Kant and Hume, whether reason is in control of or if it is the humble servant of passion. This difference regarding the human way of thinking is of great importance and is built on the different opinions of whether there exists a priori knowledge besides that which is built on the impressions by the human sensible apparatus. The question is also the intrinsic relations in the human being between reason and passion, since there does not seem to be a clear-cut border between them. This is also underscored by results in modern brain research, to which we will come back later.

Ethical behaviour is part of the daily behaviour of people, and it cannot be separated from other aspects of classification of living. *Rational behaviour* for example is a concept which is empty of content. It needs goals for the behaviour, it needs contextual apprehension and it needs imposed restrictions on behaviour. Furthermore, individual social behaviour is generally required to be fairly consistent; thus we have the problems of time, memory and causality.

Consequently the ethical principles of whatever form are seldom difficult to grasp, but it is their implication in a certain contextual and historical environment which makes them problematic. Observe here that we do not speak of ethics on the aggregate level but on the individual one. Thus the individual as well as being an acting subject with respect to the private spheres is also a part of the collective body and its composite behaviour.

Analyzing ethics consequently requires that we see the concept in relation to the intellect and knowledge. It must also be put in relation to time and memory, in relation to individual and collective perspectives, and there are surely more aspects but these are examples. Thus the attitude one sees many times, that *the ethical dimension* is something which we sometimes have to take into consideration and sometimes not, is a rather obscure picture of ethics. What is the society in the absence of an ethical structure? We can have clashes of ethical structures, we can have breakdowns of ethical structures, but it is hardly possible to think of any society without ethical structures. You can say that those who are poor are themselves to be blamed and that supporting them by collective means is damaging for those who really achieve something and add to the common wealth. This is an ethical standpoint. We can say that it is right or wrong based on different norms, but still it is an ethical position. From our analytical point of view, it is however more interesting to analyze the stability of such an ethical position if it dominates a society.

We have rather recently experienced a change in the policy towards refugees. In the author's home country, Sweden, this has led to changes in laws which make it possible to expel people, young males, to countries which the migration board claims are stable and secure for people at the same time they forbid their own personnel to go there because it is too unsafe. The authorities are allowed to use considerable force to expel people, which is clearly against all humanitarian rules, but the law allows it. So we may arrive at the ultimate ethical question: Is it always in line with humanitarian rules to obey the law, and if not, what shall we do? Are unwritten ethical standards subordinated to newly created rules to politically solve an acute problem? In the Nuremberg trials, some persons were sentenced to death since they had not opposed Hitler, although they claimed that if they had not obeyed him they would have been killed, which was most probably true.

However, prior to all analysis of the ethical nature of humans and society is the very fundamental question of how humans perceive and comprehend their environment, and we will see that there are wide varieties of approaches to that.

An intense question is whether we must trust our sensual perceptions or whether we may have some analytical a priori knowledge to revise our deficient sensual perceptions. Furthermore, we may also ask what happens when we transform our perceptions and comprehensions into logical or mathematical analysis, as we mentioned in the prologue in the discussions on Wittgenstein's Proposition 6.211.

Humans as moral creatures or calculating beasts

A question which is implicit in the myth is whether humans are moral creatures or calculating beasts. This question is particularly discussed by Aristotle and Hobbes so it can be good to start with these two, although Aristotle will have other things to say which are important for later discussions.

Aristotle

As usual in an analysis of the peculiarities of our world, it is practical to start with Aristotle – not because he is always right or always particularly interesting, but because he had Plato for a teacher and thus he had a brilliant education, for that time, in logic and deductive analysis. He also broke from Plato's idealistic analysis of the world and opened the path to modern empirical analysis. Bertrand Russell writes in his book on history of philosophy:[5]

> In reading any important philosopher, but most of all in reading Aristotle, it is necessary to study him in two ways: with reference to his predecessors, and with reference to his successors. In the former aspect, Aristotle's merits are enormous; in the latter, his demerits are equally enormous. For his demerits, however, his successors are more responsible than he is. He came at the end of the creative period in Greek thought, and after his death it was two thousand years before the world produced any philosopher who could be regarded as approximately his equal.

Aristotle touched on most aspects of nature, humans and society, and thus systematically used his scientific method in such a way that he gave a rather consistent picture of the surrounding world and society.

Ethics is thoroughly discussed in the *Nicomachean Ethics* (which will be shortened to *NE*), but he also touches on such questions in *Politics* and *On Rhetoric*.

We will not go into the material content of Aristotle's ethics but more discuss his conceptualizations and his structural positioning of ethics in individual and social life.

As usual, Aristotle starts with the very conceptualization of the issue he is going to analyze, and that is the basic virtue of his analysis. But more than that, Aristotle is thoroughly aware of the fact that some for some issues, by their very nature it is easy to find efficient and precise conceptualizations, while for others that are more obscure, the conceptual precision is less and should be less since "We must not expect more precision than the subject–matter admits of" (Aristotle, *NE*, p. 2).

The *Nicomachean Ethics* contains ten books. For our purposes, the first six books are most important, and particularly the first three.

A central question to Aristotle is whether the ability to make ethical considerations is a "gift" to the human being as a species or if it is due to breeding and social development.

The question is indeed relevant, and we have the well-known answer from Thomas Hobbes, who describes the human as a calculating beast incapable of social cooperation and at best being able to be "governed" by a strong leader (which per se is a somewhat contradictory creation). Aristotle is of the opposite opinion and claims that the human being has an ability separate from animals.

The difference between Aristotle and Hobbes is however a bit difficult to define, so we must start with Aristotle's conceptualization in order to understand the difference.

Ethics is a science very close to politics. Aristotle claims already in the sub-title of the second part of Book I that "The science of the good of the man is politics", thus ethics, both individual as well as collective, is to be considered as the science of politics. What is then the role of ethics? He claims that all human activities aim at some good; consequently the general science of the good for men is politics, and thus ethics is a sub-science with respect to rational behaviour of the individual, given the aim of achieving the ultimate good. Aristotle separates basically three government forms: the ruling of the one, the few and the many. He separates two forms, one good and one less good, for each of them. The fundamental dividing line between the good and the less good forms are on one hand whether the rulers are aiming at the good of the collective or are just interested in selected groups of the collective and on the other hand whether the single citizen looks upon the state/collective as a productive member and considers the activities of the state valuable for the individual as well or whether the individual behaves like a kind of "free rider" (Aristotle doesn't use this expression).

Thus to achieve the ultimate good, we need both the state/collective as an independent actor as well as the individual actors, and both parts should be governed by *rational behaviour* vis-à-vis the ultimate aim. Subsequently ethics in the Aristotelian sense is the science of what is rational behaviour in the aim at achieving the ultimate good.[6] In relation to the discussion in the prologue, Aristotle claims:

> Since there are evidently more than one end, and we choose some of these (e.g. wealth, flutes, and in general instruments) for the sake of something else, clearly not all ends are final ends; but the chief good is evidently something final. Therefore, if there is only one final end, this will be what we are seeking, and if there are more than one, the most final of these will be what we are seeking. Now we call that which is in itself worthy of pursuit more final than that which is worthy of pursuit for the sake of something

else, and that which is never desirable for the sake of something else more
final than the things that are desirable both in themselves and for the sake
of that other thing, and therefore we call final without qualification that
which is always desirable in itself and never for the sake of something else.[7]

(*NE*:342 Bno. 1097ᵃ)

Furthermore, Aristotle claims a clear link between the individual and collective
ethics in the sense that both have the same ultimate aim in mind but work with
different means. When we go back to Proposition 1 in the prologue, where we
showed that microscopic and macroscopic levels were logically separate only
with respect to additive aggregation, Aristotle separates two forms of ruling a
society. The one where inhabitants and the ruler try to see to the best of all, in
the case of ruling of the many, is called *politeia*. The bad form occurred when
everybody utilized the state and its affairs for their own purposes and was called
Democracy. Thus, in relation to Proposition 1, Aristotle broadens the perspective
to the total social organization where the individual accepts that the aggregate
bodies have to make asymmetric decisions in order to balance the whole. Subsequently, the interaction between individual and collective ethics is and must
be very strong but implemented in different ways:

> Virtue, then, being of two kinds, intellectual and moral, intellectual virtue in
> the main owes both its birth and its growth to teaching (for which reason
> it requires experience and time), while moral virtue comes about as a result
> of habit, whence also its name (ethike) is one that is formed by a slight
> variation from the word ethos (habit). From this it is also plain that none
> of the moral virtues arises in us by nature; for nothing that exists by nature
> can form a habit contrary to its nature. For instance the stone which by
> nature moves downwards cannot be habituated to move upwards, not even
> if one tries to train it by throwing it up ten thousand times; nor can fire be
> habituated to move downwards, nor can anything else that by nature behaves
> in one way be trained to behave in another. Neither by nature, then, nor
> contrary to nature do the virtues arise in us; rather we are adapted by nature
> to receive them, and are made perfect by habit.
>
>   . . .
>
> This is confirmed by what happens in states; for legislators make the citi-
> zens good by forming habits in them, and this is the wish of every legislator,
> and those who do not effect it miss their mark, and it is in this that a good
> constitution differs from a bad one.
>
> (ibid.:348, Bno. 1103ᵃ)

When we thus consider our question above, whether man has an "ethical" gift
or not, the answer is in a way yes, but not ethics per se; rather using it as a means
to achieve certain ends. The end in general form is in the very subtitle to the
first part of "Ethics": *All human activities aim at some good: some goods subordinate to
others.* However, to understand what Aristotle means by *good*, we must scrutinize

the difference between humans and animals and most of all the soul of humans in relation to the soul of animals. These things are discussed in *Biological Treatises* with respect to animals, particularly in "On the Motion of Animals" and "On the Gait of Animals", and in *Metaphysics*.

Aristotle counts humans as animals from a biological point of view, so his differentiation occurs when regarding the *soul* of different animals. That is why we must consider *Metaphysics*. He starts (*Metaphysics* 1990:980[a] and 980[b]):

> All men by nature desire to know. An indication of this is the delight we take in our senses; for even apart from their usefulness they are loved for themselves; and above all the sense of sight. For not only with a view to action, but even when we are not going to do anything, we prefer seeing (one might say) to everything else. . . . The animals other than man live by appearances and memories, and have but little of connected experience; but the human race lives also by art and reasonings.

In the last sentence he mentions "art and reasonings," which seems a link to Hume's distinction between reason and passion. Aristotle actually follows up this theme in *On the Soul* (1990:632 and 403[a]):

> A further problem presented by the affections of soul is this: are they all affections of the complex of body and soul, or is there any one among them peculiar to the soul by itself? To determine this is indispensable but difficult. If we consider the majority of them, there seems to be no case in which the soul can act or be acted upon without involving the body; e.g. anger, courage, appetite, and sensation generally. Thinking seems the most probable exception; but if this too proves to be a form of imagination or to be impossible without imagination, it too requires a body as a condition of its existence. If there is any way of acting or being acted upon proper to soul, soul will be capable of separate existence; if there is none, its separate existence is impossible. In the latter case, it will be like what is straight, which has many properties arising from the straightness in it, e.g. that of touching a bronze sphere at a point, though straightness divorced from the other constituents of the straight thing cannot touch it in this way; it cannot be so divorced at all, since it is always found in a body. It therefore seems that all the affections of soul involve a body – passion, gentleness, fear, pity, courage, joy, loving, and hating; in all these there is a concurrent affection of the body.

Aristotle displays here a view which is close to modern brain research, which claims that the soul in Aristotle's meaning and the body are integrated and that external events affecting the body also have physiological effects on the brain and its functions.

In "On the Motion of Animals" (Biological Treatises 1990:700[b]) Aristotle claims that the soul moves the body related to an *end* created by speculation, while animal movement belongs to the sphere of action, not speculation. By that he means that while men might move because of reflections on current events in relation to gained experiences, wisdom is thus the knowledge of certain principles and causes. For the animals, however, there is only a direct link between current apprehension and action and a memory linked to a certain thing/person/action without any further generalization.

Consequently, there is a gift installed in humans, namely the ability to grasp ends which are not directly caused by current events, and this gift is, if we interpret Aristotle's discussion on memory/reflection/experience, in its deepest sense linked to the ability of abstraction and generalization. Ethics becomes thus the science of achieving such ends in a rational way.

The Aristotelian rationality is however not the bare skeleton of an equivalence relation as in the neoclassical general equilibrium theory but of the kind we discussed in relation to epistemic cycles in the prologue; thus the rationality includes also contextual considerations.

In relation to our question of whether humans are calculating beasts reacting to events, Aristotle answers, no. Humans have through their capacity for speculation/reflection the ability to formulate ends which are separate from the current events and the current need of action, and thereby there is a need of a separate kind of analysis which takes us beyond the immediate action and into more abstract and generalized questions.

However, this is affected by differences in experiences, traditions and memory, and to change the individual's basic apprehension of the environment does not imply that plain intellectual speculation is sufficient. It has to be consistent with current living.

Thus the fairly materialistic Aristotelian view of body and soul tells us that the intellect is a part of the body; the soul is an incarnation of the newborn child, and the bodily sensations during life implies that ethics is a part of our bodily life and is integrated in our social life and experiences. Ethics are not something to shove into the analysis after more practical considerations have been done. Furthermore, ethics are not something valuable per se, but ethical principles guide our actions, and then the actions are those which are to be valued in terms of good or bad:

> Now neither the virtues nor the vices are passions, because we are not called good or bad on the ground of our passions, but are so called on the ground of our virtues and our vices, and because we are neither praised nor blamed for our passions (for the man who feels fear or anger is not praised, nor is the man who simply feels anger blamed, but the man who feels it in a certain way), but for our virtues and our vices we are praised or blamed.
>
> Again, we feel anger and fear without choice, but the virtues are modes of choice or involve choice. Further, in respect of the passions we are said to be moved, but in respect of the virtues and the vices we are said not to be moved but to be disposed in a particular way.
>
> (NE:351, Bno. 1105^b)

In Book VI, Aristotle makes a statement of utmost importance which is in line with our discussions in the prologue on the content and relevance of the neo-classical theory in economics and which is the foundation for the methodological line in this book:

> The origin of action – its efficient, not its final cause – is choice, and that of choice is desire and reasoning with a view to an end. This is why choice cannot exist either without reason and intellect or without a moral state; for good action and its opposite cannot exist without a combination of intellect and character. Intellect itself, however, moves nothing, but only the intellect which aims at an end and is practical; for this rules the productive intellect, as well, since everyone who makes, makes for an end, and that which is made is not an end in the unqualified sense (but only an end in a particular relation, and the end of a particular operation) – only that which is done is that; for good action is an end, and desire aims at this. Hence choice is either desiderative reason or ratiocinative desire, and such an origin of action is a man. (It is to be noted that nothing that is past is an object of choice, e.g. no one chooses to have sacked Troy; for no one deliberates about the past, but about what is future and capable of being otherwise, while what is past is not capable of not having taken place . . .).
>
> (ibid.:388, Bno. 1139[a])

Although Aristotle saw an ethical predisposition of the human being, the explicit ethical system was obtained by traditions, experiences and intellectual considerations, and when he discusses passions in the meaning desire of ultimate ends, he looks upon ethics as intertwined with the intellect in moulding the desires, and he ends the sixth book by writing: "It is clear, then, from what has been said, that it is not possible to be good in the strict sense without practical wisdom, nor practically wise without moral virtue" (ibid.:394, Bno. 1144[b]).

Thomas Hobbes

Thomas Hobbes is viewed as the first modern political philosopher who gave birth to the contract theory in economics. From a philosophical perspective, he is perhaps not one of the most prominent, but he is one of the first, being influenced by Galileo, to bring motion and inertia into philosophical analysis and tried to adapt political philosophy to these concepts. He was very close to Francis Bacon, a leading Platonic philosopher, but Hobbes never exhibited any deeper forms of Platonism. His analysis of the State is based on his views of man and his political and practical considerations vis-à-vis his view of man. He was accused of being an atheist, but that was not proved since Parliament dismissed the case. Nevertheless, Hobbes' writing is based on Averroes, the Muslim philosopher who brought Aristotle to Europe and claimed that after creation, God left the world to its inhabitants. Hobbes is particularly enthusiastic about geometry and the growing science particularly in Italy around Galileo, and he tries to apply a scientific method to his investigations. Hobbes is more apt to accept an inductive method; Russell, for example, pays attention to that in a positive way in a comparison with Hume, for example, who shows a thorough scepticism towards induction. However, Russell's appreciation of Hobbes' use of induction is perhaps a bit overstated, particularly when he alludes to Hume. Hobbes appears in his philosophy a bit mechanistic; with respect to social empiricism he uses induction, which is bona fide considering natural sciences, but with respect to social sciences there is no clear-cut way to apply empirical induction, which as we discussed in the prologue requires nearly atomic facts. Hobbes is basically a nominalist, which implies that he denies universalities; a group of animals, for example horses, has nothing more in common than the word *horses*. In principle, that means that definitions are always ostensive. This implies that abstract and generalized concepts based on structural definitions are not within his analytical realm.

We will come back to Hobbes in a later chapter, when we discuss contract theory, but here we will just deal with his view of the human disposition, which as we will see seems possible to link to behaviourism.

Leviathan consists of four parts: Of Man, Of Common-Wealth, Of a Christian Common-Wealth, Of the Kingdome of Darkness. Only the first part is of interest to us here. In this part, we particularly discuss the first nine chapters since they deal with the links from the sensual perception to the difference between passion and reason, ending in chapter 8 on intellectual virtues and defects and chapter 9 upon the subject of knowledge.

We mentioned above that Hobbes, following Galileo, was inspired to analyze the aspects of motion and inertia, which indeed places him among the early thinkers dealing with the aspect of motion other than natural clocks.[8] In principle, the general idea, probably taken from Aristotle or St. Thomas, is that without a prime mover, the universe is at rest. With respect to the human mind, it is at rest but set in motion by external impulses perceived by the senses. By the senses, Hobbes does not mean only the physical processes but also the impression, apprehension, of the mind: "So that Sense in all cases, is nothing but the original fancy, caused (as I have said) by the pressure, that is, by the motion, of external things upon our Eyes, Ears, and other organs thereunto ordained" Hobbes (1985[1651]:86). Later he relates his view on this to a text (used in learned societies) by Aristotle:

> But the Philosophy-schooles, through all Universities of Christendome, grounded upon certain Texts of *Aristotle*, teach another doctrine; and say, For the cause of *Vison*, that the thing is seen, sendeth forth on every side a *visible species* (in English) *a visible shew, apparition*, or *aspect*, or *a being seen*; the receiving of whereof into the Eye, is *Seeing*.
>
> (emphases in original; *Leviathan*:86)

Hobbes thus includes the mental processes creating the subjective picture in the very act of seeing. And he proceeds by defining imagination: "IMAGINATION therefore is nothing but *decaying sense*; and found in men, and many other living Creatures, as well as sleeping, as waking" (ibid.:88). From that he derives *memory* as more or less the same thing and basically linked to the Sense which is fading. Thus, experience is nothing but a "memory of many things". He, however separates between simple Imaginations: "as when one imagineth a man, or horse, which he hath seen before", and compounded Imaginations: "as when from the sight of a man at one time, and of a horse at another, we conceive in our mind a Centaure" (ibid 89). From these considerations, Hobbes moves into discussions of dreams, apparitions and visions but we proceed to understanding.

He writes:

> That understanding which is peculiar to man, is the understanding not onely his will; but his conceptions and thoughts, by the sequel and contexture of the names of things into Affirmations, Negations, and other forms of Speech: And of this kinde of Understanding I shall speak hereafter.
>
> (ibid.:94)

After defining understanding, Hobbes proceeds to the compounded understanding appearing in analysis, or as the subtitle tells, *Of the Consequence or* T RAYNE *of Imaginations*. By that, he means, "I understand that succession of one Thought to another, which is called (to distinguish it from discourse in words) *Mentall Discourse*" (ibid.:94).

First of all, the last quote displays a nominalist apprehension of the relation between humans and the environment. Our understanding is linked to our means of linguistic expression. In the deepest sense, this means that reason must reign since language must be basically consistent. The quote also expresses this view. This is contrary to the Aristotelian analysis and points more at Kant's analysis of reason in relation to "Das Ding an Sich" and "Das Ding für Sich". Hobbes' way of discussing observation and memory is certainly leading one's thoughts to our insufficient senses, which hinder us from apprehending the reality a priori.

A second comment, which strengthens the first point, is that compared to Aristotle, the link between observation, imagination and memory is rather mechanic. It has elements of Locke's "Tabula Rasa" mixed with behaviourism.

Although Aristotle did not have the current knowledge, pattern of analysis in the light of the logical/mathematical advances during the 20th century and the current means of observation, he perceives the complexity of intellect, bodily sensations and social actions. Hobbes' analysis is more or less void of such complexities. However, Hobbes' description is consistent with his answer to the question of whether humans are calculating beasts which react to current actions, which is yes. From such a description, we can expect no self-organizing ability from the individuals as a group, just chaos. The trouble is whether the ruler is from another world or is "King by the Providence of God". Ethics does not exist intrinsically in the individual but is enforced through contracts and external control.

Reason and passion

Hobbes displays a rather direct line from current observation to analysis and action. The problem with this is on one hand that he regards the observation (seeing) as uncertain and so the memory. Furthermore the reason/intellect is not treated as a complex internal relation between body and soul, passions and intellect but rather as a simple logical analysis based on a nominalist belief that the linguistic expressions also form the individual's apprehension/understanding of observed events. Thus the nominalism from a logical point of view transforms universals automatically to atomic concepts and has no room for complexities, since different creatures and items are too complex and the only relation we have to nature, except living per se, is the language. For Aristotle this is, as we understand, an impossible line of analysis.

Anyway, Hobbes' outline of the acting human is more or less what we interpret as a reflective Beast. It is also interesting that compared with Platonists, the Beast has no norm a priori which makes him lost and confused in life; a society populated with such a kind of Beast evolves most probably into chaos. Reading Hobbes in this way makes it rather similar to the reflexive human in the myth at the start of this chapter. Furthermore the way back to Paradise, the normed society, is guarded perhaps not by an angel but by the mental disposition of humans.

The interaction between ethical virtues and wisdom which Aristotle stresses is meaningless in Hobbes' analysis, but he probably agrees with Aristotle that reason without an end is empty.

Let us now move to the 18th century and to two giants in philosophy, David Hume and Immanuel Kant. Between them we have the most well-known debate of reason and passion.

In a way there are similarities between Hobbes and Kant. The latter was in his extraordinary docility to mathematics approaching nominalist approaches; however, his idealism was modified by his wider and deeper analysis and his distinction between concepts by themselves and concepts perceived. However Kant, like Hobbes, places a particular emphasis on the uncertainty of perceptions by the senses which leads to the distinction between "Das Ding an Sich" and "Das Ding für Sich". Aristotle, like Hume, admits the uncertainty of perception and apprehension, but since they also reject a priori information exogenous to the sensible perceptions, they do not require such a distinction.

Kant[9]

Kant has been of great importance to the European way of discussing space and time and the cementing of the Newtonian apprehension of space-time, so we must discuss his approach from the roots, since that will also explain his ethical conclusions.

The basic problem Kant tries to tackle with this distinction is the difference between the perceived object and the object itself, where the latter can be perceived in many different forms; thus a specific perception of an object is just one of many possible perceptions and depends on perspectives, contextual conditions and so on.

> Since we cannot treat the special conditions of sensibility as conditions of the possibility of things, but only of their appearances, we can indeed say that space comprehends all things that appear to us as external, but not all things in themselves.
>
> (Kant 1933:72)

And he continues:

> The transcendental concept of appearances in space, on the other hand, is a critical reminder that nothing intuited in space is a thing in itself, that space is not a form inhering in things themselves as their intrinsic property, that objects in themselves are quite unknown to us, that what we will call outer objects are nothing but mere representations of our sensibility, the form of which is space.
>
> (ibid.:73–74)

Kant thus separates an item as it really is, "Das Ding an Sich", from the particular perception of the item in question, "Das Ding für Sich". A first reaction from a philosophical point of view is that we have a revival of the concept of substance. This leads back to the discussion between Plato and Aristotle where Plato held an a priori attitude. A table is based on its "tableness", which is a sort of universal principle determining the basic structure of all particular things which are to be called *table*.

Aristotle has a more materialistic approach to substance. We have somehow defined a table, structural, functional or ostensive, which is the basic principle, substance, of a thing. To this we add other attributes such as colour, particularities of the form, size and similar.

One could suspect that Kant is affected, as he probably was, by the Platonic view, although he developed it into an even more abstract form, as we will see.

What Kant achieves with his distinction between "Das Ding an Sich" and "Das Ding für Sich" is that he empties the variables of real content and thus "Das Ding an Sich" becomes equal for all people, and then we achieve exactly the kind of atomic variables which we achieve in the neoclassical axiomatic structure with the Axiom of Reflexivity. The true reality will thus be possible to analyze by mathematical/logical models. From a philosophical point of view, this follows from Kant's particular kind of nominalism; he makes a clear distinction of *phenomena* and *noumena*:

> The concept of a noumenon is thus a merely limiting concept, the function of which is to curb the pretensions of sensibility; and it is therefore of negative employment. At the same time it is no arbitrary invention; it is

bound up with the limitation of sensibility, though it cannot affirm anything positive beyond the field of sensibility.

(ibid.:272)

Thus the *noumena* are empty symbols representing the sensible object without adding any factors. With respect to our discussions in the prologue on Wittgenstein's Proposition 6.211, the *noumenon* is the defined variable ready to be used in a logical/mathematical analysis. Thus we have streamlined the phenomenon in such a way that we may use it as an atomic variable suitable for mathematical analysis within the very limits of the definitions of the variable.

Kant himself is actually a bit surprised of his findings; namely that to make a logical/mathematical analysis we need to empty the phenomena of their content: "Now whence, I ask, can the understanding obtain these synthetic propositions, when the concepts are to be applied, not in their relation to possible experience, but to things in themselves (noumena)?" (ibid.:275). As we see, Kant is genuinely on the trail to Wittgenstein's Proposition 6.211 and he concludes: "The problematic thought which leaves open a place for them serves only, like an empty space, for the limitation of empirical experiences, without itself containing or revealing any other object of knowledge beyond the spheres of those principles" (ibid.:275).

Kant here in these words spells out scepticism, well in the realm of Hume's, although he starts from an abstract idealism. The mistake Kant makes is that he thinks that the mathematical/logical treatment of a system with a set of concepts is neutral with respect to the concepts; he thus rejects all attributes of the things which complicate the mathematical analysis. However, he then believes that the logical conclusions produced by the mathematical analysis are bona fide when we put these results into an empirical setting, and as a matter of fact he finds this curious, not to say strange. In the prologue we show that from the viewpoint of modern philosophy and mathematical logic, Kant's puzzlement is highly relevant and shows his analytical sharpness. Some claim that Kant was a nominalist, which is a bit misleading. His nominalism is more a methodological tool, so to speak.

There are three particular problems with Kant's view in "*Kritik der reinen Vernunft*".

The first is his approach to time, which we will discuss separately later on.

The second is that his separation of the true objects from the perceived/apprehended objects implies not only that objects are seen as nowhere dense, that is, without any structural relationships, but also that human beings are seen in the same manner.

Here we are approaching a most disturbing psychological problem of the Western world where a much-discussed question is how humans can find bridges to "the Other" to break their existential loneliness. The *otherness* is indeed a both psychological and a philosophical problem, which we will come back to. Kant however drives this problem to an extreme when he deprives the human beings' communication tools, their senses, of their meaning.

As we saw, Aristotle was keen to keep the impulses affecting the senses objective; for the sight, onto the point where the brain actively is affected, that means somewhere in the beginning of the optic nerve. He makes all the sensual impressions an interior part of humans and claims that space-time is empty of these impressions "but mere representations of our sensibility, the form of which is the space" (ibid.:74). This is an obvious juxtaposition of objective stimulus and the ability to apprehend and comprehend stimulus, which Aristotle is keen to keep apart from each other.

The third problem with Kant's text is the spatial apprehension: What is space? Space is obviously something empty furnished with forms of different kinds without the possibility of representation, except by vague, sensitive, erroneous descriptions created by the human mind. However the mathematical representation in a mathematical space gives us a true picture.

Going back to Aristotle, he was well aware of the fact that contextual conditions affect the prime impulse hitting the sense in question. The classical Greek sculptural art shows a rather perfect apprehension of the human body, and for those who have seen the statue of Zeus throwing a thunderbolt or of Poseidon throwing a trident at the archaeological museum in Athens, it is clear that a couple thousand years ago, there existed a perfect knowledge of how to reproduce the human body into a statue of the very moment of an action which is seen by the muscles of the body. The relations and stretching of the muscular machinery is exact even from a medical point of view. Thus this statue could well be some sort of a priori picture of the perfect human body, but it is a result of keen observation of the anatomy of the body, and there is no reason to believe that the unknown artist had some a priori knowledge besides the very observation and the intellectual analysis of this observation.

But there are indeed problems with human observation, even if we just limit our analysis to the very prime stimulus hitting the senses, and these two problems are perspectives and projections.

We may limit the discussion to visual perspectives, which in ancient time troubled scientists and artists since it implies that we see a distortion in lengths depending on distance. The eyes seem to automatically compensate for this in most cases, but if we have a mixture of perspectives, the eyes can be tricked.

Already Brunelleschi, Mantegna and van Eyck at the end of 14th century discovered how to project three-dimensional space on a two-dimensional surface and thus discovered the geometrical perspective, which in the beginning of 19th century was generalized by Lobachevsky and Bolyai and ended later by Riemann in the general theory of curved spaces. Thus visual perspectives are intellectually treatable. When we come to other senses like the sense of hearing, we have similar distortions due to contextual conditions. A dynamic phenomenon is the Doppler effect, which is also present to the visual sense but only with the help of instruments, red and blue shifting, depending on whether a sound is moving from or to the observer. We know that the structure of the room affects sound, particularly more complex sounds like that of an orchestra. When it comes to olfactory sense, it is physically objective that different aromas or odours interact.

Of course we know that impulses of different senses interact, but then we must reach the brain's treatment of them, so to speak, and leave the physical space outside the individual.

Thus the contextual physical conditions affect the objective impulses which hit the sensual apparatus, and this may lead to different apprehensions of the space.

Then we come to a much more deceitful aspect: the projection. We touched above on the artists from the 14th century and their discovery of the geometrical perspective and its mathematical treatment discovered by Lobachevsky and Bolyai. The discovery in art led to a fantastic development in the ability to project the space on a two-dimensional canvas. But it also led to the art of questioning the senses, which was fully developed in art during the 20th century. For example Salvador Dalí, by exaggerating or distorting certain details of a structure, created new impressions of surprise, disgust, indignation, an almost hallucinatory dream world; René Magritte makes us question our impressions of the surrounding world, paints the beauty, the mystery and the impossibility of contradictory perceptions. We got the so-called impossible figures, geometrical figures which illustrated something impossible. The Swedish artist Oscar Reutersvärd is seen by many as the first, followed by the Dutch artist Maurits Cornelis Escher. Such figures have also been analyzed in psychology.

All such pictures are intriguing for the brain to analyze but per se, with respect to the sensible impulse, they are not founded in the distortions of the brain but created outside, and as impulses the curiosities are so to speak objectively built into the picture. This means that the picture per se enforces a multitude of interpretations. Obviously, since humans are subjects, the individual brain might add or withdraw aspects of the picture, but to make a common norm of how to watch and how to apprehend the picture is not advisable.

Consequently the space which Kant simplifies, in a not admissible way we may think, by representing it with a Euclidian space grossly limits his analyses of the real world. The world contains as it seems objectively a great number of unexplainable or explainable contradictions which make a mathematical representation at best local and temporal. Generalizations based on nominalist atomic variables are seldom relevant since the limitations are too strong. In local and temporal contexts, it can be relevant within the imposed limitations, but this is almost always relevant for experimental sciences. In social sciences, particularly if we assume that the individual is a subject and thus a local final cause, general systems are almost always problematic and require extreme social inertia. This does not prevent us from seeing tendencies and developments but, following Keynes' letter to Harrod in 1938, exact mathematical modelling is not advisable.

Let us finish this discussion of "erratic" perceptions by looking at Figure 1.1, where there are some problems in describing the intrinsic relations between the boxes, which might lead to a friendly discussion during a coffee break.

The confused picture is not a matter of having the glass over five which makes all the difference but a deliberate playing with the geometrical perspective. The confusion is outside our minds, caused by projections and perspectives.

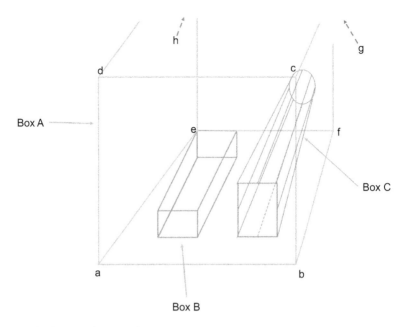

Figure 1.1 Mixture of perspectives

In some way we get the impression that Kant aims at a space like an Euclidian space, but Figure 1.1 occurs through a projection from a three-dimensional to a two-dimensional space, so it is perfectly explainable from a geometrical point of view. Consequently perturbations of my senses relative to others may not depend on my particular sensibility but are due to factors outside, belonging to the space in Kant's wording.

Kant discusses in this context a rose which differs in its appearance between different persons. These differences are claimed to depend on intrinsic processes of the human brain. First of all we must then state that all visual, tactile, olfactory and eventual gustatory sensations exist objectively outside the human being, but they can of course be perturbed by the particular circumstances of the sensation, so we have in principle the same kind of confusion as in Figure 1.1. Thus when it has passed through the receptors of the body, then the interior treatment of the person starts. But what starts? Do we have to analyze the soul and proceed into metaphysics? That is what Kant is doing. However, nowadays, natural sciences have evolved and we are, even though much knowledge is missing, in a somewhat better position to pursue the problem a bit further.

Let us however start with analyzing a bit more of our objective observations. In the simple figure of three boxes in Figure 1.1, we can see if we systematically let the eyes skim the picture that there seem to be certain regions, rather tiny, where the visual interpretation becomes uncertain and there is probably some border region to a new interpretation. We have a major reinterpretation when Box B and C change from hanging on side *abcd* to the case that Box B and C are attached to the floor *abfe* and the circle ends at wall *efgh*, but the latter is uncertain since it could end somewhere in the corner at *c*. There are however more possible reinterpretations. This is an analogy for the problem of the stability of dynamic models in general. Thus we see that when we have projections where perspectives are mixed, this induces dynamics into geometry, so to speak.

Two questions come to mind: Is the division line between uncertain areas and stable areas always the same for a particular individual, or does it vary with different focussing on parts of the picture; thus, are the stable/uncertain areas defined in the very objective picture, or is it a matter of internal decision, conscious/ unconscious decision of the spectator or perhaps both? And the second, can we isolate a factor or a group of factors internal and/or external, which is a necessary or/and sufficient condition for switching the interpretation?

These questions the author with warm heart leaves to the reader to answer.

In fact, these questions are basic to the analysis of dynamic stability and some mathematical, logical and empirical properties of such problems are discussed in Ekstedt (2015:176–216).

However Kant's "*Kritik der reinen Vernunft*" was published in 1781 with a second revised edition in 1787, so the mathematics he employed was the one of Descartes and Newton. Newton's admirable *Principia* was built on transforming objects into concepts which then were treated mathematically and produced conclusions. Kant took this technique to the universal plane.

But Kant died in 1804, twenty-two years before Lobachevsky's work on non-Euclidian spaces became known, beginning Riemann's more universal studies of spaces, and twenty years before Sadi Carnot's path-breaking article *Réflexions sur la puissance motrice du feu et sur les machines propres à développer cette puissance*, which Rudolf Clausius generalized in the 1860s on the entropy principle which fundamentally breaks down the Newtonian system as a universal system. It is a temporal and local approximation.

These two scientific discoveries shook up the scientific world from abstract philosophy to engineering techniques, and in mathematics we got the fabulous development to a great extent built on paradoxes like Cantor's, Russell's and Gödel's. The 20th-century discussion in analytical philosophy on atomic and complex variables and on irregular spaces led to the insight that mathematics as a language is a tool void of any empirical meaning.

A fascinating exchange of opinions took place at Salvador Dalí's place in Figueres, north of Barcelona, in November 1985, when the Nobel laureate in chemistry Ilya Prigogine met René Thom, the great French mathematician, in a public discussion:[10]

Thom: You should very carefully distinguish between what belongs to mathematical theory and what belongs to real systems. Mathematics has nothing to say to reality.

Prigogine: That's your point of view, it's not mine.

As we see, we have still disagreements between empirical scientists, who are inspired by the multitude of forms which can be created by abstract mathematical speculation and the mathematicians who realize the full difficulty of transforming complex variables into atomic variables.

Both Kant and Hume admired Newton, but while Hume doubted the very transformation of reality into mathematics, Kant believed that mathematics brought some a priori knowledge of the empirical world, something which Hume rejected.

However Kant's self-critical remarks quoted above show that he somehow realized the problem of first making things void of sensible matters in order to analyze the interrelations between these things ("an Sich") and then apply the conclusions to a reality where all sensible matters are restored into the things. Thus, how do we create a link between "an Sich" and "für Sich"? Wittgenstein suggests in his Proposition 6.211 that the main problem of science is not the logical/mathematical but the very transformation of real complex variables into atomic ones. But he is in the middle of the development of the 19th century mathematical revolution. Consequently we will not judge Kant too hard.

Anyway, the problem with Kant's analysis in "*Kritik der reinen Vernunft*" is that having expressed his doubts, he still upholds the distinction between "an Sich" and "für Sich", most probably as a result of his high estimation of mathematics as conveying some a priori knowledge on empirical relations which could not be analyzed outside mathematics. This was contradicted by the work of Russell and Whitehead in *Principia Mathematica*, which first showed that mathematics is one of several possible logical languages. Second, although it was painful to Russell, he developed and proved his paradox which stated the logical difference between atomic and complex variables. The third step lasted until the 1930s with Gödel's paradox and brought the final conclusion that mathematics is void of any empirical meaning, which makes it, as hinted by Prigogine above, very suitable as an analytical tool, although it must be used with care since as Thom claims mathematics conveys no primary information on empirical matters but depends wholly on chosen axioms and assumptions in the first place and on the interpretation of the conclusions into the real world. Standard assumptions like continuity and reflexivity have as we discussed in the prologue extensive analytical consequences with respect to empirical matters.

The problem which Kant has with mathematics appears very clear when he comments upon Hume's discussion on conceptualizations (ibid.:127–128) where Hume rejects the existence of concepts which are a priori and not rooted in experience, though understanding is necessarily connected to an object: "it never occurred to him [Hume] that the understanding might itself, perhaps, through these concepts, be the author of the experience in which its objects are found" (ibid.:128). We recognize in these words the quote from the discussion between Thom and Prigogine above. Kant ends his discussion with a credo to mathematics and the stable and definite natural laws; he lives in an ordered world.

> Now this *empirical* derivation, in which both philosophers [Locke and Hume] agree, cannot be reconciled with the scientific *a priori* knowledge

which we do actually possess, namely, *pure mathematics* and *general science of nature*; and this fact therefore suffices to disprove such derivation.

(emphases in original; ibid.:128)

Well, neither the mathematics nor the general science of nature showed up the believed stability for more than half a century after Kant's death.

The most serious effect of Kant's difficulties with his apprehension of mathematics is that reason is seen as the basis of humans' underlying ethical apprehension. To express it radically: humans are ethical because they are rational.

Since Kant truly believes that transforming the empirical reality is treatable by mathematical methodology, although he has some doubts, he goes on with his analysis and in ethics this leads to a general conclusion which by all means is rather modern in its settings but in reality means nothing: the so-called "Kant's categorical imperative":

Act externally in such a manner that the free exercise of thy will may be able to coexist with the freedom of all others, according to a universal law.

(Kant 2007[1795]:398)

First of all we see the universal claim, which seems to imply that there is a way to find out a universal law; that is, Kant seems to suppose that anybody actually can act in such a way that a law of such a description could be beneficial universally. Aristotle claimed that humans had some kind of "ethical sensibility" inlaid from the start, but this sensibility was moulded by experiences and memories, thus the very resulting ethics from this sensibility is dependent on both the person in question and the particular context.

Kant however goes much further in stating the possibility of a materialized ethical content which holds universally. This is from a logical point of view rather natural if we sort out any kind of sensible matters from the phenomena and leave the noumena empty of everything except its spatial coordinates.

The second aspect of Kant's categorical imperative concerns its role in economic theory. We have already mentioned this, but for completeness, we bring it into the context. If we think of the neoclassical general equilibrium theory in its axiomatic form, we can say that, given the distribution of initial endowments, the single agent maximizes the utility under the restriction of all other agents' utility functions; that is in line with the Edgeworth/Nash analysis. In this case however the moral imperative presupposes some consciousness of the aggregate solution or at least that the agents voluntarily submit to the market exchange process. Anyway, it is clear that increasing the number of agents towards infinity will take us into the Nash equilibrium, which Debreu (1982) showed is equivalent to the neoclassical general equilibrium. Thus we here see the roots of thinking with respect to the neoclassical theory. Furthermore, we can see the sometimes heard opinion that even if the individuals are void of moral sentiments, the market process will correct it.

A bit surprisingly, the critique which was presented in the prologue against the neoclassical general equilibrium theory has a certain support from Kant when he reveals his analytical doubts of the distinction between "Das Ding an Sich" and "Das Ding für Sich", but we can understand why Kant proceeded to keep the distinction. However, we do not understand why current scientists still use such a distinction, although they pretend not to deal with metaphysics.

Hume

When Hume concluded his first book of the Understanding, he evaluated what he had accomplished (ibid.:172):

> I have expos'd myself to the enmity of all metaphysicians, logicians, mathematicians and even theologians, and can I wonder at the insults I must suffer? I have declar'd my disapprobation of their systems; and can I be surprised, if they shou'd express a hatred of mine and of my person? When I look abroad, I foresee on every side, dispute contradiction, anger calumny and detraction. When I turn my eye inward, I find nothing but doubt and ignorance. The world conspires to oppose and contradict me; tho' such is my weakness, I feel all my opinions loosen and fall themselves, when unsupported by the approbation of others. Every step I take is with hesitation and every new reflection makes my dread an error and absurdity of my reasoning.

His stronger and more convinced feelings he displays on page 177:

> For my part, my only hope is, that I may contribute a little to the advancement of knowledge, by giving in some particulars a different turn to the speculations of philosophers, and pointing out to them more distinctly those subjects, where alone they can expect assurance and conviction. Human Nature is the only science of man; and yet has been hitherto the most neglected.

Hume was a predecessor of Kant, although many modern philosophers, particularly empiricists, claim Hume to be the first really modern philosopher. Particularly Hume's discussions on the concept of causality are regarded as more or less complete on a general level. Hume's scepticism with respect to scientific induction is well-known and often criticized as too harsh. But even the natural scientists have to admit the importance and the difficulty of making precise scientific concepts ready to be used even in experiments, but particularly in mathematical models. The more we discover about the interrelations in our world, the more difficult it is to transform a complex variable into an atomic one. For social sciences, such a transformation is impossible, other than within very precise limits of space and time, and we completely agree with the spirit of Keynes' letter to Harrod in 1938, which we quoted in the prologue. If we compare this letter with the exchange of opinions between Thom and Prigogine above, Prigogine's more unorthodox view of mathematics probably fits well into Keynes' opinion.

It is clearly so that Hume's scepticism seems to become more and more reasonable, but it can depend on the fact that science today is more and more the servile servant of Profitability and Power.

Hume's scepticism is revealed in the first quote by his mention of those he thinks are the strongest adversaries: "metaphysicians, logicians, mathematicians and even theologians". Those categories are in principle based on deductions from a priori postulates. Mathematics and logic were often believed to be the fundamental principles of nature. The great Newton wrote in his preface to *Principia*:

> Since the ancients (as we are told by Pappus), made great account of the science of mechanics in the investigation of natural things; and the moderns, laying aside substantial forms and occult qualities, have endeavoured to subject the phenomena of nature to the laws of mathematics, I have in this treatise cultivated mathematics so far as it regards philosophy. The ancients considered mechanics in a twofold respect; as rational, which proceeds accurately by demonstration; and practical. To practical mechanics all the manual arts belong, from which mechanics took its name. But as artificers do not work with perfect accuracy, it comes to pass that mechanics is so distinguished from geometry, that what is perfectly accurate is called geometrical, what is less so, is called mechanical. But the errors are not in the art, but in the artificers.

The thought that there exists the perfect system but we slightly deficient humans are not able to create nor even perceive it by our senses, but it is disclosed in logic, in mathematics, in geometry: this was the belief of Galileo, Newton and Kant. It started mainly with the works of Occam and Bacon and developed into nominalist ideas. Hume turns these discussions upside down by asking: How can we believe in a system which has no representation in our sensible world? He is aware of our imperfect sense and the problems of perception and comprehension and all the kind of external and internal influences which perturb our primary impressions, but how can there exist a method, void of sensible impression and void of frictions of the reality, mostly due to humans as the very central part of the reality?

Are mathematics, logic and geometry something given to humans? Perhaps this is what the myth speaks about – the reflective and the creative intellect. Hume adds also metaphysicians and theologians, which is less surprising perhaps, although St. Thomas strictly separates the physical and the metaphysical analysis and with respect to the physical analysis is a successor and partly a developer of Aristotle.

But as we already have discussed, during the 20th century the insights of the incompleteness of mathematics and logic came into scientific focus.

Having delivered the critique of the deductive sciences, however, Hume also rules out induction as a viable technique. This means the mechanical use of it. We can look at this rejection with modern eyes, which is instructive. Let us first look at Russell's well-known words in *History of Western Philosophy*:

> Hume's scepticism rests entirely upon his rejection of the principle of induction. . . . If this principle, or any other from which it can be deduced, is true, then the causal inferences which Hume rejects are valid, not indeed as giving certainty, but as giving a sufficient probability for practical purposes. If this principle is not true, every attempt to arrive at general scientific laws from particular observations is fallacious, and Hume's scepticism is inescapable for an empiricist. The principle itself cannot, of course, without circularity, be inferred from observed uniformities, since it is required to justify any such inference. It must therefore be, or be deduced from, an independent principle not based upon experience. To this extent, Hume has proved that pure empiricism is not a sufficient basis for science. . . . What these arguments prove — and I do not think the proof can be controverted — is that induction is an independent logical principle, incapable of being inferred either from experience or from other logical principles, and that without this principle science is impossible.
>
> (Russell 1996[1946]:646–647)

As late as 1948, Russell is prepared to regard the induction in empirical sciences as *an independent logical principle*. Let us look at this a bit closer.[11]

Russell's claim depends entirely on the problem of atomic versus complex facts. Hume hints at such a discussion in his distinction between simple and complex impressions but takes a different route of analysis.

The mathematical induction is based on an axiom after the Italian mathematician Peano from around 1900:

Peano's Axiom[12]

1 Zero is a number.
2 If *a* is a number, the successor of *a* is a number.
3 Zero is not a successor of a number.
4 Two numbers of which the successors are equal are themselves equal.
5 (Induction Axiom) If a set S of numbers contains zero and also every successor of every number in S, then every number is in S.

We may illustrate its use by a small example from Ekstedt (2015:90):

Proposition

Assume any natural number n ρ 3, then proposition A holds:

$$A \qquad 3^n \geq 2 \cdot n^2 + 3 \cdot n$$

Proof

For n = 3, the proposition obviously holds:

$$B: \quad 3^n - 2 \cdot n^2 - 3 \cdot n \geq 0$$

Developing B with respect to the left part (LP), we get

$$LP = 3 \cdot 3^n - 2 \cdot (n+1)^2 - 3 \cdot (n+1)$$

Inserting $n \geq 3$ gives us

$$LP \geq 3 \cdot (2 \cdot n^2 + 3n) - 2 \cdot (n+1)^2 - 3 \cdot (n+1)$$
$$= 4 \cdot n^2 + 2 \cdot n - 5 \geq 4 \cdot 3^2 + 2 \cdot 3 - 5 = 37 \geq 0$$

Thus we have proven A for the number 4 and subsequently, given Peano's axiom, that if we assume a Set Φ of natural numbers for which the condition A holds, all natural numbers $n \rho$ 3 belong to Set Φ. Q.E.D.

Thus mathematical induction leads to *implication*, which for the above case is that $n \rho$ 3 $\Rightarrow$ A is true, and the proof only concerned number 3 and the subsequent number 4, and then we applied the axiom.

The links between mathematical and empirical induction seem natural link but the impression is deceitful, and it is here that the whole problem of atomistic logic and complex variables enter. Thus, in order to use any kind of association whatsoever to mathematical induction, we must transform our variables into an atomistic setting where the real variables can be replaced by numbers. Consequently, we have the restriction that the real variables should be defined in the relevant dimensions such that they belong to non-proper classes, using the terminology of Russell's paradox. That is what happens in experimental sciences. The issue is to get repeatable experiments, and in order to do so, the variables as well as the context and environment must be defined precisely so the variables seem atomistic. In such a case we are able to convert them into a mathematical language, but the logical conclusions only hold given the precise definition of variables, context and environment.

Thus Hume's scepticism is a bit harder to get around than Russell suggests. If we look into social sciences, it won't hold to mix up the principle of induction with some form of inertia, particularly not since the main variables are humans themselves, which are to be seen as subjects and thus local and temporal final causes in Aristotle's language. Furthermore, we have Proposition 1 in the prologue, which suggests that the macroscopic levels although affected by individuals as well as groups of individuals and companies, have no logical and uniquely causal link to the microscopic levels, and the vice versa relation also holds.

In principle, Hume's analyses of human perception and apprehension are along the same lines as Aristotle. However he makes a very important distinction, which by all means can be seen as implicit in Aristotle's reasoning, but Hume expresses it clearly:

> There is another division of our perceptions, which it will be convenient to observe and which extends itself to both our impressions and ideas. This division is into SIMPLE and COMPLEX. Simple perceptions or impressions and ideas are such as admit of no distinction nor separation. The complex are contrary to these, and may be distinguish'd into parts. Tho' a particular colour, taste and smell are qualities all united in this apple, 'tis easy to perceive they are not the same, but are distinguishable from each other.
>
> Hume (2002[1740]:7–8)

As Hume describes the difference, he is close to touching on the problem of atomic and complex things, where the complex things have separating attributes while simple things do not. Obviously the mathematical analysis requires simple things which make simple perceptions, but it is a bit more problematic. Hume speaks about impressions, not things, and that means that two things, like two barrels of oil, give rise to similar impressions but for use they are of different qualities. Thus the immediate impressions require on one hand further investigation and on the other a specification of its final use. Looking at scientific development in general, new approaches have often started with new methods of measurement. Consequently, Hume's specification is not sufficient as a distinction between atomic and complex matters.

Hume uses his distinction for other purposes since impressions are the first step in forming ideas.

He then makes the distinction between the *sensation* and the *reflexion*. Now we enter the brain and the impression of whatever kind creates a sensation. This sensation has to do with direct reactions to the impression as pain, pleasure, and so on. The reflexions are based on these sensations in conjunction with the impression and are saved in the soul as a complex piece of experience and ideas such as desire, hope, pain, aversion and so on. Thus, the impression per se fades away but the reflexions on the sensations which the impressions give rise to remain in the soul. In many ways there are similarities with Aristotle's picture of the process, although it is more detailed.

The simplicity/complexity of the impressions and also the *vivacity* of the impressions determine in conjunction with memory and imagination the character of the ideas which the impressions give rise to. Thus Hume strictly maintains that the impression is the basic cause of the idea, thus an external impulse through the senses, which then is moulded into ideas of more or less complex ideas by our memory and imagination in form of precedent ideas. He categorically rules out any a priori idea; however, the impressions do not meet some "tabula rasa" but memory and imagination created by experience. Thus he does not rule out creative minds, but creations are built on experience and imagination, not some a priori existence of ideas. As such, even mathematics can work in studying different topological and dynamical patterns, giving rise to analogies. This is what Keynes alludes to in the earlier quoted letter to Harrod in 1938.

We will not go into this any deeper, but when we compare a possible ethics built on this description of how the individual forms ideas, it is indeed difficult to imagine something similar to Kant's ethical imperative.

So now we have seen already that what Hume calls a simple perception is indeed quite complex. The complexity lies in the fact that they possess differentiating attributes as well as different parts which per se is observable:

> I must make use of the distinction of perceptions in *simple* and *complex*, to limit this general decision, *that all our ideas and impressions are resembling*. I observe, that many of our complex ideas never had impressions, that corresponded to them, and that many of our complex impressions never are exactly copy'd in ideas. I can imagine to myself such a city as the *New Jerusalem*, whose pavement is of gold and walls are rubies, tho' I never saw any such. I have seen *Paris*, but shall I affirm I can form such an idea of the city, as will perfectly represent all its streets and houses in their real and just proportions?
>
> (ibid.:8)

Here at the very distinction of the prime impression, Hume distances himself from the simple empiricism. The complex impression gives rise to comprehensions which are affected by earlier impressions which may not only resemble the new impression as a whole but also separate parts of the complex and thus "distort" the objective relations between the contained parts of the new complex impression. But not only that, earlier impressions, both simple and complex, may be decoupled from what they were and combined into new ideas which are intrinsic to the mind.

But this of course implies that ideas which are created in the mind are basically created by impressions, simple or complex, but can be arranged into new ideas like New Jerusalem, which probably do not belong to the sensible world as a whole but are in part built on simple impressions or parts of complex impressions which belong to the sensible world.

Hume states:

> On the other hand we find, that any impression either of the mind or body is constantly follow'd by an idea, which resembles it, and is only different in the degrees of force and liveliness. The constant conjunction of our resembling perceptions, is a convincing proof, that the one are the causes of the other; and this priority of the impressions is an equal proof, that our impressions are the causes of our ideas, not our ideas of our impressions.
>
> (ibid.:9)

Here Hume rules out a priori ideas as well as nominalism as an analytical method per se. Furthermore, he accepts that perceptions might be different with respect to contextual structures as well as between individuals.

It is interesting that Hume's discussion comes close to household production theory in modern consumption theory. We then look upon commodities as inputs in producing services to households; thus a single commodity is seen as a potential part of a structure of services which the household ultimately demands. That means that the commodities are complexes themselves and are combined into new, more complex structures. Here we have an example of the fact that a premeditated idea in a household leads to the picking of things/services of the sensible world in obtaining the idea. The idea per se is a priori only in the sense of combinatory activities of existent items of the sensible world.

This means however that by a chain: impression, simple or complex, – sensation/reflexion – memory, imagination, Hume claims the composition of the apprehension of the surrounding world via the association of ideas brought by "*resemblance, contiguity* in time or place and *cause* and *effect*" (ibid.:12–13).

In analyzing ethics concerning individuals both with respect to structure and content, it is rather important to ask whether individuals apprehend and comprehend the same environment which they share. If we look at the neoclassical theory, as it appears in the axiomatic structure, they consider the same commodity basket which has a constant dimensionality and all commodities appear to be of positive value in all preference functions. The latter follows from the Axiom of Reflexivity. Hume's analysis however points out that an item might be used for different purposes, or can be interpreted as differently as a painting, or implies a type of function, which requires some form of learning process and similar complexities. Such things imply often that the first impressions of different complexities may differ since the impressions also require some form of analysis, or might create associations, activate memory and so on.

Moore's paradox

We now get into the neighbourhood of the moral philosopher G.E. Moore; he discussed the nature of impressions and formulated his famous paradox (1993[1903]):[13]

> *Weak Form* : $p \wedge A(\neg p)$

We can read it as "it is raining and I do not think it is raining".

> *Strong Form* : $p \wedge \neg p$

We can read as "it is raining and it is not raining".

The paradox, particularly in its strong form, seems a bit absurd. Some philosophers have interpreted it as some kind of academic joke. However, looking ahead at Gödel, we find that the strong form is well in the frame of elementary logic. Furthermore, Umberto Eco (2000: chapter 2) introduces so-called molecular meanings of a word, which means that most persons agree on a specific interpretation. However, around this molecular meaning there is a set of interpretations which are conceptually defined and which are sometimes almost contradictive to each other.

A simple example of the *weak form* is "It is raining, although it is not raining, it is drizzling". In this example we use at first a sort of universal of a set of particular forms of rain. However, this explanation is not the only one, since we here have confronted the item p with a *belief* of the contrary, so then we might also consider the nature of the belief.

The difference between the weak and the strong form of Moore's paradox is crucial. While the weak form introduces not-p as an argument of a function, we can still uphold the difference between the *thing* and the *perception of the thing*. Thus it leaves us with the possibility of separating the thing from the perception of the thing.

The weak form of the paradox is pretty important for ethical analysis, not only with respect to belief in terms of faith but also in terms of interpretations. Obviously, we then discuss primary impressions affected by memory, associations and other internal considerations.

The strong form however has two possibilities. On one hand we have an impression which we at the same time deny. That in fact is possible when, as Kant does, we employ a priori conclusions to correct the impression. On the other hand we accept the thing and at the same time we reject it. This obviously will appear when we add attributes to the thing which make it complex, and we then get the problem which Russell's paradox focuses on; namely, that while the particularities are equipped with attributes, the universal class is empty of attributes. But then Moore's expression in logical variables is an insufficient description of the paradox, which then needs a structural definition, which is delivered by Russell; namely, the distinction between proper and non-proper sets.

As we mentioned, its very form is a key result in Gödel's theorem on *formally undecidable propositions*, although Moore did not discuss logic per se. However it must be seen in the same realm as the weak form of the paradox. Let us compare it with Russell's paradox, which has this form:

$$Let\ \mathcal{P} = \left\{ x \mid x \notin x \right\} then\ \mathcal{P} \in \mathcal{P} if\ and\ only\ if\ \mathcal{P} \notin \mathcal{P}$$

Russell's paradox appeared in 1901, while Moore's *Principia Ethica* was published in 1903. Russell's antimony, as it was called, caused a lot of attention. Even Russell did not like it a lot, since it pointed towards intrinsic problems of pure logic, and as we know Gödel took the decisive step which made logic void of any empirical meaning. Moore does not mention any link to Russell, but the strong form is perfectly understandable if it's interpreted in the realm of Russell's paradox, with a distinction between proper and non-proper classes which is taken into the discussion of atomic variables and complexes.

An example of the use of the strong form of Moore's paradox would then be, when we make a general statement of cars, which is interpreted specifically to mean a brand of cars or vice versa. Such a logical structure is extremely difficult to express in simple logic since p does not represent a single well-defined item but a set of different elements, and we then in Moore's and Russell's paradoxes express intrinsic difference between elements and aggregates of elements.

A quite different interpretation of the strong form is when we simply discuss different implicit definitions of real or abstract items that do not agree; *freedom, democracy, efficiency* have many definitions, of which many seem contradictory. Looking at debates on TV gives normally good examples of the existence of Moore's paradox in its strong setting without any involvement of Russell's paradox.

Kant – Hume – Russell

We immediately see the difference in relation to Kant's distinction between "Das Ding an Sich", which is the variable definition which could be logically analyzed, and "Das Ding für Sich", which is mirroring the sensible world through the senses and emotions and thus gives only a temporal and local picture of individual perception. "Das Ding an Sich" however is a particular variable void of any attributes and consequently suitable for mathematical analysis. There is no reason to question Kant's distinction per se; we have used exactly the same distinction when analyzing the neoclassical general equilibrium theory, but we called "Das Ding an Sich" an atomic variable and "Das Ding für Sich" a complex variable.

But Kant takes a further step due to his overestimation of mathematics, which makes him simply reject attributes in all form of analytical value. In all sciences, and particularly in social sciences, the attributes in Kant's sense are those which matters.

Hume makes exactly the same distinction as Kant, the distinction between *simple* (atomic) and *complex* things/variables, but regards the complex variables as central to the scientific analysis and thus part of the scientific problem. The fact that complex variables make the scientific analysis more difficult is not an adequate issue; it has to be dealt with.

Russell, who had many problems with complex variables, which also led him to discuss the notion of *negative facts*, makes a follow-up to Hume's distinction:

> Attributes and relations, though they may be not susceptible of analysis, differ from substances by the fact that they suggest structure, and that there can be no significant symbol which symbolizes them in isolation.
>
> (Russell 2007[1956]:337)

Structure is the keyword, obviously, and having said that, *relation* is a concept central to the analysis. Kant's a priori analysis lacks all relations to the sensible world and thus has to form an a priori analysis where the variables are completely independent of each other, exactly as the commodities and agents formed by the neoclassical axiomatic structure. Kant is actually aware of this but dismisses it since it makes the mathematical analysis meaningless. But Kant also admits the problem expressed in Wittgenstein's Proposition 6.211, that we need to apply an a priori deductive conclusion based on variables void of the attributes of the sensible world and then bring all attributes to the employed variables to achieve a conclusion for the sensible world. As a metaphysical analysis it is probably OK, but as an analysis of a sensible world, particularly applying Kant's own doubts, it won't hold.

Consequently Hume starts from the very sensible world. Our senses are all that provide us with prime information that hits the sensual organs about the outer world. That does not mean that the objective, in a physical sense, gives a picture that is in any sense perfect and the same for all, since it is subject to contextual circumstances. Hume mentions the colour of a rose which varies according to the light conditions. The same we have with the fragrance of a rose which varies both with light conditions and most of all with the humidity of the air. Thus a sensual prime impression is indeed a physical reality, but the reality is a dynamic organism which implies that impressions of a thing will always be temporal and local due to contextual variations.

Then if we compare the prime impressions for different persons, which are objective impressions as regards respective individuals, we meet the problems of perspectives in a broad meaning. If we stick to roses, changes in colour and structure of background may affect the perception of nuances. The same with fragrance; the wind is different at different places in the garden, so at one place you have the full fragrance of a "Comtesse de Rohan" but at another place there is a small interference from the garbage cans, which gives a mixed olfactory experience. When we watch a landscape, the impression depends much on the focus of the spectator, and that seems to be general when we regard structures, which might also explain the distinction Kant makes between "an Sich" and "für Sich". When we look at the complex structure, it must be described by its parts, or otherwise we tend to give it a *noumen* which per se is empty of content. Think of the concept *car*. If we shall describe that in real terms, we must describe some parts and some specific relations between parts, and that might vary between persons and/or contexts. *Car* by itself, as a *noumen*, is actually not a car, and we here see the link to Russell's paradox though the concept *car* belongs to non-proper classes, since the universal set of the sets of specific cars does not belong to itself.

So a tentative conclusion would be that the perception of a complex structure is affected by the specific focus of the spectator.

Furthermore the *noumen* does not need to be mystified by talking of the eventual existence or non-existence of substances but can be seen as a concept of the universal set of subsets belonging to non-proper sets. Thus the different things/structures have to be defined somehow, ostensive, functional, structural and so on, and then we might form a universal set on the basis of such a definition, but that is empty of all information except that it must be in line with the definition of the contained particulars.

Thus Kant makes a nominalist claim that the name of the universal set of proper subsets is the true variable, but then he ends up in Russell's paradox. The fascinating thing is however that he actually wrote down his doubts, and he thereby is on the very brink of 20th century mathematical logic. We repeat once more the earlier quote: "The problematic thought which leaves open a place for them serves only, like an empty space, for the limitation of empirical experiences, without itself containing any other object of knowledge beyond the spheres of those principles" (Kant 1933:275). These lines of doubt are worthy of a great philosopher.

The art of defining and what we perceive

We have touched a great deal on the philosophical approach of nominalism versus realism, and it is therefore appropriate to say some words about these concepts with respect to the art of defining.

Underlying the debate between realists and the nominalists is the medieval discussion of the existence of universals. If we look at *physical matters*, we may ask if for example dogs or cars have some particular doggishness or carishness which is the basis of the concept. The nominalists deny such universals and claim that this is just a linguistic construction covering a group of physical items which are said to be contained in the concept in question. The realists claimed on the other hand that such doggishness or carishness exists independent of human analysis or linguistic patterns.

In some sense, we can agree with the nominalists that the name of a group of items does not necessarily have anything to do with any physical aspect or attribute which links the items in questions to each other, and our analysis of Kant's concept "Das Ding an Sich" supports this approach. The universal concept does not belong to itself; a dog is not a breed of dogs, and a car is not a brand of cars. But on the other hand if we see an animal in our normal surroundings, we can mostly tell if the animal is a cat or a dog. Even when we see very unusual dogs or cats, we can tell if it is a cat or a dog.

Thus the realist and the nominalist discussions basically concerned the relation between the reality and the linguistic descriptions of the reality and its relevance and problems. From an ethical point of view these aspects have become more and more important from two different perspectives.

On the one hand we have the efficiency and certainty of communication which has become much more complex in our day due to globalization and the integration of social and cultural structures. In different geographical areas, social groups and cultures, we define things differently. Snow and ice in northern Europe are more complex concepts than they are in northern Africa, and we can surely give many amusing examples of the confusion of words and languages. But when we come to laws, agreements and similar things, these matters are often far from amusing.

Defining children is one thing in a modern Western European city and another in the rural areas in central Africa, and this varies also over time for the same country. The author started to work at school holidays in order to have some own money at the age of 12. Tall and robust physically, there was nothing to prevent taking a job as a delivery boy for a grocery shop. Today such a thing is simply forbidden. In rural societies with a simple production structure, the concept of children is different than it is in an advanced post-industrial society. Such differences per se are not particularly astonishing, but when those rural societies become more and more integrated in a global system, we will most probably have effects far from the traditional.

The mixtures of interpretations and understanding of concepts may lead to systematic exploitations and misuse, particularly when we have asymmetries in power and wealth.

In discussing Moore's paradox, we mentioned Umberto Eco's approach that words, concepts and even signs/symbols (Eco works within semiotics) have a molecular meaning to which most people agree, but around this molecular meaning there grows a net of meanings which are due to specific contextual applications. Sometimes these meanings might be almost contradictory, although all agree on the molecular meaning.

The concept of children is certainly context-dependent. When we need a definition, what do we need it for?

When we have clashes of cultures, traditions, ethical standards and similar aspects, we must realize that this also implies that a certain concept might be interpreted differently, although we apply it to the same context.

In theoretical terms it means that for a homogenous culture, a universal concept such as children, although empty of attributes, is normally interpreted in the same way for different contexts. Thus a message will be rather uniformly interpreted. For strongly heterogeneous cultures, this is often not so, and that makes communication and information more uncertain and less efficient. We have taken different continents as examples, but this also applies to a big city, where we have subgroups and even subcultures which develop separate conceptualizations and even separate languages.

The other aspect of definitions is when we deliberately let the universal concepts imply certain aspects, often of degrading character, which spills over to the members of the concept. This is perhaps the most dangerous form of using universal concepts when we speak of nationalities, cultures and similar items. This latter aspect we will come back to in discussing ourselves and the Other.

However when we define something, a thing, a process, we utilize earlier experiences. But how do we proceed when we stand in front of something entirely new? In daily life we can of course dismiss it, but in science we cannot. The question is very interesting within economics since for fundamental thinking we still use a theory, the neoclassical theory, which was developed about 150 years ago and concerns more a medieval economy of barter than a modern money economy, which by the way cannot be integrated into the theory since the concept of money or any kind of medium of exchange cannot be meaningfully defined within the theory.

One thing is of course that we frankly say that the theory holds where it is relevant and other ad hoc theories might hold otherwise. In such a case we run into formidable logical contradictions, but this is what many seems to advocate. During the 21st century we have so far experienced a period when inflation is said to hurt economic growth and another period where we have been told that inflation is implied by economic growth. Furthermore, we have been told that the state does wrong when it interferes with the markets, but when markets fail, the state should intervene and protect the market actors, who have obviously not been able to master the markets. What the going gospel is now, in autumn 2017, is indeed hard to say.

Anyway, we stand in front of a new kind of phenomena. Umberto Eco has an amusing example of this in his book *Kant and the Platypus* (2000:241–254).

In 1798 a naturalist named Dobson sent the British Museum a stuffed animal from Australia which the locals there called *water mole* or *duck-billed platypus*. The first reactions in London were that he had become crazy or perhaps made some practical joke. However, an article from 1797 by a researcher named Collins reported a similar animal, and there were similar reports from other observers. Thus, the apparatus started to classify the phenomenon: what did they really see? The platypus is an egg-laying, duck-billed, beaver-tailed and otter-footed mammal. It took 86 years for the scientists to classify this animal, and the debate was sometimes harsh. In 1884 however W. H. Caldwell, who was in Australia to study the phenomenon on the spot, sent a telegram to the University of Sydney: "Monotremes oviparous, ovum meroblastic". In other words, the monotremes were Mammals and laid eggs. This ended the argument.

Umberto Eco (ibid.:248–249) concluded:

> What is the moral of this story? In the first instance, we might say that this is a splendid example of how observation sentences can be made only in t0he light of a conceptual framework or of a theory that gives them sense, in other words, the first attempt to understand what is seen is to consider the experience in relation to a previous categorical system . . . . But at the same time we would have to say . . . that when observations challenge the categorical framework, attempts are made to adjust the framework.

We related parts of the philosophical differences between Kant and Hume and the story of the scientific classification/understanding of the platypus is further weakening Kant's discussion on "Das Ding an Sich" and its relation to a priori conceptual understanding. Kant writes (1933:60):

> A manifold, contained in an intuition which I call mine, is represented, by means of the synthesis of the understanding, as belonging to the *necessary* unity of self-consciousness; and this is affected by means of the category. This [requirement of a] category therefore shows that the empirical consciousness of a given manifold in a single intuition is subject to a pure self-consciousness *a priori*, just as is empirical intuition to a pure sensible intuition, which likewise takes place a priori. Thus in the above proposition a beginning is made of a *deduction* of the pure concepts of understanding; and in this deduction, since the categories have their source in the understanding alone *independently of sensibility*.

Eco has given his book its title after the very hard confrontation between the process of categorizing the platypus and the idealistic ideas of Kant with respect to empirical sensibility and understanding.

This means that already the apprehension of a perception is affected by the experience and the structural understanding of the observer/receiver of the information. So, when we take the step to *comprehension* of the information when it concerns a complex item/process/event, then we, as in the case of the scientist classifying the platypus, are affected by our education, empirical experience, socio-economic and ethical structures and also of our combinatorial abilities. Thus since even the prime apprehension of a complex information is problematic and asymmetric among individuals, the deeper comprehension process becomes even more complex.

With respect to Kant, we appreciate his idealism in many aspects, but his attitude to empirical information and its complexity is unfortunately too idealistic and is leading completely wrong with respect to scientific investigations.

Furthermore, that will have consequences for the Kantian ethics defined a priori. Since our perceptions, apprehensions and comprehension of the reality by necessity are different, ethics must in its general form be based on the very acceptance of the human as a subject and *thus* a final cause but otherwise be related to social and cultural contexts and the fact that humans are creatures with social responsiveness. Consequently, ethics deals with complex matters, not with atomic variables, which means that ethics as tool to achieve a good life as Aristotle expresses it is dependent on socialization and social responsiveness.

Notes

1 I read about this myth in the late 1980s in a paper by the French philosopher Claude Tresmontant, a mimeograph, never published, on the theological foundations of John Duns Scotus. A friend, a scholar in history, later told me that this myth probably had appeared in medieval times in the Massif Central in France.

2 Faith is the intellect's acceptance of the truth.

3 Smith proceeds: "The causes or circumstances which naturally introduce subordination, or which naturally, and antecedent to any civil institution, give some men some superiority over the greater part of their brethren, seem to be four in number." The four aspects which according to Smith give precedence to some people are: (1) "the superiority of personal qualifications, of strength, beauty, and agility of body; of wisdom and virtue, of prudence, justice, fortitude, and moderation of mind"; (2) "the superiority of age"; (3) "the superiority of fortune"; (4) "the superiority of birth" (Smith 1952[1776]: 309–310).

4 One could also take a more current philosopher like Heidegger, but with respect to our discussion, he does not part from Kant in any important matter.

5 Russell, Bertrand, (2000[1946]). *History of Western Philosophy*, Routledge, London.

6 In *The Nicomachean Ethics* (1998), the translator, David Ross, makes a point about Aristotle's use of the Greek word λόγος (*logos*): "Of all the words of common occurrence in the *Ethics*, the hardest to translate is λόγος. Till recently the accepted translation was 'reason'. But it is, I think, quite clear that normally λόγος in Aristotle does not stand for the faculty of reason, but for something grasped by reason, or perhaps sometimes for an operation of reason."

This means of course that ethics is to be an analytical discourse on rational behaviour by individuals as well as collective to achieve the highest good. Thus, Aristotle regards it as belonging to the practical sciences.

7 When quoting Aristotle, we will use *Encyclopædia Britannica*, 2nd edition, from 1990. We will then for the sake of precision use the numbering they use according to the standard Berlin Greek text. So, the references will all be linked to *The Works of Aristotle Vol. I* and *Vol. II*, Encyclopædia Britannica, Inc. Chicago, London, 1990. We then shorten the references, as in this case (*NE*:342 Bno. 1097ᵃ), where *NE* stands for *Nicomachean Ethics* and Bno for Berlin enumeration. Other available texts use a different enumeration of the different subparts of the books, but to have a commonly accepted indication of subparts of the Greek text, we use the *Encyclopædia Britannica*. Occasionally, however, as in the quote from footnote 2 of the *Nicomachean Ethics* where the translator, David Ross, as in the *Britannica*

version, explains the principles of translation, we used a version of *Ethics* from Oxford World Classics (1998).

8   By natural clocks, we mean Earth's revolution on its axis and around the Sun.

9   I have to emphasize that we here discuss Kant as he appears in *"Kritik der reinen Vernunft"*; we will meet another Kant later.

10   The congress archives are available at www.dalidimension.com

11   We will base our discussion on Ekstedt (2015:89–98).

12   We use the version used in Weisstein (2000), the entry Peano's Axioms, since it is bit more pedagogical.

13   G.E. Moore (1873–1958) was one of the key figures in developing ethics along the lines of logical empiricism, *Principia Ethica* 1903. He also worked on languages and his paradox is in fact on the path to Gödel's incompleteness theorem.

Bibliography

Amoroso, L., (1938). Vilfredo Pareto, *Econometrica*, Vol. 6, No. 1.

Aristotle, (1990 [original around 334–324 BC]). On the Soul Bno. 402^a–435^a. In *The Works of Aristotle Vol. I*, Encyclopædia Britannica, Inc., Chicago and London, (Bno refers to the Berlin enumeration).

Aristotle, (1990 [original around 334–324 BC]). Nicomachean Ethics Bno. 1094^a–1179^a. In *The Works of Aristotle Vol. II*, Encyclopædia Britannica, Inc., Chicago and London, (Bno refers to the Berlin enumeration).

Aristotle, (1990 [original around 334–324 BC]). Biological Treatises Bno. 486^a–789^b. In *The Works of Aristotle Vol. II*, Encyclopædia Britannica, Inc. Chicago and London, (Bno refers to the Berlin enumeration).

Aristotle, (1990 [original around 334–324 BC]). Metaphysics Bno. 980^a–1093^b. In *The Works of Aristotle Vol. I*, Encyclopædia Britannica, Inc., Chicago and London, (Bno refers to the Berlin enumeration).

Aristotle, (1990 [original around 334–324 BC]). Politics Bno. 1252^a–1341^b. In *The Works of Aristotle Vol. II* (p. 452), Encyclopædia Britannica, Inc., Chicago and London, Bno. 1258^b, (Bno refers to the Berlin enumeration).

Eco, U., (2000). *Kant and the Platypus*, Vintage, London.

Ekstedt, H., (2015). *Money, Valuation and Growth*, Routledge, London and New York.

Hobbes, T., (1985[1651]). *Leviathan*, Penguin Books, London.

Hume, D.A., (2002[1740]). *A Treatise of Human Nature*, Oxford University Press, Oxford.

Kant, I., (1933). *Critique of Pure Reason*, Macmillan Press Ltd, Houndsmills, Basingstoke, and London.

Kant, I., (2007[1795]). Fundamental principles of the metaphysics of morals. In *Great Books of the Western World*, Encyclopædia Britannica, Chicago and London.

Keynes, J.M., (1938). Letter to Roy Harrod 10th of July, Collected Works of Keynes, available at internet http://economia.unipv.it/harrod/edition/editionstuff/rfh.34a.htm

Moore, G.E., (1993[1903]), *Principia Ethica*, Cambridge University Press, Cambridge.

Reichenbach, H., (1938). *Experience and Prediction*, University of Chicago Press, Chicago.

Russell, B., (1948). *Human Knowledge: Its Scope and Limits*, George Allen and Unwin Ltd, London.

Russell, B., (1996[1946]). *History of Western Philosophy*, Routledge, London.

Russell, B., (2007[1956]). *Logic and Knowledge*, Spokesman, Nottingham.

Smith, A., (1952[1776]). *An Inquiry into the Nature and Causes of the Wealth of Nations*, Encyclopedia Britannica, Inc., Chicago, London, and Toronto.

Weisstein, E.W., (2000). *Concise Encyclopedia of Mathematics*, CD-ROM version, Chapman & Hall, London.

2 Philosophy and economics of the modern world

The heart of the matter

In economic reality and in economic analysis, we concentrate upon a single moment, the very market exchange, which in almost all cases is irreversible.

As we thoroughly discussed before, economic theory in its axiomatic form is bona fide as an abstract description when it comes to analyzing a precise point of exchange in space-time; however, any form of aggregation relative to commodities or agents presupposes assumptions which are far from what can be even remotely representative of the macroscopic reality. Mathematically, we then build on additive aggregation which indeed is doubtful as a general method.[1] It is as if you look at a spot on a map, such as Fécant or Brighton. The spots on the map indicating the place in question contain all information about the coastline. The map of the coastline is a limitation of dimensionality; we exclude all other information. Thus, to aggregate from a point to a curve is not possible due to the increase of the dimensionality, like deriving a function, as in Table 2.1. We derive a function and get in the end the numerical constant 6. But then we may go the other way and integrate, and we realize that the two sides are incommensurable on an a priori basis.

Consequently, when we integrate a function starting from 6 we realize that there are infinitely many functions going through 6, and we may then ask how the parameters a, b and c are determined.

Thus, when we start with the very market exchange as an action and claim that we can from the nature of that action aggregate to a sort of societal optimum, it is as if we have specified the parameters a, b and c in advance as exogenous to the functions we have. Referring to some *invisible hand* obviously transfers the economic faculty to a sub-department within the theological faculty. But we instead replace the invisible hand with an axiomatic structure.

This problem is very fundamental in mathematics. If we look at the mapped coastline as a function, we may derive a certain position in relation to its relative position in the network of roads and other places. But describing the topological and physical reality at the point of the place and its neighbourhood with respect to other characteristics than an overall silhouette, in our case the coastline, is obviously impossible without more and detailed information of the very topological and physical structure.

Table 2.1 Derivation – integration

Derivation	Aggregation
$y = f(x) = x^3$	$Y = F(x) = 6$
$f'(x) = 3 \cdot x^2$	$F^1(x) = 6 \cdot x + a$
$f''(x) = 6 \cdot x$	$F^2(x) = 3 \cdot x^2 + a \cdot x + b$
$f'''(x) = 6$	$F^3(x) = x^3 + \dfrac{a}{2} \cdot x^2 + b \cdot x + c$

In the neoclassical theory, we actually start from the very microscopic point of barter with respect to a given set of commodities, and from that rather abstract perspective, we assume that it is possible to say something about the space-time development and the macroscopic conditions without any further information about the topology of the environment where the barter takes place; then, just assumptions of the preference functions and the distribution are given.

Our claim is that the singular market exchange of agents is determined by contextual conditions in space-time. As we have noted earlier, Gerard Debreu makes an annotation of the problem in *Theory of Value* (chapter 2) when he defines commodities/agents by a position in space-time. An agent i may be described mathematically as $_t^s(\precsim_i, e_i)$, a preference function and an endowment vector, indexed in space and time.

We thus arrive at the concept of epistemic cycles, which from a theoretical perspective simplifies the discussions a lot but which in reality is extremely complex.

With respect to epistemic cycles, we conclude that the judgement of the commodities is dependent on the very topology of the environment. But this means that we need to separate the commodity as a physical item/process from the commodity as just a commodity which has to fit into the apprehended structures of the consumer. The consequence of this is that the Axiom of Reflexivity does not hold.

It is obvious that we can construct assumptions of the commodity concept such that the axiom holds, and the most natural is that at the very occasion of the market exchange, when all premeditations are done, the two aspects of the commodity merge, and that is Debreu's interpretation.

The agent chooses in space-time; thus, the epistemic cycle is dated in space-time. The important thing is that we focus on action. Aristotle has already noted this. As a basis for the actual relative valuation, Aristotle uses the value of labour as an anchor, and the exchange values ought to reflect the relative content in a commodity of labour efforts. But he has an interesting wording, possibly indicating a sort of market valuation:

> There will, then, be reciprocity when the terms have been equated so that as farmer is to shoemaker, the amount of the shoemaker's work is to that of the farmer's work for which it exchanges. But we must not bring them into a figure of proportion when they have already exchanged (otherwise one extreme will have both excesses), but when they still have their own goods.
> (*Politics* p. 381, no. 1133[a]–1133[b])

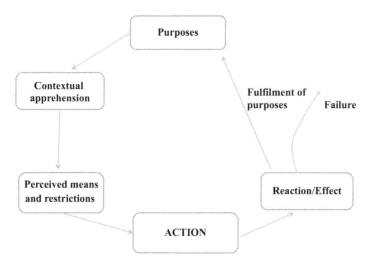

Figure 2.1 Epistemic cycle

Thus he touches on a sort of an *ex ante/ex post* reasoning. Although we may lighten the burden of a decision by different measures, we always come to the point of no return in a market exchange. To try to escape this problem by introducing a mathematical axiomatic structure which perturbs real-life economics is perhaps not the most convincing scientific route, particularly when dismissing the space-time problem, which is a definitive break with Newton. St. Paul formulated this problem: "For what I am doing, I do not understand; for I am not practicing what I would like to do, but I am doing the very thing I hate" (Romans 7:15, New American Standard Bible). Thus we are caught in circumstances, sometimes of a dynamic development of a self-chosen position which turns into a nightmare, which we somehow need to break out of, and thus the earlier comprehension of the environment falls apart and we act in ways which in some sense are rational but from a different contextual environment not understandable. Thus the human being faces an almost eternal internal struggle and torments, giving rise to sorrow and remorse. We cannot solve this, but we can at least have a discussion on the problem of epistemic cycles and choice in an effort to approach the concept of ethics.

The direction of time

We in principle avoided the space-time problem per se in our exposé of philosophical aspects concerning the structure of ethical approaches, but when we discussed the important concepts of Kant in "*Kritik der reinen Vernunft*", "Das Ding an Sich" and "Das Ding für Sich", we noted that the former concept could be understood in the light of Russell's distinction between proper and non-proper classes, which brought to our attention the distinction between atomic and complex facts. This allusion was actually supported by Kant's own expressed doubts. At the same time, we claimed that a probable explanation of

Kant's rather strange distinction was the poorly developed mathematical logic of the 18th century, which was for the 20th century philosophers and mathematicians to develop.

But that was not all. The philosophical, conceptual, logical development was exceptional during the late part of the 19th century and during the 20th century, particularly space-time and its topology.

Universal space-time has several aspects, some close to Newton and some fundamentally different. The basic change of the space-time concept occurred when Carnot and Clausius discovered the entropy concept. The Einstein–Minkowski approach was indeed important, but not as revolutionary as the entropy principle. Furthermore the development in mathematics via the paradoxes of Cantor and Russell led to Gödel's paradox, which finally cuts the direct link between mathematics/logic and the physical reality, and this basically changed the conditions for empirical analysis.

So let us just remind ourselves of the "Introitus" to Newton's *The Principia: Mathematical Principles of Natural Philosophy*. It is an admirable work but nevertheless dated with respect to knowledge and understanding.

He starts with necessary definitions (2010[1688]:13): "I do not define time, space, place and motion, as being well known to all", but he proceeds, "Absolute, true, and mathematical time, of itself, and from its own nature flows equably without regard to anything external, and by another name is called duration . . .". He then defines absolute space: "Absolute space, in its own nature, without regard to anything external, remains always similar and immovable". He then comments on place and motion, but that will become clear implicitly.

We see that Newton strictly separates time and space and, furthermore, none of the concepts has any links to the physical reality taking place within the mathematical concepts of time and space. In fact, we can imagine a four-dimensional diagram containing the three spatial dimensions plus the time dimension, and this most probably is a measurable Euclidian space of four dimensions, although Newton does not use that kind of wording. There are some difficulties with this picture which are at the bottom of the theoretical changes with respect to Newton's space-time, but that requires a different mathematics from that of Euclid and Descartes.

From a historical point of view, the first and maybe the most fundamental discovery was that of Lazare Carnot, his son Sadi and Rudolf Clausius: entropy.

As a consequence of the Greek belief of the eternal atom and thus the eternal world, there was an underlying dream of many scientists that there could be constructed a sort of eternally working system, particularly a mechanical system, a perpetuum mobile.

Lazare Carnot was a French revolutionary military engineer and member of the public safety committee 1793–94, although he opposed Robespierre. He was an able mathematician and engineer with a particular interest in mechanics and dynamics. He wrote the book *Principes Foundamentaux de l'Equilibre et du Movement*, where he chooses a different path of analysis than Newton.

First of all, Carnot was an engineer and attacked the principle of mechanics from an experimental point of view in the construction of machines. The difference between universal laws and theorizing and the factual constructions of machines is enormous. The former implies abstraction and generalization, which means that many aspects are lost in these processes of analysis. Newton derived his laws of motion with respect to rigid bodies using the concept of *force*; mathematically, he used the Cartesian vector space.[2] However, since Carnot worked with theories of machines, he regarded the concept of force almost metaphysically. Humans, animals and machines set things into motion, thus representing a force. He thus developed his principles for the concept of relative speeds, since for Carnot a physical system was a collection of physical bodies with different speeds. The momentum of bodies as well as the system per se was created by collisions (interference) of bodies at different speeds. At difference with Newton, he expressed force as mv (mass times velocity) instead of ma, where a is acceleration. In short Carnot's engineering principles were a first step to the theory of gases under different heat conditions and laid the groundwork for his son Sadi's and Clausius' explorations of the entropy concept. Furthermore, Newton assumed a universal inertia space which Lazare Carnot did not; he treated it as an analytical concept. There exists, according to him, a counter-resistance to all actions, but that is an empirical matter and due to collisions of bodies at different speeds. That was, as a matter of fact, a decisive step from the perpetuum mobile of the Newtonian system to the later developed world of birth and death.

We have dealt with Lazare Carnot since he deviated from Newton in his conceptualizations, although his immediate scientific results did not. His conceptualizations brought the minds of his successors onto new paths, which Sadi Carnot and Clausius exploited and found the entropy principle, which today is of the highest possible importance, in physics of course but also with respect to economics and to moral considerations.[3]

Technically, the entropy principle deals with a general process of increasing disorder. It is mostly known as a universal process, although it is perhaps most important for microscopic processes. Although it is a universal process it is neither uniform nor continuous, since the entropy may decrease locally. Let us look at a trivial example.

When we make a quiche, we want of course to heat the oven with the minimum use of electricity or gas to bake the quiche. But we know that we have heat losses due to the heating of the environment. Thus, the heat losses are examples of waste which decreases the volume of useable energy, provided non-renewable energy use, and thus also an increase in entropy. We consequently increase the order of life in baking a quiche, we fulfil our desires, but at higher electricity consumption than just the one needed for the baking, which increases the universal entropy by an amount bigger than producing the quiche per se.

But then we could isolate the oven better, in order to increase the baking efficiency; first we may be able to isolate the oven better at very low costs, but then when we must use other materials, different constructions and so on, so the resources of manpower and electricity increase. Consequently we find a situation where the gain in entropy increases from the use of the oven is lower than the marginal increase of entropy in the total production of ovens. Since entropy basically is based on changes in the distribution of energy which in a physical sense is heat – we can for example look at global warming as a measure of excessive waste of energy – thus with respect to energy use we have a very interesting measure with respect to energy production, complex but significant, EROI, which means energy return on investments (in energy production). This answers the question of how much energy we can forecast producing per one unit input of investment in a certain kind of production method.

But the entropy concept is deeper than that. Our example of making a quiche can be enlarged. We put in human work, natural resources, electrical energy into the making. All of this can be converted into energy equivalents; natural resources need to be extracted and refined and transported, and we can of course specify very fine. But if we then look at the sum of these partial energy equivalents and compare it with the energy which we get from eating the quiche, we will find the energy cost is considerably higher. So, who pays? We do, in buying the ingredients for the quiche, the electricity and the use of the oven and the kitchen utensils. Yes, that is correct, but most probably we will find energy costs which are unpaid, and who pays them?

Thus the basic message concerning entropy is: *If you have a global system which contains different subsystems and you increase the entropy in one subsystem, the proportional loss for the global system is higher.* That is not an economic statement; that is not a political statement. That is a statement concerning the basic physical conditions which make it possible to live on Earth.

As such, it is of highest possible ethical potency. There is no philosophically, religiously or politically created ethical system which does not have to face the problem of entropy with respect to human creativity and human production activities.

Those political, economic and opinion leaders who dismiss this problem are at variance with the very living conditions in the world.

Space-time

Another important aspect of philosophical thinking which appeared during the late 19th and the early 20th century was the changed realization of space and time concepts. Although they are linked to the relativity theory, they are not as fundamental as the exploration of the entropy principle, which actually can be seen as a universal time concept although a bit difficult. But the main finding of the 20th century is that time and space are more closely linked to each other than Newton thought; he regarded them as a separate dimensions. However, when we regard physical time it really doesn't matter if we work according to Newton or with the Einstein–Minkowski approach. What matters is that we have an observer who is a human being, and then we have an interface between the physical space and the social space.

Let us just say before we plunge into the time-space of Hermann Minkowski that clock time is not time itself but a measure of time. What we choose as a measure is not that important either in time or in space. "Give me a place to stand and I will move the Earth", exclaimed Archimedes, but modern physicists shrug their shoulders and answer, "Just choose one."

But human impressions and understanding and human actions are not relative but absolute for the person in question, and it is actually at this very point that ethics, imagination and creation come into consideration. The universe, time and space are not continuous, but the human mind creates them continuously. This is the basic message which we will discuss.

In the appendix to this chapter, we explain Hermann Minkowski's time-space, which was the ground for Einstein's special relativity theory. We will not use the more intricate physical results but just discuss space and time when we have the fastest signal. Einstein later used the speed of light, but for our needs we just say that in any event, there exists a fastest signal, which may vary between different events.

For example, if presidents Macron and Putin meet officially and announce this via press conference, the signals, the messages, reach the general public almost at the speed of light, but if they very discreetly meet in Plzen, in the Czech Republic, with utmost secrecy, it would take a considerably longer time to reach the public due to the changed mode of information, in which we also count obstacles such as secrecy, remoteness with respect to classes, cultures and other possible obstacles for information such as ignorant journalists, ideological matters and whatnot. The physical choice of light is not suitable in the social space since it is one-dimensional, thus atomistic, and in the social space signals are almost always complex.

Let us use exactly the same explanation for Figure 2.2 as in the Appendix in order to avoid any mistakes caused by different wording.

1   The W-axis represents the physical space, although at a universal level. Thus the three-dimensional space is compressed to one dimension. Different points on the W-axis thus represent different subspaces at a physical distance from each other. We then assume some kind of distance measure for the physical space, like the meter or similar.
2   The T-axis represents the time dimension on the universal level. We may define a measure; normally this is seen as the speed of light, but for our purposes, we assume that there exists a signal of maximum speed. In astrophysics it is the speed of light, but in a socio-economic space we may think of another.
3   To explain the hyperbola Θ we need an observer located at (W_0, T_0). It is also important to observe that the W-axis through (W_0, T_0) represents *now* for the observer in that point. Obviously, we may think of (W_0, T_0) as a particular historical point in space-time with respect to current now when reading this.

4 Given the maximum signal speed, the distance $[(W_0, T_0) - (W_0, T_1)]$ represents one time unit, which in a vacuum on the universal level is one light-year.

5 Assume that the physical subspace is (W_1, T_0) and that the observer watches this. Due to the distance $[(W_0, T_0) - (W_0, T_0)]$ it takes some time for the signal at maximum speed to convey the information of W_1 to W_0. Thus the information is conveyed to the observer when W_1 has advanced to (W_1, T_2). This means that if we imagine that the subspace W_0 and the subspace W_1 move at the same speed, the maximum signal speed, when W_0 has advanced to (W_0, T_1), we will observe the W_1-space when it has advanced to (W_1, T_2).

6 Consequently the $\Theta - \Theta$ hyperbola represents the entire physical space W which uniformly moves forward at the maximum signal speed, and we have an observer at W_0. Subsequently this observer will observe subspace W_1 when it has advanced to (W_1, T_1) at a future date T_3. We can thus make similar analyses for all points and make the hyperbola $\Theta - \Theta$ representing the world when in the future the subspaces in W can be observed from (W_0, T_1). That means that all points within the hyperbola can be ordered in space-time, while those outside cannot.

Thus, as long as our observations are limited to one-dimensional atomistic light-signals, the discussion with respect to Figure 2.2 so far is hardly anything to write home about, since we do not care about the physical proceedings, which we have in the Appendix. But if we transfer this reasoning of Figure 2.2

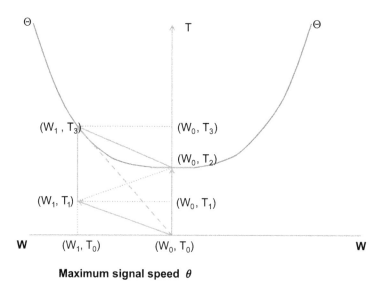

Figure 2.2 Space-time

to the social space, where we deal with complex signals, the approach becomes theoretically explosive.

Let us go back to the concept of epistemic cycles. Our decision to act is based on historical information, traditions and apprehension of the current situation; our action creates some form of reaction which might be positive or negative with respect to our goals or desires. All this takes place in the time-space. As long as it concerns the buying of two kilos of potatoes, this theoretical apparatus may seem a bit exaggerated, but when we discuss the buying of a villa or taking a new job, things become different. Keynes is said to have said something like, "I want it if I get it now, but if I have to wait I will change my mind."

In order to have a meaningful time concept, we need some sort of event in space. In Figure 2.2 we have indicated the world which moves; obviously it is assumed to move forward along something we call the time axis. Events in space are observed and define something which we can call *before* and something we can call *after*, and thus simple logic induces us to assume that there is something we call *now*. If we start at *now*, it seems to mean a moment of observation. From that we may define before and after. But as we see according to our dating with the help of the time axis, we may ask ourselves how the observer can deduce that the signal W_1 at T_2 in reality occurred earlier at time T_0. So, how on earth can human beings be able to develop theories like the one Herrmann Minkowski did in 1908? We basically only have our senses. It is obvious that practically speaking, the knowledge that light had a limited speed, as shown by Michelson and Morley in 1887, is enough to construct Figure 3.5. Besides that, we must have some sort of almanac at W_0, and that almanac cannot be based solely on some abstract time concept; it has to be based on physical events in W_0. The point is that the time concept per se cannot be what Newton suggests in the quote above: "Absolute, true, and mathematical time, of itself, and from its own nature flows equably without regard to anything external, and by another name is called duration" (2010[1688]:13). It is exactly here that Lazare Carnot makes an essential contribution when he changes the focus from the static force to the differences in speed which is the basis of time. Changes in speed imply a space of bodies which change their position, and this is the creation of time. Thus the observer at W_0 has an agenda which is due to the local special movements at T_2, and that makes the observer fit to date the events also at W_1. This has nothing to do with relativity, but it is an answer to Archimedes' cry for a place to stand. Lazare Carnot does not mention Archimedes' exclamation, but he defines absolute time as the time which has a fixed point of measurement, like Greenwich for example.

In modern physics such a time concept is natural and William Unruh (1995:24) expresses this:

> It is precisely this conflict between a mutable notion of time and the absolute and unitary notion of time inherited from Newton that has caused consternation and confusion. This confusion came about not because of

any innate violation of the sense of time that we are born with. Time for children is flexible and changeable, and certainly need not be the same here as it is there. Throughout our early years we were taught the lessons of Newton. Time was something out there, something that our watches measured, and something that really was the same everywhere. We learnt while very young that our excuse to the teacher that our time was different from the teacher's time was not acceptable.

Thus we can now state that there must exist a sort of time concept in W_0 for dating an event at W_1. It does not need to be the same as in W_1, but we get a sense of the concepts before and after. *Now* is a problem, but it must fall out from a logical analysis based on accepted axioms. Certainly we need some other assumptions of some average speed, although not necessarily constant and that the light chooses the quickest way. To some degree such matters can be experimentally tested for the universal neighbourhood, but assuming it globally seems a bit adventurous.

So let us now concentrate on the observer in W_0 who started the whole trouble. We are then talking of a human being, who may use a machine constructed by human creativity and intelligence. Can we say that he or she is entirely happy about our efforts to explain time so far? Unfortunately this is probably not the case, and the quote from Unruh above partly explains why. Unruh comes with the shocking claim that time is not the same even for the same individual at all times, and he links the child's unhappy fostering into Newtonian time by the teacher's behaviour, which was linked to standard clock time.

Assume that we can make a small sailing tour on a leaf at the water surface on a pond. We may also assume that our weight does not affect the leaf significantly with respect to other leaves, which are floating around. In the beginning there is no wind, but currents are created by branches of trees around falling into the pond. The leaves move in a random way (like a Brownian motion), and we can then tell where we have been, but this gives no idea of where we are going. Thus there can be no expectation with any probability distribution other than the rectangular since the moves are of limited length.

For those who have studied probability theory, there is also a widely used example of a drunkard stabilized by a lamppost at the other side of the street of where the entrance of his house is. He is so drunk that the probability of the direction, circle around, is rectangular. Given the average step length and the distance to the entrance door, we may now calculate the probability of reaching the door after a certain time. Thus from the point of view of our inebriated fellow, the direction of the next step is completely unknown, but it is limited (the difference from the other example is that he probably does not know where he comes from).

In such world there is probably a universal time concept like entropy, but this can hardly be disaggregated to the microscopic level.

When we look at both of these examples, Newtonian time seems to be a bit too abstract. Even the entropy increase seems to be easier to handle. Using the implicit time concept of Minkowski where time is linked to relative spatial movements can work in a very formal sense, but unfortunately it requires an observer who has some kind of almanac.[4]

Immanuel Kant had a lot of trouble with the time concept since his a priori world erased any form of meaningful universal time concept, but he regarded time as a coherent organizing principle for ephemeral sensual experiences:

> Time is nothing but the form of inner sense, that is, of the intuition of ourselves and of our inner state. It cannot be a determination of outer appearances; it has to do neither with shape nor position, but with the relation of representations of our inner state.
>
> (Kant 1933:77)

The Kantian standpoint on time can be and is criticized pretty hard, but nevertheless it is interesting in searching for a social time concept.

The most interesting philosopher with respect to time is Henri Bergson, who in *Time and Free Will* links time to Hume's concept of causality. As we discussed with respect to Aristotle, memory and structural compositions create a basis for analyzing future possibilities, thus the past is linked to now, which creates expectations concerning the future.[5]

Causality requires some sort of continuity of space-time, and we are led to assume such continuity by the duration of matter, forms and the multitude of actions in space-time which can be ordered. The latter aspect may seem a bit curious, but although the surrounding actions may seem confusing and random, they compose a sort of carpet of continuity in space-time which induces us to assume continuity in space-time with respect to causal structures. However, this is a rather courageous assumption.

Let us look at a more dramatic example from literature, the crime novel *The Bride in Newgate* by John Dickson Carr, published in 1950.[6]

In the opening of the novel we meet two central figures, Richard Darwent and Lady Caroline. Darwent had been sentenced to death for killing a nobleman in a duel. Nobilities could duel, but not private men. Lady Caroline had received an inheritance on the condition that she married, which was not her wish to do. So, she decided to marry a man sentenced to death, and that man happened to be Richard Darwent. During the preliminaries one hears a couple of horses aiming for Downing Street 11, the house of Lord Castlereagh, Minister of Foreign Affairs.

The marriage ceremony, however, is brought to a happy end for Lady Caroline, who only had to wait until 08:00 for her inheritance. Before that, however, a messenger arrives to say that Darwent's two cousins were killed in the Battle of Waterloo, which happened to have taken place before Darwent's duel with the nobleman, and at that time he was actually Marquise de Arwant and thus had full permission to duel. Thus, the logic of the events was turned completely around, outside the knowledge of the two concerned. We can illustrate this in Figure 2.3.

When time goes by, *now* is revised with respect to known history, which sometimes confirms the believed state of the world and sometimes not. Thus,

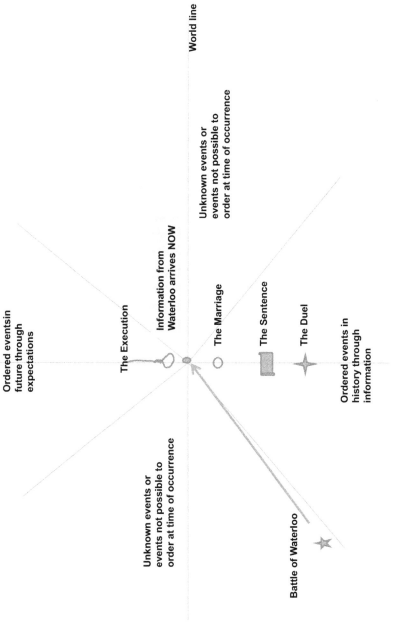

Figure 2.3 A space–time illustration

when *now* evolves in time, we learn about states of the world which have earlier been hidden. This means that we sometimes have to reinterpret history with respect to new knowledge. From that moment, we transcend into a new causality structure and a new logic of events.

In the case of *The Bride in Newgate*, the Battle of Waterloo was unknown when the duel took place; the information arrived after the duel but before the planned execution. Thus, in *now*, our knowledge of the general state of the world is at its minimum. We might say that in *now*, the direction of time is the most uncertain. For the future, we judge the direction by structural knowledge and probable inertia of behaviour, and our historical knowledge is ordered both temporally and locally according to explicit or implicit norms formed by the present physical/socio-economic structures. But if we look at knowledge, repetitiveness of mistakes, cruelties and so on, time sometimes seems to go backwards or stand still. Time as a concept in human lives is not equivalent to the actual measurement of time.

Looking at Figure 2.3, we realize that time is irreversible, bringing in causal structurers into the time concept of Einstein and Minkowski, which is reversible per se. Thus, with respect to the Newtonian construction of time, a shift to the Einstein–Minkowski approach places the problem of the direction of time within the individual and society due to physical and social actions. If we go to the pure physical world, we may believe in a universal process of increasing inertia, which obviously gives us a universal direction of time, although uncomfortable. But this general concept of time built on increasing entropy cannot be disaggregated since we on the microscopic level have local processes of both increasing and decreasing entropy for different subsystems.

To add causality into social space-time is consequently absolutely necessary, and it replaces Newton's thought of a deterministic time dimension. But we must then remember Hume's distinction that causality means a lack of determinism and the introduction of chance (Hume p. 93).

The conclusion of our discussion is that the human time concept must be linked to changes of the space as suggested by Minkowski, and furthermore it must also be linked to a set of perceived causal processes based on implicit assumptions of continuity and duration of space.

However, the causal processes of importance are those which the individuals take part in, and this is what Unruh means: The child knows that time is variable and soccer is different from riding with respect to time and the perception of time, but when going to school, the child plays no part in the logic which is exogenous depending on clock time, and furthermore coming too late means unpleasantness.

It is also interesting here to allude to Smith's discussion of subordination with respect to the increase in wealth. An increase in wealth implies that different properties mean different kinds of causal processes which the individual must be part of; it can be physical maintenance, social duties, public responsibilities and so on, which are implicit in ownership and control of property. But we may also suspect that decreases in wealth means fewer causal processes in which the individual is engaged. Thus, with respect to imposed logical processes following from the development of society and economic environment, the individual will increasingly lack control and means of influence, and consequently development of society will become increasingly exogenous. Social alienation will increase. This implies that we may suspect that from an abstract point of view, poor people are less connected in time-space then wealthy people. This may of course have consequences for behaviour and general responsibility for self and environment.

Thus, adding causal processes in which the individual takes part to the time concept will give the individual a place in time-space which also includes the social space. We will come back to this aspect.

A last aspect of the Minkowski diagram and which has been strengthened by the story of Richard Darwent and Lady Caroline is in relation to epistemic cycles. We decide our actions on the basis of purpose, apprehension of context and perceived restrictions. Still, we may fail due to a change in circumstances, as in the case of the reports from the Battle of Waterloo. Then it is not just a change of events, but we may have a complete change of logic, which might cause revision of purposes as well as the revision of our understanding of the context. Thus, when we for example draw a decision tree, we make assumptions of the environment and of possible routes of decision which are limited, but as time goes by (i.e., as events happen), the whole environment for the prospective decision changes. As of December 2017, the UK Leave negotiations with the European Union seem to be a good example of a situation where several different apprehensions of current conditions as well as appropriate expectations have systematically gone through a process of change which has implied that the logic of the negotiations has become different from what it was as late as some months ago. Certainly such changes are followed by accusation of lying, false information and double agendas. To an outside observer, it is clear that information was somewhat foggy, but most information which is relevant today was also relevant some ten months ago. Thus what has happened is that the judgement of the consequences differed, although whether that was due to neglecting reactions from negotiating partners, ignorance of the asymmetry of pulse and tempo of socio-political and economic processes or pure dishonesty in promoting private or group agendas is hard to say.

This aspect illustrated by Figure 2.3 is however of outmost importance when we later on discuss the role and suitability of public organizations. It is important not that it can replace deterministic thinking as in the case of decision trees but sooner that it creates an awareness of dynamics and the stability of complex processes where deterministic thinking per se has little relevance. Obviously we can draw a decision tree at any time based on current knowledge in order to clarify our own thoughts, and that is sensitive and good, but to treat such tools as giving information or new insights is parallel to claiming that mathematics contains information about the world. The basic question to work with is our own apprehension and comprehension of the dynamics of the world, and for that we must be prepared to change some of the logic we earlier have believed in. Thus we leave the event-based analysis where events contain no structural load to look at events with respect to possible structural compositions. The events are then treated as conditions, some sort of "axioms" which affect our logical analysis.

The neoclassical trap: lessons from Arrow's paradox

From our discussions in the prologue, economic theory has a long way to go in order to integrate the microscopic world and the macroscopic. The path is not through inventing some additional technical assumptions of mathematical character but through cooperating with other social sciences in order to catch the mysteries of the human societies.

The mystery lies in the very fact of the human being a subject and a final cause, and consequently additive aggregation is not relevant.

We saw in the prologue that starting from a pure barter economy, we had an inescapable rift between the microscopic level and the macroscopic, and we also saw that this was the reason for Arrow's paradox; that is, the analysis of a barter economy with people who are on one hand aware of the interdependence between individuals and on the other hand aware of and able to manipulate the aggregate level will imply that there exists no general equilibrium in the neoclassical sense.

But we also showed that introducing money and money values in analytical practice makes *de facto* both commodity values and individual incomes possible to analyze additively. Thus, although money is an anomaly in neoclassical theory, the principle of additive aggregation so to speak is incorporated with a non-equilibrium analysis in a way that from a theoretical point of view at least, we do not have the slightest idea about the analytical effects. We theorize as if it was true.

The interpretations of Arrow's paradox and the sloppy treatment of additive aggregation have compromised economic research in several ways. But let us start with repeating what Arrow's paradox actually tells us: *If we in the neoclassical type of market allow the individuals to behave contradictory to the neoclassical axiomatic structure, a neoclassical general equilibrium cannot occur. Thus, all the axioms of the neoclassical axiomatic structure are necessary to imply a neoclassical general equilibrium.*

This result is normal for logical paradoxes. If we take Russell's paradox for example, the paradox has its roots in the fact that items, which can be represented as logical variables, can be of two kinds: atomistic and complex. Cantor's non-accountability paradox occurs because numbers can be of two kinds; on one hand they can be used for annotations/signs of positions in a space, and on the other they can be used for accounting. The basic problem these paradoxes approach is that if we have one bowl with three apples and two pears and one with two oranges and four bananas, we can have this addition sentence:

$$3ap + 2pe + 2or + 4ba = ???$$

So what is that?

But if we set ap = pe = or = ba = Fruits (fr); we will have

$$3fr + 2\,fr + 2fr + 4fr = 11fr$$

But on the other hand if we define a concept "fruit salad" (fs), we may have

$$3ap + 2pe + 2or + 4ba = 1fs$$

So, when can you abstract a problem in such a way that you can use numbers as representatives for the physical items? In the prologue we mentioned that Jean-Baptiste Say rejected the use of prices and money as representatives of the values of commodities, other than locally and temporally. This little mathematical exercise is illustrating the deeper principle on which he builds his rejection.

Seen in this way, Arrow's paradox is quite natural and a kind of correlate to the neoclassical axiomatic structure and the proof of the existence of general equilibrium.

The problem is that there is confusion about what the general equilibrium really means. Here we have pointed out that Gerard Debreu from the very beginning was aware that commodities and individuals exist in space-time and that it is not a Euclidian space.

In his discussion on space-time topology, Roy Douglas concludes that even from a point of view where we disregard the processes of the conscious human mind, it is hard to see that the Universe displays any global continuity:

> The (global) Hausdorff property certainly simplifies the mathematics of our models; unfortunately, it is also an entirely inappropriate restriction for models of space-time, precisely because (as we have seen) it is a strictly global constraint, in spite of any naive intuition to the contrary.
>
> (Douglas 1995:180)

The quote from Douglas is extremely interesting since it takes its start in the physical space. The Hausdorff property is absolutely essential for concepts of continuity, additive measurability and thus aggregation. A Euclidian space, we might say, is a measurable Hausdorff space with a defined metric. We have criticized the neoclassical construction of the market space, which is the commodity space, where agents are vectors, with respect to the dimensionality aspects. When we introduce a commodity into the market space, which is not derived from existing commodities but is a new dimension, we break both the conditions of the Euclidian metrics and the Hausdorff property. Furthermore, when we criticize the Axiom of Reflexivity in the neoclassical axiomatic structure, it is from the point of view of neighbourhoods. When we accept the notion of *structures*, it actually means that a certain commodity might belong to different neighbourhoods which are disjoint and of different dimensionality, which breaks the Hausdorff property. This is not in any sense mystical but an effect of rejecting atomistic commodities and presuming that all commodities are complex.

Douglas discusses from a universal physical perspective, but we add the conscious human mind with memory and expectations. That will imply that an individual may perceive a continuous space-time with respect to an epistemic level, but in fact the human being per se is the fundamental source of instability in physical and social space-time. This follows the assumption that the human being must be regarded as a subject and consequently a final cause. We are now in the neighbourhood of the deepest questions with regard to artificial intelligence, which we will return to.

Structures and structural compositions

Let us first notice the notion that lexicographic preferences and their character implicitly introduce structural compositions among the commodities with respect to a single agent as well as to the society. In fact, our whole approach to the markets, commodities and production/consumption is based on a structural approach. This follows directly from our claim that commodities and agents are not atomistic variables but complex, which means a limitation with respect to substitutability. Furthermore, the dimensionality problem which is annoying in the case of atomistic variables is devastating with respect to structures, though the problem of zero hits us with maximum force and furthermore we get the problem of *negative facts*.

Let us return to the epistemic cycles and a relatively typical Western European family and its formidable organizational problems. Let us say that the central bank decides to raise the interest rates significantly or take other costly measures to curb borrowing. Our family realizes that they are not able to pay interest and mortgages. They have to move to a small two-bedroom apartment in the other end of the city. What does that mean to the family with respect to other dimensions of life, to other epistemic cycles? A macroscopic theory may well display a nice continuous picture through averaging individual effects, but bringing in other local and temporal conditions raises doubts of the relevance of such pictures.

We addressed in the prologue our two basic propositions 1 and 2, from earlier books. Proposition 1 says that commodities are almost always complexes and thus there exists no possibility of additive aggregation, since we have no unique price vector, and subsequently no general equilibrium when all individuals reach their individual optima as the society also reaches a social optimum. But on the other hand, in Proposition 2 we are told that if we pass on to use money values as *representatives* for commodities in the aggregation process, the analytical result for the real economy in Proposition 1 will not hold.

Furthermore if we have a goal such as "maximizing the financial surplus" or "minimizing the financial costs" given restrictions in financial terms, then we may very well imagine the existence of a set of individual optima which are unique to a certain universal optimum, and these are measurable in the same way as any aggregate optimum. This follows from the fact that in equilibrium, the utility-maximizing problem given income and prices is equivalent to the cost-minimizing problem given utility. The theoretical problem is that Proposition 1 is based on a rejection of the Axiom of Reflexivity and implies that we have no unique measure for the link between real commodities and the preference space. Thus, we cannot say anything about the utility-maximizing problem other than locally and temporally, and thus we must reject additive aggregation. Consequently, the cost-minimizing problem has no utility-maximizing counterpart, which implies that the cost-minimizing problem is always possible. Since money values are atomic facts, any optima is always true, and furthermore additive aggregation is always allowed, but it carries no links whatsoever to the real welfare problem.

Thus an economic analysis based on money values, outside general equilibrium, on the macroscopic level has no a priori logical links to the microscopic levels. Subsequently macroscopic events or conscious politics will affect the microscopic levels, but these effects are of structural character and are furthermore most probably irreversible.

Our family has been forced to change their mode of living, but this is not an atomistic fact in a Euclidian space. It is a structural event which affects the whole decision structure of the family. If we think in dimensionality terms, we will most probably have some new dimensions while some will disappear and the family will apprehend a different dimensionality.

But if we now look at the two sides of the macroscopic discussion in question, the decision makers decide on a set of variables and parameters which are completely different from the decision space which is comprehended by the individuals whom the decision affects. This alludes in the deepest sense to the meaning of Arrow's paradox when he introduces new types of agents in the neoclassical axiomatic structure which are able to negotiate the aggregate results, implying that additive aggregation does not hold.

Thus, if commodities and agents are structural complexes, the dimensionality problem and the art of measurement will turn out to be quite different from what we experience when we work with a predetermined Euclidian space where we use the mathematics of Newton and Descartes. We come across the mathematics of *topology*.

Topology deals with the characteristics of spaces and the possibilities of moulding a space in a continuous way. A simple example is when we write on one side of a piece of paper, which is seen as a two-dimensional space, and want to go on writing on the other side. We must then make an exogenous operation to turn the paper, utilizing a third dimension which is not present in the two-dimensional space of a side of the paper, which we write on. Thus we know that the two-dimensional side exists embedded in a space which has more dimensions than the page we write on.

One of the very first problems we run across in topology is the problem of zero, which takes us to the consequential problem of "negative facts". During the 20th century, Bertrand Russell introduced the possibility of negative facts.

In logic we denote an item as a variable, *a*, for example, defined as an atomic fact. Then we have the simple rule: *either a* or *non-a*. It is called the law of the excluded third. In the neoclassical axioms, this is arranged by the axioms and the commodities are defined only in the positive orthant. This means that we can create different kind mathematical analysis, which is nice and well behaved.

Obviously, the notion of *non-a* relates somehow to the notion of empty space, Ø. Let *a* denote some brand of cars. Non-*a* means then that there is no car of the desired brand; the number of such cars is zero. Although the meaning of this is obvious for atomistic variables, it is not so for complex variables, which require a structure.

The problem of zero

Let us assume n variables $x_1, \ldots, x_n$. Let us furthermore assume a function F over the n variables: $F(x_1, \ldots, x_n)$. For $n = 3$, we may write $F^3(x) = ax_1 + bx_2 + cx_3$. Thus we have three different variables represented in three different dimensions. In Figure 2.4 we illustrate a point of $F^3(x)$:

Thus the equation $F^3(x)$ defines a vector $(x^a_1; x^b_1; x^c_1)$, and this could define a corner in a box, as is indicated in the left side of Figure 2.4. However we can say that the *c* dimension is void; that is, the empty space, zero. In that case, as is shown, we could still define a function $F^2(x)$ which defines a vector illustrated in the right side of the figure as $(x^a_1; x^b_1)$. So what we do is that from an abstract point of view, we think of a space which potentially can be moulded freely with respect to dimensions and the dimensions are independent, as shown in Figure 2.5a and b.

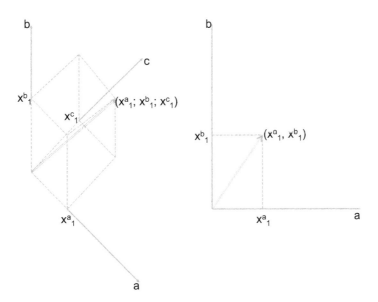

Figure 2.4 Reduction of dimensions

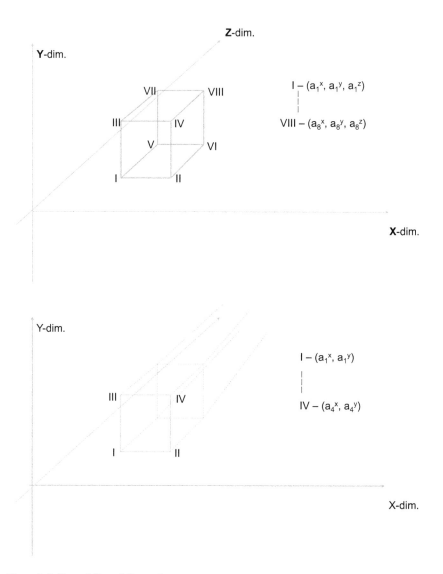

Figure 2.5 Potentiality of dimensions

We see from this figure that the three-dimensional figure in Figure 2.5a can be seen as a realization of the imaginative third dimension in Figure 2.5b. Thus we draw on a paper the two imaginative figures with different dimensionality.

Let us first say that this is an exemplification that an abstract point in a space has relations to all possible realizations of the space with respect to dimensionality. This is a central thought in abstract topology and necessary for understanding the concept of space as well as the concept of paradoxes.[7]

Let us first start with the so-called tiling theorem (Alexandroff 1961:1–2). The tiling theorem implies that we take a surface like that bounded by points I–IV in Figure 2.5b and cover it with (very) small areas; when we are well inside the boundaries, these small areas are just two-dimensional subsets, but when we come to the border, say the line between points II and III, we suddenly realize that we are on the brink of a precipice and we get in contact with a new dimension. The simple conclusion is that any singular point in an abstract space has "contact" with or has a neighbourhood of all the dimensions of the abstract space. Normally we think of an ordinary physical space, the three-dimensional Euclidian space, and if we spot a point of a blackboard, which we call the origo in a two-dimensional diagram, we immediately can imagine a third dimension with an axis through the origo. But from a mathematical point of view, there are no possibilities to form a path from the two-dimensional surface to the three-dimensional box. The other direction from higher to lower dimensionality is possible in certain cases when dimensions merge, like space and time in astronomy, or in the case of a Möbius strip or a torus.

If we transform these considerations to an axiomatic analysis, we never attain these dimensional borders in an ordinary logical analysis well inside the axiomatic structures, but if we think of Figure 2.1, they appear when we translate our results into a multidimensional reality. Thus the axiomatic structure reduces the dimensionality, but it does not reduce our intuition or our imagination, as in Figure 2.5b when we see the two-dimensional quadrant but can well imagine the three-dimensional box of the figure. In the physical reality which we can handle without more sophisticated instruments, the imagination is normally kept within proper frames, but when we analyze complex abstract systems, it is much more difficult to keep the feet well buried in the soil when we transform abstract analysis to the real world.

Another problem, which is some form of dual to the one we have discussed, is the *ex ante/ex post* problem in relation to structures.

As we said, for the human mind the imagination of extended spaces is indeed a marvellous gift. It is possible to think of different kinds of physical spaces and particularly perturbations of these spaces, but we have also the gift of thinking of abstract processes in other spaces, like the social space, cultural space and so on. In economics there have appeared papers on the mathematical optimization of husband/wife, optimal decision of suicide and similar things. We raise a number of factors which affect some behaviour and then try to create functional relationships. Although the author is not frightfully impressed by behaviouristic theories, it obviously could be a form of additional tool, at least to other forms of analysis. But – and here comes a big *but* – to make such an analysis, we have to make proper mathematical presumptions/axioms of the space where these kinds of functional relationships will work. The fundamental problem which we have to deal with is irreversibility. In production theory this is sometimes named the putty-clay problem. As we quoted in the first chapter, Aristotle is well aware of it in ordinary trade. When we have bought a commodity, our structural relations are changed, both to the commodity in question and in principle to all other commodities.

If we think of a house, we can think of that with respect to a fourth dimension, time; the house is subject to an ageing process. We can also, at least in principle, think of the house in relation to probable demographic changes or infrastructural changes. Thus we add other dimensions to the three physical ones, but we can never think of a house in reality in a two-dimensional way. Thus when we reduce the dimensionality of a structure, normally the structure vanishes. Adding dimensions will change the total structure, but the original one is still there as a substructure. Consequently zero when we interpret it in a structural way is a quite remarkable concept.

Zero or its technical sign, $\emptyset$, means the empty set. But looking at it, we may ask with respect to human society if zero food and zero diamonds are equivalent. If one says that these are not the same, then we must make models which can handle the two kinds of zeros in an appropriate way. But the mathematical problem is the trivial one if we regard public policy and measures which are asymmetric in the way that some people have to struggle with the problem of lexicographic preferences and some people do not need to bother. Then we are in for structural changes at the individual level, and when we have broad developments like technological changes of a certain character and/or globalization affecting production and consumption structure, we will have changes of the macroscopic structures which most probably will be asymmetric.

The asymmetries will then probably affect big groups of individuals but also change the conditions for public policy and other parameters in the society. Then we are in for huge structural changes which are very difficult to understand since they affect not one societal structure but many different ones with respect to dimensionality, degree of aggregation and character.

What is important is that the public policy, its definitions, goals, implementation and effects with respect to structural problems of the society, is not generally logically consistent with rational actions on lower aggregate levels per se. Proposition 1 in the prologue gives that result which basically stems out of the fact that we regard individuals as subjects and final causes. Adam Smith claimed that the growth of wealth required a higher degree of subordination, and that is certainly true, but we could easily enlarge this to say that the higher the degree of social and cultural integration we have, the higher the degree of subordination to the collective good must be required. Thus the social and cultural integration also enlarge the market penetration of the society and consequently increases the individual wealth, but this cannot be separated from what we might call the collective wealth which actually lies in the increased integration.

This aspect is completely outside any possible social interpretation of the neo-classical general equilibrium theory, and this also is true with respect to Adam Smith's formulation.

Consequently, the economic dimensions of the society are impossible to cut out from the rest of the social dimensions. Furthermore, sacrificing some social dimensions in order to make the market dimensions simpler to model is a completely inadequate thought, since no one has information about the full social structure. Even those who seem to benefit from such model restructuring cannot judge the coming repercussions.

Negative facts

In line with the discussion of the interpretation of zero in a structural sense, it follows per automata the problem of *negative facts*. Negative facts were first an intuitive thought by Bertrand Russell in the beginning of the 1920s. He was never able to solve the problem entirely, and he was much criticized by other philosophers.

In elementary logical language, negative facts are certainly an anomaly, and so it seems with respect to ordinary language. A negative item is impossible; of course we have such as negative temperatures, but that is just a matter of formulating a particular measure. A fact is attached to a physical composition of the physical space in some sense; then we could say, "I am tired" or "I am not tired", but negation just means absence and does not relate to the concept of tiredness.

However, during the time since Russell first started to discuss the problem of negative facts, mathematics and natural science have made incredible progress. Today we are talking of negative matters, and in the universe we have both black holes and quasars, which are contrary phenomena. At a more daily level, we can think of positive and negative poles in electricity and magnetism, and if we do not think about that in coupling the wires, we will have unpleasant problems. Thus we are not talking of contradictive phenomena but contrary ones.

A negative fact implies that its existence affects something else in a counterproductive way. It is not something mystical; on the contrary, it is very simple. Unstructured noise is not only the non-existence of meaningful sound of some kinds; it may also be unhealthy with respect to our ears. Listening to a string quintet of Mozart which is disturbed by noise is not particularly enjoyable. But still, unstructured noise might be meaningful and valuable as an element in an artistic composition with respect to paintings and photos. It is easy to think of an exhibition containing war paintings like *Guernica* or photos from wars where the unstructured noise might be effective in the holistic experience of the exhibition. That means that a negative fact is not negative per se but in relation to a particular structure.

When we have electric poles anodes and cathodes, we may have a pleasant electric circuit in between, but direct coupling leads to electric breakdown. With respect to magnetism, the same poles lead to repulsion while different poles lead to attraction.

Thus negative facts appear in relation to complex structures, but not when we have atomic facts. Furthermore, the effects of negative facts might be different for different structures.

In economics, the standard theory seems to define both the commodities, goods or services, per se as defined in the positive orthant and so also the produced utilities of the commodities. Defining the commodities in the positive orthant is acceptable since from the production side, they exist in a physical sense. To define the produced utility in the positive orthant is remarkable when we think of commodities as structurally defined. Indeed, it is hard to think of it even if we try to decouple commodities from any structure. Stigler and Becker wrote a famous article, "*De Gustibus Non Est Disputandum*", where they take the structural view of household production theory. In their conclusion they say:

> Addiction, advertising, etc. affect no tastes with the endless freedom they provide, but prices and incomes, and subject therefore to the constraints imposed by the negatively inclined demand curves, and other results. Needless to say, we would welcome explanations of why some people become addicted to alcohol and others to Mozart, whether the explanation was a development of our approach or a contribution from some other behavioural discipline.
>
> (Stigler and Becker 1977:89)[8]

The household production theory separates the commodities per se and the "utilities" of the consumer. Thus the commodities are chosen to fit in to the utility structure which is "produced" by a combination of commodities together with the household's efforts in housing, dinners, social gatherings, free time activities, work travelling and so on. Bringing in some new dimensions of commodities implies structural changes to some degree.

What Stigler and Becker are aware of is that their structural approach is simple in the meaning that they avoid deeper socio-psychological explanations but build on just observables and inertia of structures. From that point of view, their approach fits into our concept of epistemic cycles. It is however obvious that if we enlarge our analysis to contain interpersonal relations and with respect to macroscopic levels due to social responsiveness, we must look at our sister sciences within the social and behavioural area.

Important however is that a structural approach of whatever design concerning the real world must take into account that some matters which threaten the existing structure may be defended as negative from a preference/utility point of view. Therefore, it is natural to regard the produced commodity basket defined in the positive orthant while its "utility" content is defined over both the negative and the positive orthant; thus mathematically we have a relation, as in Figure 2.6.

Consequently there exists no unique price level.

We have commented now and then on the inadequacy of the neoclassical theory, but the fact that the neoclassical theory fosters a non-structural and even anti-structural thinking is probably one of the most devastating defects of the theory.

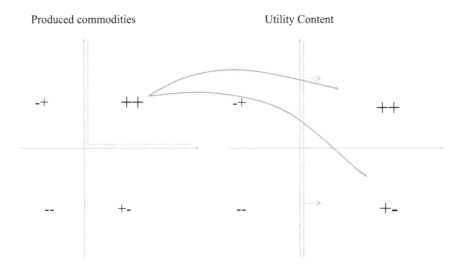

Figure 2.6 Relation between commodities and utilities

Conclusion

The developments during the 19th and 20th centuries in analytical philosophy, mathematics and the natural sciences change the approaches to modelling the world. Science realized that the abstract mathematical analysis gave no information per se of the empirical reality. The abstract modelling had to be framed by limitations, precise conceptualizations and precise local and temporal purposes. We could say that most of all, through the discovery of the entropy principle, the dream of universal a priori models ended once and for all. Unfortunately, economic theory became obsessed with a kind of Newtonian equilibrium thought which was developed mathematically to an impressive intellectual achievement. Sadly to say, this was a colossus with feet of clay. Its axiomatic underpinning is so obviously asocial, not to say antisocial, that it contradicts not only empirical findings in other social sciences but also findings by economic research.

To build a macroscopic theory on the fundament of the neoclassical axiomatic structure is both logically erroneous and ethically doubtful, to say the least.

Appendix on space-time

Diagrammatic explanation of Minkowski space-time

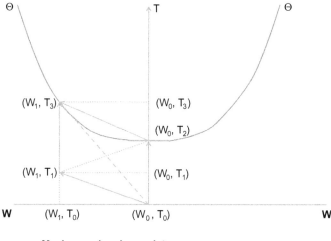

Diagram A.1 The general space-time situation

1 The W-axis represents the physical space, although at a universal level. Thus the three-dimensional space is compressed to one dimension. Different points on the W-axis thus represent different subspaces at a physical distance from each other. We then assume some kind of distance measure for the physical space, like the meter or similar.

2 The T-axis represents the time dimension on the universal level. We may define a measure; normally this is seen as the speed of light, but for our purposes, we assume that there exists a signal of maximum speed. In astrophysics it is the speed of light, but in a socio-economic space we may think of another.

3 To explain the hyperbola Θ we need an observer located at (W_0, T_0). It is also important to observe that the W-axis through (W_0, T_0) represents *now* for the observer in that point. Obviously, we may think of (W_0, T_0)

as a particular historical point in space-time with respect to current now when reading this.

4 Given the maximum signal speed, the distance $[(W_0, T_0) - (W_0, T_1)]$ represents one time unit, which in a vacuum on the universal level is one light-year.

5 Assume that the physical subspace is (W_1, T_0) and that the observer watches this. Due to the distance $[(W_0, T_0) - (W_0, T_0)]$ it takes some time for the signal at maximum speed to convey the information of W_1 to W_0. Thus the information is conveyed to the observer when W_1 has advanced to (W_1, T_2). This means that if we imagine that the subspace W_0 and the subspace W_1 move at the same speed, the maximum signal speed, when W_0 has advanced to (W_0, T_1), we will observe the W_1-space when it has advanced to (W_1, T_2).

6 Consequently the $\Theta - \Theta$ hyperbola represents the entire physical space W which uniformly moves forward at the maximum signal speed, and we have an observer at W_0. Subsequently this observer will observe subspace W_1 when it has advanced to (W_1, T_1) at a future date T_3. We can thus make similar analyses for all points and make the hyperbola $\Theta - \Theta$ representing the world when in the future the subspaces in W can be observed from (W_0, T_1). That means that all points within the hyperbola can be ordered in space-time, while those outside cannot.

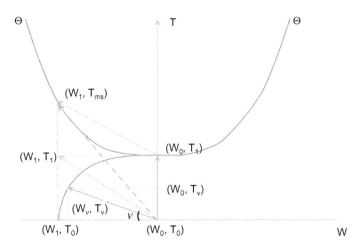

Diagram A.2 Distinction between spatial distance and time distance

1 We use the same basic diagram as A.1, but here we particularly study the conditions at (W_0, T_0), $(0, T_1)$ and $(W_1, 0)$. Let us look at the vector (W_v, T_2). Geometrically the points of the vector depend on the angle v.

2 When the angle $v = 90°$, we have the relative maximum signal speed, and when $v = 0°$, the relative signal speed is 0. But this is equivalent to say that at $v = 90°$, all mass is transferred to maximum signal speed, and when $v = 0°$, we have only the special dimension.

3   Thus (W_v, T_v) represents vectors of the subspace (W_1, T_0) at different relative speeds in fractions of the maximum signal speed. Consequently the mass, *potential energy*, of the subspace (W_1, T_0) is transferred to dynamics, *kinetic energy*.

4   Let us assume a measure of the maximum signal speed, **c**. We then have the distance between (W_0, T_0) and (W_0, T_1) of **c**T. The curve from (W_1, T_0) to (W_0, T_1) created by the vector (W_v, T_v), letting the angle represent different fractions φ of **c**, thus $0 \le \tau \le 1$. Consequently, the point (W_0, T_v) is decided by φ**c**, where φ varies between 0 and 1.

5   When we look at the curve created by (W_v, T_v), this represents the subspace (W_1, T_0) at different relative speeds as a fraction of the maximum signal speed. At $\varphi = 0$, we have the two subspaces (W_1, T_0) and (W_0, T_0) at the same relative speed and we have space-like conditions for the two subspaces; i.e., a world equivalent to Newton's. When φ increases to 1, subspace (W_1, T_0) has been transformed to pure light, as indicated where the curve described by (W_v, T_v) cuts the T-axis. The subspace (W_1, T_0), however, is seen in (W_0, T_0) as light from (W_1, T_1) when it has reached (W_1, T_{ms}). This is indicated by the diagonal from (W_0, T_0) to (W_1, T_{ms}).

6   *Consequently we have two distances to pay attention to in space-time: the spatial distance and the time distance set by the maximum signal speed.*

7   Furthermore, we have a direct relation between the two kinds of distances described by the transformation of spatial subspaces into light, as described by the vector (W_v, T_v). Without proceeding to the astrophysical analysis, we only mention the hypothesis of the general relativity theory $e = mc^2$, where e represents energy, m stands for physical mass at rest (potential energy) and c is the speed of light. Light is seen as an electromagnetic movement. Thus, when we accelerate the subspace (W_1, T_0), it will appear at (W_0, T_0) as the mass is compressed as illustrated by the curve described by the vector (W_v, T_v) at different speeds. At (W_0, T_0), the subspace (W_1, T_{ms}) will appear as light.

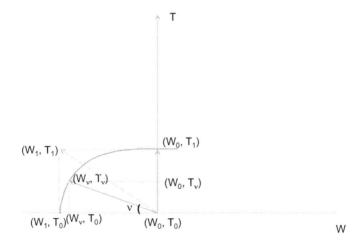

Diagram A.3 Illustration of distortion of mass

1 Let us now look more carefully at the curve created by the vector (W_v, T_v) and a relative speed as a fraction $0 \leq \varphi \leq 1$ of the maximum signal speed. The perpendicular point on the X-axis of (X_v, T_v) is (X_v, T_0). We then get two subsets: first, the rectangle created by the vector and the X and T axes, which we may call the M-space. Then we have the area limited by the curve from (W_1, T_0), (W_v, T_v) and (W_v, T_0), which we may call the E-space.

2 We can see that increasing the fraction φ diminishes the M-space and increases the E-space. However, this distortion of the M-space is not detectable for an occasional observer at the subspace (W_1, T_0), only from an observer at the subspace (W_0, T_0).

3 Thus the M-space may stand for the mass in motion and the E-space is the portion of mass at rest which is transformed to kinetic energy in the universal space, light when $\varphi = 1$.

Notes

1 Keynes rejected additive aggregation in economics 1903 in a speech to the apostles in Cambridge. (Ekstedt 2015:50).

2 First Law: Every body perseveres in its state of rest, or of uniform motion in a right line, unless it is compelled to change that state by forces impressed thereon.

Second Law: The alteration of motion is ever proportional to the motive force impressed; and is made in the direction of the right line in which that force is impressed.

Third Law: To every action there is always opposed an equal reaction: or the mutual actions of two bodies upon each other are always equal, and directed to contrary parts.

3 The general technical expression for entropy is a statistical measure: $H(X) \equiv -\sum_X p(X) \cdot \ln[p(x)]$

where H(X) is the degree of disorder of a variable X. In Ekstedt (2015:278) a small example is developed.

4 We do not want to give the impression of some kind of solipsism, but the fact is that if we base our theories on empirical knowledge, we always have to have in mind the observer and the surrounding conditions of the observation. This is not necessarily comparable to solipsism, although we have to question the relevance of theories which presuppose a universe where people do not exist or observe. Assuming that we may think like God does not impress.

5 In Ekstedt and Fusari (2010:117–119), there is a more comprehensive analysis of Bergson's thoughts.

6 This example was also discussed in Ekstedt and Fusari (2010:120–123).

7 We will base our further short discussion of these aspects on Paul Alexandroff's fundamental little book *Elementary Concepts of Topology* from 1932, published in English 1961. The book is astonishing for its mixture of intuition-based thoughts and precision in explanations, and much of modern mathematics of abstract spaces is necessary for the understanding of physical space-time as well as the extension of mathematics into the non-physical space as for example social spaces.

8 Stigler, George J. and Becker, Gary S., (1977). De Gustibus Non Est Disputandum, *American Economic Review*, Vol. 67, No. 2, pp. 76–90.

Bibliography

Alexandroff, P., (1961). *Elementary Concepts of Topology*, Dover Publications, New York.

Aristotle, (1990 [original around 334–324 BC]). On the Soul Bno. 402[a]–435[a]. In *The Works of Aristotle Vol. I*, Encyclopædia Britannica, Inc., Chicago and London, (Bno refers to the Berlin enumeration).

Douglas, R., (1995). Stochastically branching spacetime topology. In S. Savitt (ed.), *Time's Arrow Today: Recent Physical and Philosophical Work on the Direction of Time* (pp. 173–188), Cambridge University Press, Cambridge.

Ekstedt, H., and Fusari, A., (2010). *Economic Theory and Social Change: Problems and Revisions*, Routledge, London and New York.

Ekstedt, H., (2015). *Money, Valuation and Growth*, Routledge, London and New York.

Hume, D.A., (2002[1740]). *A Treatise of Human Nature*, Oxford University Press, Oxford.

Kant, I., (1933). *Critique of Pure Reason*, Macmillan Press Ltd, Houndsmills, Basingstoke, and London.

Minkowski, H., (1909). *Raum und Zeit* (Space and Time). Vortrag, gehalten auf der 80. Natur-Forscher-Versammlung zu Köln am 21. September 1908, Druck und Verlag von B.G.Teubner, Leipzig und Berlin, available at internet https://de.wikisource.org/wiki/Raum_und_Zeit_(Minkowski)

Newton, I., (2010[1688]). *The Principia: Mathematical Principles of Natural Philosophy*, Snowball Publishing, available at internet www.snowballpublishicng.com

Stigler, G.T. and Becker, G.S., (1977). De Gustibus Non Est Disputandum, *American Economic Review*, Vol. 67, No. 2, pp. 76–90.

Unruh, W., (1995). *Time, Gravity and Quantum Mechanics: In Times Arrow Today: Recent Physical and Philosophical Work on the Direction of Time.* Ed. Steven F. Savitt, Cambridge University Press, Cambridge.

3 Economics and ethics in economic theory

Action and remorse

François Villon: *Poésies Diverses*

The debate between Villon and his heart[1]	Envoi
I get the heartache, you the injury and pain	*Want to live? – God give me the strength –*
If you were just some poor crazy idiot	*It's necessary. . . – What is? –*
I'd be able to make excuses for you	*To feel remorse?*
You don't even care, all's one to you, foul or fair	*Lots of reading – What kind? –*
Either your head's harder than a rock	*Read for knowledge*
Or you actually prefer misery to honour	*Leave fools alone – I'll take your advice –*
Now what do you say to that? –	*Or will you forget? – I've got it fixed in mind –*
Once I'm dead I'll rise above it –	*Now act before things go from bad to worse*
God, what comfort! – What wise eloquence –	*I've nothing more to tell you –*
I've nothing more to tell you – I'll survive without it –	*I'll survive without it.*

François Villon knew the bitterness of the world in the middle of the 15th century. Starting off to become a priest, although from rather poor circumstances, he soon became a thief, a robber, a murderer, a whoremonger, who the night before he was to be hanged wrote:[2]

> *My name is François*
> *that's my curse*
> *Born in Paris*
> *close to Pontoise*
> *Some yards of cord*
> *the neck will know*
> *the burden of my arse*

Villon will partly be the key to our discussion of ethics of economic action and the subsequent effects on individuals, and also collectives of individuals, perception – apprehension – comprehension, with respect to future actions.

Like St. Paul, we do what we don't want and we know what we shall do but fail to do it. In theory, choices should be rational and simple, but in reality, some decisions fill us with anguish and afterwards our actions fill us with remorse. We want a better world, yet we are trapped in structures which make us feel like mice in a treadmill where we lose our will. Aristotle saw ethics as part of the fundamentals of life, but economic theory regards us as automata and indeed we sometimes feel like that. We discussed the problem of time in the previous chapter, and although life from a microscopic point of view may currently seem both stable and reversible, we know from bitter experience that changing macroscopic structures creates new restrictions and new risk factors for us.

We also discussed unexpected information. Although we agree with Keynes in *Treatise on Probability* that it is not rational to take into account events which are very improbable, we have to be aware that the more complex a causal system becomes, the higher the probabilities that improbabilities occur due to sheer complexity, since increasing dimensionalities of a causal system induce risks and uncertainties which are not even in the assumed space of outcomes. Ethics and rationality require that we are reasonably able to make priorities, but when structural changes occur, like that in the example concerning Richard Darwent and Lady Caroline, it sometimes does not only change probability distributions but the whole space of outcome and possibly also the entire causality structure. This will turn earlier priorities into uncertainty of the context and even of self.

But there is an even more important factor, and that is the complexities of aggregate levels. In modern society, there are several levels of aggregation, which produces some sort of services and control systems and implies taxes. Thus in western democracies, the complexity of individual and collective interdependence by necessity increases. We could say that this is a parallel to what Adam Smith touches on when he claims that the degree of subordination increases when individual wealth as well as the collective wealth increase.

Furthermore, the decisions at an aggregate level are per se independent of the single individual/family and thus can be seen as an act of God, which may break any individual epistemic cycle. But that also goes for the production sector. A removal of a factory or bankruptcy may create severe social problems. The problems of the so-called Rust Belt of the American Midwest have lasted for a considerable time now, and no replacement is in sight. The current administration has some promises that investment in obsolete coal technology would do the trick, although most market actors have reasonable doubts. Who decides what an obsolete technology is? Well, market valuation is sovereign. Investing in the production of Berliner coaches drawn by eight horses is certainly an elegant way of travelling. The rather vulgar communication structure today makes them a bit hard to sell, but who knows? Given the long-run climate and energy development, they might be back sooner than the coal technology from yesterday.

There is no reason to plan for totally unexpected events, but on the other hand, the complexification of structures leads to a creeping feeling that the unexpected might occur. Furthermore, when structural dependence increases, events which earlier were almost atomistic in the sense that they had very small repercussions may become more important, with respect to indirect effects due to complexification. Then we suddenly come to the point where the claim "This sort of event is very improbable to occur when I consider my context" has to be followed by the question, "Will the occurrence of such an event anywhere affect me indirectly through its repercussions?" We then take a step from the microscopic area to a macroscopic framework; this problem is exactly what is fundamental to the use of terror and how a handful of desperate people could change the path of a society. From a probability point of view, we must then change our attitudes. The probability that lightning should hit me twice during a year is extremely small, but it ought to be a rather substantial probability that somebody in Britain or Europe should be hit twice during a year. The second question will guide the macroscopic processes while the first on the microscopic. Already here we see the potential conflict, namely that those who want to dimension the ability of macroscopic decisions/actions on the basis of the individually experienced probability structures do not actually see, or maybe not prefer to see, the eventual following repercussions.

But as already has been said, such kinds of evolvement may occur through gradually increasing complexities of a causal system, both with respect to dimensionality and also with respect to the character of the causal dependence.

Thus, as for Villon, our life is full of bad decisions, not perhaps per se given the believed context, but because we should have earlier realized that time goes by, "panta rhei", and our decision was based on insufficient updating of knowledge and information – or worse based on prejudice and biased valuation of received information.

What is ethics? What is rationality?

Villon is an ethical mystery himself, being one of the most important poets of his century as well as one of the greatest ever. His life was that of a rascal and a villain. But he is very clear about his situation; he is aware of the implicit causality or logic of his actions and his social behaviour, but on the other hand, he displays the deepest remorse for his situation. Villon displays in his poetry the man in constant fight with his heart, although his earlier life sets out an almost deterministic route. In fact, few poets penetrate the anguish of the heart in relation to the cold determinism of contextual reality. But we can see the confusion. The cold attitude of his rational self meets the upset heart, which points out dimensions of his life and actions which are never brought into his rational self.

Aristotle claims that ethics and rationality are integrated since he saw the individual as a whole; soul and spirit incarnated in a human form. The economic rationality concept is *in toto* defined outside the mind of the agent; it is a simple equivalence relation between the outside choice space and the interior preferences such that the individual in the end ceases to be a subject and a final cause. Thus, when Aristotle speaks about ethics as being the tool of rational behaviour in order to obtain the highest good, his use of rationality is fundamentally different from that of economic theory. But that also means that using the concepts of ethics and rationality in relation to the real world implies contradictions in space-time due to changing complexity.

We remember the myth introducing Chapter 1. The reflexive intellect makes us realize a rather scary reality, and the fear fills us with emotions which make us insecure and doubting our abilities in two ways. On one hand, we doubt ourselves, which makes us ready to escape or turn to some desperate "Eat, drink and be merry, for tomorrow we shall die" feeling, which we recognize from history, literature and our hearts. On the other hand, there is another fear which Nelson Mandela put his finger on: the fear of our actual strength and abilities and where that may take us.

Fears govern our rationality, and our intellect is the humble servant of our emotion and fears. At best the intellect can modify and put things into proportion, and that is perhaps a kind of meta-rationality which we achieve by education and analytical training.

The heart of the matter

In economic reality as well as in economic analysis, we concentrate upon single moments, namely the very market exchange, which in *almost all*[3] cases is irreversible.

As we thoroughly discussed before, economic theory in its axiomatic form is bona fide as an abstract description when it comes to analyzing the precise point of exchange in space-time. However, any form of aggregation relative to commodities or agents presupposes assumptions concerning the constancy of space-time which is far from what can be even remotely representative of the macroscopic reality. The expression *ceteris paribus* is all right but meaningless when we work with pure statics, since we then present the immediate result from a single interaction. In comparative statics it might give us information of the working of the model given appropriate inertia, which should be specified since *ceteris paribus* is not a theoretical concept but an empirical statement signalling the possibility of inertia. For dynamic models the system stability is dependent on the actual *sensitivity* of the parameter structure and we may for some structures have substantial shifts in the system behavior due to small perturbations. Imposing broad restrictions as *ceteris paribus* reduces the economic/social analysis to a mathematical exercise. Mathematically, we can always assume additive aggregation, but that requires very precise specifications, and as a general method it is very doubtful.[4]

From an ethical point of view, there are two important results of our earlier results vis-à-vis economic theory, which we summarized in the prologue. First, we rejected the Axiom of Reflexivity since that single axiom forced all variables to be atomic variables and dismissed complex variables for the analysis of market exchange. Second, we showed Proposition 1, which tells us that there is no a priori logical connection between microscopic and macroscopic decisions, which also explains Arrow's Impossibility Theorem.

The Axiom of Reflexivity implies that for any binary choice, we have *Independence of Irrelevant Alternatives*, meaning that there can be no structural dependencies between either agents or commodities. Before entering an analysis of this, we must repeat that if we interpret commodities as Gerard Debreu (1987[1959]) does, namely that commodities at different space-time segments are different commodities, then the axiom holds. On the other hand, we lose any kind of intertemporal or interspatial interpretation, and the whole general equilibrium exercise becomes more or less meaningless as a scientific empirical tool.

Consequently, when we reject the Axiom of Reflexivity, we open the analysis for complex variables and thus for structural dependencies. Ethically, that means that we judge a commodity, or choice alternatives in a broader meaning, a preference relation without any structural meanings, to commodities, choice alternatives, which are valued due to their structural dependencies.

Thus the base for *consumption choice* is not the commodity as a physical item, be it a thing or a process, per se, but its structural role with respect to the consumer's context. *The producer* does not produce structural roles but physical items or processes.

This is the essential logical reason why general equilibrium in the neoclassical sense is not only meaningless to discuss but also deeply erroneous to speak about.

As we saw in Chapter 1, Kant's introduction of the concept "Das Ding an Sich" is an example of the same mistake; we empty the concept of all physical content and expect the mathematical treatment to give us some a priori empirical information per se, which is independent of all contextual relations.

The advances of mathematical philosophy during the 20th century have closed this possibility once for all. Logic and mathematics are a valuable intellectual tool but empty of any kind of a priori empirical information.

Consequently, when we reject the Axiom of Reflexivity we end up, in principle, in two different ethical problems, the consumer problem and the producer problem, which have little to do with each other. It is obvious that producers can adapt to certain well-documented and inert social structures; furthermore, they may even change, or at least hope to change, consumption structures to benefit of themselves. Fashion in general is a very good example of this.[5] However, this is also the source of the basic uncertainty of any kind of productive investment.

The ethical rift between the consumption side and the production side implies that the automatic link between the consumption choice and the income side becomes dubious. Although we are not Marxists, we agree with Marx that this rift between the consumption side and the production side makes sense of the expression that the worker is alienated from the production result, which does not occur in a barter economy but in a money economy. Thus it is true that increase in general demand increases the possibility of selling one's production, but taking into consideration changing income distribution, structural developments with respect to demand and/or technology, an increase in production followed by an increase in labour demand is indeed uncertain. If we take for example technological changes, Hume and Ricardo have realized that these could have both positive and negative effects on labour demand, but the introduction of neoclassical thinking closed this discussion by asserting that there was an a priori link between asymmetric technological change and increase of alternative production by applying the so-called Say's Law, which not even Jean-Baptiste Say himself believed in.[6]

It also implies that a stubborn refusal to realize the inadequacy of the neoclassical theory has deep-going ethical implications with respect to the scientific standard of economics. It will obviously not be impartial when evaluating empirical information, and it will be biased with respect to political ideologies. An interesting thing to note at this point is our reference to the Soviet economists/mathematicians Makarov and Rubinov (1977) in the prologue, and their claim that the neoclassical theory could not discriminate between the neoclassical form of market economy and the Soviet command economy. The reason why they could draw this conclusion is that they realized that the momentary character of the neoclassical axioms, given Debreu's clarification of dating commodities, required a dynamization of the theory, which is necessary if we shall add the production process as in the Newman and Gale approach. Thus, we cannot leave the price mechanism to the metaphysical "invisible hand" but it must be handled either by the capital market or by the state authorities.

When we come to Proposition 1 in the prologue, this is in fact only a correlate to the rejection of the Axiom of Reflexivity and Arrow's Impossibility Theorem. It tells us that there is no a priori logical link between the optimality of individual choices and that of the macroscopic levels.

Thus, from an ethical point of view, we have a rift between the microscopic and macroscopic level as well as between different macroscopic levels.

This implies that if we have a social organization of different levels of aggregation combined with complexities implying structural dependencies, we can expect ethical conflicts on one hand between different individuals and on the other hand between different levels of aggregation. Thus a coherent action on any aggregate level as well as an individual level requires a certain amount of subordination. Furthermore, direction of measures to a particular level of aggregation requires information which is adequate for the level. Information designed for more aggregate or disaggregate levels is not relevant. For example, if we work at a communal level, information has to be relevant with respect to precisely that particular group of actors since it contains relevant sets of goals, restrictions, relations to other levels and so on. Thus, the relations between a commune and a kind of federal level such as the EU are different from those of the state, for example, and that creates substantial complexities within the public sector, which by themselves may create intricate problems.

The debate on privatization which has dominated the political spheres for the last three or four decades has to a large extent among economists been based on theoretical results acquired by a mathematical analysis of the neoclassical axiomatic theory. Such results are neither right nor wrong from a scientific point of view, with regard to the precise interpretation of the axioms, but they are meaningless since no empirical answers can be achieved that way.

This also shows the ethics of scientists. We have earlier discussed Wittgenstein's Proposition 6.211 in *Tractatus Logico-Philosophicus*. To achieve a logical conclusion in manipulating a model, proposing that a logical structure is empty of any information of the empirical world implies that the precise empirical meanings and limitations of the axiomatic structure must be explained. Thus, we know that *all* axiomatic structures require atomic variables to be adequate in a logical analysis, but we also know that *almost all* (in a mathematical sense) empirical variables are complex. Thus an axiomatic structure *has to* contain implicit limitations with respect to the empirical aspects it should concern. Therefore, the misinterpretations of Arrow's Impossibility Theorem which signals the anomaly between the neoclassical axiomatic structure and an economic modelling which contains definitions not obeying this structure, but in line with more empirically founded behaviour, is not only a mistake from a logical point of view but also ethically erroneous.

Rationality and causality in space–time

In earlier works we have introduced the concept of *epistemic cycles*, which we discussed in the prologue. Since agents as well as commodities are complexes, the actions of the agents and the use of commodities are structurally and contextually dependent. Consequently, we need a rationality concept which allow for this enlargement of the theoretical base.

It might seem a bit tricky to keep the concept of rationality, but this is actually essential in order to keep economics possible to analyze within a scientific frame. It should be clear from earlier chapters that we follow an Aristotelian approach and regard humans as subjects and final causes. This implies that we can never reach the intrinsic reasons for an agent's decision, but given the decision, we have to assume that the action is relevant with respect to the decision. Thus we follow the approach to rationality as *purposeful action.*[7]

This is a very important attitude. It is actually to proclaim that the very doubtful *principle of revealed preferences*, which falls out automatically from the neoclassical axiomatic structure, is a vital principle of disequilibrium analysis, although this is an assumption concerning individuals and not an a priori axiom and thus subject to empirical investigations. As economic scientists, we cannot have a norm for what is a rational decision vis-à-vis apprehended structures and context when we work with complex variables. However, we can discuss rationality, given a known decision, knowledge about goals and restrictions and the induced action.

The problem, whether rationality can be seen as a normative concept or not, was central to the trial some years ago of the Norwegian mass murderer Anders Breivik, who killed 77 people. In the psychiatric investigation, the psychiatrists divided themselves into two groups. One claimed that to commit such a crime, a person must be mentally disordered, and the sentence should be compulsory psychiatric care for an undetermined amount of time. But the approach which underpinned the sentence was that Breivik was perfectly capable of handling daily life and making time-consuming and complex plans for his crimes, which showed that his daily life was not affected by his antisocial opinions which he shared with people publishing their opinion of different pages on the internet. This is also in line with Joachim Fest's works on Hitler, particularly *Inside Hitler's Bunker: The Last Days of the Third Reich* [*Der Untergang*] (2002), which was also the basis for the film with same title. It is also apparent in the many versions of notes taken from "Hitler's table talks" that Hitler was a quite boring mediocre "*besserwisser*" with rather standard views on life in general, except of course in those dimensions which concerned his "mission" in the world.

The commentaries to the film *Der Untergang* were quite interesting in Sweden, and I think it was the same for other Western European countries. A rather substantial group of film critics and also ordinary people were shocked that Hitler appeared as quite an ordinary man while they presumably imagined a kind of monstrosity. We also saw these kinds of comments with respect to Breivik; a surprise that even when he was actually planning his crime, Breivik appeared as ordinary, a bit shy and lonely, but on the whole a "one of us" person. The frequent shootings in the USA reveal often that nobody has any suspicions about the perpetrator in advance.

Consequently we cannot assume that rationality has some ethical qualities per se.

These examples show the two modes of thinking regarding rationality which we may call Kantian and Humean respectively. The Kantian thinking starts from a belief that there exist some a priori truths and ethical behaviour, and rationality is to adapt this truth and ethical behaviour. Thus the decision as well as the action are seen as a unit and must be subordinate to the a priori true world.

The Humean way of thinking starts from the assumption that our senses give us the "true" and only world to relate to; thus perspectives, perception, apprehension and comprehension in the Aristotelian sense will direct our emotions, "passions", which will govern our intellectual decisions and rationality with respect to the perceived and comprehended context. Thus the ethics of the decision is separated from the rationality of the action.

According to the concept of epistemic cycle, we see that the concepts *ex ante* and *ex post* fall out quite naturally from Hume's approach to rationality. We act, but the action is followed by some kind of reaction which might imply that the cycle is closed or that we fail to achieve our scopes. If we fail, we have to ask why and in some sense reconsider purposes, contextual apprehensions or our perception of means and restrictions. This implies that the *ex post* considerations will result in a somehow changed behaviour in future decisions, but not only that. The decision in the first case might change the whole logic of further decisions/ actions with respect to the dimensions involved.

Let us look at the neoclassical expected utility approach to realize this. This is built on the fact that we act in an environment which is variable, and we must have some opinion of possible outcomes and attached probability distributions. The agents' behaviour per se is, however, the usual kind related to simple barter optimization and is therefore static and foreseeable. However, when we pass over to a kind of disequilibrium analysis, the fellow agents' reaction to my decision is perhaps the most important uncertainty factor of all. A certain decision may in fact induce fellow agents to realize matters which also change their behaviour, which means not only going back and trying to "correct" contextual apprehension and our perception of scopes and means and come back with a new decision/action, but the whole logic of decisions within those relevant dimensions might also be changed. A very simple reason could be that fellow agents' apprehension of space-time is changed.

Unfortunately this is also the case if we succeed in closing the epistemic cycle, succeed with our purposes. This can be interpreted as having been right in our different judgements, but if so, it is by no means sure to be repetitive since environment and fellow agents have a changed space-time.

Thus the epistemic cycle is dated in space-time. As we discussed in Chapter 2, our own actions affect space-time locally and change the conditions for further actions. Our story in Chapter 2 of Richard Darwent and Lady Caroline shows how the complexity of decisions, information and structural problems coincided, resulting in a completely unforeseen outcome and changing the whole future logic of life for the involved parties. The important thing is that we focus on action. By necessity, actions affect the environment when we have a structural ordered world/society. Here the neoclassical theory, and by all means the Kantian static a priori thinking, is most deceitful since our actions are in general irreversible. It is true that there are microscopic situations where we might almost have reversibility, par preference in experimentally designed situations, but from a macroscopic perspective almost all actions are irreversible.

Aristotle touches on a sort of an *ex ante/ex post* reasoning, as we mentioned earlier. Although we may lighten the burden of a decision by different measures, we always come to the point of no return in a market exchange. To try to escape this problem by introducing a mathematical axiomatic structure which perturbs the real-life economics is perhaps not the most convincing scientific route.

Thus we are caught in circumstances, sometimes of a dynamic development of a self-chosen position which turns into a nightmare which we somehow need to break away from, and thus the earlier comprehension of the environment falls apart and we act in ways which in some sense are rational but from a different contextual environment are not understandable. Thus the human almost eternal internal struggle and torments giving rise to sorrow and remorse. We cannot solve this, but with the help of our experienced old friend François Villon, we can at least have a discussion on the problem of epistemic cycles and choice in an effort to approach the concept of ethics from Hume's standpoint that the intellect is the obedient servant of passion.

From our discussions in the prologue, economic theory as well as general social theory has a long way to go in order to integrate the microscopic world and the macroscopic. The path is not through inventing some additional technical assumptions of mathematical character but through cooperation with other social sciences in order to comprehend the mysteries of human societies.

The mystery lies in the very fact of the human being a subject and a final cause, and consequently additive aggregation is not relevant, particularly over time, when reactions and counteractions might have sprung from completely different epistemic cycles.

We saw in the prologue that starting from a pure barter economy, we had an inescapable rift between the microscopic level and the macroscopic, and we also saw that this was the reason for Arrow's paradox; that is, the analysis of a barter economy with people who are on one hand aware of the interdependence between individuals and on the other hand aware of and able to manipulate the aggregate level will imply that there exists no general equilibrium in the neoclassical sense.

The immediate conclusion, of course, is that if we dismiss the aggregate levels as containing some sort of mysterious superhuman "world spirit", all ethical systems must include both individual levels as well as the aggregate levels. But since there are no a priori logical connections between the microscopic levels and the macroscopic levels, the ethics must be of different character. This means from a pure abstract point of view that ethics on the micro and macro levels may well be partly consistent, but since we may assume consistency intrinsically, the difference in definitions and dimensionality must most probably imply inconsistencies and contradictions between the two levels. Thus we cannot expect one axiomatic system to solve ethical conflicts between the levels.

It is at this very point that the foggy concept of money enters. As we know, money is an anomaly in neoclassical theory, which deals with barter. However, in the very state of general equilibrium there exists a consistent relative valuation of the different items which we call commodities. This relative valuation might be expressed as real numbers, which we may give the name *prices*. But these prices are not to be compared with what we call prices in the real world; they are only a mathematical measure which works for one and only one specific occasion, namely general equilibrium, and at that occasion the numerical values are of course possible to aggregate additively, since they are defined in a Euclidian space. But the deceitful moment comes when we leave the simple Euclidian space when it concerns commodities in relation to the apprehended utilities, and treat agents as complexes and subjects as final causes. They do not form a unique Euclidian space from the consumers' point of view, since the dimensionality of the commodities differs. From the production point of view, they might still form a Euclidian point of view since we can talk about physical items; things and probably many kinds of services can also be seen as items in relation to income/ outlay matters, but it is a bit more complicated. Anyway, there is a distinct difference between the consumption side and the production side. However, when we transform consumption items to money values and assume that all consumption decisions are rational, we are able to aggregate the money values irrespective of the underlying complexities of commodities. Money values belong to non-proper classes and are subject to the same kind of intrinsic contradiction as we find in Cantor's Unaccountability Theorem, namely that money can be used for accounting but also representatives in an Euclidian space, and that means that additive aggregation is allowed. Subsequently, we seem to get a logical a priori link between the microscopic level and the macroscopic.

This is almost a kind of a mystery, although from a mathematical point of view it is evident. But if we think of all papers written on the problem of welfare comparisons and the usual claim that GDP is not an aggregate welfare measure but an accounting measure concerning the money turnover in an economy with respect to production and consumption of commodities, we actually state what is mathematically evident.

But it is deceitful particularly when discussed in media and politics, because if we assume some inertia of a social system, we can of course claim that a change in GDP represents a change in incomes and consumption, private or public, and if we assume all positive numerical changes are beneficial to the society and the numerical changes seem to fulfil the Pareto condition for an economic change. There is however a problem with even this humble attitude, and that is that leaving the atomistic economic world of the neoclassical theory, we plunge into a complex world of structural links and dependencies concerning the relations of the agents, relations between commodities and relations between the microscopic and macroscopic entities.

Commodities are linked to each other in their use, ordinary complementarities, but also with respect to effects. The petroleum used for making plastic bags and the petroleum used in cars have different external effects. The fact that all producers and all consumers are actually populating the same earth creates all these effects. The usual definition of economics as a science which deals with the allocation and distribution of scarce resources cannot be reduced to a simple timeless and space-less exchange but concerns physical, social, demographic and cultural reality. No commodity, no productive resource, no production activity, no consumption activity can escape this reality. That is why we have to distance ourselves from all kinds of metaphysical believes and postulations. We have also to realize that time and space is in a sensual reality possible to measure and analyze.

Consequently, all concepts regarding welfare, efficiency and productivity are basically in touch and affect all dimensions of this earthly/human reality.

Arrow's paradox, the market principle and public government

We have claimed, Proposition 2, that introducing money and money values in analytical practice makes *de facto* both commodity values and individual incomes possible to analyze additively. Thus, although money is an anomaly in neoclassical theory, it appears that the use of money as a medium of exchange is adequate in disequilibrium analysis. But when we use money values as measures of commodities, the principle of additive aggregation is also automatically incorporated into the disequilibrium analysis, contrary to our assurances that no such measure theoretically exists more than locally and temporally. Using monetary values as a general measure concerning complexes which are structurally linked to each other in a way that, from a theoretical point of view, we have not the slightest idea about creates a theoretical anomaly since the normal assumption in a science which uses any kind of measure is that this measure is exogenous with respect to the analysis. We are reminded of the quote from Jean-Baptiste Say in the prologue concerning measuring the area of the pyramid of Ghaize and the value of a camel respectively. Say was to my knowledge the first who observed this theoretical problem, and he says later in his book:

> It is obvious, therefore, that one cannot form an idea of the value of a commodity from its estimate of money price, except during a space of time, and within a space of territory, in which neither the denomination of the coin, nor the value of its material, has undergone any change; else the valuation will be merely nominal, and convey no fixed idea of value whatever. . . . In comparing values, the denomination of coin is useful only inasmuch as it designates the quantity of pure metal contained in the sum specified. It may serve to denote the quantity of the metal; but can never serve as an index of value at any distance of time, or of place.
>
> (Say 1834[1803]:311)

We can see that Say has an approach similar to Gerard Debreu. It is remarkable to see how, in order to reach some kind of analytical results, economists forget about the restrictions in the use of money values and also that we are in a disequilibrium economy. If anybody claims that we live in an eternal equilibrium – prove it! Unfortunately, it is impossible to prove because we then leave physics and enter metaphysics, and then we have a similar discussion as we had with respect to the Kantian concept of "Das Ding an Sich."

Our critique of the neoclassical theory is exactly the omission of structural complexities, and that is not remedied by some general macroscopic modelling dealing with monetary values. In the 1970s the so-called Keynesian theory was criticized for lacking a microscopic underpinning, and that critique was correct since the current economic theorizing was unable to understand the structural changes which took place and was deep-going. However, the fundamental mistake was the belief that this was remedied by inserting the neoclassical theory to cover both the microscopic and the macroscopic levels. The mistake was even more amazing, not to say absurd, since the so-called Keynesian modelling at that time was built on the IS-LM modelling invented by Hicks and others to be some compromise between the neoclassical theory and Keynes' critique, which was at least to some extent accepted.

Consequently, any kind of disequilibrium theorizing must accept that there are no such things as general equilibrium or a universal concept containing all agents, all markets and all aggregate levels. There are of course partial equilibria of more or less dissipative character.

Since we deal with physical, social, demographic structures, these have to be particularly addressed with respect to some general accepted ethical goals, and then we use the Aristotelian approach to ethics as a means to achieve the highest good.

But such an analysis is not possible to perform in economics as a narrowly defined academic subject taught as in standard American textbooks; rather, economics has to be seen as a part of social and political sciences within a changing physical world.

Such a change of attitudes will subsequently have an effect on traditional economic concepts such as efficiency, productivity and growth, and money values have to be considered as the friars of Salamanca emphasize; they are mirroring the relative supply-demand conditions locally and temporally. Profits and investments measured in money have to be valued according to their structural consequences and ethical relevance.

The expression *ethical relevance* means that we do not advocate some kind of communist kind of distribution or allocation of resources; the market principle is indeed valuable as an instrument of valuation. Profit and salary are important incitements, but they are not the only ones. Investment does and must contain risk-taking and even "animal spirit" to conquer uncertainty and the hard process of entering a market. But the market principle, contrary to the promises of the neoclassical theory, is not intrinsically stabilizing but highly unstable since economic power can be used for monopolizing, and in that way it undermines the whole market process. This is also emphasized by the neoclassical theory, it is said, but that is a truth with some modification since the problem will not even appear within the neoclassical axiomatic structure. This means that the "market principle" needs a corrective outside the market itself, and that is what we call the public sector. The economic role, so to speak, of the public sector is on one hand to correct anomalies of the market and also to protect important physical, social and cultural structures. The discussion of whether the public sector shall be marketlike is a complete misunderstanding of the market principle. The public sector can use the market principle as a means to obtain some goals, increasing competition for example, but that is not a general principle; it can also use monopolization as a means. The workings of the market and the public sectors are completely different and must therefore not be juxtaposed. The latter statement implies that efficiency of the public and private sectors must be based on different criteria. The market is not a place of analysis; it is a place for immediate action. The long-run needs crave investigation, analysis, trial and error processes, failure and success. In this evolution the market principle is an important part, yet just a part. Economists have to get over their obsession with economics as the most sophisticated social science due to its formalization since that formalization is on the whole built on a shaky axiomatic structure which lags behind modern mathematical logic and sticks to the mathematics of Newton and Descartes, which by itself is impressive but not sufficient for our scientific needs.

The problem however is that the population who forms the market also forms the public sector and has to reach some kind of agreement of how the public sector should be created. We discussed in Chapter 1 a first step from a kind of Leviathan without a ruler to an ordered society in an example from the Icelandic Sagas. In this example, we saw that the change of rules also changes the valuation of abilities. Thus, the protection of farmers reduced the value of fighting skills (at least, according to the law), while the laws by Eirik Jarl protected property obtained and farming skills. Thus the introduction of a public law is seldom, if ever, neutral towards all individuals. In Chapter 5 we are going to discuss government and governance more in detail, particularly vis-à-vis democracy, but here the principal links between the collective, public decisions and the market and its concepts of growth, efficiency and so on will be discussed.

In the aftermath of Arrow's Impossibility Theorem, there have been many different kinds of discussion of global efficiency in a market system within a socio-political system. These discussions are generally erroneous with respect to Arrow's theorem, but nevertheless the issues should be addressed. We have Hobbes' start of contract theories but we also have the more organic Aristotelian and Humean approaches to the socio-political level based on the fact that humans by nature are social creatures. The weakness of the contract theory is obvious, since we then presume some kind of "King by the Providence of God". That is historically seen a fact that such principles have existed and actually more or less exist currently, but it is one alternative way of looking at government. We also have the principles of the French revolution; Liberté, Egalité, Fraternité, which is quite a different way of looking at the public/collective government. We have the principles spelled out in the Constitution of the United States, which has some similarities with the French principles, but there are also differences. Irrespective of which form of government we choose or are forced into, the simple fact is that a collective government in control of an area with its population has the means of coercion, which forces the population to subordinate to principles of governance. We consequently may discuss the relation between the public goals, means and principles of governance with respect to concepts like growth and efficiency, both intrinsically as well as globally. We should also discuss it vis-à-vis the market principle with respect to asymmetries and contradictions, but there is little point in discussing the public sector by taking the market principle as a norm since that principle adapts to virtually any kind of public government. Such discussions are generally based on a belief that the market system is described by the neoclassical axiomatic structure and consequently become a bit esoteric.

The interpretations of Arrow's paradox and the sloppy treatment of additive aggregation have compromised economic research in several ways. But let us start to repeat what Arrow's paradox actually tells us: *If we in the neoclassical type of market allow individuals to behave contradictory to the neoclassical axiomatic structure, a neoclassical general equilibrium cannot occur. Thus, all the axioms of the neoclassical axiomatic structure are necessary to imply a neoclassical general equilibrium.*

This result is normal for logical paradoxes. If we take Russell's paradox for example, the paradox has its roots in the fact that items, which can be represented as logical variables, can be of two kinds: atomistic and complex. Cantor's unaccountability paradox occurs because numbers can be of two kinds; on one hand they can be used for annotations/signs of positions in a space, and on the other they can be used for accounting.

Seen in this way, Arrow's paradox is quite natural and a kind of correlate to the neoclassical axiomatic structure and the proof of the existence of general equilibrium.

The problem is that there is confusion about what general equilibrium really means. Here we have pointed out that Gerard Debreu from the very beginning was aware that commodities and individuals exist in space-time, and that is not a Euclidian space.

We are reminded of our discussions in Chapter 2 on space-time. Furthermore, in his discussion on space-time topology, Roy Douglas concludes that even from a point of view where we disregard the processes of the conscious human mind, it is hard to see that the Universe displays any global continuity.

It is also interesting to see, relative to our exposé of some philosophers, we could criticize Kant's discussion on "Das Ding an Sich" on virtually the same ground as we criticize the neoclassical theory. Kant's analysis is based on Descartes' and Newton's mathematics of the 17th century. An analysis with the help of the mathematical tools of the 20th century makes the problems more realistic and accepts a world full of linguistic and perhaps also real paradoxes.

With respect to Arrow's paradox, Howard DeLong (1991) claims that he refuted Arrow's paradox. However, we agree that DeLong refuted the interpretations of Arrow's theorem, or most of them in any case, but as we see here we cannot refute Arrow's Impossibility Theorem given the neoclassical axiomatic structure; on the contrary, we may claim that most of *the interpretations of the theorem are irrelevant.*

Consequently, the neoclassical theory is rather deceitful in the sense that although it might have some relevance at the microscopic level, it has no relevance whatsoever at the macroscopic level since it is based on mathematically inadequate axioms in relation to empirical experience.

On the other hand, such anomalies are very suitable for those who interpret a theory for ideological purposes. When looking at the neoclassical theory, we can specifically mention the so-called rational expectation approach, an approach which may work with respect to well-defined market segments but which is inadequate at the macroscopic level.[8] Another catastrophic inadequacy occurred when economic scientists were led to define a concept like *natural unemployment*, where just the concept per se is antisocial. Suffice to say, the root of that concept comes directly from the assumption that the economy would attain general equilibrium if people were not as stubborn as they are, but looking at the economic world as a subset of the social, cultural and the political world there might exist other explanations.

The fundamental role of Arrow's paradox is that it proves the irrelevance of the neoclassical theory applied to the macroscopic level. This is the only conclusion we can draw from Arrow's Impossibility Theorem. Any further reference to the real world is inadequate both from an empirical and a theoretical point of view.

Efficiency, growth and welfare

Underlying Arrow's Impossibility Theorem is the thought of a global efficiency concept, Pareto optimality, which appears in the neoclassical general equilibrium. It tells us that we have achieved full distributive efficiency of a market economy, given a distribution of initial endowments. Further exchange of marketable goods is impossible without worsening the welfare for at least one agent. As a correlate, we have that any action of barter is Pareto-sanctioned if one person gains without anybody else's welfare being worsened.

As such, this efficiency concept is formidable in its simplicity and its universality. According to the neoclassical axiomatic structure, Pareto optimality is always achieved in general equilibrium and therefore we are accustomed to regard it as an economic concept, but that is too restrictive. Pareto optimality is obviously a social concept which also in theory could be applied to a disequilibrium analysis, but then in wider social frames; practically difficult – indeed yes, but there is no a priori reason why it should not be possible to have some kind of social application of the Pareto concept. Unfortunately, if we see it as a general efficiency measure, a thought like that breaks down due to our structural approach. The Pareto criterion is when interpreted generally a subjective concept; in a partial sense, we can of course use it for specified dimensions such as incomes, purchasing power, health status according to specified aspects, education and so on. Generally speaking, aspects which are not defined in money values are better than those which are. Obviously, such aspects as distribution power in a society have value in discussing general welfare policy and allocation matters, but such matters as distribution of access to health care, education, nutrition and similar give a picture of the difference between different classes and groups to develop their abilities. Most countries today make such enquiries and have done so for decades. However, the Pareto criterion still hovers in discussions of public policy with bearing on general efficiency, which lacks any theoretical meaning.

So, we live in a world where all equilibria are local and temporal and consequently more or less dissipative. Technically speaking, from a mathematical point of view, we can think of the concept of equilibrium where we have varying inertia of the parameter structure due to socio-politico-economic inertia, thus eventual stabilizing forces are to be found within the entire social context. From a scientific point of view, economists have to understand perturbing socio-economic factors, at least those which are more or less generic to an economy. If we look at the latest decades, we find for example the induced austerity policy which has been accepted as a tool to gain a balanced economy. At the same time, it has created massive unemployment, particularly among young people, and a huge redistribution of incomes and wealth to the benefit of the richest segments of the population. How this could have proceeded in a democracy without many experts protesting and warning of the risk of social upheavals in different forms is indeed a mystery. The myth of the independent world of economy based on rules separated from the social life has perhaps been too strong for the minds of economists and other social scientists. Anyway, it should be clear that the market economy as a system of thoughts or ideology based on the medieval barter economy has no stabilizing role in a society, but on the other hand the market system is an efficient way to bring prosperity through a maximum diffusion of the means of exchange, money.

It is interesting to read Hume's praise of the money economy because he focuses on the very diffusion process and warns against reducing the medium of exchange thus creating annoyance for the population. When looking at the austerity and the sometimes perverted focus of inflation reduction, we are certainly bound to conclude that scientists advocating such policy have ideological reasons to favour certain groups at the expense of others, which we will come back to in Chapter 6.

We know from history that social instability and eruptions harm economic affairs and investments more than anything speaking for the entire society. However, it is clear that some people may gain from the destruction of social stability; how and to what extent varies with the context.

Thus we can rule out any global *economic* efficiency concept. What we have done by rejecting the Axiom of Reflexivity and thus additive aggregation is separate consumer efficiency from producer efficiency and furthermore separate microscopic efficiency from macroscopic efficiency.

Production efficiency

In order to proceed, we just remember the general definition of efficiency and productivity. *Efficiency* is, as most people have learnt, based on the degree of goal fulfilment given resources devoted to the goal in question, while *productivity* is based on a particular production output or income per physical resource unit or cost unit during a time segment.

Generally, productivity is used as a kind of measure of efficiency both on the microscopic and the macroscopic level. This is quite correct with respect to the neoclassical theory but is unfortunately used even for non-equilibrium analysis, although goals are not defined with respect to different sectors. Thus, defining efficiency and productivity as we did above does not imply any logical a priori link between the two concepts.

Let us look at a standard case. In industrial activities we have, broadly speaking, a goal to maximize the financial surplus given the costs of the activity. The financial surplus will cover pure profit for the entrepreneurs/owners, depreciation of capital and hopefully further reinvestments and new investments. This must hold irrespective of the form of ownership; obviously we can skip the profit for the entrepreneurs/owners and transfer it to new investments, but this is more a contextual question than a general one. Thus we get some standard expressions for different kinds of productivity measures per chosen time unit:

1   $Pr_{TC} = \dfrac{TR - TC}{TC}$ Total Cost productivity

                      TR – Total Revenue; TC – Total Cost

2   $Pr_{L} = \dfrac{TR - TC}{L}$ Productivity per labour unit

3   $Pr_{LC} = \dfrac{TR - TC}{w \cdot L}$ Productivity per labour cost

With respect to our industrial activity, all three productivity measures reflect the efficiency concept reasonably well, though the goals of the activity are implicit in the numerator.

However, the analytical meaningfulness of the measures is more doubtful.

As we see, the measures all concentrate on relative prices, basically three types of prices – product prices, input prices and wages – and the classical debate of whether wages or commodity prices are most flexible is the only sensible discussion to intonate in order to discuss profitability. The measures above represent gross profit to total costs, gross profit to labour quantity and gross profit to gross wage costs, but there are two other measures: gross profit to invested capital and gross profit share. The latter is interesting since it also might be related to liquidity position. Traditionally in Sweden, for example, the discussion between trade unions and employers' organizations has focussed on the factor of income distribution, both gross and net, given the risk/uncertainty environment for the industry. In Ekstedt (2015:235–253) these matters are discussed more extensively, but let us here say that all those measures based on prices implicitly assuming some kind of *ceteris paribus* with respect to real structural changes are indeed doubtful from two reasons. First of all, they have generally regarded capital as the fixed factor in the short run and labour as the variable (although this is changing now); the second problem has been that researchers have most often used aggregate data which tend to cover structural shifts, both intrinsically of sectors as well as between sectors. One structural feature of the last three or four decades has been the outspoken labour hoarding. It takes place both in heavy capital-intensive production as well as in labour-intensive service production, and it is not an aggregate parallel development for all sectors but varies from sector to sector. A very clear sign of increased labour hoarding is increased pro-cyclical variations in productivity, but, for example, Basu and Kimbal (1997) observed for the Chilean industry that such variations tended to decrease when the level of aggregation increased, particularly among export sector industries where trade cycle variations of different sectors were different. Such kinds of structural evolvements imply that labour forces become a semi-fixed factor, mostly due to an increasingly heterogeneous working force and the increased specialization of jobs.

The obvious effects are that factor income distribution becomes more variable, thus inducing a higher risk of liquidity stress. From Ekstedt (2015) we take Figure 3.1, which shows an ultimate effect of this structural development.

The curves $(Q/L)_1^*$ and $(Q/L)_2^*$ show the physical labour productivity at fully flexible labour in the short run while $Q_1(L)$, $Q_2(L)$ and $Q_3(L)$ are attached to the short-run fixed labour force, L_0^1, L_0^2 and L_0^3 respectively. Consequently the long-run increased labour productivity takes place at the price of higher short-run variations of the productivity and consequently also the profit share, thus inducing higher risks for liquidity stress. Let us assume that L^* and L_2^* represent the optimal utilization rate of capital. We can then see that due to higher variability and profit share, the companies tend to choose a lower investment rate;

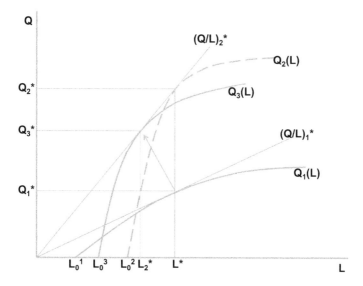

Figure 3.1 Development of structural unemployment

thus, in L^* for example, they do not invest to an optimal investment volume of Q_2^* but go for Q_3^*. The distance between L^* and L_2^* will then be an increase in structural unemployment.

If we think of this as a general feature for an economy, we understand the concept of structural unemployment and also permanent unemployment. Those who talked of "natural unemployment" realized at the end of the 1980s and the beginning of the 1990s that "natural laws" were due to regular changes which could not be explained by price information. We see from Figure 3.1 that the problem of physical structures does not necessarily imply that the wages need to change per remaining worker. Furthermore, relative prices do not need to be changed in order to have these effects.

Table 3.1 partly underscores the structural aspects with respect to reasons why profitable small industries in Sweden hesitate to expand the size of the company. We can see that the two most important factors are competition and lack of suitable labour, and these aspects are of course related to each other.

In Ekstedt and Westberg (1991: chapter 2) and Ekstedt (2012:144–151) there are more extensive discussions of these problems.

From this example, we can see how devastating the neoclassical thinking is in its avoidance of dealing with structural matters, and this avoidance is not a matter of ignorance of economists per se but the very fundamental feature of the neoclassical theory. Unfortunately the so-called Keynesians have kept the most fallacious feature of all, namely the simple additive aggregation of commodities and agents in money terms.

Table 3.1 Reasons for not expanding the company

	Number of employees	
	10–49	*50–249*
Competition	32.0	41.9
Insufficient demand	9.7	13.3
Profitability of the company	13.9	13.4
Access to the credit market	14.2	12.1
Access to external share capital	10.0	5.9
Lack of suitable labour	33.0	26.8
Access to relevant infrastructure	5.8	6.6
Insufficient capacity of fixed capital	13.1	12.4
Owners' lack of time	26.4	–
Laws and bureaucracy	23.7	14.5

How can we discuss important moral features like permanent unemployment if we keep the methodological features of the neoclassical theory, omitting all structural relations of an economy?

Let me give one more example of these theoretical anomalies in mixing neo-classical and Keynesian thinking and by all mean Marxian thinking, since none of them observe these problems in general.

At the end of the 1980s, the Swedish car manufacturer Volvo had experienced international success. They wanted an analysis of different kinds of strategic problems, so two master's students made an enquiry with me as their supervisor. Among other things, they found some very interesting features of the development with respect to internal risk features.

We can discuss the finding in relation to the simple Table 3.2 (Ekstedt 2013:200). We have limited the table to just two countries to emphasize the principles involved.

First, we observe that Volvo has had enormous success in the world market and in the US. But a closer look at the figures reveals a considerable increase in market risk. In 1963, Volvo mainly produced for the internal Swedish market. That implied that factors affecting demand as inflation, increase in wages and political measures affected both sides, so to speak, both the cost side and the income side, to almost equal extent. But if we look at the situation in 1963, we see that the production share of US demand is bigger than Swedish demand, while at the same time the market share in the US market is tiny and probably easy to damage while the market share in Sweden is rather comfortable. Thus Volvo faces a situation where the exogenous factors, in relation to Sweden, have become more important compared to the internal factors. This means that while Volvo's wishes with respect to governmental policy were practically in line with their customers on the Swedish market, this was not the case in 1987. Thus the growth of Volvo had changed the

Table 3.2 The development of Volvo

	Sweden %		USA %	
	1963	*1987*	*1963*	*1987*
Share of production	85	17	< 5	25
Market share	35	25	≈ 0	1.8

risk structure of the company, and when we remember the fact that Volvo's development was in no way unique or extreme for Swedish export development, we can draw the conclusion that the opinion of the major Swedish industry with respect to what was seen as an appropriate macroeconomic policy had changed. These changes had nothing to do with ideology or theoretical considerations but were due to structural changes of the demand structure and were implicit in the growth of the producing companies on the export market.

But if we put together these two effects, illustrated in Figure 3.1 and Tables 3.1 and 3.2, we may come to an interesting question. Sweden is an extremely foreign trade–dependent country, and competitiveness in the international market is a necessity. However, the export sector does not increase its demand for labour; the maximum was reached in the beginning of 1970s and has since then had a diminishing trend.

Thus the hopes for labour demand are the service sector, broadly speaking, and the public sector. But the service sector has got its own kind of heterogeneity of labour and thus has a problem with different types of labour hoarding, since the labour share is relatively than bigger the service share. The building sector is more vulnerable to financial conditions and to variations in household expectations than the export sector. The public sector is a bit different but is bound to balance restrictions due to the huge export sector. Thus the question is: Where does the necessary labour demand to absorb permanent unemployment come from? We should need new expanding production sectors, but the aggregate demand of Sweden seems too small and the competition in the international market is hard, and a general expansion there is almost impossible, other than in exceptional cases.

Thus Sweden has come to the paradoxical situation where the unemployment rises because the labour supply is too small with respect to the narrow sector distribution of the Swedish aggregate production. For increasing the labour demand, we need a broader spectrum of production sectors, but that is risky due to a small population. We can solve it in the long run with immigration, but in the short run that causes social unease for the moment because of the idea that the immigrants steal Swedish jobs, and populist parties can see their chance.

The interesting ethics in these discussions of structural changes is within economic science and economic policy with respect to what kind of methodological approaches are chosen. Given a neoclassical approach, the questions raised above will not even appear.

Given a Keynesian approach, to a large extent it depends on whether we use additive aggregation with respect to money values and analyze broad aggregates. We see that it is absolutely necessary for macroeconomic studies to have a microeconomic underpinning, not in the sense of incorporating the neoclassical thinking but of analyzing structural peculiarities and developments.

Disregarding economic, social, political and cultural structures in understanding economic development and problems has long been a significant feature of economic theorizing. Now, in the shadow of social unease and threats to global warming, we have come to the conclusion that going on in this ignorance is unethical.

Necessity and choice possibility[9]

When we enter a discussion of epistemic cycles, we have to immediately realize that generalizing the concept into some common epistemic cycle for a group or for a society will enable us to return to some axiomatic structure for that group, given structural assumptions and particular behavioural idiosyncrasies. This is for better and worse. It is good in the sense that sensitive mathematical analysis of particular social groups and their dynamic interaction may render deeper insights into the composition of the society. However, standard aggregate assumptions out of empirical consciousness, next to prejudices, will add nothing to science. This means that it is necessary for economists to utilize knowledge from all social, medical and physical sciences. The real trouble with the whole approach of epistemic cycles is the success/failure to close the cycle. As we see, the analysis leading to an action is on the whole controlled by the agent. After the action, however, the agent must wait for the reactions from other individuals, organizations and so on which decide the final outcome of failure/success. However, that is completely outside the control of the agent. What we do in the neoclassical structure is that the so-called axiom of choice defines an equivalent relation between the outer space of the choice alternatives and the inner space of preferences which is numerically equivalent, and that washes out the problems of the uncertainty of reactions, so to speak. Furthermore, all choice alternatives as well as agents are void of any structural relationships.

In Ekstedt and Fusari (2010) and Ekstedt (2013), we have claimed that although rationality according to the neoclassical *axioms of choice* is extremely doubtful, we will have the interesting result that by imbedding the neoclassical axioms within the concept of epistemic cycles, we may to a large extent claim that all agents are rational in the axiomatic sense, although it is now the last step before action when all the contextual considerations are done and we just stand in front of the very choice space which is now considerably less than before the contextual considerations. The fact is that we now can apply Debreu's indications in chapter 2 of *Theory of Value*, so we can define an agent indicated above as

$_t^s(\precsim_i, e_i)$, but then we must remember that before that, we have the complexity illustrated by the epistemic cycle.

Following Aristotle, our understanding of the exterior world is completely based on observation, direct or indirect. Implicit in the concept of observation are of course instruments and experimental designs. We are reminded of our discussions earlier on Hume's concept of causality and his scepticism, the emptiness of empirical understanding intrinsic to mathematics or logic and the problem of projections.

We will keep away from the internal mind of the individual and just stick to some trivial observable patterns. Humans seem to have several forms of memory and combinatorial algorithms; modern neurology and brain research seems to maintain that the human brain is physiologically affected by external events and experiences. However, to these general outfits we should remember the interesting discussion Arthur Koestler has in his book on *The Act of Creation* discussed in Chapter 1. Koestler's views are somewhat parallel to Hume's in an intricate way.

So, what happens after agent's action? We will bring the *ex ante/ex post* analysis of the old Stockholm School from the 1930s to the 1960s. We will simply have to ask if the epistemic cycle will or will not be closed.

There are mainly two aspects to keep in mind. First we have Hume's analysis of causality in its full complexity, which implies that there is always a possibility for the epistemic cycle to be closed irrespective of the relevance of the preceding analysis. Due to inertia, for example, an explanation based on the goodwill of *gnomes* may have equally good explanatory power as the most intricate empirical-logical investigation in a particular case. The important thing, however, is that when the epistemic cycle is closed, this is most often interpreted as a proof that the analysis, of whatever character, was *true*.

The second aspect concerns the situation when we replace the atomic neoclassical theory with a structural approach which theoretically has some surprising effects. Let us first see what a structural approach really means.

Let us look at a standard Western European family with teenagers living at home. Such a family is involved in many structures. If both the parents work, they have then different obligations, expectations and judgements vis-à-vis their short- and long-term views of their job development. Assume they have a house, which represents financial obligations, time consumption, social interactions and through that eventual social obligations. They have children, which means they are drawn into their education, leisure time, planning, driving to and fro, short-run and long-run expectations and fear, and only God knows the complexity; add to that parents, friends, hobbies and so on. All this creates separate structures of purposes, choices and decisions, some interdependent, some seemingly independent of one another, *but all are interacting*. For such a family, exogenously forced changes with respect to jobs, housing or infrastructure for example may cause major structural shifts in their social, cultural or psycho-social patterns.

That means that if the epistemic cycle fails, the agent obviously has to reconsider the left side; the purposes, the contextual apprehension, the perceived means and restrictions. Since we now face a complex structural composition of substructures, we end up in the result that changes in some substructures may have discontinuous effects on other substructures as well as the total individual situation. This is very important to keep in mind when we analyze the relations between the microscopic and the macroscopic level and when we allow for aggregate measures which have no direct logical links to any microscopic structure but affect all microscopic structures to a higher and lower degree and are asymmetric.

We leave the explanation of the epistemic cycle concept, which obviously can be applied on aggregate bodies which are decision makers. But when we analyze macroscopic and microscopic levels, these kinds of considerations are at the bottom of our thoughts. It also implies, which I leave to the reader to formulate a proof of, that we might have local reversible changes at the microscopic level but never at the macroscopic.

The heading for this section is *Necessity and Choice Possibility*. When we deal with the neoclassical general equilibrium theory, the commodity space is defined over the positive orthant in the n-dimensional Euclidian space. In the general case, we have no distinction between necessity and choice possibility, other than perhaps some difference in the form of the preference function.

There is, however, an example which mostly is regarded as a degeneracy (Arrow and Hahn 1971:405) which leads to non-convexities. It can technically be dealt with in order to attain *a neighbourhood* sufficiently close, of a sort of general equilibrium, but as Arrow and Hahn admit, the fundamental problem is hardly solved.

Lexicographic preferences can be thought of from many perspectives. They imply that we rule out any form of substitutability between certain alternatives, thus there exist no price relation at which alternative α will be substituted for β. I suppose there are some conservative music lovers who at no price difference will choose heavy metal music instead of string quintets by Mozart.

Such examples are frequent with respect to individual choice, but we also stand in front of a much deeper philosophical problem.

In Ekstedt (2013:162–163) we presented the basic problem, but here we just shortly present the technical problem in order to discuss the more intricate structural details.

In Figure 3.2 we have three indifferent curves, which as usual denote the substitutability conditions between the commodities $\mathbf{X}$ and $\mathbf{Y}$. However to the left of the vertical line at $\mathbf{X}_0$ the curves are dotted, indicating that there are no substitution possibilities irrespective of price relations. That means that the consumer actually must have the quantity $\mathbf{X}_0$ of the commodity $\mathbf{X}$ before any consumption of commodity $\mathbf{Y}$ is possible.

Let us first notice that the notion of *lexicographic preferences* and their character implicitly introduces structural compositions among the commodities with respect to a single agent as well as to the society. In fact, our whole approach to the markets, commodities and production/consumption is based on a structural

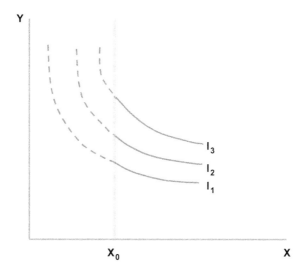

Figure 3.2 Lexicographic preferences

approach. This follows directly from our claim that commodities and agents are not atomistic but complex variables, which means a limitation with respect to substitutability. Furthermore, the dimensionality problem which is annoying in the case of atomistic variables is devastating with respect to structures, and the problem of *zero* also hits us with maximum force, as well as the problem of *negative facts*, which we discussed in Chapter 2.

Let us return to the epistemic cycles and a relatively typical Western European family and its formidable organizational problems. Let us say that the central bank decides to raise interest rates significantly or take other costly measures to curb borrowing. Our family realizes that they are not able to pay interest and mortgages. They have to move to a small two-bedroom apartment at the other end of the city. What does that mean to the family with respect to other dimensions of life, to other epistemic cycles? A macroscopic survey may well display a nice continuous picture through averaging individual effects, but bringing in other local and temporal conditions raises doubts of the relevance of such pictures; the average picture presupposes basically additive aggregation, while in real life the variance and the existence of extreme cases can be as worrying as rather common cases from a social and political point of view.

The two basic propositions in the prologue, which are seemingly at variance with each other, will thus have some interesting ethical consequences. Proposition 1 concerns barter, which means that it deals with matters of the real world and the ranking of their intrinsic representation of the individual, where we claim that since the matters of reality are complexes, their intrinsic representations of the individuals are different. But the difference in representation does not affect the supply and demand conditions per se since the real matters, be they goods or services, have to be bought irrespective of the different intrinsic individual representations. Subsequently from a structural point of view, there is no unique price vector with respect to individual representations, and consequently the market process which is based on money values is not logically attached to the barter process per se.

Thus we come to Proposition 2, which claims that the market process based on money values may well lead to temporary equilibrium, but that has logically nothing to do with barter in utility/welfare terms; it is based on liquidity matters. Consequently, the money values are more attached to the structural interpretations of those who are well equipped with the medium of exchange. Thus, the prices of the market process are asymmetric with respect to the structural needs of the agents, and this is basic to the emergence of exploitation and the modern form of slavery. Thus the so-called liberal economy has per se no particularly ethical load, but it must be exogenously controlled if collective ethical goals are to be achieved.

This is basically the reason why the macroscopic and microscopic levels cannot coincide to a grand general optimum for all levels of aggregation. An economic analysis based on money values in a disequilibrium economy has on the macroscopic level no a priori logical links to the microscopic levels since goal formulations are necessarily different. An almost logical correlate to that claim is that no exogenous action by an aggregate body affecting underlying microscopic levels is symmetric with respect to the agents. As we claimed above, the price system per se is structurally asymmetric, and that implies for example that so-called market conform means are also structurally asymmetric. That does not mean that the latter are unsuitable; perhaps on the contrary, if the deciding bodies are aware of the asymmetries.

In Chapter 1 we started, as one should, with Aristotle and accepted his claim that ethics was a tool to rationally achieve the highest good in a society. However, Aristotle accepts that individuals are at variance with respect to perception, apprehension and comprehension of the physical and the social reality. The State is therefore seen as a kind of mediator between individuals by controlling and completing individual decisions, but Aristotle also claims that there are better and worse States dependent on the collective frameworks of the state. Thus, contrary to the Kantian view that there exists some a priori true reality accessible through logic and mathematics, humans have to fight everywhere and every time to achieve the good society, whatever that can be.

An economic interpretation

When we pass over to an analysis of complex social variables, these are almost always linked to each other through particular structural compositions. That implies that a particular item may have different roles in different structures.

When entering a structural analysis, the mathematical concepts of empty space and negative space have to be reconsidered, since on one hand the lack of one dimension for example enforces a different structure compared with the case that the dimension exists. Furthermore, the negativity of an item has a structural meaning in the sense that it counteracts the existence of certain structures.

From an economic point of view, this also explains the difference between Proposition 1 and Proposition 2. Proposition 1 deals with personal utilities in the form of physically defined commodities, be they goods or services in a broad sense. Proposition 2, however, deals with money values. It is most probable that all individuals do not demand only those commodities which are positively appreciated by all fellow citizens; thus we have contradictions. From a social point of view, this may lead to unease, not to say chaos. According to Proposition 1 such a contingency is possible and analytically definable, while it is not according to Proposition 2. Consequently, only looking at aggregates of money values implies that many structural anomalies are hidden.

Vespasianus' expression *"pecunia non olet"* comes to mind, as well as Thorstein Veblen's analysis in *The Theory of the Leisure Class*.

Sometimes one hears a saying that those matters which can be subject to mathematical analysis are so-called hard facts and consequently reliable, while other matters which are more difficult to express mathematically and require proper assumptions and limitations are seen as soft facts and consequently unreliable and emotional.

Our analysis shows that such a division in analytical modes shows more of a lack of mathematical and logical understanding.

Some comments of ethical character

According to the neoclassical general equilibrium theory based on Arrow/Debreu's axiomatic structure, we may have a kind of dual interpretation of ethics. The axiomatic structure works in principle as a flea market where people walk around supplying the junk they have brought from their wardrobes and look for what others have brought. People engage in bidding, and this goes on until no one can improve his or her utility. So, in a way, all people have to agree on a common solution; that is the reason why the individual and social optimum coincide. We could describe such a process as chaotic and furthermore that anyone and everyone has an individual veto with respect to the global solution. In this case, it is hard to see an ethical dimension intrinsic to the very exchange process.

However, we can reformulate the exchange process in emphasizing the parallelism between the general equilibrium and the Nash equilibrium.[10] Nash equilibrium implies a situation where all individuals optimize their respective utility functions, given all others' utility functions. In such a case, we may link it to Kant's imperative: act always so that your action could be seen as a general law. Thus the behaviour postulated by the axiom is the common law.

The problem of course is that this is purely static since the actions are performed within a closed space, which brings us to the problem of dimensionality that we mentioned earlier. As we then noted, a change in dimensionality leads also to revaluation of relations in the commodity basket. An additional problem is that commodities are to be seen as complexes, which underscores the problem with changing dimensionality of the commodity space. When we add social and cultural differences, both general equilibrium and Kant's imperative run into problems. Thus the barter process is released from all social and cultural links by the axioms and ethics is once and for all given a priori, which could be interpreted as being in line with Kant's idealism. This also accounts for the production process if we link a Neumann-Gale model to Arrow/Debreu.[11]

We must, however, be aware of the fact that economic factors are immensely important for the rise of social, cultural and ethical conflicts due to differences in the distribution of purchasing power as well as the demand and supply structures, which imply competing modes of resource utilization and allocation. These factors are simply not there in the axiomatic structure. Thus the link we may make to Kant's ethical imperative is purely of formal interest, and besides that, of no relevance. Although we may be critical of Kant's imperative, it indeed has more depth and complexity than just some formal similarities.

The neoclassical general equilibrium analysis, when we interpret it (as Debreu) as a temporal and local picture of the actually fulfilled exchange actions, is of course always correct in some sense. The problem, however, is that there is no connection between any two temporally and locally defined equilibria (if such can be detected). So, in this case, we have to plunge into a disequilibrium analysis for which the axiomatic structure does not hold and cannot even be thought of as some kind of abstract theoretical norm.

The second interpretation is an eternal equilibrium with no changes in the dimensionality of the commodity space, and we have already discussed its relevance both for the very content of the axiom as well as for the implications in reality.

People living in an eternal general equilibrium have less power to affect their lives than we have to affect a slot machine to give us a jackpot. Furthermore, the axioms grant their behaviour to be appropriate with respect to the market process in which all conflicts are eliminated. Luigi Amoroso, in his famous overview of the works of Vilfredo Pareto, calls attention to the *antisocial* features of Pareto's theory.[12]

> In general the meaning of obstacles is that economic goods are limited; thus until violence and fraud, theft and donation are excluded, a thing cannot be had except by giving in exchange for it one of equal value pro tempore; that every product is the result of a certain combination of the factors of production in harmony with the laws of techniques, as they are known pro tempore; that legal order and the economic organization fetter individual actions; and so on. . . . It is at this point that the crux of Pareto's system becomes apparent. The internal forces of the economic system are not

susceptible of a theoretical representation as simple, elegant, and universal as is the case for the applied forces. They are not only, as for the material macrocosmic systems, forces of conservation, by which – to express it elegantly – the dead city dominates through inertia the living city; they are also directed forces or forces of impulsion, through which the living city forms or attempts to form the city of the future. The internal forces, therefore, are History, they are even Ethics and Politics, something powerful, but vague and indistinct, which is not susceptible of mathematical representation; an expression of the freedom of the will, which does not allow itself to be enclosed in the meshes of a mechanical representation, and, because it is mechanical, determinist.

A problem seldom discussed in economics is the *anonymity*. Adam Smith's example with the butcher is intuitively appealing, and we seldom realize its significance. In fact, the axiomatic structure institutionalizes that we live in a homogenous society from cultural and socio-economic perspectives. The modern market economy is global, which means that commodities as well as different production modes are judged by different cultural idiosyncrasies, which obviously add to the complexity of the commodities.

The analytical clarity of the neoclassical theory is therefore an illusion. It is "bought" by sacrificing essential factors and features of the reality.[13] The biggest "mistake" is that all commodities and utilities derived from them are defined in the positive orthant, which means that a society is by definition free from conflicts intrinsic to the character and differences in use of the commodities. We showed earlier that this feature depends on the fact that the commodities are assumed to be demanded as the very physical items defined in atomic terms. We have earlier noted several other peculiarities which are not prevalent in the reality, but then follow from squeezing in the reality into a too-simple axiomatic structure, which brings clarity and elegance to the analysis but which makes the economic analysis completely unfit for analyzing the real world economics.

"In the long run we are all dead"

Keynes' famous expression is indeed deceitful. It is like the answers of the Oracle at Delphi, which were always true since they could be interpreted differently in different contexts. Such is the case with the expression by Keynes; however, reading for example *The Economic Consequences of the Peace* or the discussions on his pamphlet "The Economic Consequences of Mr. Churchill" and the return to the gold standard rules out all trivial interpretations.

Keynes was deeply aware of the social and political world, and although he was a wealthy patrician he was both aware of and worried about social misery. He also saw quite well economics as a sub-science within the other social sciences, particularly sociology, and understood clearly that social unease was devastating for investment and growth; for him, unemployment was a key factor in social unease. His final chapter of *The Economic Consequences of the Peace* is remarkable in its clarity with respect to socio-economic analysis.

Thus we cannot interpret his saying that economic planning and policy only concerns the current living people.

To understand Keynes, we have to realize that he was not a neoclassical economist. As a matter of fact, there is not even the slightest possibility of finding any kind of compromise between Keynes' philosophical approach and that underlying the neoclassical theory. It is a question of *contradiction in terms*.

The expression "In the long run we are all dead" has to do with Keynes' understanding of social, cultural and economic structures. A family hit by long periods of unemployment faces often a successive social and cultural depreciation which affects those living now and eventually those to come, and the offspring will be raised under degenerating social and cultural structures which has severe effects for the future.

This attitude can be contrasted to Hume's joy of the money economy bringing a multitude of cultural impulses. Keynes sees the same as Hume, but he also sees the degenerate side of it.

The point is that we have to break the curse of social heritage, and dreaming of long-term plans solving problems in fifty years or so is completely meaningless.[14] Long-run deals with future living conditions are to dream about, but to effect them, you have to act now. The climate problems which the earth faces are certainly a long-run problem already becoming a rather short-run one in some dimensions; this is an example which called for action many years ago.

But here comes the problem of Hume that the intellect is the humble servant of passion. Both Aristotle and Hume, however, envisage the possibility that intellect may foster our passions, and the myth we had in the introduction also envisages such a possibility. We will later discuss this further in relation to a paper by Immanuel Kant in 1784 about how humans must leave self-inflicted immaturity.

The neoclassical theory in its claim of being a general theory is more or less cementing this self-inflicted immaturity.

Stability, creativity and inventions and social goals

Stability as a technical concept of mathematics deals with systems of dynamic equations which have a parameter structure allowing for a convergence of variable values to certain relations and levels in a predetermined system of measurement. What about economic stability with respect to such a definition?

It is hard to say. Isn't it?

When listening to political debates, the word *growth* is much more frequent. Words like *the need for inventions* and *innovations* are often as much emphasized as economic stability, particularly in a country like Sweden which is extremely dependent on foreign trade and international competitiveness. We are sometimes a bit bewildered about the eventual content of the words.

In economics we have a few growth models which appear in analytical form. The most advanced is the Neumann-Gale model which given absolute flexibility and substitutability can appear to handle unbalanced growth but lack of flexibility and substitutability is bound to deal with balanced growth. In either case, we can see problems with respect to economic stability in reality.

But what do we mean by economic stability? First of all, we must remind ourselves that stability is a dynamic concept; it concerns changes in space-time. Second, we must remind ourselves that economic actions, which have macroscopic effects, are almost always irreversible. Third, we must remind ourselves that averages imply additive aggregation, which we reject.

When we look at these three rather restrictive limitations, we may wonder if economic stability is at all possible to model mathematically without dropping those limitations. Anyway, it is not possible to analyze within the realm of the Euclidian space.

If we look at the neoclassical axiomatic structure, economic stability is rather well defined. The neoclassical market economy is stable as long as the Pareto optimum holds. So, does that mean that we can regard so-called Pareto-sanctioned changes in an economy out of equilibrium as some kind of convergence process? No, unfortunately not. When we are not in equilibrium, either we have to have a certain kind of distribution as a norm or there are infinitely many distributions which may fulfil any general equilibrium. But that is of course presupposing an economy void of any structures.

When we have an economy imbedded in social, cultural, political and physical structures and whatnot, characters, stability and stabilizing actions are often seen as structure-preserving. Whether that is good or bad is of course a different question, as we learnt from history. When we take an economic perspective, dealing with production, consumption, financial matters and economic policy, things are not easier. It seems good to support what seems to be traditional and important national sectors to ease the pressure from international competition, but that may only be wasteful as we may hold up a necessary structural change.

To think of structure-preserving as stability is tempting, but we know that is a pretty dangerous definition. An example from the 1960s is the then-world leading Swedish producer of calculating machines, Facit. These machines were able to do addition and multiplication, subtraction and with some problems also division, and they had a weight of around 12 kilos. The company did not care about electronics and consequently went bankrupt in two years.

Thus the two dangerous words with respect to that kind of definition of stability in a simple sense are *inventions* and *innovations* caused by human creativity. New knowledge takes us to new levels, but that only means that we need new ladders.

Looking at the world today, we see the two strong tendencies of "stop the world, I want to live in peace" and those saying we must have a new world where we can exist. The contradictive forces of the dead city and the living city, if we allude to Luigi Amoroso, are always present but constantly changing their shapes. What we can say is that economic policy systematically favourable to particular groups in a society is seldom, not to say never, beneficial to social and/

or economic stability. We will come back to these questions when we discuss the concepts of anomie and saturation.

With respect to ethics, we have the legitimate demand for human security; partly, it seems, in contradiction of the legitimate instinct for development and creation. The contradictive appearance should not however be exaggerated. It is often a matter of time before new structures are incorporated, but clearly there is a need for the public sector to ease the transformation, particularly when earlier education and experience become obsolete.

Thus individuals themselves are the fundamental source of uncertainty; this is mostly not in an unethical sense, but by performing perfectly legitimate activities which imply structural changes which are of an asymmetric character with respect to individual abilities. We analyzed earlier an example where firms' necessary striving to maintain competitiveness could lead to permanent unemployment if it was a generic feature of the economy. In this case, the unethical dimensions often occur in the economic-political area when we explain the phenomenon as unimportant or dismissing it altogether, declaring it "natural unemployment". This is mostly attached to ideological statements but nevertheless unethical in its diminishing of people's dignity; in fact, it is dehumanization. When it occurs in research, it compromises the very fundamentals of science.

Inventions and innovations are necessary for the growth of society, but they change the structures. This aspect never even occurs in the neoclassical axiomatic structure, but it is the one which causes most of the trouble because we are dealing with real humans and real production and consumption. That is not built on atomic variables but complexes which are linked differently to different societal structures, and that creates social inertia of a different kind; sometimes it has to do with regional changes, sometimes with technological changes making some human abilities more demanded and some less demanded. If we look at the climate problem and global warming, the technical knowledge in a narrow sense is there to reduce emissions, but the implementation of the techniques has generally large production, infrastructural and demographic effects which make it difficult from a political point of view.

If we look at another sector which was implemented quite easily without any deeper thought, the IT sector, we now see the problems coming. I am sure there are more to come, for better and worse, but that is almost completely unknown since the implementation of new abilities is due to technical achievements while law-making, control and supervision have to somehow be arranged after the acute problems have occurred. The easiness with which IT systems are perturbed is indeed remarkable. Presently, a 16-year-old boy with a rather old stationary computer is in court, accused of causing a breakdown of the Swedish banking system which lasted for several days in spring 2017. Customers were told by the banks that their security systems were very good and almost completely secure. Sic!

We will come back to this problem when we touch on human intelligence versus artificial intelligence.

As a conclusion, we can say that the effect of rejecting the neoclassical axiomatic structure and proposing Propositions 1 and 2 is that we cannot have a growth process, only build on individual market initiatives, but we need the corrective force of a collective agent defining overall social goals for the economy in question. We certainly know that there is an ideological fight, and some people want to be liberated from all types of collective influence. To be frank, this is often based on a very limited apprehension of the world, which might be understandable from an emotional point of view, but particularly when it occurs among the wealthiest groups, it induces allusions to greediness without spatial and temporal perspectives, often built on fear.

In Chapter 2 we touched on the concept of entropy and the enormous effects its discovery had for the apprehension of physical space and time. The concept is also of great theoretical interest as a measure of order/disorder. In Ekstedt (2013:203–205) it is shown that the principle is underlying the Allais paradox dealing with expected utility theory. It has also been used in economics, particularly by the Dutch economist Henri Theil as a method of studying changes in income distribution, and we can also use it for studying industrial concentration. The technical definition is built on probabilities, and it is defined in Chapter 2.

However, one physical application is interesting for social sciences merely as a mode of thinking, though it is difficult to define for practical use. It is the fact we can see when we use pipes in the lawn to heat the house or the water we use: geothermal energy from the surface of the ground. After a couple of years, the lawn will be in extremely bad shape due to the lowering of the ground temperature. That is due to the very principle which Lazare Carnot discovered and which started the research from which Rudolf Clausius could later derive the more general theory.

We have two containers A and B, where we assume B is inside A and A is almost completely isolated from the environment. In Figure 3.3 we have also added some instrument/machine C, which transforms heat from the environment of B in A to the interior of B.

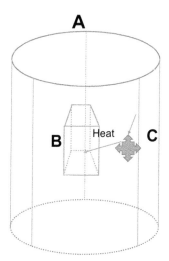

Figure 3.3 Illustration of the entropy principle

We may then increase the heat in B by lowering the heat of its environment in A. But then we will arrive at a result which tells us that the heat increase in B will be lower than the heat loss of its environment in A. Thus we have a total loss of heat due to the operation which is bigger than the gained heat in B.

If we now allude to the use of entropy as a measure of order, lowering entropy means increasing order/concentration with respect to some matters, while increasing entropy means lowering the order/concentration of the matter in question. Universally speaking, we reach maximum entropy when energy is evenly distributed in the universe, which means an unpleasant temperature of $0°K \approx -273.15°C$. But if we use this analogy in social sciences and apply the reasoning in Figure 3.3, it gives rise to many exciting applications. Take slavery, for example, used for building the civilization of the Southern US as it is shown in glamorous Hollywood productions. Its effects were not only devastating for African individuals but also for the existing African cultures and civilizations, which were pretty advanced. There are many other examples for illustration. However due to the problem of measurement, this figure of thought cannot be used analytically but only in analogy forms. We may hope that anthropologists and ethnologists may develop some crude measures which might be used, at least for methodological development. In economics it is mostly used as a distribution measure, but Nicholas Georgescu-Roegen used the entropy concept for environmental effects of production, and that should be more used within economics. If we apply figures, the production of human good uses our nature in some respect, which is the basis of the cost of the product, but there is a surplus use/waste of resources which always occurs in some form. It includes so-called external effects but is much larger and involves human, social cultural and environmental costs. For example, one problem of peculiarities is that production output and the costs underlying the prices are generally linear, dependent of the production volume, while many other indirect effects of the types mentioned are exponential through accumulative effects and structural changes. Making paper out of Amazonian forests induces one to think of such differences of processes, not to mention the complexity of the effects of diminishing the forests of the Amazon.

The reference to the entropy process and the examples of thoughts it induces leads our thoughts to the problem of organic processes, and it is natural to look at the market process of a money economy, as interpreted by radical market liberals, as an organic process where the atomic item of Money becomes the primary factor of human goals, without any relation to underlying utilities.

But money is an ethical neutral factor, as the friars of Salamanca pointed out when they allowed money trading, and they built on St. Thomas Aquinas when asking, "Is the goodness or badness of action due to its object?" He answers:

> It seems not. 1. An action does not seem to derive goodness or badness from its objects, for the object of an action is a thing, and evil is not in things but in the use of them by sinners, as Augustine says in *On Christian Doctrine*.
> (Aquinas 1988[1271]:568)

Thus the market economy, as proposed by radical liberals, implies that social life is transformed to an organic process with no relation to any human will or intellect. Humans are seemingly transformed to animal machines of an Aristotelian kind; that is, observation is directly linked to action. This seems also to be in line with some market economy proponents who tell us that the market economy is void of any exogenous ethics but will always choose the right ways.

Notes

1 François Villon, (circa 1455), *Poésies Diverses*. Original French text available at http://poesie.webnet.fr/lesgrandsclassiques/poemes/francois_villon/le_debat_du_c_ur_et_du_corps_de_villon.html; English translation by Galway Kinnell available at www.scribd.com/document/249185989/Poems-of-Francois-Villon

2 Like a cat with nine lives, Villon survived. His friends succeeded, on the very execution day, in getting him free but he was ostracized from Paris. When, how and where he died is unknown.

3 We will use the expression *almost all* frequently. That should be interpreted to mean that we really believe *all*, but our knowledge is limited, so we cannot grant that the All-operator $\forall$ holds.

4 Keynes rejected additive aggregation in economics in a 1903 speech to the apostles in Cambridge (Ekstedt 2015:50).

5 When it comes to fashion, production has to be planned approximately two years before the clothing line is launched. Thus, the commercial strategy has to be streamlined for that occasion under considerable uncertainty, and when the particular fashion is launched, economic benefits or losses are almost immediately apprehended by its reception among some leading personalities. The film *The Devil Wears Prada*, from what I have learnt from Mrs. Paula Ekstedt, fashion designer, gives a reasonably good illustration of the current fashion creation technology.

6 I have argued that claiming that Say had anything to do with Say's Law is grossly erroneous when reading Say's total analysis. Say's writings which could be interpreted as "Say's Law" have more to do with the standard Marginal Propensity to Consume, although a bit more implicitly expressed than Keynes does.

7 I am grateful to Dr. Anna Ekstedt, psychiatrist, for fruitful discussions on this subject, bringing me into touch with different approaches to brain and psychiatric research. I therefore conclude that refusing rationality in the immediate sense of neoclassical theory, which is just a logical concept of consistency, can only be relevant when we have severe cases of psychological disorder.

8 This example is particularly discussed in Ekstedt (2015:53–63).

9 For a comprehensive analysis of these concepts, I recommend Fusari, Angelo, (2014). *Methodological Misconceptions in the Social Sciences*, Springer, Dordrecht, Heidelberg, New York, and London, and to some extent also Ekstedt, H. and Fusari, A., (2010). *Economic Theory and Social Change Problems and Revisions*, Routledge, London and New York.

10 Debreu, Gerard, (1982). Existence of general equilibrium. In K.J. Arrow and M.D. Intrilligator (eds.), *Handbook of Mathematical Economics, Vol. 2*. North-Holland Publishing Company, Amsterdam and New York.

11 It is important to mention the production sector since the conditions there are implicit to the Arrow/Debreu setting. But it is possible to make it implicit through a Neumann-Gale model. In Makarov and Rubinov (1977) it is proved that an optimal trajectory under certain conditions coincide with an Arrow/Debreu equilibrium. The ethical aspect which comes to mind then is child labour and underpaid work utilizing poverty.

12 Amoroso, Luigi, (1938). Vilfredo Pareto, *Econometrica*, Vol. 6, No. 1.

13 In Ekstedt (2015) chapter 1, Mill's vision on Utilitarianism is compared with Jevon's effort to formalize utilitarianism into a consistent mathematical approach, and although he does in it a sensitive and intelligent way, we can see how he must sacrifice important features which Mill discusses in order to have a consistent mathematical structure.
14 It reminds the author of a conference at the Belgian Central Bank in the beginning of the 2000s when a famous economist analyzed the British tax base for the coming fifty years. He didn't have Brexit as one of his scenarios.

Bibliography

Amoroso, L., (1938). Vilfredo Pareto, *Econometrica*, Vol. 6, No. 1.

Aquinas, T., St., (1998[1271]). What Makes Actions Good or Bad?, *Summa Theologiæ*, 1–2, 18–20. In *Selected Writings* (pp. 565–611), Penguin Classics, London.

Arrow, K.J. and Hahn, F.H., (1971). *General Competitive Analysis*, Holden Day Inc., San Francisco.

Basu, S. and Kimball, M.S., (1997). *Cyclical Productivity with Unobserved Input Variation*, National Bureau of Economic Research, Working Paper 5915.

Carr, J.D., (1950). *The Bride of Newgate*, Harper and Brothers, New York.

Debreu, G., (1987[1959]). *Theory of Value*, Wiley, New York.

Debreu, G., (1982). Existence of general equilibrium. In K.J. Arrow and M.D. Intrilligator (eds.), *Handbook of Mathematical Economics, Vol. 2*. North-Holland Publishing Company, Amsterdam and New York.

DeLong, H., (1991). *A Refutation of Arrow's Theorem*, University Press of America, Lanham, New York, and London.

Douglas, R., (1995). Stochastically branching spacetime topology. In S. Savitt (ed.), *Time's Arrow Today: Recent Physical and Philosophical Work on the Direction of Time* (pp. 173–188), Cambridge University Press, Cambridge.

Ekstedt, H., (2013). *Money in Economic Theory*, Routledge, London and New York.

Ekstedt, H., (2015). *Money, Valuation and Growth*, Routledge, London and New York.

Ekstedt, H. and Fusari, A., (2010). *Economic Theory and Social Change Problems and Revisions*, Routledge, London and New York.

Ekstedt, H. and Westberg, L., (1991). *Dynamic Models for the Interrelations of Real and Financial Growth*, Chapman and Hall, London and New York.

Fest, J., (2002). *Inside Hitler's Bunker: The Last Days of the Third Reich*, Macmillan, Basingstoke and Oxford.

Fusari, A., (2014). *Methodological Misconceptions in the Social Sciences: Rethinking Social Thought and Social Processes*, Springer, Dordrecht, Heidelberg, New York, and London.

Georgescu-Roegen, N., (1971). *The Entropy Law and the Economic Process*, Harvard University Press, Cambridge, MA.

Koestler, A., (1970). *The Act of Creation*, Richard Clay Ltd, Bungay, Suffolk.

Makarov, V.L., and Rubinov, A.M., (1977). *Economic Dynamics and Equilibria*, Springer Verlag, Heidelberg and Berlin.

Say, J.B., (1834[1803]). *A Treatise on Political Economy; or the Production, Distribution, and Consumption of Wealth*. Grigg & Elliot, 9, North Fourth Street, Philadelphia.

Wittgenstein, L., (1974[1921]). *Tractatus Logico-Philosophicus*, Routledge and Kegan Paul, London.

4   Faith and axiomatic structures

Codex Regis Stanza

Now Garm howls loud | before Gnipahellir,[1]   47
The fetters will burst, | and the wolf run free;
Much do I know, | and more can see
Of the fate of the gods, | the mighty in fight.

The sun turns black, | earth sinks in the sea,   55
The hot stars down | from heaven are whirled;
Fierce grows the steam | and the life-feeding flame,
Till fire leaps high | about heaven itself.

Now do I see | the earth anew   57
Rise all green | from the waves again;
The cataracts fall, | and the eagle flies,
And fish he catches | beneath the cliffs.

In wondrous beauty | once again   59
Shall the golden tables | stand mid the grass,
Which the gods had owned | in the days of old,
. . . .

Then fields unsowed | bear ripened fruit,   60
All ills grow better, | and Baldr comes back;
Baldr and Hoth dwell | in Hropt's battle-hall,
And the mighty gods: | would you know yet more?

More fair than the sun, | a hall I see,   62
Roofed with gold, | on Gimle it stands;
There shall the righteous | rulers dwell,
And happiness ever | there shall they have.

The Utopia, the Faith, gives us hope even in the darkest times and there, in the Valley of Death, it is perhaps the only link to the living world which we have. Suppress the Faith, the Dream and life vanish. Death is inevitable but life is mighty – it is grandiose! When we reach the outer end of our solar system in our dreams, we meet the terrible God of Death, Pluto, who plagues and terrorizes our minds, but what is he? He is completely insignificant, a trivial composition of stones and ice. We turn around and watch the wonderful blue planet; looking closer, we see the fresh green colour and dreams are born. We turn around once more, but we don't care about Pluto and we look instead at the magnificent universe with stars, galaxies, nebulas, black holes and quasars illustrating the eternal variations of *creation* and *death*, where the two are twins and each other's precondition. We are filled with dreams and visions like the *Voluspo – the Wise-Woman*.

I am writing these lines 10 September 2017, 14.05 CET, while keeping half an eye on the TV with reports of Hurricane Irma hitting Florida at full strength. An army officer, a retired general, is helping the elderly and the disabled to find shelter at the brink of Irma's full outburst. He tells about preparations and strategies, gives pieces of good advice to refugees and so on, but he finishes by saying, "Irrespective of what we do and have done, Mother Nature will win the first quarter with death and devastation, but we hope to win the second quarter with rescue and help." When I listened to this man, who seemed tired to the bones, wet and with a plagued face, my mind turned to the spirit of the Hávamál, which is central to the vision of Voluspo: you understand the consequences of the fight, but you do your duty and use the strength of the incarnation of your body, mind and spirit to fight for the right cause. Then you can proudly meet your fate with dignity.

Stanzas 74–76 of the Hávamál teaches us:[2]

> The half wit does not know that gold
> Makes apes of many men:
> One rich, and one poor,
> There is no blame in that.

> Cattle die, kindred die,
> Every man is mortal
> But good name never dies
> Of one who has done well.

> Cattle die, kindred die,
> Every man is mortal:
> But I know one thing that never dies,
> The glory of the great dead.

"*Assensus intellectus veritati*"[3]

Faith, a word which we in science try to avoid, is perhaps one of the central words to be used to explain much social analysis of individual actions and social choices. The referendum in 2016 on the UK leaving the European Union was, when we look at it in retrospect, hardly based on cold intellectual analysis, on economic and political pros and cons. Rather, it was based on emotional sentiments and beliefs poorly underpinned. Faith is the basic sentiment underlying most scientific revolutions and innovations. Faith and ideals are the central forces driving humans for better or worse.

But faith is linked to our perception and comprehension of the surrounding world, and thus it becomes a viable part of the research process – not in the logical part of the scientific analysis but in the definition of the research problem, the imposed restrictions and assumptions. Keynes says that the entrepreneur is driven by animal spirit; this spirit is based on faith, dreams, ideals, visions, which are outside the realm of reason and logic. Any thought outside a conventional structure has to be intuited well before any logical proof exists. By intuition, we do not mean the kind of a priori intuition proposed by Kant but an alternative way of looking at the world based on associations, metaphors and analogies.

Arthur Koestler (1970) discusses the act of creation. He looks at the creative thought as a conjunction of three abilities of the human being: Pathos, Logos and Bathos.

A triptych which often is present in the creative mind: Logos stands for reason, logic, coherency of concepts, scientific analysis, while Pathos is the ability to feel sympathy and to understand the pain of our fellow brothers and sisters. Bathos is the ability to realize the absurdities, the surrealism of the world, and

Picture 4.1 Bathos – Logos – Pathos

Source: Albert Engström (1965[1901]), En Bok, Bonniers, Stockholm

laugh about it. Thus both Pathos and Bathos create perspectives of the outside world which create thoughts that are possible to use for scientific purposes. Logos has no part of creativity, which is intrinsic to its role as a rational/effective language.

There are also other approaches to the problem of creative versus scientific thinking. When Thomas Brody (1994) discusses the philosophy underlying physics and thereby introduces the concept of epistemic cycles, which we make extensive use of, means that the scientific discussion is not separate from coffee talk in the way that it is loose and not particularly consistent. But it has to be like that in order to free the mind from its tight logical coat and be a bit more spontaneous, in order to see concepts and methods from other perspectives.

We mentioned in Chapter 1 the French expressions *l'esprit de finesse* and *l'esprit de géométrie*. The former may use Bathos and Pathos in intuitive thinking, while the latter is the systematic logical analysis of coherent concepts.

We also mentioned Hans Reichenbach (1938) and his distinction between the *context of discovery* and the *context of justification*, where the former refers to *l'esprit de finesse* while the latter is used to link our thoughts to the language of conventional knowledge.

We have to regard the incarnated human, to use a theological language of spirit, soul and body, and attempts to separate them will in the end lead astray.

The neurologist and brain researcher Antonio Damasio takes one step further the mystery Koestler is alluding to:

> My hypothesis, then, presented in the form of a provisional definition, is that *a feeling is the perception of a certain state of the body along with the perception of a certain mode of thinking and of thoughts with certain themes.*
>
> (original emphasis; Damasio 2004:86)

And he proceeds:

> If feelings were merely clusters of thoughts with certain themes, how could they be distinguished from any other thoughts? How would they retain the functional individuality that justifies their status as a special mind process? My view is that feelings are functionally distinctive because their essence consists of the thoughts that represent the body involved in a reactive process. Remove that essence and the notion of feeling vanishes. . . . What makes thoughts "happy"? If we do not experience a certain body state with a certain quality we can call pleasure and that we find "good" and "positive" within the framework of life, we have no reason whatsoever to regard any thought as happy. Or sad.
>
> (ibid.:86–87)

Thus, a proposition exists before the means of logical proof are in place. In fact, it exists independently of any logical analysis whatsoever. How is it created? Is it a divine revelation, or is it a part of explainable processes belonging to the physical world? I heard an interview with the late Norwegian composer Egil Hovland, who wrote music for many hymns together with the poet Britt G. Hallqvist, of which one is particularly beloved. He was asked in a TV program what he felt and thought when he composed the music to that hymn. He answered: "I did not compose it. It was revealed to me. I have a photo of one of my children choirs and these children were released from the paper and appeared as tones on my music paper." His description is very emotional and there is no reason to doubt that the hymn was composed in a particular emotional state, but it was certainly moulded by his musical education and genius. It is interesting however that he places the creation outside himself because we all experience sometimes in particular situations that somebody else is there to govern our actions. Sometimes we talk about angels. There are certainly processes in body and mind which are hidden or disguised in such a manner that our intellect cannot grasp them by a simple reasonable analysis.

Observe in the quote from Damasio that he regards the feelings as essential for the body in the *reactive process*. This is an extremely interesting attitude. We have already discussed Aristotle and Hume with respect to the perception/apprehension phase, while comprehension is something more complicated and involves experiences, memory and combinatory ability; we can say that mostly it concerns an intellectual analysis. If so, the perception/apprehension concerns more the emotional instinctive reactions and thus has more direct effect on the alertness of body, a direct link in preparing for the reactive process.

Both Aristotle and Hume are in the neighbourhood of such a view, although they do not have the same neurological background as Damasio. What is important is that we have in principle two receptive patterns: the first emotional, more or less instinctive apprehension, and the secondary more conscious intellectual comprehension, but which also uses more fundamental emotions and "passions" in Hume's meaning. The first question, then, is whether these two patterns support each other or whether they can occasionally contradict. The second question is that if the two patterns might contradict, in that case is there some pattern dominant for actions, or does it vary? The two questions lead to a third, quite natural question: whether the two patterns may in some way become interdependent over time.

Aristotle and Hume, both but a bit differently, link apprehension and comprehension to individual heritage and upbringing, particularly the phase of apprehension, while intellectual analysis and combinatory ability in conjunction with memories and experiences are more important in the phase of comprehension. But this means that as time goes by, intellectual patterns become habitual reactions.

This is particularly important with respect to holistic thinking. Skilled composers working at the borderline of emotions and intellectual analysis may experience this. If we look again at Hovland's answer, we can see him reading the text from Hallqvist, which is very beautiful and has a very distinct although discrete rhythm. He is moved and watches the text as a whole, which creates an idea of the start, and he finds that the rest is just to fill in, which is due to his experience and deep knowledge of theory and practice of composition. I have based my guess on descriptions of Mozart's way of composing by Hildesheimer (1980) and Einstein (1964). Even if Hovland does not have the gigantesque gestalt of Mozart, it is probably the same kind of principal process.[4]

It is important to understand that logic is empty of any aspects of reality, while emotions are directly linked to reality. However, this is not the outside reality but perception as a montage over a complicated emotional background created by conscious, half-conscious and unconscious emotional experiences of different strength, which Hume claims and which is to a high degree supported by Damasio. Thus, with respect to our questions above, we can probably with some confidence say that in a "competition" between the intellectual and the emotional apprehension, it is not even a match; the intellect resigns immediately. Contradiction in the sense that it has effects on the individual probably appears in the step from apprehension to comprehension, and it is also in this step that the intellect may mould the emotionally affected apprehensions. But the reason why the intellect may affect emotion is based on the fact that the intellectual analysis displays deeper structures, which in its turn has an emotional load which may affect the individual. Thus, to simplify the reasoning: the first apprehension is linked to apparent emotional values, while the more careful analysis using the intellect may display other emotional goals of importance, and this is why the intellect may affect the actions of the individual. However, a trained intellect with some understanding of self's reactions may integrate some generic logic concerning areas where the individual is very active, emotionally and intellectually. But basically, our thoughts are where our heart is.

We can never know what is going on in our fellow's mind. What Damasio and other brain researchers have understood is that psychological and social experience directly affects our brain in a physiological way. If so, all we have learnt from Popper is doubtful when we come to research incorporating individuals. If humans are to be seen as subjects and final causes, then they also per definition escape a closure of an experimental situation, which is possible when we deal with objects. Furthermore, the link between observable actions and their causes is to a great extent hidden. Of course we can in many cases on good grounds assume a certain inertia, but that is not possible to generalize; it is local and temporal.

When we take the possible inertia as a reason why we could use probability theory as a tool in forecasting human behaviour, we must be aware of the fact that nobody could tell about the reasons why an earlier inertia is broken.

Consequently, we have a problem that *reason* can almost never be used to explain human behaviour, simply because that *reason* is a secondary process in the human decision. The first process is some type of mixture between emotions, particularly viable experiences and similar. As our discussion of the example of discontinuous time with respect to Richard Darwent and Lady Caroline in Chapter 1, we cannot assume continuity of space-time, and reading Hume's comments on the difficulty of isolate causes even in simple cases makes the difficulties worse. With respect to Hume's scepticism with regard to reason, he says:

"By this means all knowledge degenerate into probability; and this probability is greater or less, according to our experience of veracity or deceitfulness of our understanding, and according to the simplicity or intricacy of the question" (Hume 2002[1740]:121). We fully accept Hume's scepticism when it comes to sciences involving humans, and from what we understand of natural sciences, particularly physics, they are approaching the social sciences in the sense that the very experimental design is an endogenous factor in the experiment. This is mostly due to the fact that the size of the object of study is of less magnitude than Heisenberg's uncertainty relation, a magnitude of approximately 10^{-35}, and the physical impact of the experimental design will most probably affect the experiment at a bigger magnitude. Probability judgements will only do if we exactly know the intrinsic probabilities of the investigated particle, which to my understanding is not the case.

Consequently we have in social sciences two sources of scientific uncertainties: on one hand we have the problem that humans are subjects and thus local final causes, and on the other hand the persons who are performing a scientific study are also endogenous to the study themselves.

Looking at the illustration of Wittgenstein's Proposition 6.211 in the prologue, we find that because causality is irreversible, we have to make restrictions which are just temporal and local, and thus we are basically prisoners of social dynamics. Consequently the belief that we find some kind of an a priori individual by removing disturbing environmental aspects in making the individuals comparable in some particular dimension is doomed from the very beginning since we then disregard the structural role of the environmental aspects vis-à-vis the specific individual. Reaction patterns of the individual are structurally dependent on the environment and changes in that environment.

Thus, modern brain research suggests that trying to isolate the brain from the body is equally impossible as trying to isolate the body from the brain. As the title of one of Damasio's books, *Descartes' Error: Emotion, Reason and the Human Brain*, it is claimed that the saying that "we Think therefore we Exist" should be reversed: "we Exist therefore we Think". The theological concept of incarnation is actually practical when we speak of human beings. The incarnated human, mind, soul and body, should be seen as a unity, and that is the ground for speaking of humans as subjects and local final causes.

Back now to the expression "*assensus intellectus veritati*": our intellect must consent to the truth. We discussed Moore's paradox in Chapter 1, and this expression seems even more paradoxical.

Let us see what the intellect can consent to. We use Aristotle's chain: perception, apprehension, comprehension.

We have earlier mentioned that even perception in an objective sense could be problematic due to differences in perspective, environmental disturbances and individual deficiencies in the sensual apparatus. These problems are however of minor importance. The first problematic point is when the objective perception is transformed to an apprehension. As we have already mentioned, this step is affected by emotions due to earlier experiences which might be strong enough to perturb the perception. An example is the exaggerated fear of snakes where even rather far-fetched associations with snakes affect the behaviour of an individual; obviously there is no intellectual analysis of whether the believed apprehension correctly interprets the objective perception.

The first impression of a phenomenon is seldom linked to an intellectual analysis, and this means that while some people are not willing to go deeper in analyzing the first impression, some others do, and this may create an epistemological difference between people.

When we proceed to the step from apprehension to comprehension, the intellect must in some way be involved. But that is also due to big individual differences in education, informational basis, and emotional affections with respect to religious and ideological beliefs attaching the perception to individual hopes, fears and wishes and similar aspects. In science we have paradigms which have a tendency to perturb the analysis, not perhaps from a pure intellectual point of view but with respect to conventionality, money and career reasons and similar.

Consequently, when we deal with complex perceptions/impressions, the road to a somewhat common-sense comprehension could be rather rough. In Umberto Eco's story of the platypus, the time from perception to a common-sense comprehension among scientists was 86 years.

From a scientific point of view, these "disturbances" are not exogenous to the individuals but intrinsic and actually form the personality of the individual.

So, when we look at the understanding of a complex perception, it seems possible that through intellectual analysis and communication with others, we can at least narrow the window for possible comprehension, but I doubt that we can bring it to common acceptance.

Thus we have to go to the other side of the problem, namely when the specific comprehension should be used for human actions.

When we listen to political debates on TV, it is remarkable how concepts, theories and knowledge can be of use in different interpretations. We had to take some pains to analyze Moore's paradox in Chapter 1, but looking at a TV debate, we will have loads of declarations placing even the strong form of the paradox as conventional propositions which are supposed to be believed. Most such propositions do not appear in direct form but with some delay between the first and the second step, usually less than a couple of minutes, and it appears in different words.

Some years ago, I was in a conversation with a leading regional politician on the newly published plans for commuter traffic between my place and Gothenburg, circa 70 kilometers. The plan was to replace trains with buses. I regretted this, but he motivated the decision by saying that while trains did not pass the places where people lived, the bus could do that. The argument was OK so I did not oppose it. Then, after approximately 30 seconds, he added that furthermore the bus would take the motorway, so it would not stop between my place and Gothenburg. When I revealed some puzzlement with respect to the logical consistency of the arguments, he was genuinely surprised, as if he had not thought about such an aspect. This man was absolutely not stupid, nothing of the kind, but he was defending a political decision and heaped up arguments of whatever kind against my feeble criticism. I believe it was a way of natural instinct to kill every kind of protest in its very cradle.

That brings us to the concept of consistency and/or rationality. Obviously, with respect to the real problem, the arguments contradicted each other, but above that we can probably find a kind of "power logic" of persuasion. It failed in this very example, but given a little longer time between the two propositions and a different atmosphere, more intensive and antagonistic, both the propositions could have done their job in persuading different groups that did not care for logical consistency. Thus, when we look at the concept of rationality, we must think of different layers of a problem where we have different kinds of logical consistency, particularly when it comes to politics, power and economics. This follows from the need for politicians and leaders of companies to persuade and convince people with very different apprehensions/comprehensions of a particular aspect in a society. That means that there is no single logic, no clear-cut common understanding of the concept of rationality. In this aspect it is very interesting to study different interpretations of Arrow's paradox, where some regard the neoclassical approach to rationality as The Rationality.

So, we have arrived at a position where we roughly understand the realm of Faith, but what on earth is Truth? The old Catholic expression probably refers to the Gospel of St. Matthew, chapter 25. The point is that if someone says he follows Christ, then his behaviour and actions should be in line with that. Thus, a proposition gains its truth through its consequences for human actions. This is particularly explicit in the gospels and epistles in the Bible, but it goes for all propositions concerning the empirical world. A proposition gains its meaning in its structural role of the real world. That is also the implicit consequence of the fact that mathematical/logical propositions per se have no empirical meaning whatsoever. This is also the message from neurology and brain research, what we above called the incarnated human, namely the unity of body, mind and soul. The thought is effective if it causes an action.

Thus, if we now try to interpret the expression *"assensus intellectus veritati"*, we could say that Faith must lead to actions which are understood because they are in line with the foundations of the specific Faith. If the Faith does not lead to action, it is void of any relevance for the empirical world and could be dismissed. If the Faith leads to action, the action must be logical with respect to the Faith.

But interpreted in this way, the expression per se does not distinguish different kinds of Faith with respect to ethical qualities; we just talk about logical consistency and the unity of thoughts and actions. Thus a Faith cannot be judged per se but only through its consequential actions and their empirical consequences.

Consequently, the principle of free speech is indeed a radical principle and needs constant attention with respect to the development of society in different dimensions. Persuasive propaganda is a social action which certainly has consequences; however, the ethics involved may be judged in one way now and in another way in the future. Thus, the only way the principle of free speech and freedom of media can work is when we have complete transparency of public power. Secrecy of public authorities must be governed by crystal-clear principles and supervision must be entrusted to independent groups of citizens.

In Chapter 3 we mentioned the trial of the Norwegian mass murderer Breivik. Some psychiatrists claimed that he was mentally ill due to his perverted opinions and should be sentenced to mental care. However, another group of psychiatrists claimed that Breivik's opinions were in line with opinions announced in media, particularly the internet, and that given acceptance of these public opinions, his behaviour was quite rational in his goal to kill as many people as possible. The court chose the latter attitude and sentenced Breivik to jail since he was not to be seen as mentally ill at the time of the crime so he could not behave consistently.

The verdict was consequently in the line of our interpretation of the expression "*assensus intellectus veritati*".

What we have said suggests on one hand that faith and the emotions are a form of filter for the intellect and furthermore they have a conservative effect on the personality, while the intellect/reason per se does not have such conservative effects. On the other hand, however, from a physiological point of view, the brain seems to register and adopt emotionally strong psychological and social events. Thus the brain is affected, from a physical point of view, which implies a continuing change of the personality for better or worse. The department of Neuroscience at Cambridge writes on their homepage:

> Epigenetics is the study of how a set of reversible heritable changes in the functioning of a gene can occur without any alterations to the DNA sequence. These changes may be induced spontaneously, in response to environmental factors, or in response to the presence of a particular gene.
> . . .
> The contribution of genetics to the understanding of cognition and psychiatric disorders has tended to focus on gene polymorphisms. However, although there are increasing numbers of genetic polymorphisms under investigation, they are still unable to account for much of the variance seen in many psychiatric illnesses. In contrast, gene-environment interactions can account for much more of the aetiology of psychiatric disorders. For example, schizophrenia is only 50% concordant in genetically identical (monozygotic) twins, while the severity of different "life-events" is known to predispose some people to certain psychiatric disorders. It is now established in animal and human studies that some environmental events can induce long-term developmental changes in chromatin structure through various mechanisms such as histone de-acetylation and DNA methylation of non-coding sequences, which produce long-term silencing of transcription. Since most human brain development occurs postnatally, the brain more than any other organ is under strong social and environmental influences that can have long-lasting effects on brain function and wellbeing.[5]

Thus reason expressed in terms of logic and mathematics has the formidable complex of human body, soul and spirit to handle, more complex than any theoretical exogenous to the human being. The struggle with this complex is not external to the individual but intrinsic to every person. We are discovering the world, the universe around us, and we do it skilfully, but perhaps we should pay more attention to the interior journey.

Holism versus atomism

Before we say some words more on Kant's and Hume's conflicting views, we must dig a bit deeper into the question of holism and atomism. We have up to now looked at atomistic variables at variance with complex ones, where the latter needs to be seen with respect to a certain structure in order to be interpreted correctly. But we are aware of the many researchers who look at *atomistic research* at variance with *holistic research*. We are not entirely convinced that we understand this distinction. Arthur Koestler, who we discussed vis-à-vis understanding by using the triptych Pathos-Logos-Bathos, makes this difference. He then basically emphasizes the need for both logical understanding as well as emotional, social and cultural understanding. Often, concepts like qualitative research are contrasted with quantitative research and rationalism is looked upon as a kind of a simplifying atomistic concept.

Henri Bergson discusses an analysis of the whole in relation to the contained parts of the whole, which is close to the more formalized mereology mainly developed by the Polish philosophers Stanisław Leśniewski and Alfred Tarski.[6] Mereology was an attempt to get around Russell's paradox, but since the very paradox induces a structural analysis, mereology is a bit redundant. Bergson's analysis however describes hierarchies of structures, which is of course in the natural line of development. Bergson, also in line with Hume, emphasizes intensities of experience as an element of structural understanding. He takes an example of a needle tickling your palm: increasing the pressure, it hurts a bit; increasing the pressure still more, it really hurts and you must do something about it, as it interferes with your needs. Increasing the pressure again, the pain will be affecting your entire body. Here Bergson describes a process that is far from additive, and although the pressure increases, it might be described as a kind of continuous additive process. The sensitive experience is not so but goes through different layers which send different kinds of signals to the brain. The reaction goes from just noticeable and very local to a pain that completely affects body and mind as a general factor of your well-being.

In the discussion of atomism and holism, such examples are mentioned in order to separate the two kinds of thinking: a sort of quantitative rational thinking is contrasted with a qualitative holistic thinking. But if we look at Bergson's needle example, this is not something qualitative or holistic. Electronically, there are rather easy techniques to replicate such "intensity" measurement – perhaps not exactly replicating the experience of the single individual, but the principle is rather simple. Furthermore, through modern brain science it is now known that intrinsic electrical and chemical processes of the brain can be measured so that such kinds of events/reactions will be analyzed with different scientific methods and design.

What is disturbing with the classification of atomism/holism is that the latter concept seems to be completely undefined, and it seems almost as if some proponents also understand metaphysics and ideologies as a part of holism. In such a case, holism seems to become a method; we have to understand the universe before we can understand the individual. I certainly believe that Arthur Koestler is on the right track to something important when he emphasizes that to find different dimensions of thought, you need to take in different kinds of perspectives, and that is clearly in line both with Aristotle and Hume. This process is not scientific per se. If we think in a standard logical scheme we have a possible procedure:

> Observation → Intuitive analysis → Statement of a proposition → Attaching the intuitive language to the common scientific language, forming measures → Logical analysis and proofs → Empirical testing with respect to relevant reality → Temporary and local acceptance

Thus the statement of a proposition often falls outside the strict scientific work, and that also goes for intra-scientific discoveries. They are often triggered by observations and intuitive thinking outside the measurable and logically consistent standard procedure. But when we are convinced that our intuitive proposition is worth going on with, we have to find a standard scientific form for expressing the proposition. This step might be extremely difficult. In order to communicate science – and that is one of the main tasks – we need to connect our variables and structures to expressible and in some way measurable entities and forms. The central task is thus to work with the scheme outlined in Figure P.3 of the prologue and which is based on Wittgenstein's Proposition 6.211. In the earlier related story by Umberto Eco about the problems of classifying an item, the platypus, within an existing standard of classification, the classification in this case may not affect the scientific study per se but is more getting things properly ordered. In the 18th century, the Swedish botanist Carl von Linné made an enormous work of classifying flowers into groups, subgroups, sub-subgroups and so on, a classification which is still used, although there have been many revisions. This classification is however passive in the sense that it does not reveal any analytical and dynamic relations, at difference for example with Darwin's theory.

The research process thus has two parts: the anticipation of a problem seen in a structural composition, which is mainly governed by earlier experiences and emotional predispositions, and then the translation of the problem into an analytical form possible to handle logically, where the transition from one part to the other is the main difficulty. Earlier, we discussed logical paradoxes where logical consistence breaks down and the only way to discover the proper content of these intriguing figures is to be meticulous with respect to logical consistency and conceptualization.

If we take the greatest genius of all time, Mozart, we hear him adapt to musical norms of his time at the same time as he breaks them. The forms were not a hindrance; he did not really care for them in his creation, but they were practical since they gave him an understandable language. It is interesting to study his Adagio and Fugue in C minor, K. 546, where he makes some efforts to merge the contrapuntal of Bach with his own musical language. It required quite a different musical form with a multitude of dissonant parts, foreboding more the post-romantic music than the romantic era.[7]

The proposition by Wittgenstein, to which we often return, sends us a clear warning that the logical analysis per se is not the important part but the conceptualization and the general design of the analytical basic pre-suppositions or axioms. But this step is sometimes blurred by the unnecessary antagonism between holistic and atomistic analysis. This antagonism has led to some sciences avoiding mathematics *in toto*, while at the same time simple statistical averages are seen as useful information.

In principle, if we look at Keynes' work, he was able to grasp a kind of holistic picture of the aggregate economy using logic and sometimes mathematics, but at the same time he could write his letter to Harrod, which we quoted in the prologue. This gives us a hint that atomism/holism is not a productive categorization. Later macroeconomic research, which is said to develop a sort of Keynesian model, uses models of utmost mathematical complexity, which seems far from the spirit of Keynes in his letter to Harrod.

However, concerning these things I had a discussion with the rather well-known Swedish sociologist Johan Asplund some ten or twelve years ago over a beer in his home town, Lund.[8]

He was extremely pessimistic about the prospects of science in general and social sciences in particular. The general attitude of current research is characterized, he claimed, by two principles: the search for the *Holy Grail* and the *chaff-cutter*.

Science is looking for some magical item/variable/approach/knowledge which solves the entire research problem; the general theory par preference. It is a dream and we can see it through history. Plato created a general approach defining the existence of an eternal truth. Kant refined it and made it more workable. Galileo developed a philosophy of a mechanical world à la Averroes, and Newton believed in showing the eternal beauty of God's creation in its mechanics. Many famous scientists have claimed that their approaches are the final words of understanding. But in the end Aristotle appears, Carnot/Clausius appear, Max Planck appears, Gödel appears, Keynes appears and so on. The Holy Grail is indeed troublesome to find, so maybe we should be satisfied if we could come to some local and temporal results which seem robust.

The *chaff-cutter* is almost a correlate to the search of the Holy Grail. We have to be careful not to miss anything, so we cut the adequate reality which we study into finer and finer parts, hoping that in some of the pieces we can find the *thing* which solves everything. From this perspective, it has been amusing to follow the fight between the string theorists and particle theorists in physics.

The fundamental question underlying the chaff-cutter problematics is the relation between the macroscopic reality of some form and the microscopic realities within that form. A purely holistic approach is not a solution to this problem. What it has to do with is understanding the relations between the microscopic and the macroscopic levels. These are neither completely dependent nor completely independent of each other. We have already discussed this in relation to Propositions 1 and 2 in the prologue, and we have emphasized the importance of structural compositions. Thus one could loosely say that, simplifying to two levels, the microscopic and macroscopic levels mutually define each other. So neither the holistic approach nor the atomistic approach per se solves the problem. In physics, the fight between particle physicists and string physicists seems to have been less accentuated after some evidence of the Higgs boson effect was detected: an item was found which affected the existence and behaviour of other "particles" and which has a mass which is dissipative at a rate due to its (particle) environment. While strings are multidimensional, the Higgs particle induces an element which is dissipative but obviously depending on environmental structure. Whether we use one concept of fixed dimensionality which is affected by and affecting the environmental dimensions or a concept of many and variable dimensions which adapt to and affect the environment and its dimensions seems more a difference in expression than in substance.

Nevertheless, the word *particle* is a bit annoying in physics since different experiments deal with different definitions of particles, so they are generally incommensurable.

Since Democritus, who had a relatively sophisticated approach to atoms, we have been used to seeing atoms as the smallest kind of building material, but this was opposed in different ways by Plato and Aristotle; the latter claimed that the elements were continuous. Without going too much into the history, we can say that the concept of atoms has been corrupted by the metaphysical question of a creator. Newton for example had a very trivial opinion of atoms, causing rather devastating critique from Leibnitz.

A key question is the acceptance of the void, and that is what actually puzzled Aristotle. He rejected the atom hypothesis on the ground that it required the acceptance of void spaces. We have in Chapter 2 discussed the problem of zero and claimed that zero when we discuss structures is not represented by the empty space, $\emptyset$, but by a new structure. The thermodynamic laws help us realize that energy cannot be destroyed but may be of different forms. Thus, burning a house implies heating of the environment which propagates to wider areas and in the end the total universe.

This is as when we are making a car excursion to the sea shore and use a map like in Figure 4.1.

The car map is of course very practical and the information is reduced to the most essential. But it does not tell anything about what kind of nature you will meet on arrival at your destination.

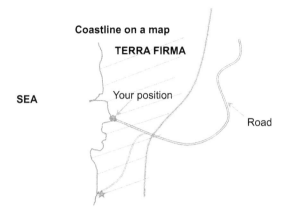

Figure 4.1 A coastline map

Picture 4.2 The beach

It can be like Picture 4.1 or it can be like Picture 4.2.[9] The map gives you no information.

The point is that from the map, you can never create any information about structures omitted from the map if you do not have that information exogenously given. Consequently, starting from a derived point, an atom, a particle or whatever at the microscopic scale can obviously give us information which

Picture 4.3 The non-beach

is of highest importance with respect to structural analysis. Building a bridge requires utmost care in choosing materials, but not knowing the form of the bridge leaves you bewildered with respect to the use of materials.

Thus the belief that we will find the Holy Grail with the chaff-cutter is fundamentally wrong, as is the belief that the Holy Grail can be found in the study of forms without relating it to material facts. It is the interaction between the microscopic and the macroscopic reality which is the crucial thing and which gives meaning to both microscopic and macroscopic studies. The great biologist D'Arcy Thompson, whose work on growth and form is scientifically revolutionary, writes:

> We call a thing *big* or *little* with reference to what it is wont to be, as when we speak of a small elephant or a large rat; and we are apt accordingly to suppose that size makes no other or more essential difference, and that Lilliput and Brobdingnag are all alike, according as we look at them through one end of the glass or the other . . . .
>
> All this is true of *number*, and of *relative magnitude*. The Universe has its endless gamut of great and small, of near and far, of many and few. Nevertheless, in physical science the scale of absolute magnitude becomes a very real and important thing; and a new and deeper interest arises out of the

changing ratio of dimensions when we come to consider the inevitable changes of physical relations with which it is bound up. The effect of *scale* depends not on a thing in itself, but in relation to its whole environment or milieu; it is in conformity with the thing's "place in Nature", its field of action and reaction in the Universe. Everywhere Nature works true to scale, and everything has its proper size accordingly.

(original emphases; Thompson 1992:16–17)

What we are doing in a theoretical model for example is that we postulate the relative scale of size, of importance or whatever we use the model for, but then the model is locked. We can obviously use it if we assume, and prove, local and temporal inertia of the piece of reality we study, but then we have to remind ourselves that appropriate inertia can be created by limiting the environmental effects, and that is only possible at the smallest microscopic level. The more aspects we try to cover by the model, the more aggregated it will be, and subsequently the rise of increased relationships with the environment will surely not be linear but supralinear of some magnitude. This is the basic starting point of the discussion of complexity as a theoretical concept. And when we have reached this far in our thoughts, we start to doubt the very existence of the Holy Grail.

Hume's and Kant's conflicting views

We noted in Chapter 1 the difference between Hume and Kant with respect to the relation between reason and passion. Following our analysis of the Latin expression *"assensus intellectus veritati,"* we need to look at this difference again.

In Chapter 1, where we discussed the difference between Kant and Hume, we did so with respect to a form of universal relation. Kant's a priori intuition preconditions the intellect in relation to almost eternal categories which settle the foundation for the intellectual analysis. Hume on the other hand claims that "the intellect is the humble servant of passion". But our analysis of the Latin expression above suggests that there is a more complex relationship between intellect and passion (in Hume's sense). Let us therefore go back to our concept of *epistemic cycles*.

An epistemic cycle is directed towards some kind of action. We have illustrated it in Figure P.4 and it contains the steps contextual apprehension, perception of means and restrictions which in conjunction with purposes create the conditions for action. The reactions will close the cycle when the purposes are achieved, or we will have a failure. From what we have discussed, we can say that locally and temporally, we have a kind of intuited understanding of categories involved. This is based on both emotional and intellectual experiences, which creates preparedness for the current action. This is probably what we could call an a priori understanding from the point of view of current action; we thus think of a joint emotional and intellectual process creating an experience. It is interesting here to see the difference between individual and collective epistemic cycles. A reasonable hypothesis is that the importance of the intellectual analysis increases in collective decisions since the individual emotional/intellectual experiences become more disparate. However, that is not convincing since historical events, as for example the one Keynes envisages in the end chapter of *The Economic Consequences of the Peace*, where the population is united by emotions created by common experiences. Amartya Sen (2002:76) discusses it with respect to how disparate individual preferences unite in moments of crises. Alexis de Tocqueville in his book *Democracy in America* discusses the principles of American democracy in relation to the free market system and comes to the conclusion that the "median voter", a sort of minimum denominator with respect to different political dimensions, will dominate. Thus the individual structures of preference concerning self may sometimes be correlated to individual structures of preferences concerning the working of the collective bodies. Subsequently the theories of the "median voter" are probably true in some cultures but not true in others. But in the end, when we have a representative democracy or some kind of dictatorship, we must be aware of the fact that there are individuals who interpret the will of the people, and they are subject to Hume's relation of passion and intellect. But when we reach supranational organizations like federal levels, organizations like UN and NATO, the intellectual analysis has a much more important place since compromises must always be based on intellectual considerations.

As of this writing, the Brexit process has reached a critical level, and it is interesting to see Britons complain of the formalism of the EU delegation and its lack of flexibility. However, the British delegation negotiates from a nationalistic perspective where the nationalism forms a rather emotionally united perspective, while the EU delegation negotiates for twenty-seven different countries, some of which have conflicting views in other dimensions; thus there is hardly an emotional "glue" on the EU side while there is one on the British side.

Consequently, when we leave the individual level, the emotional impact becomes less important the higher the aggregate level. If we go back to times of Kant and Hume, the influence of aggregate bodies was great when it concerned war and peace, much greater then today, when the democratic influence works in favour of peace. On the other hand, in other aspects the aggregate influence is much more differentiated and widespread today. Thus in the meeting between the individual and the collective bodies, there is an asymmetry in relation to emotional load, knowledge of rules, intellectual understanding and so on, which varies most between individuals and has a tendency to create alienation. This also affects elections and referendums in an unforeseeable way since the collective organizations are expected to handle relevant affairs according to equality among the citizens and types of affairs according to rules, thus rather independent of emotional aspects, which vary between individuals. The individuals, however, look at the collective affairs from a rather narrow perspective and might be affected by education and information. Thus, the Aristotelian discrepancy between the good and bad arts of ruling, when it comes to ruling of the many, the good – *politeia* and the bad – democracy, deals exactly with the intellectual aspect of the consequences of the individual decision in a social frame. We come back again to the fact that the individual is a final cause, and from an emotional point of view that means that *the Other*, except for the nearest circle of family and friends, is next to an object. Thus the socialization process is at the same time an intellectualization process.

If we look at this in view of election campaigns, we can see the implicit fight between the use of emotions and the use of intellect. We can also see the implicit fight between confrontation and unification. It seems that an intellectual approach needs to be underpinned by emotional arguments in order to be successful; to use emotional arguments to those who are unable or have no interest in the intellectual arguments is indeed risky.

Thus when we come to the individual role in the creation of aggregate decisions, we have a rather complex interplay between passion and reason. At the aggregate level, reason must rule since we must balance between different emotional standpoints. However, the individual tends to judge the aggregate decisions from an individual point of view where immediate emotion often rules the intellect. So, we have a rather intricate relation between Kant's and Hume's view in the problem of going from a bad form of ruling the many to a good form.

Kant actually addressed this problem in a famous article from 1784, with the title "*Beantworten der Frage: Was ist Aufklärung?*" This gives rise to some interesting questions which are central to the link between individual and collective ethics.

"*Beantworten der Frage: Was ist Aufklärung?*"[10]

In *Berlinische Monatsschrift* in September 1784, there appeared a text by Immanuel Kant with the above title. It is somewhat remarkable for two reasons. First, it is at least partly at variance with Kant's more deterministic appearance in "*Kritik der reinen Vernunft*", and second, it is in the line with the freedom principles of the forthcoming French revolution.

Thus Kant discusses the word *Aufklärung* which is a name for the cultural/ philosophical period which we call the *Age of Enlightenment*. So Kant answers the question "What is Enlightenment?" and the beginning of the text is magnificent. There are several English translations, but we use the one Columbia University provides.[11]

> Enlightenment is man's emergence from his self-imposed nonage. Nonage is the inability to use one's own understanding without another's guidance. This nonage is self-imposed if its cause lies not in lack of understanding but in indecision and lack of courage to use one's own mind without another's guidance. *Dare to know!* (*Sapere aude.*) "Have the courage to use your own understanding," is therefore the motto of the enlightenment.
>
> Laziness and cowardice are the reasons why such a large part of mankind gladly remain minors all their lives, long after nature has freed them from external guidance. They are the reasons why it is so easy for others to set themselves up as guardians. It is so comfortable to be a minor.

Kant's text has a twofold purpose: on one hand he discusses the individual ability to act as a mature/responsible citizen and on the other hand a society where individuals are to be seen as mature/responsible. It is constructive to relate Kant's text to Aristotle on one hand and Machiavelli on the other with respect to purpose and conclusions.

Thus the second aspect in Kant's paper is in line with Aristotle's distinction between good governance and bad governance and the necessary conditions for good governance which is beneficial to the whole society, to individuals as well as the collective.

The three forms Monarchy, Aristocracy, and Politeia are the good forms which are beneficial to the collective as well as the individuals in the society. The three forms Tyranny, Plutocracy and Democracy are the bad forms of governance where the rulers only serve their own interests, whether groups or individuals. We will discuss these forms more extensively in the next chapter.

We may also relate to Machiavelli, particularly his book *Discourses on the First Ten Books of Titus Livius*, where he discusses the efficiency of governance with respect to the contextual conditions. When he discusses *The Prince*, he does not follow the same line of thinking as Aristotle but concentrates on the question of how the prince should stay in power, which is obviously is a different question, although he arrives at partly similar conclusions as in the *Discourses*. In the *Discourses* he has the republic as the basic form of governance, but he also deals with the question of efficiency of governance when the contextual conditions are difficult, such as wartime or social unease. Then there could be a need for limiting the power to a few, but only within limitations of time and limitation of issues.

The varying conditions of governance are also noted by Amartya Sen (2002:76), indicating that governance and the conditions for governance change with respect to exogenous pressure, such as warfare, famine and natural catastrophes, which is in line with Machiavelli. But Sen also discusses the efficiency of the principles of market exchange, noting that under normal conditions, the preferences of individuals are very dispersed, making both economic and political aggregation difficult, while in crises they narrow:

> When distributional issues dominate and when people seek to maximize their own "shares" without concern for others (as, for example, in a "cake division" problem, with each preferring any division that increases her own share, no matter what happens to the others), then majority rule will tend to be thoroughly inconsistent. But when there is a matter of national outrage (for example, in response to the inability of a democratic government to prevent a famine), the electorate may be reasonably univocal and thoroughly consistent.

At variance with Aristotle and Machiavelli, Kant does not start his analysis from the aggregate forms of governance but from the individual. We have in the prologue stated a proposition implying that there are no automatic logical links between macroscopic social behaviour and microscopic social behaviour.

We realize that there are close links between these two levels, but these links are not built on some axioms, and the aggregation of individual behaviour cannot be expressed in simple additive forms.

It is exactly here that Kant's paper on *Aufklärung* enters.

The underlying problem is the *control of the controller* or *the governance of the government* or similar expressions of this principle. Thus Kant's text takes the stance in the very fact that humans are subjects, and as such final causes, in Aristotle's terms. Humans are subjects, but human organizations are not. That means that irrespective of which kind of organization of governance we have, the ultimate control lies in the hand of a group of individuals who are representatives of the collective. But a correlate of this is that the people populating the governing organization are of the same kind as those who are governed. Thus the collective needs to control those who are in control, but as we discussed before, laws, ethical principles and contracts are not the actors. They can point out the direction of an action, but the decision to act is an individual decision.

Kant's text is particularly exiting since it appeared some years before the French revolution.

Kant thus discusses self-imposed *Immaturity* [*Unmündigkeit*], as when the individual refrains from taking necessary responsibility for the public sphere and just obeys and follows, and from cowardice or laziness consents to submit to others' judgement without reflection.

To take the full step into *Maturity* [*Mündigkeit*] might be costly and even dangerous. It has little to do with individual intellectual/cultural/physical abilities but with moral courage.

For the individual to enter the state of full personal maturity it is, as Foucault states it, a conscious courageous act to use his/her *Understanding* [*Verstand*] independently not only for the strictly private sphere but for the public sphere.

Kant mentions an example of a public servant who has to perform his duties, but then reflects over the duties and their structures and is prepared to tell the chiefs about inconsistencies and malpractices. We talk today of something we call whistle-blowers, but that is not what Kant means. He means natural everyday critical reflection of one's duties and decisions and a preparedness to communicate anomalies to superiors. The whistle-blower comes in when things have gone too far.

After having discussed the individual aspects of coming out of the strictly private sphere, being mature enough to take a responsible place in the public sphere and analyzing [*räsonniert*] contextual problems on different aggregate levels, independently and due to the individuals' intellectual capacity and understanding, Kant says further down in the paper:

> Thus a public can only attain enlightenment slowly. Perhaps a revolution can overthrow autocratic despotism and profiteering or power-grabbing oppression, but it can never truly reform a manner of thinking; instead, new

prejudices, just like the old ones they replace, will serve as a leash for the great unthinking mass.

Nothing is required for this enlightenment, however, except freedom; and the freedom in question is the least harmful of all, namely, the freedom to use reason publicly in all matters. But on all sides I hear: "Do not argue!" . . . I reply: The public use of one's reason must always be free, and it alone can bring about enlightenment among mankind; the private use of reason may, however, often be very narrowly restricted, without otherwise hindering the progress of enlightenment. By the public use of one's own reason I understand the use that anyone as a scholar makes of reason before the entire literate world. I call the private use of reason that which a person may make in a civic post or office that has been entrusted to him.

Thus Kant envisages that the only way to have a good society, irrespective of the governance principle, is through individual maturity and courage. His concrete discussions in the paper vis-à-vis his own time concerns religious freedom but also the possibility of freedom from religion. In the last section of his paper, however, he enters the deepest core of his argument:

But only a ruler who is himself enlightened and has no dread of shadows, yet who likewise has a well-disciplined, numerous army to guarantee public peace, can say what no republic may dare, namely: "Argue as much as you want and about what you want, but obey!" Here as elsewhere, when things are considered in broad perspective, a strange, unexpected pattern in human affairs reveals itself, one in which almost everything is paradoxical. A greater degree of civil freedom seems advantageous to a people's spiritual freedom; yet the former established impassable boundaries for the latter; conversely, a lesser degree of civil freedom provides enough room for all fully to expand their abilities. Thus, once nature has removed the hard shell from this kernel for which she has most fondly cared, namely, the inclination to and vocation for free thinking, the kernel gradually reacts on a people's mentality (whereby they become increasingly able to act freely), and it finally even influences the principles of government, which finds that it can profit by treating men, who are now more than machines, in accord with their dignity.

We have two pictures: the myth from Chapter 1 and, here, Kant's text on enlightenment implies that an aggregate ethics is wholly due to a discontinuous/metaphysical step by the individuals populating the collective. If so, our next two questions must be: (1) whether there is a way in which a development towards such a step can be created in a physical sense; that is, conscious measures taken by the collective and/or the individuals; (2) whether and where to find the obstacles against such a development. In the last quote we find the deepest problem: "Argue as much as you want and about what you want, but obey!" This is however not only a problem of the enlightened king but also a trap of the liberal society.

Herbert Marcuse addresses this problem in *A Critique of Pure Tolerance*, where he claims that if the liberal society evolves into an oppression of minorities of the type Kant formulates, this will in the end corrupt the liberal society into some kind of the dictatorship of the "silent majority", whatever that can be and who interprets its will, where uncomfortable opinions are allowed but must never have any effects of the governance. As we mentioned earlier, this thought is present in Alexis de Tocqueville's *Democracy in America*, where he claims the liberal society based on the market principle will evolve into the hegemony of the mediocracy.

Marcuse means that the revolutionary minority should be obliged to re-educate the silent majority. Thus in Kant's terms, the people who have taken the step into maturity must re-educate the others. Tocqueville has no such ideas but sees as an inevitable development of the reign of the mediocracy.

"Thou shalt . . ." versus "Thou shalt not . . ."

Ethical principles start with either "Thou shalt . . ." or "Thou shalt not . . .". Moses' commands contain two distinct "Thou shalt . . ." commands: "Remember the Sabbath day, to keep it holy" and "Honour thy father and thy mother". The rest belongs to the type "Thou shalt not . . .": "Thou shalt have no other gods before me", "Thou shalt not kill" and so on.

When we compare these two constructions, we see immediately that "Thou shalt not . . ." is precisely defined while "Thou shalt . . ." is much more diffuse with what we are expected and not expected to do. The so-called Golden Rule, which Christ tells, appeared early in many religions. Confucius in China is interesting since he formulates both the negative and the positive variant:[12]

> Positive: One should treat others as one would like others to treat oneself
> Negative: One should not treat others in ways that one would not like to
>   be treated.

As we see, the negative variant is of a given dimensionality limited to the realm where we can say no to a certain action, but it does not exclude indifference or passiveness. The positive variant is unlimited with respect to dimensions since it also may involve unknown dimensions and thus could imply a social dynamics, particularly if we look at human beings as socially responsive. Thus the negative variant is suitable for a law, and consequently Kant's categorical imperative will fit under this principle.

The positive variant sort under the Chinese concept "*ren*", which has the meaning of benevolence, perfect virtue, human heart and similar. Confucius discusses also this with respect to the behaviour of the ruler. He then comes close to Aristotle and his classification of good and bad rulers: if the ruler lacks "*ren*", it is difficult not to say impossible for the people to behave humanely.

This means that expressions of the negative type, "Thou shalt not . . .", identify precise actions and not dimensions of actions. A precise action, to kill, is as it stands a universal statement, but does not tell about respect for other people's living conditions. Thus bad salary and bad working conditions might shorten a person's life, although no one has actually killed the person. "You shall not steal" is also rather precise, but it does not imply "Care about others' belongings", nor does it rule out "Do not care about others' belongings".

The positive variant is much more difficult to define for two main reasons: on one hand, a positive action can take place in many forms which are normally affected by the contextual situation, and furthermore there has to be an interaction between the "acting" and "receiving" part. Thus in a sentence like "You shall not steal", given reasonable common definitions, the non–action can be defined irrespective of the context and it also concerns only the potentially acting part. A positive form like "You shall be generous" requires social interaction and common understanding of the context in order to be effective.

The Kantian imperative is thus very interesting in this perspective: that we shall act in such a way that our behaviour can be promoted to a common law. If we as Kant suggests have an a priori definition of good behaviour, the imperative does not need any social interaction to adapt to.

Look at the sentence "Be generous to others". It is virtually impossible to have an estimation of the dimensionality: physical and/or psychological support vis-à-vis a specific context, active spiritual support in endeavours, being a good listener and so forth. Thus we have the question of what and who *generosity* shall be related to, the "actor" or the "receiver" of generosity. It cannot, I think, be seen as an act of generosity for Sweden to send five obsolete snowploughs to Zaire, apart from the scrap value. Furthermore, the contextual situation must be defined in conjunction between the "actor" and the "receiver".

Consequently, the negative form of the command above is much more simple and narrowly defined than the positive, which implies active socialization with a theoretically undetermined outcome. Furthermore, while the negative form of the command above normally does not make any structural changes, the positive form will most probably imply that. Consequently, looking at humans as creatures which are socially responsive, the positive form has a meaning.

Utopias: dictatorship and/or evolution

Historically there has been produced a multitude of utopias. We started with the Prophecy of Voluspo. The producers of such prophecies of utopia have not necessarily meant it as something to believe in but have used it for illustrating moral principles. We have basically two principles of utopia: one is the lost Eden, a kind of myth which we used in the beginning of Chapter 1, and the other principle is how we create New Heavens and a New World. The Prophecy of the Voluspo may be an example.

But what is a bit funny and which has had philosophical significance is that we are able to imagine a kind of world that includes justice, moderation, social responsibility and similar virtues. Aristotle, Confucius, Jesus Christ, Mohammed, and to some extent also Buddha emphasized similar virtues for a good life both individually as well as parts of a good society. On the other hand, we have the deadly sins which are similar for most religions and cultures.

Of course there are exceptions, but generally speaking, most cultures and religions, at least with respect to internal affairs, seem to be quite content with a moderate, tolerant and responsible way of living if we read the annals.

But there are radicalized views based on some beliefs that we have from the birth a kind of picture of the perfect world and we strive for that. One of the most radical ones is the Gnostic idea that there was a fight in heaven and the devil was thrown out and had to build his kingdom on Earth. One possible logical consequence of such a belief, which is also practiced among some groups/sects mostly in the USA but also in Europe, is that if you have the right faith, usually some sort of "Christian" faith, you do not need to care about this world whatsoever. You have no moral obligations, since this world is the home of the devil.[13]

However, we also have utopias based on a belief of a balanced world, in some or all aspects. There are mainly four such utopias which are interesting. One is the liberal market theory with its axiomatic formulation in the neoclassical approach. The Marxist (Hegelian) theory of a historical evolution through attaining contradictory extremes finally comes to rest in a classless society where all individual capacities are met but the distribution of needs is based on necessities which are objective and accepted by all. We have in the prologue mentioned that the final communist state and the final general equilibrium of the neoclassical theory are practically equivalent. The latter however is unable to explain the evolution of the initial endowment into some commonly accepted distribution.

If we look at Jesus Christ, he seems a bit difficult to categorize. In the Gospel of St. Matthew, chapter 20, he approaches a Marxian state where all have the same salary irrespective of how long you worked during the day. On the other hand, in the Gospel of St. Luke, chapter 19, he tells the story about the three servants who got ten, five and two pounds respectively to manage. The first two succeeded in enlarging the sum while the third because of fear hid the resources. The two loyal servants received the same appreciation while the third one, who had got the smallest resources but hid it, was rejected. Do your duty irrespective of your ability and assets.

The two stories most probably deal with different aspects of life, but still they seem intriguingly contradictory.

It is interesting to see that under most utopian thinking, there is an assumption that humans accept each other as equals and with respect to the society fulfil the sentiments. Aristotle advocates that it is necessary to obtain the perfect state, when it comes to the ruling of the many, *politeia*.

The great Jesuit priest Pierre Teilhard de Chardin, who was a great palaeontologist, developed a vision from the very birth of life on earth in his book *The Human Phenomenon*, which is a sort of mixture between the Marxian/Hegelian historical development and a developed Darwinism, including biological mutations and discontinuous jumps. However, he combines this with a spiritual development including mutations and jumps with respect to ideas and abilities of apprehending the world. His vision implies that we have now come to a stage in the development of the human brain that we are able to rise above the narrow individual perspective and understand the social aspects of our own lives; such a development is asymmetric with respect to individuals, but when there is a certain "critical mass" of individuals, we will have a new framework for thinking and analyzing the world.

The utopia of Teilhard de Chardin seems to be implicit in Aristotle's *politeia*, but it is also some form of aggregate dynamics of Kant's paper on enlightenment which we earlier discussed.

What perhaps is interesting is that the neoclassical theory is rather unique in the sense that it dismisses the possibility that individuals care about aggregate levels, but this led to Arrow's paradox.

Another form of utopia where the end solution is the same as for Teilhard de Chardin is *The City of the Sun* by Tommaso Campanella. He does not envisage a clear way to obtain the utopia other than Christian behaviour. The utopic organization is a city where all have their decided places in society. Ruling the city is not superior to being a farmer or a craftsman, and all share the production result in relation to necessary and objective needs. The utopia of Campanella seems a bit static, so therefore it is a bit of a surprise when he in his defence of Galileo Galilei stresses the necessity of freedom of speech and development.

If we look at other traditions than the Christian, where I also see Islam and Judaism belonging to the same complex of faiths, we have Hinduism and Buddhism. They advocate the achievement of a balanced mind, which means non-evilness but at the same time passiveness; however, it is better to be good than evil, since the ultimate balance is when mind and body are in conjunction with the development of the universe.

The Chinese have two main and well-known approaches; the teaching of Confucius and that of Lao Tsu/Lao Zi. The latter's teaching is similar to the teaching of Buddha, while Confucius is a bit more interesting for Europeans since he is prior to Aristotle (551–479) and is rather similar to him both with respect to ethics in general and also with respect to the relation between the individual and aggregate level(s). As we mentioned above, he formulated the Golden Rule long before Christ. The society he envisages is a balanced society, like that of Campanella, although being an aristocrat he has more of a classless structure. However, for him the true aristocrat is more a philosopher, an observer of reality and someone who advocates temperance and modera-tion, so I would say that he comes close to the City of the Sun.

The revolutionary tendencies we seldom meet in utopias; they are more descriptions of the perfect society either as states or as an end result of an evo-lutionary process. We have however Hobbes' Leviathan and the Marxian class struggle. Hobbes' revolution comes however out of a contract; the beasts of Leviathan are prepared to make a contract with a sort of dictator to sort out the mess. But if such a consciousness exists, why cannot we negotiate other forms of ruling than dictatorship? Furthermore, if the dictator is recruited from the ordinary beasts, I can see little hope of any improvement. Hobbes may have read Aristotle, but perhaps not the *Politics* too closely.

The Marxian class struggle, a revolutionary cleansing of the table, is indeed hard to understand since they start with a Hegelian deterministic historical process and then suddenly the individuals must start helping the mighty universal deterministic process; being aware of their class belongings, they start a revolution. Is the knowledge of this necessity and time of start also deterministic, or is it an act of free will aggregated to a collective will? If the latter, the optimal timing of the two processes is clearly a problem.

The so-called contract theory in economics, including the principal agent problematics, are certainly an advancement at the microscopic level, where the negotiating agents and eventual principals are facing a well-defined environment and are trying to optimize goal functions. However, as a macroeconomic tool it requires full information not only of objectively observed structures but also of possible apprehended structures; that is, analysis of possibly involved differences in epistemic cycles. The theory is an effort to obtain a kind of structure which overcomes Arrow's paradox and traces some paths of analysis back to Arrow's paper from 1963 on "Uncertainty and the Welfare Economics of Medical Care". There he outlines some problems of individual behaviour with respect to publicly provided utilities. The contract theory often suggests privatization to cope with some of the problems Arrow discusses. Experiences, however, shows that privatization as such has other problems, which suggests that the optimization principle and the principle agent approach works within limitations for some areas, but sometimes the strong asymmetric incitement structures on the producer side vis-à-vis the consumer side lead to problematic consequences. We will not go into this further since that takes us into technicalities which are outside our scope, although there are very clear ethical but also ideological connotations. The important thing however is that the contract theory and the principal agent theory are based on the neoclassical axiomatic structures where experienced problems of the reality are dealt with by inducing more implicit as well as explicit postulates for the aggregate working of the theories.

In general, utopias, irrespective of the current structure, envisage a kind of ideal state like the New Jerusalem without presenting any form of dynamic process for how to reach there. As we have seen, the establishment of "what is" is indeed problematic, and to claim a utopia without any links to possible current structures is a bit esoteric

Utopias, however, although not a creation of political realism, may have a much more important role and a much more fantastic/dangerous role. They are dreams which may create life, hope, faith, action, cooperation. Utopias or dreams can be fought only at the price of destroying life and creating desperation, but they may on the other hand prepare the individual to sacrifice and take lives.

Our society today seems to lack knowledge of the utopias and their role. We think we are rational when we stick to theories of rational man beyond any relation to practical life.

Arrow's paradox once again

Our interpretation of Arrow's paradox concerns the neoclassical axiomatic structure when one changes atomistic agents and commodities to complexities. The paradox itself has no bearing on reality but is a meta-axiomatic analysis.

This means that results for complexities gained by assuming atomic variables are only acceptable when precise definitions and limitations are presented, as in physical experimental designs. If this is not done, the analysis becomes ideological and/or metaphysical and is thus irrelevant from a scientific point of view. This is an ethical condition with respect to science. Speculations and ad hoc models are certainly of vital help in forming possible propositions, but to claim that the theory/modelling may have relevance even as a picture of the reality is a step which in social research is almost always inadequate.

This is the deepest meaning in the 1938 letter from Keynes to Harrod we quoted.

Arrow's paradox per se, however, tells little about the degree of complexity when we allow agents to negotiate, being aware, affected by and eventually interfering with the aggregate levels. The Kant/Hume discussion reveals that we deal with complicated emotional and intellectual structures; ethical aspects are sometimes difficult to understand due to the complex interrelations between agents as individuals, agents as group/class members and agents with respect to repercussions of collective measures and/or events.

Basically, Arrow's Impossibility Theorem suggests that no general theory exists and that solutions of problems are only local and temporal with varying inertia.

The expression "*assensus intellectus veritati*" has a clear significance if interpreted as saying that if a faith/belief/emotional standpoint is verified by the intellectual analysis of its empirical relevance and possible consequences, it can be regarded as true. Thus we find here a way of the intellect moulding the passions which seems important, though Aristotle and particularly Hume as well as modern brain research indicate that the emotions/passions are the key factor in human decisions.

From an ethical point of view, we repeat our quote in Chapter 1 from Aristotle:

> It is clear, then, from what has been said, that it is not possible to be good in the strict sense without practical wisdom, nor practically wise without moral virtue.

Notes

1 THE POETIC EDDA; Volume I: Lays of the Gods: VOLUSPO: *The Wise-Woman's Prophecy* Translated by Henry Addams Bellows 1936, www.sacred-texts.com/neu/poe/ The enumeration refers to Codex Regis, the "Royal Parchment Manuscript", from the 13th century. It was written before Snorre Sturlasson wrote his prose version, which nowadays is called Snorre's Edda or the Prose Edda. Voluspo is the prophecy of the final war, Ragnarök, between the Gods and the evil Giants where the world reaches its end. But after that, there appears a new world. As we understand, there are strong links to the myth of

Armageddon in St. John's Revelation. I have enumerated the verses differently than in the internet version by Henry Addam Bellows from 1936. The order is a bit different and according to more recent research. Those verses which are left out are doubtful; the text is in some cases defective, in other cases probably misplaced or generally doubtful with respect to origin. To help me, I have used a modern Swedish edition interpreted by Professor Emeritus Lars Lönnroth, who bases his interpretation on research at the University of Frankfurt which has been ongoing since 1997: *Kommentar zu den Liedern der Edda*. It is currently published by Universitätsverlag Winter in Heidelberg by Beatrice La Farge, Klaus von See and others.

2 The English translation is taken from www.anomy.net/havamal/ *Hávamál* means *The Words of Odin* and is from the Elder or Poetic Edda. There are many translations, but I have chosen the W.H. Auden and P.B. Taylor translation, as it is to my opinion closest to the original Icelandic text.

3 Faith is the intellect's acceptance of the truth.

4 One may think of *Ave Verum Corpus*, which Mozart is said to have composed in the office of his music editor as a repayment of a loan; it took him one hour.

5 www.neuroscience.cam.ac.uk/research/cameos/GeneticBrain.php

6 Bergson, Henri, (1912). *Tiden och den fria viljan* [Time and the Free Will], Wahlström and Widstrand, Stockholm.
Tarski, Alfred, (1983[1955]). *Logic, Sematic, Metamathematics*, Hackett Publishing Company, Indianapolis.

7 Mozart was a keen student of Bach, and in April 1789 he visited Leipzig for three days and took the opportunity to copy choir music in particular.

8 Johan Asplund was born in Jakobstad, Finland, in 1937. Unfortunately he did not write in English but Swedish and German. He mainly analyzed the urban society, and there is a compilation in Grönlund, Bo, (2002). *New Urban Theory: Developed by 'Non-Architects'*, Kunstakademiets Arkitektskole, Copenhagen. Asplund is in many ways remarkable. He is affected by the German sociologist Ferdinand Tönnies, and he basically deepened the Aristotelian attitude of humans as social creatures. He claimed that humans generally, except in pathological cases, were *socially responsive* (Asplund 1991). This is clearly a development since he then brings in an active element in the more passive concept of the human as a social being. I may tell that we had a thorough discussion on the concepts of epistemic cycles which fit into to the concept of social responsiveness since it focuses on action and is thus a theory of observables. His most famous book is *Det Sociala Livets Elementära Former* [*The Elementary Forms of Social Life*]. Personally I find his first book *Mättnadsprocesser* [*The Processes of Saturation*] (1967) and *Storstäderna och det Forteanska Livet* [*The Metropolis and the Fortean Life*] the most interesting from an economic point of view, since he analyzes social processes which directly affect socio-economic behavior and thus affects the market process. The concept *Fortean* is after the American author Charles Hoy Fort. It deals with the necessity of the individual to be seen by others, to be defined by the outside world and to be remembered after death, so here we have the link to the quoted poems of Hávamál. There has been a lot of metaphysical ideas with respect to the concept, but Asplund treats it in relation to the ability to receive *social responses*. The current phenomenon of individuals who expose the most private parts of soul and body in public can be analyzed within the realm of the Fortean concept. We will come back to this in chapter 5.

9 Photos: Barbro Ekstedt: Fécant in France and Palafrugel in Spain, respectively.

10 Our discussion of the paper is affected by Foucault's lectures at College de France, January 1983, which was published in Swedish in 2015.

11 Kant, Immanuel, (1784). *What Is Enlightenment?* [*Beantworten der Frage: Was ist Aufklärung?*], Columbia University, New York, available at internet www.columbia.edu/acis/ets/CCREAD/etscc/kant.html

12 Shankar, Padma, (2013). *Recalling Confucianism for Sustainable Development*, available at internet www.slideshare.net/drpadmashankar/confucius-kung-fu-tzu

13 Gnosticism is ruled out in the Catholic Church and most Protestant churches in the Apostles' Creed when saying "I believe in God the Father Almighty, maker of heaven and earth", which rules out that anything in Creation can be evil per se.

Bibliography

Asplund, J., (1967). *Mättnadsprocesser* (Saturation Processes), Argos Förlag AB, Uppsala.

Asplund, J., (1991). *Essä om Gemeinschaft och Gesellschaft*, Bokförlaget Korpen, Gothenburg.

Bergson, H., (1912). *Tiden och den fria viljan* (Time and the Free Will), Wahlström and Widstrand, Stockholm.

Brody, T. (1994). *The Philosophy Behind Physics*, Springer Verlag, Heidelberg and Berlin.

Damasio, A., (2004). *Looking for Spinoza: Joy, Sorrow and the Feeling Brain*, Vintage, London.

Einstein, A., (1964[1945]). *Mozart: Människan och verket*, Bokförlaget Aldus/Bonniers, Stockholm.

Engström, A., (1965[1901]). *En Bok*, Albert Bonniers Förlag, Stockholm.

Foucault, M., (1983). *Styrandet av sig själv och andra* (Le Gouvernement de soi et des autres) Lectures at Collège de France, Paris, 1982–1983. Here Lecture 5 January 1983 is used.

Hildesheimer, W., (1980[1977]). *Mozart*, P.A. Norstedt & Söners Förlag, Stockholm.

Hobbes, T., (1985[1651]). *Leviathan*, Penguin Books, London.

Hume, D.A., (2002[1740]). *A Treatise of Human Nature*, Oxford University Press, Oxford.

Kant, I., (1784). *What Is Enlightenment* (Beantworten der Frage: Was ist Aufklärung), English translation available at internet www.artofthetheory.com/what-is-enlightenment_immanuel-kant/

Koestler, A., (1970). *The Act of Creation*, Richard Clay Ltd, Bungay, Suffolk.

Machiavelli, N., (1983[circa 1524]). *The Discourses*, Penguin Books, London.

Reichenbach, H., (1938). *Experience and Prediction*, University of Chicago Press, Chicago.

Sen, A., (2002). *Rationality and Freedom*, The Belknap Press, Cambridge, MA, and London.

Tarski, A., (1983[1955]). *Logic, Semantic, Metamathematics*, Hackett Publishing Company, Indianapolis.

Thompson, D.W., (1992[1942]). *On Growth and Form*, Cambridge University Press, Cambridge.

5 Collective ethics and forms of government/governance

Retirement of Diocletian at Salona, as told by Edward Gibbon[1]

Diocletian, who, from a servile origin, had raised himself to the throne, passed the nine last years of his life in a private condition. Reason had dictated, and content seems to have accompanied, his retreat, in which he enjoyed for a long time the respect of those princes to whom he had resigned the possession of the world. It is seldom that minds, long exercised in business, have formed any habits of conversing with themselves, and in the loss of power they principally regret the want of occupation. The amusements of letters and of devotion, which afford to many resources in solitude, were incapable of fixing the attention of Diocletian; but he had preserved, or at least he soon recovered, a taste for the most innocent as well as natural pleasures, and his leisure hours were sufficiently employed in building, planting, and gardening. His answer to Maximian is deservedly celebrated. He was solicited by that restless old man to reassume the reins of government, and the Imperial purple. He rejected the temptation with a smile of pity, calmly observing, that if he could shew Maximian the cabbages which he had planted with his own hands at Salona, he should no longer be urged to relinquish the enjoyment of happiness for the pursuit of power.

In his conversations with his friends, he frequently acknowledged, that of all arts, the most difficult was the art of reigning; and expressed himself on that favourite topic with a degree of warmth which could be the result only of experience. "How often, was he accustomed to say, is it the interest of four or five ministers to combine together to deceive their sovereign! Secluded from mankind by his exalted dignity, the truth is concealed from his knowledge; he can see only with their eyes, he hears nothing but their misrepresentations. He confers the most important offices upon vice and weakness and disgraces the most virtuous and deserving among his subjects. But such infamous arts, added Diocletian, the best and wisest princes are sold to the venal corruption of their courtiers."

A just estimate of greatness, and the assurance of immortal fame, improve our relish for the pleasures of retirement; but the Roman emperor had filled too important a character in the world, to enjoy without allay the comforts and security of a private condition. It was impossible that he could remain ignorant of the troubles which afflicted the empire after his abdication.

Few persons of power have expressed the difference between self in power and self in private conditions as Diocletian, the great emperor (244–312 AD) who made a fundamental organizational and administrative restructuring of the whole Roman Empire. Although some of his work vanished almost immediately after his abdication, much of it is still at the bottom of the organizational and administrative framework of Western Europe.

The quote from Gibbon on Diocletian's retirement makes the difference between individual and collective ethics plain, but it is in a form that we seldom understand. Diocletian, who is said to have ended the classical Rome, was also a Grand Caesar of the stature like Augustus, Vespasianus and Marcus Aurelius, and as such was worthy of being declared god-like. Despite this, he admits his very human difficulties to govern a state, as any modern president or prime minister might do in our times.

Collective ethics concerns a vast number of individuals and groups with different goals and different means and, at difference with the neoclassical axiomatic structure, which are well aware of the fact that collective decisions indeed concern themselves as individuals and as members of different groups. Furthermore, they all want to affect the aggregate level to their advantage.

Since the Emperor, the Government, the Parliament and the People consist of persons, human beings of flesh and blood, the governance of the collective body, the State, is invented, decided and implemented by people who have different epistemic cycles, both intrinsically in relation to different dimensions of the governance and obviously vis-à-vis others. There are certainly traditions and historical experiences which may guide the persons in power, and there are rules defining the frames of governance. But history can be obscured by differences in interpretations and even in some cases by plain rejection of verified experiences, as for example the Nazi-organized Holocaust. There are also some leaders today who simply refuse to accept commonly realized but uncomfortable facts, sometimes by referring to "fake news". But most of all, as Diocletian points out, the governing body needs to be informed, and where does the information come from? Those surrounding the emperor have their own agendas and may mould their information according to that.

Diocletian was interesting in that he understood both the role of Rome as an empire and the particulars of its structure in different dimensions, and he also understood the very key problem of governance, which we are still struggling with.

His reformation of its organization and its bureaucracy was based on an understanding of the different conditions and needs of various parts of the empire and also an effort to make the empire sustainable even after his death. His reforms were, as far as I can understand, one of the earliest efforts to implement a conscious decentralization of decisions and implementation, a sort of subsidiary principle. He thus divided Rome into four parts, where two parts were governed by two Prime Caesars and two were governed by Junior Caesars, who were each subordinate to a Prime Caesar. The macroscopic reorganization failed immediately after Diocletian's resignation; nevertheless, his bureaucratic inventions were more viable and we see parts of them even today in Western European bureaucracy.

It was on one hand a very interesting experiment, and on the other it was remarkable since Diocletian was a true autocrat and would easily have pursued the line of European kings in the 17th and 18th centuries of being "King by the Providence of God", or as was the case in Rome, that the emperor became a god. Diocletian was of simple birth and had reached the ultimate power by hard and sometimes harsh efforts, and unlike other rulers, he never forgot that he was human. He also realized that the human mind is often corruptible by pompousness, ceremonies, spiritual rituals and the naked power of violence. Perhaps that's why he was not murdered but resigned when he was exhausted by the reality and boredom of governance.

The opening quote from Gibbon shows a man of great analytical ability and down-to-earth sense and reason.

Collective and private conceptualization and interpretation

In the prologue, we ended up in Propositions 1 and 2 stating that for a barter economy, there were no simple additive links between the individual and the collective levels, and furthermore that the introduction of money implied that individual cost-minimizing optima given any budget could be aggregated to a sort of society optimum with no bearing on the individuals and the actual collective welfare. Such an optimum is just an accounting result irrespective of distributional and allocation considerations. Consequently, the main logical links between the individual and collective levels are due to socio-economic, cultural and political matters.

However Proposition 1 also tells us that any decision of the collective body will, most probably, affect the individuals in an asymmetric way and will furthermore be imposed like an exogenous event. Some individuals will be able to take measures with respect to an expected collective decision, while some will not. Since the effects are asymmetric, the secondary effects will often concern structural changes for individuals and groups which are hard (not to say impossible) to calculate without deep-going knowledge of the structural composition. Generally speaking, the more general a collective measure is, the more accentuated the structural effects will become.

If we take for example the privatization discussion, the main reason for privatization is to increase efficiency, it is said. In earlier discussions, it is shown that if we reject the Axiom of Reflexivity and thus also additive aggregation, we end up in a situation where the collective bodies may have quite different goals. Furthermore, we have shown that the two kinds of efficiency concepts, internal efficiency of an organization and allocative efficiency of a society, should be solved by a kind of market economy, and these two efficiency concepts should become commensurable and possible to aggregate additively. It is thus necessary that the neoclassical structure holds in reality.

Consequently, when we reject the empirical relevance of the neoclassical axiomatic structure, we also break the logical link between so-called X-efficiency and the allocative efficiency of the society. Subsequently, privatization, implying a shift from public production to private production, implies most probably a difference in the ultimate goals of the organization in question. It also implies that financial surplus is not related to the ultimate goals of the aggregate level, and this implies that we must find other measures of X-efficiency than the productivity measures based on money values. The so-called Baumol's cost disease, when public service rises in costs due to the lack of technical evolution, is an interesting example of cost increases due to technical advancements.

If we think of a piano concerto by Mozart, the time of playing it is longer now than it was during Mozart's days due to the richer sound of modern pianos. Mozart himself was much involved in trying to improve the sound of the current pianoforte, so he would probably not mind the development. If then the payment to the pianist is constant per hour, the price of listening to a concert will actually *rise* with respect to the technological improvement of the instrument.

Another example, which was discussed during the 1990s, concerns the increasing daily costs for hip operations shows the difficulty of choosing measurements norms in health care.

In Figure 5.1 we measure the daily average costs for hip operations at a clinic. We have assigned operations with the old technique with P^A and with the new technique P^{Bn} and P^{Cn}.

We see that the new technique implies that more patients can be treated, but at a higher cost per day. In our example, the average daily cost per operation will rise from 17.5 coins to 22 coins. Thus, if we measure the daily costs of the clinic without registering how many patients we can treat, we end up with higher daily costs, but if we use the measure daily cost per patient day, we have a lower cost, 11 coins. If health care was now a private enterprise, we could call this a productivity increase, but if health care is collectively financed via taxes, we must raise the taxes. In this case, the bureaucrats were not used to the new conditions,

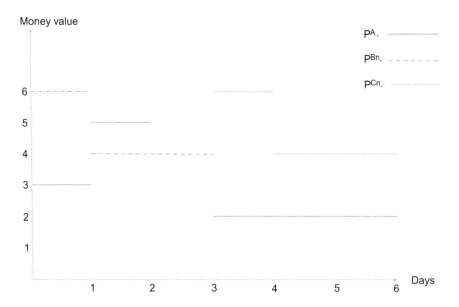

Figure 5.1 Daily average costs for hip operations

so the information given to the electorate was that we had higher costs for hip operations and that productivity measured in average daily costs for the clinic was deteriorating. Of course, this caused an ideological debate, which stopped concerning this very sector when the full picture was given.

Consequently, we can say that it is always good to calculate, but it is even better to know also which kind of conceptualization and which kind of measures it is appropriate to use.

We may take an example from education concerning the misuse of new technology in order to reduce costs. The author's home commune decided some ten years ago to decrease the number of teacher lessons in mathematics and replace them with some fancy calculators which the pupils received from the commune. My son, who was then a teacher in maths at Chalmers University of Technology, discovered that students from his home commune could not understand the principle of rational numbers, which are fundamental for mathematics, since they had the belief that rational numbers were an old-fashioned way of writing fractions and consequently the same as decimal fractions.

Thus, reducing all kinds of efficiency discussions to financial surplus is indeed a way of making the short way to the reign of "idiocracy", or as Hávamál tells us, quoted in Chapter 4:

> The half wit does not know that gold
> Makes apes of many men

Picture 5.1 Volenti nil impossibile

The professor at a technical high school to the students after a test

"If you gentlemen don't improve your skill in mathematics,

I will not, if necessary, hesitate to fail ninety percent of you."

A VOICE: *"WE AREN'T THAT MANY."*

Source: **Albert Engström**, author and artist, (1965[1920]), *Bläck och saltvatten*, Albert Bonnier, Stockholm.

From a pure accounting point of view, there is no difference between the microscopic and the macroscopic levels. However, while the individual is a subject, the collective is not; it is instead a composition of subjects which from a formal point of view implies that the collective belongs to proper classes in the terms used in Russell's paradox. That means, as we have showed, that simple additive aggregation does not hold, but even more simple statistical measures as averages and variance are problematic to use (we have touched on this several times) because equality between two subjects in some dimension may be of different structural importance between the two subjects. We used to say in political discussions that democracy must be built on majority decisions, and that must be a sound principle, but when we come to certain dimensions in a society, a stubborn additivity principle may lead to a democratic breakdown if for example a substantial minority loses its confidence in the collective. Politics is the art of what is possible; that is, we have to realize structural limitations, but at the same time, we must perhaps say that compromise is the true soul of democracy. Some of the interpretations of Arrow's paradox have led to discussions of the efficiency of democracy, where simple economic efficiency measures are used. Beside the irrelevance of such interpretations of Arrow's paradox, the problem of efficiency is like discussing the efficiency of raising children, the efficiency of speaking with friends, the efficiency of watching ice hockey.

Thus measures relevant at the microscopic level do not always fit the collective level. The concepts used at the microscopic level do not always have the same definition. Simple statistical concepts as average and variance are generally hard to interpret when we deal with the macroscopic level and cannot use additive aggregation.

In our exposé of some philosophical aspects, we found that the very problem of perception, apprehension and comprehension of the sensible world may create different interpretations of a certain object or process. The very elementary perception, although it can be regarded as objective per se, of contextual conditions and difference in perspectives makes the very perception differ between agents. To this comes the intra-personal aspects of memory, epistemology and ontology. This means that any thought of making some kind of engineering model of aggregations is doomed. We have also alluded several times to the glorious times when the Newtonian universal stability was ruling the minds of scientists and philosophers. Today we realize that humans themselves are the basic factor of uncertainty; physical reality is governed by thermodynamic laws making events in time and space irreversible. The social and cultural reality is constantly affected by human actions which affect other persons as individuals but often also aggregate structures of different kinds, which makes individual actions in the socio-cultural space irreversible. Our experiences and memories are not rigid bodies but are constantly being moulded and interpreted according to new experiences, and new experiences are also being comprehended according to earlier experiences.

Any social theory must take social and cultural irreversibility as a fact, given the current standard of knowledge within psychiatric and neurological research. Obviously, as we have earlier pointed out, we may look at well-specified situations where actions are almost reversible due to their slight interactions with the environment. But such inertia can never be aggregated, as we claimed in our discussion on derivation/integration. Thus the inertia of individual structures can be seen as diminishing the higher the interaction with the environment is, and this also is valid for aggregate decision bodies which will even more increase uncertainty on the individual level, although the uncertainty will be asymmetrically distributed among the individuals.

Obviously, we can use words for classes of structures which are so broad that they cover changing structures to a great extent. A concept like a "democratic state" can cover a great variety of kinds of democracies of very different characters. Let us take a fresh example directly from the oven, so to speak. The revision of this chapter is made 18 January 2018. The day before, in the great opening debate of the year in the Swedish parliament, the prime minister suggested that so-called gang criminality, which has plagued the suburbs of the three biggest cities, should be fought by using military units. This is indeed a remarkable suggestion both for constitutional reasons and with respect to Swedish traditions. If such a decision would be taken, which I hope not, that would be a remarkable change in the structure of the Swedish democracy, but still I suppose that we can use the word *democracy*.

The problem is implicit in our use of Russell's paradox: the words and concepts concerning the reality are complexes, which can also be used to hide specific uses of a certain kind of a structural change.

There is much written in political science by using concepts covering a wide variety of interpretations, but one forgets that using a common word for a complex is in fact similar to Kant's problem of "Das Ding an Sich", namely that we empty the concepts of their sometimes even almost contradictory potential meanings. A complex must, in scientific analysis, be defined with most of its variety of contextual meanings, as is done in thesaurus dictionaries, because using common general classes of concepts may hide structural problems and changes. If we allude to the earlier quoted 1938 letter from Keynes to Harrod, we can say that abstraction will give no further information or true meaning of a concept per se. It will help us to develop a structural/functional analysis of the involved concepts, given some sort of general understanding of the concepts, but that means that the analysis per se is just to be seen as a tentative understanding of causal forms and gives no precise empirical information. To have precise empirical information, we need, as claimed earlier, to transform the concepts to almost atomic facts to use in repetitive experiments. Thus social sciences can never develop the kind of precise understanding as is possible in some natural sciences, although we can use logical/mathematical techniques in the tentative causal analysis.

But most of all, we must be aware of that using a concept with respect to an individual is normally quite a different story from using the same concept with respect to a collective.

Collective decisions – cultural and social homogeneity – knowledge

When we enter the problem of collective ethics, that is, the ethics of governing organizations which consists of many individuals and their variety of understandings and preferences, we also have to consider how words are used in order to trigger a collective action. The Prologue of St. John's Gospel says:

> And the word flesh became and dwelt among us, and we beheld the glory of him, glory as of the only begotten Son from the Father, full of grace and truth.[2]

We can link this to the expression "*assensus intellectus veritati*", which we discussed earlier and interpreted as when we mould our faith and beliefs with intellectual analysis, and if they hold, we can act as if our faith and beliefs are true. This is actually what is illustrated in the epistemic cycle. Beliefs, faith, ideas, dreams have to result in action to be satisfactory to the individual: *the word has to become flesh*. We do not have to interpret it in a biblical sense but as a human experience, and since we are all parts of different structural compositions, our actions must be guided in such a way that the epistemic cycle is completed.

But it is in these considerations that the ethical analysis comes in, and we can apply ethics as a rational tool to achieve the highest of the human being, which means that the good is structurally sustainable.

Our discussion of the paper by Kant on the enlightenment, in the preceding chapter, showed that Kant claims that in order to achieve the highest good in the Aristotelian meaning, the epistemic cycle of the "mature" individual contains active dealing, opinion and action concerning the aggregate government/governance. But if we then apply Kant's ethical imperative, the problem of social and cultural homogeneity floats to the surface. What Kant says is that a "mature" individual must also take part in the political and socio-economic processes on various aggregate levels; but then, if we imply that the mature person shall act ethically so that the action could be used as a common law, the question arises, "mature" in relation to what? Thus we can expect that it is easier to arrive at a common rule of some basic structure of ethical attitude in a rather homogenous society than in a society with a multitude of social and cultural subgroups. Cécile Laborde (2001) discusses this problem with respect to the thought that there exists a specific French culture to be separated from English culture, American culture and so on.[3] She arrives at the result that the internal variations of subcultures were larger than the variations of alleged differences in national cultures. If we use our way of analysis, superficially speaking, her findings show that the French cultural elite, who were mainly in

Paris and who apprehended the friction to foreign cultures, tended to pick elements of the local, regional cultures in such a way that the "aggregate French
culture" thus created had very little bearing on any of the local and regional
subcultures in France.

An interesting, partly adverse discussion comes from Peter Stirk (2010), who
relates an opinion by a German constitutional theorist, Josef Isensee, and the
former German Chancellor Helmut Schmidt:

> In Isensee's words, "Autocratic systems can satisfy themselves with the legal
> [*staatsrechtlichen*] definition by citizenship, because the unity is granted by
> the authoritarian compulsion [*obrigkeitlichen Zwang*]" (2004:65). Democra-
> cies required (and continue to require) something more. They required
> social and cultural homogeneity in a way that authoritarian states did not.[4]

The difference between Laborde and Isensee is both notable and significant.
Obviously, Isensee's approach is consistent with the Kantian ethical imperative,
when we have a clear norm. That norm could for example be just a kind of
aggregate, as Laborde discusses. But given Laborde's claim that cultural variations
within France are larger than the differences between foreign cultures and the
standard aggregate culture reached by some form of cultural cherry-picking by
the elite in Paris, we would either end up in a multicultural France or a breakdown of all aspirations of having a national culture, which could, according to
Isensee and Schmidt, be a threat to the French democracy.

But we reach a still deeper problem when we come to the distinctions made
by the sociologist Norbert Elias (2000), who separates *culture* from *civilization*.
The former word is, according to Elias, linked to cultivation and creation, while
the second word is linked to standard modes/patterns of life. We could link culture to some form of ontology of a society or subgroups of a society, while with
respect to civilization we can speak of an urban or a rural civilization or maybe
aggregates such as European, American or Chinese civilization. Thus the bor-
derlines with respect to cultural differences need not follow the borders between
different civilizations. Generally speaking, ontological differences concern religious and ideological matters and ways of regarding fundamental questions of
humanity and human life, while differences with respect to civilization concern
behavioural rules in social contexts, organization of society, administrative modes
and patterns, and similar. The author lived in Belgium for many years and found
some minor differences in behavioural rules between individuals and rather big
differences in administrative patterns, but when it came to religious and ideological questions, thus ontological differences, both Sweden and Belgium were
similar concerning rather deep-going internal differences between groups and
classes, which were probably deeper than between corresponding groups/classes
in the two countries.

It is interesting how right-wing nationalistic groups cooperate over
national borders, which should be almost like a contradiction in terms,
superficially speaking. However, if we think of an exclusion process in the

respective countries based on education, social stigmata of different kinds, persons with a generally lower rate of participation in the workforce, lower incomes and education in relation to some kind of average, the trans-border cooperation is more understandable. Those groups which are to a great extent socially excluded from their respective societies still have a form of social identity through their nationality and their rights as citizens, so they tend to emphasize that, in contrast to those groups which benefit from globalization and have access to institutions and labour and other markets, even in other countries. Most of all, such marginalized groups tend to emphasize their nationality in contrast to immigrants who come from outside and get access to the labour market which is excluding themselves in spite of their nationality. The eventual positive dynamics of immigration is just theoretical whim in their opinion. When such excluded groups form parties in the EU, they pay less attention to the nationalistic dimension, which is not a separator anymore, and pay more attention to the fight against established groups who are defining the norms irrespective of country and who are excluding them, according to their views.

Formally, it can be seen as a contradiction, but it is just a different form of emotional logic.

Education, which gives increasing knowledge of known facts and relations of the world and increasing abilities in languages, mathematics, music and physical activities, is fundamental for the individual's analytical ability to master the surrounding culture and civilization as well as for further scientific studies. Perhaps the two most important educational dimensions should give a general understanding of social and cultural life and preparation for the general access to the labour market. Generally speaking, education is extremely important with respect to both ontological factors and civilization factors. To some extent, education consists of the four elements of indoctrination, culture, breeding and analytical training; what is what is sometimes difficult to say.

The most alarming "cultural" differences within a country normally have to do with ontological differences, since the differences with respect to civilization dimensions are easier to adapt to. Furthermore, the most notable form of ontological differences seems to appear in relation to education. Thus, there are probably fewer ontological differences between an educated Christian and an educated Muslim than between an educated Christian and an uneducated Christian. The same thing holds with respect to different nationalities as well as supporters of different football clubs. Consequently, it is suggested by such a hypothesis that the nationalistic approach per se has rather limited value as an explanation factor of the behaviour of nationalistic extremists; instead, it has to do with underlying factors which have to do with exclusion/inclusion processes in a society.

In economics we mostly speak about income and wealth distribution as the most important factors for social differences, but education is perhaps at least as important, although it is seldom studied in economic empirical investigations of general character. In the 1970s the Swedish Ministry of Health and Social Affairs initiated a national interdisciplinary enquiry of the conditions of children during childhood and adolescence.[5] In the study, 16,000 households with children were randomly selected and were asked to keep a diary for three months with respect to some dimensions, among which consumption patterns were included. The enquiry was extremely expensive and it has never been repeated at that size. Nevertheless, from an economic point of view, we could relate consumption patterns to income, education of the highest educated in the household in months, age, size of city and some more variables. With respect to income and education, we could define a sort of elasticity concept for education and income. Crude measures, but in the line of Keynes' letter to Harrod, quoted in the prologue, they gave us indications but not any precise answers; the results were discussed in conjunction with sociological and also some psychological investigations. The consumption groups are those used in official statistics and are not entirely consistent. Table 5.1 gives some results where we compare education elasticity with income elasticity. The elasticity concepts are defined in the usual way; let y represent income, e education and c_i the particular consumption group.

Then we get:

$$\varepsilon_y = \frac{\Delta c_i}{\Delta y} \cdot \frac{y}{c_i} \quad \text{and} \quad \varepsilon_e = \frac{\Delta c_i}{\Delta e} \cdot \frac{e}{c_i}$$

y – income

e – education, total in months

ci – consumption group

The income elasticity ε_y tells us how much the consumption will be affected by 10% change in income. For example, tobacco consumption in Table 5.1 will increase with 10×1.11, which is around 11%. The education elasticity ε_e works the same way; if the total education in months increases 10% in the household, we see from Table 5.1 that tobacco consumption will decrease with around 20%. I leave to the reader to contemplate the figures in Table 5.1.

We have to remember that the figures relate to the early 1970s and are probably rather specific for Sweden. But still they are interesting since they signal that education has a considerable effect on consumption patterns, different from income. We should also be aware that the effect changes over time due to changes in relative prices, demographic changes and the social role of the different consumption groups. An example is foreign travels, where the charter industry has had both diminishing prices and changes in the modes of travel which have made knowledge of language less important. But although it is old, we have seldom access to such rich empirical material, and it shows the importance of education as a factor almost comparable to income but implying a different structural effect.

Table 5.1 Consumption effects by income and education

Commodity Group	Income Elasticity	Education Elasticity
Health and beauty care	0.98	0.30
Recreation	1.57	0
Clothing	1.36	−0.36
Food	0.67	0
Tobacco	1.11	−2.01
Alcohol	1.34	−0.37
Housing	0.64	0.54
Furnishing	1.15	0.30
Toys for children	1.37	0.34
Voluntary additional education	0.35	1.68
Literature	1.04	0.43
TV and radio	1.84	−0.81
Domestic travels	1.69	−0.31
Foreign travels	1.74	1.40
Restaurants/Hotels	1.76	1.18
Entertainment, music halls and similar	1.67	−2.67
Weekly allowances for children	0.41	0
Cinema and theatre	1.85	0
Social interaction, invitations, visits	0.9	2.07
Day care for children	0.15	1.06
Telephone and post	0.55	0.98
Gifts	1.31	1.8
Insurances, saving schemes	1.15	0

When we look at the individual, we can find one basic question concerning the basic structural requirement: How much control of their own life does the individual think is possible to achieve? Thus, we may ask which goals are feasible in the short and long run, we can make judgements of restrictions and we can make judgements of possible counteractions to our actions. When we look at primitive cultures which had to fight hard and uncertain Nature, the usual explanation was to claim that different gods governed different sectors and we have to please these gods in different ways. The individual controlled only a rather narrow part of the immediate space-time. Today we know more of the causal structures which are affecting us, but that also means the differences between a poor, uneducated class and a relatively rich, educated class have widened. This creates rifts in society where some have a rather high level of control over their lives while others even have less control over their lives, compared with historical times, due to higher degrees of social interaction. Working with a monthly paper which was sold by homeless people, the author could see their deep fatalism and hopelessness, but on the other hand, when a more

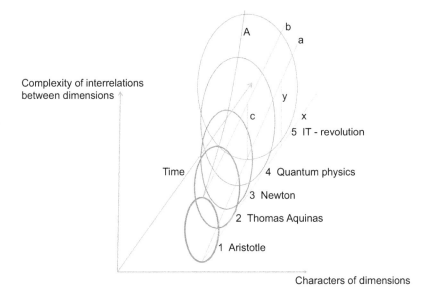

Figure 5.2 The complexification of society

or less regular job or somewhere to live more steadily opened a "window" of hope, their vitality, purposefulness and hope immediately increased. The social welfare system for such groups is necessary to some extent, but what they really need is purposeful activities which give hopes and dreams. Unfortunately, such programs are more expensive for the society in the short run than to just pay people off in hopes that they will die from overdose or internal fights.

A tentative picture of different perceptions of society's complexity is in Figure 5.2. Let us think of slices of time from now and in the direction of the timeline. We may start sometime around Aristotle and go forward to the present day.

We do not need to look at time as continuous since we are looking at some form of intellectual development. In fact we can have jumps, backward travels or black holes, so the time axis is used only to order historical states, slices. Consequently, we look at the figure as a two-dimensional space moving in the direction of the timeline, where we cut out five numbered slices. The two dimensions denote the number of relevant dimensions affecting life and the complexity of relations between the dimensions. The latter depends on the degree of integration of economies, cultures, social and judicial contacts and so on.

The diagram looks like standard diagrams in mathematics which include some measure and measurement, but this is not the case here. The slices denote a dimensionality and complexity; the width of the slices is the maximum perceived dimensionality while the height denotes the maximum perceived complexity. Thus the different slices describe how perception and the dimensions can be completely different between the slices, thus in no. 1, Aristotle analyzed certain dimensions, some of which might have occurred in no. 2, which is Aquinas' time slice, but some might not.

Consequently the helpline *A* denotes the complexity of analysis of the trained minds during Aristotle's time, while the helpline *a* denotes the complexity of analysis of the untrained minds. We thus see that *a* increases by necessity due to the increasing dimensions that must be mastered for ordinary life; to handle a cell phone seems to the author a giant analytical effort, so we have made this increase linear. But when we come to the trained mind, it has to master a supralinear development. Consequently we can see by the distance *c* that the complexity of Aristotle's analysis is still superior to much analysis going on in slice no. 5, the IT revolution days. But fortunately/unfortunately (difficult to say), the distance from ordinary life complexity of analysis, illustrated by *a*, to the maximal complexity perceived by trained minds has increased very much compared to the situation in Aristotle's days.

If we use dramatic words, we could say that this development shows a gradual alienation of ordinary society from science concerning the physical and social conditions affecting ordinary society. So, while Aristotle might reach some form of macroscopic convergence to a happy world, through an ethical standard, that is perhaps more difficult today; local and temporal slices of stability may be the best which can be achieved.

We will come back to these questions when we discuss the concepts of *saturation* and *anomie*.

Forms of government

Kant's paper from 1784 is indeed remarkable in many ways since it invites so many types of interpretations. It can be read in the spirit of "*Kritik der reinen Vernunft*", but we can also read it in a prerevolutionary way and get quite different feelings and intellectual associations.

Thus, to interpret Kant, we must take into account that he lived in a monarchy ruled by a benevolent and enlightened but still autocratic king; he actually suggested that the government should be open to public control and criticism which should trigger social and political changes. This is not a man sitting and controlling whether the mathematical calculus adds up to "Das Ding an Sich" of the a priori world. No, this is a man tired of non-action who is ready to take to the barricades to defend democratic values and human rights. We have criticized his a priori concepts, but instrumental to our critics were his own doubts, which he overcame due to the insufficient logical and mathematical tools he worked with. Still we must criticize him, although perhaps more his followers not completing Kant's analysis by updating the mathematical and logical tools. There are problems in his analysis which we must be constantly aware of.

But we love his article from 1784, and let us now proceed his analyze of governments by looking at a conversation from circa 486 BC, which was approximately contemporary with Kant with respect to the intellectual clarity and general spirit.

Aristotle discussed the three modes of government: of the one, of the few and of the many, with respect to good and bad variants.

In Herodotus' third book, *Thalia*, chapters 80–82, there is a famous exchange of views between three Persians, Otanes, Megabyzos and Darios, where each of them presents his preference for the three modes, respectively.[6] With respect to what is happening today in the Middle East, Eastern Asia, the USA and Europe, it is interesting to read this text from around 500 BC with great care. Today, we have recently experienced the Arabic Spring, bringing hope of democracy, of freedom to develop one's abilities, of freedom from fear, ending in confusion and blood. In the United States we can see an elected leader who has autocratic ambitions and is prepared to break up established democratic governance for a power based on nothing but prejudice and emotional whims. In Sweden and most of Europe, totalitarian movements are trying to take over the streets, bringing us back to the darkest periods of European history. In England, the nationalistic strive to be unique and better leaders of a government of the local elite similar to Herodotus' and Aristotle's definitions of aristocracy and oligarchy, which due to selfishness are not able to negotiate for their country in a consistent way; instead, they seem to give preference to their own selfish purposes.

The background to the three speeches is that the three speakers, together with six other prominent men, were discussing the future mode of government in Persia after the death of the Persian tyrant Cambyses. All nine men were highly respected, and the three speakers were particularly held as men of highest reputation.

After the three speeches the group voted, and the majority chose a monarchy and Darius as king. Thus the speeches were held at the very peak moment of the hour of destiny for Persia. Whether or not the speeches as related by Herodotus really took place or are some sort of compilation of a larger discussion, whether the three speakers were the most prominent representatives of their respective opinions is of little importance. The speeches reflect the arguments à la mode for the group involved and for the intellectual class at that time.

First out as speaker is Otanes (*Thalia*, chapter 80) who recommends that the management of public affairs should be entrusted to the whole people, thus democracy, not politeia in Aristotle's meaning.

"To me," he said, "it seems advisable, that we should no longer have a single man to rule over us – the rule of one is neither good nor pleasant. Ye cannot have forgotten to what lengths Cambyses went in his haughty tyranny, and the haughtiness of the Magi ye have yourselves experienced. How indeed is it possible that monarchy should be a well-adjusted thing, when it allows a man to do as he likes without being answerable? Such licence is enough to stir strange and unwonted thoughts in the heart of the worthiest of men. Give a person this power, and straightway his manifold good things puff him up with pride, while envy is so natural to human kind that it cannot but arise in him. But pride and envy together include all wickedness – both of them leading on to deeds of savage violence.

True it is that kings, possessing as they do all that heart can desire, ought to be void of envy; but the contrary is seen in their conduct towards the citizens. They are jealous of the most virtuous among their subjects, and wish their death; while they take delight in the meanest and basest, being ever ready to listen to the tales of slanderers. A king, besides, is beyond all other men inconsistent with himself. Pay him court in moderation, and he is angry because you do not show him more profound respect – show him profound respect, and he is offended again, because (as he says) you fawn on him. But the worst of all is, that he sets aside the laws of the land, puts men to death without trial, and subjects women to violence. The rule of the many, on the other hand, has, in the first place, the fairest of names, to wit, *isonomy* [author's emphasis];[7] and further it is free from all those outrages which a king is wont to commit. There, places are given by lot, the magistrate is answerable for what he does, and measures rest with the commonalty. I vote, therefore, that we do away with monarchy, and raise the people to power. For the people are all in all."

Thus Otanes advocates a system were the ruled and the rulers were equals and that the government was open to public control.

The next speaker is Megabyzos (Thalia, chapter 81), who advocates setting up an oligarchy. Aristotle some 180 years later distinguished between oligarchy and aristocracy, and here Megabyzos basically means aristocracy of Aristotle's description.

"In all that Otanes has said to persuade you to put down monarchy," he observed, "I fully concur; but his recommendation that we should call the people to power seems to me not the best advice. For there is nothing so void of understanding, nothing so full of wantonness, as the unwieldy rabble. It were folly not to be borne, for men, while seeking to escape the wantonness of a tyrant, to give themselves up to the wantonness of a rude unbridled mob. The tyrant, in all his doings, at least knows what is he about, but a mob is altogether devoid of knowledge; for how should there be any knowledge in a rabble, untaught, and with no natural sense of what is right and fit? It rushes wildly into state affairs with all the fury of a stream swollen in the winter, and confuses everything. Let the enemies of the Persians be ruled by democracies; but let us choose out from the citizens a certain number of the worthiest, and put the government into their hands. For thus both we ourselves shall be among the governors, and power being entrusted to the best men, it is likely that the best counsels will prevail in the state."

Megabyzos' arguments rests on the assumed foolishness of the unknowledge-able mob. Thus in some sense he takes up some of the dimensions in our earlier discussion on education, complexity and the heterogeneity of the society, which make Isensee and Schmidt discuss the necessity of social homogeneity of the democratic state.

The last speaker is Darios (*Thalia*, chapter 82), who advocates monarchy.

"All that Megabyzus said against democracy was well said, I think; but about oligarchy he did not speak advisedly; for take these three forms of government – democracy, oligarchy, and monarchy – and let them each be at their best, I maintain that monarchy far surpasses the other two. What government can possibly be better than that of the very best man in the whole state? The counsels of such a man are like himself, and so he governs the mass of the people to their heart's content; while at the same time his measures against evil-doers are kept more secret than in other states. Contrariwise, in oligarchies, where men vie with each other in the service of the commonwealth, fierce enmities are apt to arise between man and man, each wishing to be leader, and to carry his own measures; whence violent quarrels come, which lead to open strife, often ending in bloodshed.

Then monarchy is sure to follow; and this too shows how far that rule surpasses all others. Again, in a democracy, it is impossible but that there will be malpractices: these malpractices, however, do not lead to enmities, but to close friendships, which are formed among those engaged in them, who must hold well together to carry on their villainies. And so things go on until a man stands forth as champion of the commonalty, and puts down the evil-doers. Straightway the author of so great a service is admired by all, and from being admired soon comes to be appointed king; so that here too it is plain that monarchy is the best government. Lastly, to sum up all in a word, whence, I ask, was it that we got the freedom which we enjoy? – did democracy give it us, or oligarchy, or a monarch? As a single man recovered our freedom for us, my sentence is that we keep to the rule of one. Even apart from this, we ought not to change the laws of our forefathers when they work fairly; for to do so is not well."

Herodotus refers to a discussion which brings an eternal central question onto the table: *Since the system of governance obviously can be treated in a good or bad way, how shall we grant that we end up in good government and governance, irrespective of the formal system?*

Furthermore, we can see that all the three speakers aim at a government form which leads to the best results for the collective as a whole, and the basic problem seems to be the corruption of power and the search for individual power and wealth. We can read that none of the three speakers referred to any form of government/governance per se as preferred by the gods or fate, but it was a matter of the influence power had on the individual ruler(s).

We see that Diocletian pursued the same kind of thoughts in retrospect of his own government/governance of Rome some seven hundred years after Herodotus.

Albert Engström, a Swedish satirical author and artist from the beginning of the 20th century, illustrates the sentiment of power:

Picture 5.2 Podestas iudicialis

The newly examined Bachelor of Law, after twelve years of persevering work, standing on the University stairway telling the World:

"Now, damn it, the Swedish people will be judged!"

Source: **Albert Engström**, author and artist, (1965[1920]), *Bläck och saltvatten*, Albert Bonnier, Stockholm.

Both Megabyzos and Darios presume that we can leave the government to a man or a group of men who are wise and good persons, who want nothing but the best for the collective they rule. Here it should be said directly that Darios, who in the end was selected as king and made Darios I, really became a very good king who reorganized Persia to a state very similar to a modern welfare state. But that was in a sense possible due to the less complex reality of that time. Diocletian was also a good emperor, but his complaint is that the complexity of the Roman Empire is such that the qualities of the emperor were of less importance; the same goes for Megabyzos' speech. Furthermore, due to the built-in asymmetric power relations where the emperor was seen as god-like and the aristocracy had special privileges, complaints were next to blasphemy, particularly if the people or the mob is described as Megabyzos does. Otanes states as the very baseline that "the people are all in all", and this is for better and worse.

Consequently, Otanes does not refer to the perfect person but to a system of openness and control. This can be misused, it is true, but transparency and open control imply that the citizens do not necessarily need to go through the Kantian metamorphosis and come out of self-imposed immaturity. If so, that does really imply something extremely beneficial in a democracy, but it may trigger bloodshed in an oligarchy and monarchy due to the implied asymmetry of people.

Alienation – anomie – anonymity

Karl Marx stressed the alienation of the workers with respect to the product of their work, and according to our discussion of money, we have an alienation process between the real economy and the money economy. First of all, there are no logical links between some kind of social optimum based on money values and some kind of social optimum with respect to welfare in real terms, if such could actually exist, which is doubtful from a technical point of view.

Second, the barter economy, where the neoclassical theory starts, is, if we shall believe Hume's description in his praise of money and the money economy, local and most probably mainly non-anonymous. A money economy, on the other hand, allows people to trade over large areas and thus becomes anonymous. This anonymity means not only that no one knows with whom they are trading. It particularly has to do with the fact that modes of living, modes of production and consumption will not be known as they are in a barter system. We said earlier that the money system grows out of a social development in an interactive way. Discovering new societies may lead to better infrastructure, increasing trade, but when volumes increase, new modes of payments become necessary. In Sweden during the 17th century, when the Crown had to finance wars and needed soldiers, the society was thoroughly reorganized, and as a consequence taxes had to be collected in money, not in kind. To get money, the Crown gave land to the nobility in exchange for accepting taxes on selling at the city markets, which were where trade was allowed.

Today, when commodities are made and sold all over the world, there is no link whatsoever between the structural composition of the local circumstances of the producer and the consumer.

A third particularity of the modern money economy is that the importance of humans as a mean of production is diminishing. During the aftermath of WWII, we generally looked at the substitutability of capital and labour as a matter of price relations; this is not true anymore. Modern production capital grants flexibility, commensurability, consistency and precision in a way which often is superior to human labour. The author had the opportunity to look at a fashion designer's computer program where the designer could create fashion collections quite apart from existing ones, and in a couple of days, they were ready to be sent to test production. If accepted, within a very short time, mostly due to delivery times of fabrics,, the collections could go into mass production.

If a coil of paper is produced in northern Sweden, the manufacturing process is supervised by only a few workers. It is aimed for, say, Liverpool, England. It gets a code and is loaded automatically on a special trailer, where it has a particular place. The trailer is loaded on a train-wagon and transported to Gothenburg, where the trailer is reloaded on a ship bound for Zeebrugge, Belgium, where it is reloaded at a warehouse (approximate area $50 \times 700 \ m^2$) to a particular place bound for Manchester region, then loaded to a similar trailer for a ship bound for Liverpool. During this process from Northern Sweden to Liverpool, there is only one person who deals in some way with the coil, and that is the man handling the elevator truck in the warehouse. But there are of course lots of people supervising the computer system.

So in this case, almost all the labour force has been shifted from a variable production factor to a fixed one, and that also goes for the designers' laboratory with respect to assistants.

From the consumer's point of view, I can have a manufactured suit made to my measurements in the same time as it would take to have modifications made to a prefabricated suit with my approximate measures. Thus the new capital will increase the choice possibilities and the quality of clothes for common people, who cannot afford a tailor-made suit.

Thus we have to realize in economics that the substitutability between labour and capital is very limited. Furthermore, technology invades most production sectors even in low-paid countries and in traditional service sectors. However, its purpose is not substitution but a change in production structure due to new aspects of some technological applications.

The fashion designer is very happy, but the implication is that she will need fewer assistants/dressmakers, and we can imagine the many people working with loading and stevedoring for the paper company which were replaced. But there is a very small probability that there could be a price relation between labour and capital prices such that long-run investments would switch back to a more labour-intensive production in most sectors if we discuss a society with mass production. A generally labour-intensive production would imply a highly asymmetric society where just a small group of people would have the benefit of having choice possibilities like we have today. Maybe Western societies are on that track; the enormous shifts in wealth distribution without a corresponding rise in risky new capital could be a sign of increasing class differences, and we also note that increases in actual slavery are significant in many low-pay countries.

We sometimes speak about the reservation wage; the wage which is necessary to induce people to work and which is due to the level of social contributions. We have today a different kind of "reservation wage", and that is when modern and advanced capital takes over production, not so much that it is cheaper but enough to increase the quality of production. Earlier we had a move of companies from rich to poor countries which was only due to the wage relation between poor and rich countries, but now quality aspects endogenous to the capital matter more in combination with the education of labour.[8]

Consequently, although world employment rises as a consequence of education and increased competitiveness, the present global trends develop towards a diminishing labour intensity without a corresponding rise in the relative labour price, when we take into account both the increased quality of labour and the increased permanent unemployment. Thus, this means that an increasingly larger group of people will simply lack access to the labour market at wages which they can live on, including necessary means for uncertainty and pension planning. Even worse, large groups of young people will have more and more delayed introductions to the labour market.

We thus come to a state of anomie at the societal level. *Anomie* means that the collective norms in a society are weak, unclear and of little guidance to the individual, and mutual solidarity becomes low. Durkheim however works with two relations between the individual and the collective (Marks 1974): *organic solidarity* and *mechanic solidarity*. To start with the latter, Marks (1974:354) has a quote from Durkheim:

> What justifies this term is that the link which thus unites the individual to society is wholly analogous to that which attaches a thing to a person. The individual conscience . . . is a simple dependent upon the collective type and follows all its movements, as the possessed object follows those of its owner.

Mechanic solidarity is thus exogenously imposed on the individual: I am a Swede and have the rights of Swedish citizenship because I was born here. Even this is in fact not altogether true. If I am an immigrant with permanent permission to stay, in the public registers and the legitimation card I will have a personal number based on birth date plus four numbers. This will give me all rights as a Swedish citizen, including voting in local and regional elections. So we can just ask persons whether or not they possess the four last numbers. Thus the mechanic solidarity is linked to the *ius soli* principle. *Organic solidarity*, on the other hand, is built on a multitude of mutual links between people: Durkheim mentions trade unions, where links are built by similarity in work conditions, a common "enemy", dependence on each other in the work and eventually more dimensions.

Durkheim's thoughts were later enlarged, particularly by Robert K. Merton (1938), contemporary with Alva and Gunnar Myrdal in Sweden, who took a more biological view in their classification of useful and non-useful persons. We give a lengthy quote from the beginning of Merton's 1938 paper to settle the difference between his attitude and Alva and Gunnar Myrdal's social engineering attitude.

> There persists a notable tendency in sociological theory to attribute the malfunctioning of social structure primarily to those of man's imperious biological drives which are not adequately restrained by social control. In this view, the social order is solely a device for "impulse management" and the "social processing" of tensions. These impulses which break through social control, be it noted, are held to be biologically derived. Nonconformity is assumed to be rooted in original nature. Conformity is by implication the result of an utilitarian calculus or unreasoned conditioning. This point of view, whatever its other deficiencies, clearly begs one question. It provides no basis for determining the nonbiological conditions which induce deviations from prescribed patterns of conduct.
>
> In this paper, it will be suggested that certain phases of social structure generate the circumstances in which infringement of social codes constitutes a "normal" response.
>
> The conceptual scheme to be outlined is designed to provide a coherent, systematic approach to the study of socio-cultural sources of deviate behavior. Our primary aim lies in discovering how some social structures exert a definite pressure upon certain persons in the society to engage in nonconformist rather than conformist conduct. The many ramifications of the scheme cannot all be discussed; the problems mentioned outnumber those explicitly treated.

Thus, if we see the society as a bunch of people who have predetermined biological determinants, and on top of that we have a utilitarian and/or social-Darwinist approach to social engineering, it is rather natural that we may imagine some biologically determined "baseline quality" of people who have proper possibilities to survive. There is however a rather tricky little problem, and that is what we tried to convey in Figure 5.2. If the complexification of the society increases, we may think that this is caused by the biological qualities. If we believe that the biological development is to a high degree independent of the complexification, we obviously must heighten the "quality baseline" and sort out more individuals. That is the Myrdal problem.

Merton's approach signals an endogenous problem of the social organization which may cause its own problems. This endogenous problem may take many forms. We have touched on how the economic system from the production side "produces" permanent unemployment, which creates a group of people dependent on the social welfare network and the benevolence of others. Let us go back to our discussion of baseline collective ethics of not dehumanizing people in rejecting their being a final cause. The author was for some years Chairman of the Board for a street paper sold by homeless people. We offered also some judicial, educational and housing services. During my conversations with our sellers, I became aware of the fact that many of them refused to go to the social authorities to get the help they were publicly granted. The reason was that they were treated like children and were told how to be and what to do. They felt dehumanized, inferior human beings. Is such behaviour from the society, through their servants, due to a biological explanation of their clients' situation, or is it due to a social explanation? If it is the latter, their behaviour is obviously counterproductive.

The current trend within production technology is clearly promoting anomie in the very sense that an increasing number of people lack access to the labour market.

We may ask whether a redistribution of wealth and incomes in the world would affect this current trend. I am afraid that that is not the case. Surely the total number of employed in the world would be employed when the production sector increases, but we already see that many so-called third world countries have developed an intellectual elite which, technologically speaking, is well on the same level as the corresponding one in Western Europe or may even be higher. Thus these countries will rather quickly reach the same conditions as Western Europe. Obviously the current threat of global warming may drastically change these kinds of deterministic speculations, but unfortunately it will probably be other consequences of asymmetric poverty. Anyway, the poor countries that succeed in leaving hopelessness will from a production perspective rather soon be technologically advanced. So, our problem will remain: a large part of the population will not have access to the labour market, and thus we will have a successively smaller financial elite who can live in luxury conditions while the larger part will be forced to starve or sell themselves for cheap money to the elite. But another scenario is of course that we will have a distribution system of money to spread consumption possibilities. The question is whether such a system is linked to a system of distribution of participation of work or not. It is easy to see problems with both alternatives.

This brings us however to a different approach to anomie which Asplund (1967) suggests when linking *anomie* to *saturation* in the meaning of weariness of life. He thus discusses the degree of repetitiveness in different dimensions of life. Since he enlarges the concept of social beings into social responsive beings, he introduces an active and dynamic element. The responsiveness decreases as repetitiveness increases. That is of course the same as saying that when we have reached an earlier formulated goal, we need to reformulate the goal in order to keep our activity level. He formulates some propositions (1967:101–106);[9] one concerns the activity level of a social organization in relation to new stimuli, the second concerns the solidarity of a group and the third is linked to Pareto's theory of elites.

The first proposition is originally divided into two, but we here give an explanation of the concepts used which emanate from the second proposition.

1   A social organization tends to have an optimal activity level. It can be a productive organization, a social group of some kind or a society as a whole. A new stimuli will then cause a reaction of trying to adapt the new stimuli

towards the earlier optimal activity level; by modifying its effects on the activity level, thus we arrive at

Proposition A: *Negative emotional affects are generally experienced when the resulting activity level differs considerably from the earlier optimal activity level; positive emotional affects are generally linked to changes in the activity level towards the optimal level.*

2   Proposition B: *If two individuals, groups or societies cease to provide each other with new stimuli, their mutual interaction and approval will decrease at the advantage of an interaction and approval of a third party, if the latter implies exchange of new stimuli.*

Correlate: *Interaction implying exchanges of new stimuli maintains or increases the solidarity within a group, while interaction implying exchange of saturated stimuli diminishes the solidarity.*

3   Proposition C (Pareto): *An elite which maintains closeness and refuses to open up for persons outside the elite who have characteristics which could complete characteristics represented in the elite* – ceteris paribus – *will collapse.*

Propositions A and B tell about the balance between saturation and security. Within a rigid structure, people tend to be saturated if access to new stimuli decreases, but on the other hand, when new stimuli are introduced, these new stimuli must be possible to incorporate in the current structure without causing the bewilderment of norms and patterns. If we look at immigration, we meet different reactions, positive and negative. Immigration may cause positive effects which are seen at the macroscopic level in the form of filling vacant fields in the labour force, such as in health care, specialist jobs and unqualified jobs. On the other hand, at the microscopic level, immigration can create uncertainty due to language or different patterns, which per se do not need to be representatives of cultural differences. There is a tendency to claim cultural differences when the concern is behavioural differences due to differences in climate, topography or demography, which per se can imply also cultural differences. Often, however, these differences are nothing but different ways of behaviour that anyone would display if moving between the areas in question. The author and his wife live in the countryside on the western coast of Sweden, but when we lived in Brussels, we were in the middle of the city. We realized then that we had two lives: one when we were in Sweden and one when we were in Brussels. These two lives were completely different. It had nothing to do with cultural expressions, but with different possibilities and accessibilities.

However, different patterns, differences in language and so on may create fears and xenophobia, particularly with those who in some way are vulnerable and have weak structural links to the society as such.

We will come back to this in Chapter 7 when we discuss *otherness*.

Asplund makes a connection between saturation and anomie. It is rather easy to understand anomie in relation to excluding production technology developments, but Asplund also sees a different link. This is built partly on Durkheim and partly on Robert Merton's development (1938) of the concept of anomie. We may mention also that Bessette and Fage (2012) discussed the same aspects, but partly at variance with Merton.

As said, Durkheim started with linking anomie to weak or non-existent norm systems which made the individual uncertain with respect to himself and to the social environment and which could emanate in suicide. However, he also discovered a positive form of anomie in the trade unions where workers stuck together around clearly defined goals which were at variance with much of the power structure. These trade unions were in one sense excluded socially, but in another sense they were also excluding since they formed a rather clear norm system within their own realms. Thus we have two mostly distinct subgroups with different ethical norms and also partly different cultures. On the other hand, those who did not belong to any of the groups could have a rough time.

Merton developed the latter theme in analyzing social subgroups based on differences in goals for self-realization. If we do not share the conventional goals of life of the social environment, we could either distance ourselves from the society into social isolation or we could revolt. In the latter case, the action may attract other dissatisfied persons, and we may have a development towards a kind of subgroup. Bessette and Fage criticize Merton for being too much affected by the particulars of the American situation where, according to Bessette and Fage, a conventional structure with respect to forming goals for the individuals is ruling to a higher degree and the spread around this is narrower. In Europe, the spread of patterns of behaviour and cultural expressions is wider, there are more distinguishable class differences with respect to education, income and occupation, and these class differences are of more social importance, according to Bessette and Fage.

There is a saying, which perhaps goes back to Durkheim: It is not so that you are criminal and thus you are socially rejected; instead it is your behaviour that is rejected, and therefore you become a criminal.

The author worked in the middle and end of the 1970s with some projects for the Swedish Crime Prevention Board, particularly with drugs and black markets. There were particularly two studies which became important and which remained in mind: A. Benabud (1957) and G. Lundquist (1970).

Benabud (1957) studied the social effects of alcohol and cannabis use and misuse in Morocco and Northern France, respectively. In France, alcohol was the socially accepted drug and cannabis was not accepted, while in Morocco it was the opposite. He found that in both countries, the use of the unaccepted drug had strong medical effects, social rejection, criminality and so on. The accepted drug was used at a controllable level by the majority of the population, but in exceptional cases it led to non-acceptable behaviour and/or negative physical and psychological effects, which were treated by the health care system.

Lundquist (1970) made a five-year longitudinal study of, on one hand, one hundred persons from Stockholm who had the attention of the authorities for alcohol abuse and were forced into medical or psychiatric care. This is the A

Table 5.2 Summarizing notations in public registers for the A and C groups

Type of notation	A group	C group
1 Dead after five years	5	19
2 Notes on alcohol abuse as a main or contributory cause of death	5	0
3 Public notes of alcohol abuse, police or health care	100	0
4 Medically observed alcohol damages	Slightly above average	Much above average
5 Class belonging (Sweden has three classes, I, II, III, of which I is the highest and III the lowest)	III 100 out of 100	I 90 out of 90
6 Income level	100 out of 100 below social help level	90 out of 90 belonged to richest quartile
7 Notations in criminal records	100 out of 100	0

group. On the other hand were ninety persons who had voluntarily searched for help at the alcohol clinic at Karolinska University Hospital in Stockholm. This is the C group. The two groups were followed by the notations in different public registers.

Lundquist found the following, which we summarize in Table 5.2.

Concerning point 1, eight deaths in the C group were suicides; no death in the A group was a suicide. The C group visited the clinic under the condition of strict privacy and in search of help for generally defined problems. Later sociological investigations indicated that abuse in the higher income groups was more damaging, though these persons could afford to buy strong alcohol, while the ones in poorer groups could mostly afford "people's beer" due to high taxation of the alcohol content in the beverage.

Table 5.2 is a brutal description of a segregated society with different norms for different groups. This is of course not surprising, and we can see it with respect to tax evasion and embezzlement. The #MeToo movement has also brought attention to sexual harassment as an assumed natural means of exercising power by certain individuals. There are many more areas in which we can see a multitude of norms for the same offence.

The more stratified the society becomes and the more apparently hypocritical it is to preserve a form of respect for the superior and the class which claim they have to face the burden of responsibility for the society, the more uncertain will norms probably become, also increasing the risk for hostile subgroups in the society against the society itself.

To curb such a tendency, there are only three kinds of defence, which are partly intertwined: transparency of power, equality and coherency of the legal system, and equality with respect to ethnicity, gender and class with respect to access to the labour market and the consumption market.

However, when Asplund speaks about a link between saturation and anomie, it contains the aspects of class and group differences with respect to norm systems and with respect to socialization/de-socialization. He can still be interpreted on a more general level as attacking the problem of "consumerism", and this can be used for rich as well as for poor countries.

Let us start with the rich society growing richer. In our more abstract discussion in the prologue, we mentioned that economic growth comes two ways: on one hand we have increased quantities of the different commodity dimensions that we have in the existing commodity baskets, and on the other hand we have a growth of the dimensionality in the commodity basket. It is evident that the former quantitative growth fosters saturation quicker than the latter. Thus the film *Grandmother's Father-in-Law Comes to Town* can been seen as a very good film both by the general public as well as the critics, but it is most probable that *Grandmother's Father-in-Law Comes to Town 5* is not met by the same enthusiasm. Thus a growth of dimensionality of the commodity basket is necessary to counteract consumers being saturated too quickly. However, there is another aspect, which is the traditional definition of consumption being the ultimate goal of the production where labour is the most important production factor. Thus we see consumption as the goal to fulfil utility/welfare while labour is the means, thus a disutility. This approach underlies both traditional neoclassical consumption as well as the household production approach. In a simple barter society, it may be that way, where the bare necessities of survival must be produced. But in the modern money economy, this is a rather strange view of the economy. First of all, the kind of work we do is almost the sole provider of our status, at least in Europe. In the USA, it seems that success in financial terms is the most important, and thus the consumption standard automatically increases with respect to social status. But in Western Europe with different traditions, for good and bad, the kind of work we do per se is the bearer of social status signals. Furthermore, our jobs very often imply a widening of social contacts and access to different kind of networks which are important not only for the job per se. If we look upon the human being as a social responsive creature, the job will be equally important as off-job time. Consequently, we have to have an integrated view of the individual at work and in leisure time.

This means that possibilities of advancement and/or increased freedom at work or changing jobs are stimuli which may increase the individual activity level and counteract saturation.

Taking this into consideration, we can see that increased global competition and increased monopolization in conjunction with higher complexity of explicit laws and implicit rules may imply that saturation process increases though new stimuli generally do not imply higher activity levels.

The current movements of nationalism and regionalism are of course to some extent a consequence of this, but if such movements reach their goals, they would most probably accelerate the saturation processes even more and potentially increase the stratification of the society. Austerity policy probably also works in this way, thus reducing not only the dimensionality of the commodity space but the dimensionality of life.

From an ethical point of view, these problems of saturation and anomie are very troublesome. Since we are discussing structural features of the interrelations between the macroscopic and microscopic levels of the society, we have a difficult problem of time preference and the fact that there are unquestionable short-run gains for certain groups as there are losses when we try to isolate a country or region of some types of influences; thus we have asymmetries which have to be treated at the public level. It is obvious that if we have strong antagonistic subgroups, we will have problems. The remedies to that probably must appear before such antagonism has been developed.

If we separate people into nations, classes, ethnic groups, ethically applying Kant's imperative intrinsically will increase the process of saturation in the respective group.

The so-called Golden Rule, that one should treat others as one would like others to treat oneself, is interesting since it has an open form. The Kantian imperative is a universal binding law and becomes thus limited in time-space. The Golden Rule has an open form and is implicitly unlimited with respect to dimensionality. But while the Kantian ethics can be formalized, at least theoretically, in an explicit rule, the Golden Rule must always be intrinsic to the individuals.

Notes

1 Gibbon, Edward, (1786). *The History of the Decline and Fall of the Roman Empire*, Vol. 2, BASIL, Printed for J.J. Tourneisen, pp. 145–147.
2 John 1:14. The English translation is taken from www.biblescripture.net/Prologue.html
3 Laborde, Cécile, (2001). The Culture(s) of the Republic: Nationalism and Multiculturalism in French Republican Thought, *Political Theory*, Vol. 29, No. 5, October, pp. 708–727.
4 Stirk, Peter M.R., (2010). Multiculturalism and the concept of the state. In Maria Dimova-Cookson and Peter M.R. Stirk (eds.), *Multiculturalism and Moral Conflict*, Routledge, London and New York. In the quote it is referred to: Isensee, Josef, (2004). Staat und Verfassung. In Josef Isensee and Paul Kirchhof (eds.), *Handbuch des Staatsrechts der Bundesrepublik Deutschland*, Müller, Heidelberg.
5 The economic investigation was presented in Andersson, Åke E., (1975). *Barnmiljö och samhällsekonomi* (Childhood Conditions and Economics), Socialdepartementet (Ministry of Social Affairs), Ds S 1975:11, Stockholm.
6 *The History of Herodotus*, By Herodotus. Trans. George Rawlinson. The English translation is provided by The Internet Classics Archive, http://classics.mit.edu//Herodotus/history.html To have the correct chapter numbers, I have used a Swedish translation: Herodotos' från Halikarnassos, (1871). *Muser eller Nio Historiska Böcker*. Trans. Fr. Carlstedt, L.J. Hiertas Förlag, Stockholm.
7 *Isonomy* means equality before the law and of civil/political rights.
8 Some years ago, the Swedish company Sandvik moved some of its production to China but had to move it back due to a better educated labour force. This will of course change over time, but it is interesting that Sandvik obviously paid little attention to the wage differentials.
9 Since it there is no authorized translation of Asplund (1967) to English, I cannot quote him. Thus I present the propositions and the concept used with respect to my understanding.

Bibliography

Andersson, Å., (1975). *Barnmiljö och samhällsekonomi* (Childhood Conditions and Economics), Socialdepartementet (Ministry of Social Affairs), Ds S 1975:11, Stockholm.

Asplund, J., (1967). *Om mättnadsprocesser*, Argos Förlags AB, Uppsala.

Benabud, A., (1957). Psychopathological aspects of the Cannabis situation in Morocco, *Bulletin on Narcotics*, Vol. 9, pp. 1–16.

Bessette J.M., and Faget, J., (2012). *Approces sociologiques de la delinquance*, available at internet www.leconflit.com/article-approches-sociologiques-de-la-delinquance-2-106819543.html

Elias, N., (1991). *Sedernas Historia* (The Civilizing Process, Vol. I. The History of Manners). Atlantis, Stockholm.

Gibbon, E., (1786). *The History of the Decline and Fall of the Roman Empire*, Vol. 2, Basil, Printed for J.J. Tourneisen, pp. 145–147.

Herodotus: The History of Herodotus. Trans. George Rawlinson. The English translation is provided by The Internet Classics Archive, available at internet http://classics.mit.edu//Herodotus/history.html

Laborde, C., (2001). The Culture(s) of the Republic: Nationalism and Multiculturalism in French Republican Thought, *Political Theory*, Vol. 29, No. 5, October, pp. 708–727.

Lundquist, G., (1970). *Alkoholberoende och alkoholsjukdomar*, Almqvist & Wicksell, Stockholm.

Marks, S.R., (1974). Durkheim's Theory of Anomie, *American Journal of Sociology*, Vol. 80, No. 2, pp. 329–363.

Merton, R.K., (1938). Social structure and anomie, *American Sociological Review*, Vol. 3, No. 5, October, pp. 672–682.

Myrdal, A. and Myrdal, G., (1935). *Kris I befolkningsfrågan* (Crises in the Population Question), Bonniers, Stockholm.

Stirk, P.M.R., (2010). Multiculturalism and the concept of the state. In Maria Dimova-Cookson and Peter M.R. Stirk (eds.), *Multiculturalism and Moral Conflict*, Routledge, London and New York.

6 Money, financial structures and ethics

A poor man is seldom trusted: "What's wrong with you? Why are you poor?"

The latter question is the common question, the hard question and the question without an answer. Pay if you have money, otherwise go. Vices acceptable for the wealthy are devastating for the poor. Why are you smoking? Why such an expensive TV? A poor man stealing is a criminal while a wealthy man has committed an act of recklessness. The poor man has no credibility – Pay or Go! When the poor man can get money he is free for an eternity, a dimensionless possibility of choice, time does not exist, now is forever.

Once a well-educated, wealthy entrepreneur, your wife left you and took the children and you lost the house, you started to drink; sitting in your small apartment trying to forget, you lose the grip of your company, you are late with paying the bills, the wolves snap at your back.

You must leave your company; money vanishes, mostly in gambling halls. You end up in the street. You look for a cheap flat in a lousy district, but since you now constantly have an air of distillery around your body, nobody will care to let out anything to you.

You have to get money no matter what. Because money is your only friend and you do whatever is necessary to get close to this friend, your police record enlarges. You: the once mighty boss, who is now a creature, who has no will, no significance. Your life is random. There is no need for the wristwatch you long ago left to the pawnbroker, since the true clocks of yours are hunger and thirst. Death or life is insignificant; it makes no difference.

There are many variants, but in the end, money is the only friend you may have as long as you live your misery. Remember, you are not a human being to whom anybody has a moral obligation, so at least you don't need to care for such bullshit.[1]

"*Pecunia non olet*"

The expression by Emperor Vespasianus, when criticized for taking a fee for visiting the small houses of convenience in Rome, is certainly true and is perhaps the fundamental difference between money and barter. This difference is also the basic foundation for the social effects a monetarized economy will have.

The basic analysis of Vespasianus' saying we can find in Thorstein Veblen's *The Theory of the Leisure Class*. It does not matter how you made your money, but when you have it, you may let your money make your ego.

Thus the money economy implies a certain kind of anonymity in economic exchange which is not present in barter. In a medieval village barter dominated; salaries were paid in quantities of corn, meat and similar. In such a village, the production and consumption were integrated and so also the earning and spending. The society was strictly regulated in classes, and moral issues were defined by the church and the ruling class in conjunction. Thus when Adam Smith envisages the principles of subordination, he builds on the traditions from the medieval society.

To understand the social role of money during those times we have to go to David Hume's essays, particularly, *On Commerce*, *On the Refinement of Culture and Art*, and the one *On Money*. The key characteristic of money according to Hume is just the separation of productive decisions/actions and consumption activities, which makes people flexible in space and time and furthermore increases the anonymity of production and consumption. This implies that social/moral sentiments/judgements affect economic matters less directly and become more diffuse but also increase individual liberty.

When we look at the neoclassical theory and its axiomatic structure, the measure and measurement of the economy both on the microscopic and the macroscopic levels are implicit to the very working of the economy. That is why we do not need money in the neoclassical economy. However, when we change the distribution of resources by some sort of exogenous action, we also change the basis of measure. But how should such a redistribution of resources take place in a barter economy? If we look at the neoclassical theory, it is very foggy in regard to this question. The only way is some kind of "lump-sum" redistribution which is done outside the market sphere and consequently cannot be foreseen and accounted for by the agents. It is indeed a revolution since it redistributes the "initial endowments" which is said not to affect the price level since the agents cannot foresee the redistribution, but forgetting that, this also implies that all preference relations must be assumed the same in order to not affect the prices. If preference relations were different we would of course have a new equilibrium.

Thus, comparing with Marxism, we have earlier said, alluding to Makarov and Rubinov (1977), that the neoclassical theory cannot distinguish between a centralized price mechanism and the one which in the theory is suggested to represent the market price mechanism. When it comes to questions of distribution and redistribution, both the neoclassical theory and the Marxist theory suggest some form of revolution. The neoclassical one is assumed to be less bloodstained than the Marxist one, but it is easy to imagine that when people wake up in the morning and find that the new tax implies their resources have been diminished, they will not be satisfied with the fact that their neighbour has got substantially more and will take some action of whatever character. So, what Marx does is he draws the right conclusions from the static theory when he looks at it in a social perspective; he simply does not believe in another form of invisible hand, so we have one governing the equilibration and one governing the redistributions.

It is exactly here that we see the interface between money and the real (barter) economy. Through bringing in the anonymous supply-demand principle, the money will always tend to change price vectors through technological innovations, through changes in the structure of the society, through habits changed by fashion, and thus the valuation of endowments changes as well as profits. The only rational protective behaviour of producers to save the status quo, is actually price cartels or monopolies. Nowadays, this can be either on the financial side or the production side.

The difference between Smith's subordination principle and Hume's enthusiasm for the increased penetration of money in the society is that a money economy brings inventions and innovations; it brings hopes for entrepreneurs and it brings growth, which per se changes distribution, allocation and the working of the society. Therefore the chapter on the refinement of luxuries and art is also a part of his praise of money. By luxuries he does not mean vanities, but common nice things which could light up the plain living in the decoration of homes, going to craftsmen in other villages to buy nice chairs and similar things. It is true that Hume saw problems with the monetized society, but his main feelings seem to have been very positive. There is progress, there is mobility, and new dimensions of the human mind will develop; such thoughts dominated Hume. It is not a coincidence that the chapter before the one on money had the title *Of the Refinements of Art*.

> But after men begin to refine on all these enjoyments, and live not always at home, nor are content with what can be raised in their neighbourhood, there is more exchange and commerce of all kinds and more money enters into exchange. The tradesman will not be paid in corn; because they want something more than barley to eat. The farmer goes beyond his own parish for the commodities he purchases, and cannot always carry his commodities to the merchant who supplies him. The landlord lives in the capital, or in a foreign country; and demands his rent in gold and silver, which can be transported to him. Great undertakers, and manufacturers, and merchants, arise in every commodity; and these can conventionally deal in nothing but in specie. And consequently, in this situation of society, the coin enters into many contracts, and by that means is much more employed than in the former.
>
> (Hume 2002[1740]:55–6)

Here the anonymization process is clearly hinted at, and mostly in a positive way. Hume lived during his life in London, Scotland and France, and one may certainly understand his enthusiasm for money as a tool of deliberating humans with respect to settlement in space.

Hume also mentions remote areas in eastern Germany where the state still receives taxes in kind, which according to Hume hampers growth and development of the states in question substantially.

The money economy requires mass consumption to meet inventions and innovations. At this point, both Marx and the neoclassical theory go astray. It can be appropriate to go back to the friars of Salamanca. Martín González de Cellorgio wrote in the year 1600 (Grice-Hutchinson 1952:109):

> Since money is not real wealth, and since what is noble ever attracts what is the base, our gold and silver has been drawn away by what is truly wealth. And this we would prove more particularly to those who claim best to understand the reason of the state, when they falsely assert that the wretched poverty of this Kingdom is due to the large quantity of money to pay for the wars in Flanders and in other states belonging to the Crown of Castille. The sad error, for in truth all our evils proceed from our own idleness and from the great diligence of foreigners, who by their industry take out ten times more gold and silver than all our Orders in Council.

Although the transformation from the barter economy to a money economy is a huge step with respect to the functioning of the economy; it seems as if few economists, except David Hume, have been really interested in this development from a scientific point of view, neither with respect to economic science nor with respect to anthropological issues. I mention Hume, but the friars in Salamanca also stressed the importance of money with respect to creating and maintaining a state. The latter, however, mostly were concerned with money in commercial matters and also moral aspects with respect to the just price, usury and conditions for the poor.

Hume's approach has however been developed by Fernand Braudel in his major work of Civilization and Capitalism, where he devotes a chapter to the historical role of money and the transformation of barter into money economy.

Braudel (1992[1979]:437) makes a significant comment:

> For the same process can be observed everywhere: any society based on an ancient structure which opens its doors to money sooner or later loses its acquired equilibria and liberates forces that can never afterwards be adequately controlled. The new form of interchange disturbs the old order, benefits a few privileged individuals and hurts everyone else. Every society has to turn over a new leaf under the impact.

Further on, he concludes (ibid.:239):

> Money is of course the symptom – as much as the cause – of the changes and revolutions in the monetary economy. It is inseparable from the movements that bring and create it.

Consequently, the monetization of a society is a step in development which is integrated in the socio-economic, moral and cultural evolution, and thus there is not one money system but many, mirroring the particularities of the different societies.

One of the few current economists who has actually observed the broader anthropological problem, Ibrahima Sy (2013), in his study on income distribution in Senegal, has been able to statistically hint at the anthropological problem.

It is interesting to compare the quote from Braudel with Sy's results.

Sy compares a statistical "objective" methodology and a subjective methodology in analyzing poverty in Senegal, which means that he asks people questions according to a predetermined questionnaire but also does more unstructured interviews orally in remote areas. People in different areas were asked about their individual perception of their economic status in relation to needs and in relation to other people. As a kind of side result, Sy could show that when comparing rural areas, where barter prevailed to a high degree in contrast with urbanized areas, where the money economy was predominant, he found that people's subjective perception of economic status in rural areas was that their economic situation was better than was the case when so-called objective methods were used. In urban, monetized areas, the subjective answers were regularly suggesting a worse situation than was showed by the objective method.[2] Here of course we have an interaction between monetization and urbanization, but as Braudel suggests, we can probably not separate the two processes in any way. Consequently, Sy's results have to be regarded as a joint effect of an integrated development, and as such we can probably look at the results as indicating further effects of socio-psychological character as consequences of the joint economic and demographical changes.

From this perspective, the neoclassical theory is remarkable in its anomaly. As late as the end of the 19th century, it was developed as a fundamental economic theory which had prevailed for more than a hundred years and was built on the principles of a *barter economy*.

Furthermore, the thoughts implicit in the mainstream theory of economic policy, concerning both short-run and long-run issues, are often in line with the neoclassical theory. This makes it void of social aspects and implies reversibility of social and political processes, and furthermore, it lacks any coherent measures in space-time.

An example is the austerity policy in Europe where the behaviour of the financial organizations can be best characterized as usury and cheating *in flagrante*. That brings us to the question of who pays the time contracts in the monetized world, which we later will discuss.

Pecunia non olet is indeed as important as it was for Vespasianus; perhaps the odour is not that important but other aspects of a more sinister quality with respect to moral characteristics are.

Neoclassical theory, money and structures

We have seen Hume's enthusiasm for money as liberating humans both in space and mind, and that is to some extent true and understandable. But reading Braudel, the problem arises to a greater complexity by magnitudes. Money is a part of a social and cultural process where the monetized economy "both is a symptom and a cause", as Braudel puts it, in relation to the development of the society.

If we just look at the neoclassical economic theory and the mainstream theory as well, money has a minor role, which indeed does not mirror the fundamental importance which Fernand Braudel, a historian, attaches to it. Why?

In the prologue, we have already given the answer implicitly: marginalism versus structures. The neoclassical axiomatic structure is first of all of a universal claim in the same manner as Plato's true world or Kant's a priori world; thus it is a static eternal world which, from a vulgar human perspective, lacks time. Thus it rejects all kinds of structural relationships and Arrow's paradox must not exist, since that wipes out the axiomatic structure.

Historians, however, study the rise, the inertia and the breakdown of social, political and cultural structures and from this perspective the monetary penetration of societies becomes a matter of highest importance.

But not only the neoclassical economists are to blame; the so-called Keynesian economists have created their variants of the IS-LM theory and studied the impact of money within very narrow frames without noting Keynes' philosophical works or political books and pamphlets, such as *The Economic Consequences of the Peace*, which points at an understanding of economics within substantially broader social, cultural and political frames. Perhaps such frames are more difficult to use in order to build an academic career, but we speak about Universitas; we cannot study everything in the whole world at the same time, but at least we must place our subject in the world and study its relations to its environment. We cannot wipe the structural complexities from our consciousness. Money is obviously such a complexity, which should attract a similar structural interest among economists as among historians. As we have already hinted from Arrow and Hahn (1971:356–357):

> Keynes wrote that "the importance of money essentially flows from it being a link between the present and the future," to which we may add that it is important also because it is a link between the past and the present. If a serious monetary theory comes to be written, the fact that contracts are indeed made in terms of money will be of considerable importance.

From our Propositions 1 and 2 in the prologue, we can conclude that money matters, but it has nothing to do with some real welfare optimizing of the macroscopic level. Furthermore, monetary policy will affect the real economy but in an asymmetric way, which means that the macroscopic effects must be completed with information on underlying microscopic structural effects in order to be acceptable from an ethical perspective.

But the real equilibrating mechanism in space and time is the simple fact that with money and money contracts, there is no need to transport the physical commodities to the place where the contract is made. This is actually an issue which the friars of Salamanca deal with quite a lot. Luís Saravia de la Calle, writing 1544, starts his analysis "Of the Just Price" (Grice-Hutchinson 1952:79–80):

> Excluding all deceit and malice, the just price of a thing is the price which is commonly fetched at the time and place of the deal, in cash, and bearing in mind the particular circumstances and manner of sale, the abundance of goods and money, the number of buyers and sellers, the difficulty of procuring the goods, and the benefit to be enjoyed by their use, according to an honest man.
>
> I have said "in the place", because the mere change from one place to another raises or lowers the price, according whether the merchandise is abundant or scarce there. . . .
>
> I have said also "in the place". For we have to consider the place where the contract is arranged, not where the goods are situated. Merchandise in one place is consigned from another where the contract is drawn up, and ownership is transferred from there. If I buy spices in Genoa being myself in Milan, and agree on the price and pay for the goods in Milan, the just price is the price current in Milan, . . .
>
> I have said "at the time", for time alone raises and lowers the price of a thing. Thus it is clear that wheat is commonly worth more in May than in August, solely on account of time. . . .
>
> The mere abundance or scarcity of goods, merchants, and money raises or lowers the price, as bargainers at fairs know by experience.

Thus the equilibrating forces with respect to prices lie in the fact that the invention of money makes it possible to sell possessed commodities to some people while buying other necessities from other people, and furthermore the contract can be closed in one place while the actual quantity of the commodity is in quite a different place. Thus the equilibrating market process is not a matter of *an invisible hand* but lies in the very character of money exchange; although they do not mention the word *arbitrage*, it is in the very centre of some of the authors, such as Tomás de Mercado and Francisco Garcia. (Grice-Hutchinson 1952:96–108).

With respect to the friars of Salamanca, they also show how money exchange could equilibrate money (gold, silver) values between places where it was abundant and where it was scarce. A reason for the economic decline of Spain was that they had monopoly access to the New World, where gold and silver was abundant, and thus they could buy cheap from Flanders, Rome, Germany and England, where commodities were abundant but gold and silver scarce (Grice-Hutchinson 1952:98–99); consequently, when prices rose in Europe, the stream of gold and silver ran short. There was thus an equilibration, but at the price of a new disequilibrium, namely that Spain had sacrificed its own development of production.

The central concept in the neoclassical theory is, as we have seen, that if we have a function $y = f(x)$ in Euclidian space which is convex and continuous, we know that if the derivative $f' = 0$, there is a function that has reached a state which we may call a sort of equilibrium. This can be enlarged to a system of many equations. This result leads to the construction of a Homo Œconomicus who fulfils the conditions of the Euclidian space, where the commodities are transformed to axes and the agents to vectors of the space. Through this construction, the economists can explain the relative valuation of commodities from a mathematical point of view in a general equilibrium. This can with some effort be enlarged to include the pricing of the factors of production. Although this is not allowed by the axiomatic structure, we can imagine a converging path of the economy towards equilibrium based on marginal changes until the derivatives have taken the value zero, and it goes under the name of *marginalism*.

The explanation does not entirely differ per se from, for example, the explanations by Luís Saravia de la Calle, a Dominican friar in Salamanca, in his 1544 book *Instrucción de mercaderes*. But for the mathematical analysis of both the macroscopic and the microscopic universe, it seems adventurous, particularly when money, in daily meaning, is the medium of exchange, and the fact that this needs a particular axiomatic construction, "Homo Œcumenicos", while de la Calle wrote of the practical needs for businessmen.

The difference is that while in the neoclassical theory wipes out all friction involved in trade, we actually do not need money as a friction-diminishing factor, which further means that the financial sector is unexplainable within the neoclassical theory. Friar Luís Saravia de la Calle explains that practical businessmen need money but can do without the *invisible hand*. The latter would have sounded a bit heretic to his ears anyway.

Let us go to the current explanations at Wikipedia, where we get an acceptable definition of marginalism.

> Although the central concept of marginalism is that of marginal utility, marginalists, following the lead of Alfred Marshall, drew upon the idea of marginal physical productivity in explanation of cost. The neoclassical tradition that emerged from British marginalism abandoned the concept of utility and gave marginal rates of substitution a more fundamental role in analysis. Marginalism is an integral part of mainstream economic theory.

Furthermore, it is said:

> The doctrines of marginalism and the Marginal Revolution are often interpreted as a response to the rise of the worker's movement, *Marxian economics* and the earlier *(Ricardian) socialist* theories of the *exploitation of labour*.[3]

Thus Wikipedia says that marginalism was an ideological response to, most of all, Marxian economics. The intention was obviously to scientifically prove that market prices were set with respect to the highest possible internal efficiency of the producer as well as with respect to the highest allocative efficiency, and the basic vehicle for this was the junction of supply and demand of commodities.

Surely this is indeed underlying the discussions of the friars of Salamanca, whose discussions of these matters seem to be similar to a non-mathematical analysis of the neoclassical approach. There are however two fundamental differences between the two approaches. The friars of Salamanca did not need any *invisible hand*, but they needed money in daily terms.

The quotes above show that the Salamanca friars discussed local and temporal equilibria; furthermore, they separated the place of the contract and the location of the commodities. Their analysis of supply and demand is purely microscopic, and consequently the market exchange depends, as de la Calle expresses it: "The mere abundance or scarcity of goods, merchants, and money raises or lowers the price, as bargainers at fairs know by experience."

No metaphysical *invisible hands* here, but on the other hand, prices are local and temporal.

When it comes to macroscopic matters, Spain had learnt the bitter lesson, as Grice-Hutchinson points out at the very beginning, "that the value of money is fickle and that gold and silver are not synonymous with wealth". The long-run investment in productive activities is not necessarily linked to the present consumption level, and furthermore, the distribution of wealth was an important aspect.

Thus investments are not something which follows logically from a certain level of demand; they need an explanation taking into account other categories of variables.

Financial system: necessity, structure and output

Basically we could say that the financial system in broad terms distributes liquidities in different ways. The baseline is set by Jean-Baptiste Say when he points out the difficulties in using a diamond necklace to pay for purchases in a grocery shop. The need for liquidity varies in space-time, and we mentioned earlier the principle of lexicographic preferences to emphasize that a liquidity shortage per se can lead to unpleasant revaluations of wealth. Thus the basic role of the financial system is to facilitate the clearing of supply and demand for liquidity. That might be a check-credit or a mortgage on a house; bureaucracies and conditions are different, but the basic principle is the same. The key elements of such a transaction are the eventual security presented by the borrower, the future payment ability of the borrower and the agreed-upon price, the interest rate, which is paid to the lender.

Historically, the interest rate has caused much fuss. Aristotle was against it, Mohammed was against it, St. Thomas Aquinas was against it. Those who dogmatically and ideologically opened up for interest on loans were the friars of

Salamanca, which we mentioned in an earlier chapter when they pointed out that a thing or a pricing process was not evil per se but depended on purpose in moral terms. Thus we have the standard picture:

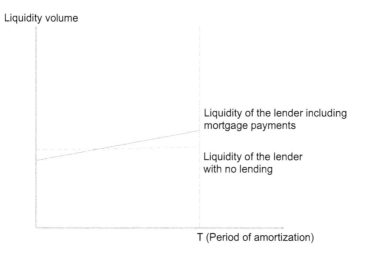

Figure 6.1 Price of liquidity

The ordinary explanation of the interest rate is that it is the price for waiting. Lending out money implies a risk, and the interest is a sort of price for that. The Salamanca friars, living in a much more dynamic and expansive time than was the case before the Renaissance, saw also the financial business as a basis for ventures.

Nevertheless, at the macroscopic level, the financial sector may work in many different ways. The most important matter is to realize the character of money per se. By definition, money is the most liquid asset since everybody uses it as liquidity. It is a form of measurement, not for some intrinsic valuation of commodities but of liquidity paid and saved. It is used to denote the price of commodities and other assets, and it is used as the basis for money contracts.

Thus money, of whatever form, gains its liquidity from its acceptance by the public as a medium of exchange. This in its turn gives money a role as a measure, not of real values but of nominal prices and nominal contracts concerning the future as well as historically. It is important to emphasize the concept *nominal* since any form of manipulation in order to create a real valuation will be asymmetric with respect to space-time and the agents.

A small example: In the beginning of the 1970s, the author bought a fantastic HP-55 calculator. The price was SEK 3,500. At the same time, when we had our Friday relaxation, my wife and I often bought a tin of Russian chatka crabmeat, priced around SEK 6. Today we may buy a calculator of the same capacity as the early 1970s HP-55 for a price around SEK 150, while a similar tin of chatka crabmeat bought online has a price today of USD 104, which is around SEK 840. Thus the price of the specific quality of calculators in question was 23 times more expensive in, let us say, 1973 than today. But on the other hand the chatka crabmeat, a tin of the same size, is 140 times more expensive compared to what it was 1973. Thus any kind of so-called real price calculation starts from a precise definition of the commodity basket; whether or not we make some further manipulation of averaging in different ways plays no principal role. Nominal prices mirror the exact market pricing at a specific point in space-time, and since we have shown that market price relations are only local and temporal, but with different inertia which increases if we work with aggregates of commodities, the so-called real prices are only appropriate for a specific definition of the commodity basket at a point in space-time. Thus using it inter-temporally, for policy for example, will induce asymmetric effects in relation to current nominal prices.

Consequently, an intertemporal contract will be signed in relation to one precise commodity basket while eventual future payments will be made in relation to different commodity baskets. This certainly will affect our judgement of so-called austerity policy, but we will come back to that.

Money implies that we change the physical structure of exchange, which means that barter develops into anonymous markets which were of entirely different socio-economic and ethical effects. Martín de Azpilcueta Navarro reflected sadly in 1556:

> Certainly in one way it [money] was a very necessary invention; and yet, in another, I doubt whether it is really so today, for it destroys souls through avarice, bodies by great dangers upon the sea, and even whole fleets (in which it is transported) by fearful tempests and shipwrecks.
>
> (Grice-Hutchinson 1952:89)

The reason for this is of course that the concept of arbitrage can be enlarged to larger areas of space-time. If by money per se we add to these effects the improved technological possibility of using arbitrage in general, not only with respect to financial assets, Navarro's reflection makes even more sense, particularly with respect to the souls.

We mentioned earlier the works of Ibrahima Sy on income and wealth distribution in Senegal, how in the same country there existed areas which had almost a barter economy and other areas were urban money economies.

When we look at poor countries from an investment point of view, we find areas where the potential profits are relatively easy to achieve due to particular kinds of resources which can be developed quickly with respect to mining, agriculture, tourism, suitable labour for some purposes at a cheap price, and particular forms of demand which need to be filled by investing in particular technology, to mention some areas and dimensions. In these areas you can get quite decent returns quickly with relatively small investments. But then there are other areas or dimensions which might be of considerable interest with

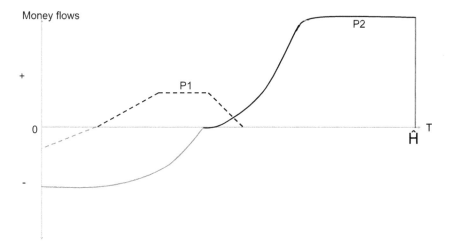

Figure 6.2 Investment horizons, discount rates and expected rates of return

big returns on a more long-run basis and which require costly investments in infrastructural, educational and social structures, although they might well be of a private character. These types of investments are by their very nature more risky and of longer run.

In Figure 6.2 we illustrate two projects, P1 and P2. We can then calculate all probable incomes, costs and risk factors and arrive at a certain expected rate of return for each project respectively which will vary with the chosen discount rate, DR. Then, depending on the existing alternatives to the two projects, we may choose a DR as a norm for ranking. Consequently, the ranking of the two projects will switch at a particular DR⋆. So when DR > DR⋆, P1 will be preferred to P2, and when DR < DR⋆, we will prefer P2 to P1.

The discount rate used is specific with respect to potential investors, but generally we can say that investors with access to the global market concerning both real and financial investments are operating with rather high discount rates which favour short-run projects with rather small long-run positive impacts for the poor country in question. It also mostly has the result that big projects are separated from the social and cultural environment by regulating physical and informational contacts between the specific project enclave and the rest of the society. In the 1990s, we had a widespread debate of this phenomenon with respect to Indonesia, which happened to have a period of very high GDP growth only to see it deteriorate and vanish when the interest of foreign investors disappeared. A continuation would have implied rather huge investments in infrastructure and education but was also risky from the view of foreign investors.

If we look at most developed countries, particularly in Europe, Japan and Korea, the economic growth of companies has mostly taken place in conjunction with the state and its development. In Sweden, for example, heavy manufacturing companies such as LME, ASEA (ABB), car producers such as Volvo and Scania and in the airplane industry SAAB, had their demand granted to a substantial part by the public sector, which was directing public investments to these companies. Obviously, when a certain level of development is reached, companies can develop in a more competitive environment of advanced economies, with high internal demand.

Consequently, the postulation that poor countries should develop quickly with respect to real and decently distributed welfare by opening to the international market actors is a rather doubtful one. The catastrophic history of the Democratic Republic of the Congo, one of the world's richest countries with respect to natural resources, reviews a battlefield of foreign interests underpinned by local "princes" and foreign military help.

The easiness with which money moves is obviously for better and worse, which we will come back to.

Money

We have so far used the concept of money in an abstract form, but what is it in a physical sense? One of the most thorough discussions of this question appeared as a book in 1802 by the British banker and MP Henry Thornton. His *An Enquiry into the Nature and Effects of the Paper Credit of Great Britain* is a classic and is still a matter of discussion.

It appeared during the Napoleonic wars, and Thornton was concerned with the chaotic financial situation in England; in this he was supported by David Ricardo, who in 1826, ten years after Thornton's death, sketched out the system which evolved into the Bank Charter Act of 1844, which also became the structural condition for the Quantity Theory of Money. We are leaving that behind us now and as it seems go back to a system similar to the one Thornton criticized, Real Bill.

In fact the dreams of Bitcoin seem a resurrection of precisely Real Bill, but in cyber form. From what is written on the internet, which is not completely consistent, Bitcoin is a decentralized system based on the number of actors and transactions. Internally, Bitcoin is defined as a kind of code which keeps the macroscopic value increasing at a constant pace to a maximum of 21 million Bitcoins. As far as we understand, the increase of Bitcoins is independent of the number of transactions or agents using it. We also understand that the use of Bitcoins can be linked to the ordinary market system, implying varying relative prices and varying currency values. So, if we then pay with a number of Bitcoins to an agent who must pay in usual currencies, Bitcoin has to be convertible. That means that with respect to currencies, Bitcoin has to adapt to changes in the relative prices; also, since the total value is given, Bitcoin is open to relative changes in currencies. The same also goes for relative changes within a certain currency. But what is more interesting is that Bitcoin is emitted at a rate which is independent of the growth of the number of users and the number of transactions.

We then will then have an equilibrium growth where the value of Bitcoin will be the same for each user and for each transaction, given the distribution among users and given the structure of transactions:

Set

ΔB – Growth of number of Bitcoins per time unit
ΔU – Growth of number of Users, given distribution, per time unit
ΔTr – Growth of number of standardized Transaction per time unit

We will then have a path where the total value of Bitcoin will be the same over time and the individual values of transactions will be the same:

$$\Delta B = \Delta U + \Delta Tr + \Delta U \cdot \Delta Tr$$

Thus we get an equilibrium trajectory where the macroscopic value of Bitcoin, let us call it Θ, will imply that the distribution of values of Bitcoin will be unaltered, as will the relative prices.

When $\Delta B < \Theta$, we will have a deflationary pressure; that is, the value of Bitcoin in relation to commodity prices will increase. And when $\Delta B > \Theta$, we will have an inflationary pressure; that is, the value of Bitcoin in relation to commodity prices will decrease. The relative price level and distribution among users will not be affected per se, but if there are debt contracts in nominal prices, we will have both relative price effects if preferences are not exactly the same, and we will have changes in distribution between debtors, creditors and others. Furthermore, relative price changes will as usual have distributional effects if we do not assume preferences to be the same and the introduction of new commodity dimensions will also have relative price changes.

Thus we have exactly the same functioning as the Quantity Theory of Money:

$$M \cdot V = P \cdot Y$$

Where M is quantity of Money
V is number of transactions per time unit
P is the Price level
Y is the physical quantity of market commodities

Thus, *ceteris paribus*, an increase in M will have an inflationary pressure, while a decrease of M will have a deflationary pressure.

What is nice to observe with respect to Bitcoin is that the conditions for attaining the growth trajectory are actually the same as for the general equilibrium trajectory, according to the neoclassical theory. So, indeed, Bitcoin has a theoretical underpinning. In my searches on the internet, I can read certain opinions from alleged economists who are somewhat strongly against Bitcoin and who call it something like the worst fraud ever. If so, I expect the same judgements with respect to monetary theory built on the Quantity Theory of Money and those who eagerly defend austerity policy without regarding real growth and distribution.

Bitcoin is interesting in the sense that it reflects the eternal search for some fixed values. Somebody – God, the Demiurge or the invisible hand – must be able to arrange some fixed values; it is like the dream of absolute time and absolute speed ending up in *perpetuum mobile*. The only problem is that human beings are subjects and thus local and temporal final causes.

However, Bitcoin calls to mind the so-called Real Bill principle which Adam Smith advocated but Henry Thornton resolutely rejected.

The Real Bill is simple, and as is said in the name, money relates to an imagined real value. Each bill in circulation must have its value defined in gold. With such a principle, anyone could open a bank and print paper bills. The Bank of England, however, was the only bank in England allowed to engage in foreign operations. In the late 18th and early 19th centuries during the Napoleonic wars, the uncertainty of the agents increased and there began a hoarding of gold and Bank of England notes, which were seen as secure, particularly in the English countryside where the Bank of England did not operate and people found local and regional banks a bit unsecure. This hoarding was so strong that it threatened the circulation of Bank of England notes, which in turn threatened the liquidity of London commerce as well as foreign affairs. On one hand, Thornton wrote his famous book, and on the other hand he was called to lead a parliamentary commission to clean up the financial chaos of London. As we see, the principle of Real Bill was similar to that of Bitcoin. However, the rigidity of this system led to the creation of a market of shadow money or *almost money*.

We have earlier quoted Arrow and Hahn (1971) on the lack of a theory of money in economics. From Propositions 1 and 2 in the prologue we can understand that a universal and coherent theory of money cannot and will not be achieved due to the logical contradictions between money as an item and the real items. Swedish economist Knut Wicksell commented regarding the mid-19th-century debates between the banking and the currency schools,

> I already had my suspicions – which were strengthened by a more thorough study, particularly of the writings of Tooke and his followers – that, as an alternative to the Quantity Theory, there is no complete and coherent theory of money. If the Quantity Theory is false – or to the extent it is false – there is so far available only one false theory of money and no true theory.
>
> (Wicksell 1936[1893]:xxiii)

Thornton makes a very simple explanation. Strictly speaking, any kind of bill is a debt obligation. Somebody must pay some liquidity at the presenting of the obligation. If you have trust in this, you can always accept a bill one year ahead at an interest of 5% as liquidity today. Thus any paper, bond, bill or liability can be accepted as near money and can be traded on the market.

Thus Thornton separates two kinds of papers which can serve as money: *papers of forced circulation* and *papers capable of circulation* (we call PCC). The former is legal money, but the latter is any kind of debt obligation in which the market actors have confidence. Thus in principle I can pay with company shares, state or private bonds or bills. The only condition is that I am confident of their bona fide. Nowadays this has grown into a jungle of financial instruments: options, futures, swaps and whatnot.

During the time of Adam Smith, who advocated a Real Bill approach, it was normally thought that the only security underlying legal money was gold and that was the only money, but Henry Thornton enlarged it in principle to any kind of security used in business transactions. This was not a theoretical speculation but a fact from his experience as a banker for one of the biggest banks in London: Down, Thornton and Free. Moreover, his father had been and his brother was governor of the Bank of England.

Henry Thornton's point is that while the law money has a given supply and circulates in all groups of agents, papers which are not law money but have the ability of circulation vary in "supply" as a means of exchange and are also asymmetric with respect to different groups of agents. Furthermore, while the velocity of circulation of legal money was variable but relatively stable, the PCC were very variable and could even in principle almost cease to exist due to variations in economic activity. Two things were sympathetic: that the contract only involved the two active parties and that the papers were interest-bearing.

Thornton describes the difference between money based on law and money capable of circulation in his critiques of Adam Smith's version of the Real Bill principle, basically concerning the circulation of money/papers/securities:

> The error of Dr. Smith, then, is this: – he represents the whole paper, which can easily circulate when there are no guineas, to be the same in quantity with the guineas which would circulate if there were no paper; whereas, it is the quantity not of "the thing which circulates," that is, of the thing which is *capable* of circulation, but of the actual circulation which should rather be spoken of as the same in both cases. The quantity of circulating paper, that is, of paper capable of circulation, may be great, and yet the quantity of actual circulation may be small, or *vice versa*. The same note may either effect ten payments in one day, or one payment in ten days; and one note, therefore, will effect the same payments in the one case, which it would require a hundred notes to effect in the other.
>
> I have spoken of the different degrees of rapidity in the circulation of *different kinds* of paper, and of the consequent difference of the quantity of each which is wanted in order to effect the same payments. I shall speak next of the different degrees of rapidity in the circulation of the *same* mediums at *different times:* and, first, of bank notes.
>
> (Thornton 1939[1802]:96)

The quote from Thornton is extremely important since it draws an analytical border between two types of medium of exchange. The law money is accessible for all agents and granted by official authorities and with a risk factor approaching zero, but the papers which are capable of circulation are mostly used in business transactions and have no official grants other than a degree of expected risk, which is basically set by the agents themselves in conjunction with general open information.

Thus when we look at money from a more general point of view, we have two sorts: legal money, which everybody has access to; money of forced circulation. It can be controlled by the authorities. The other sort concerns papers of assets and liabilities, which are capable of circulation. The public control of the financial system depends on two things: the proportion between the two types of money and the degree of public control of the asset/liability market. Thus the latter type of money is convertible into the former and thus affects the velocity of legal money, as it normally appears in the Quantity Theory of Money.

There is from a distributional point of view a difference between the two kinds of money. Legal money is what you are mostly paid in salary and what you use in shops. It can be physical money or plastic cards or Swish (a peer-to-peer money transfer app, popular in Sweden), prices are noted in legal money, and external trade involves exchange rates in different kinds of legal money. Assets and liabilities are also noted in legal money.

PCC requires trust. You may use bonds, options, swaps or whatever, but basically it boils down to the trust you have in the paper and in the proprietor of the underlying debt or asset. This must in the deepest sense fall back on the liquidity of the asset/liability in the near or the future horizon. Thus, PCC has to be backed up by either background securities or sufficient inflows of incomes.

Consequently, these two kinds of money are directed towards two different market segments with respect to income and wealth: legal money for all classes and PCC for the more wealthy classes and industry. Today in most Western European cities, it is virtually impossible to buy an apartment or a house if you do not have substantial assets combined with high income. This spillover to the housing market is based on renting flats, meaning that rent will rise, preventing young people with no helping parents and with moderate/low incomes from getting decent housing.

To see the more intricate consequences, we need to say some more on inflation.

There are two kinds of inflation. First we have the one which we mentioned in relation to Bitcoin and the Quantity Theory of Money, concerning the relation between general price levels, even at constant relative prices. Thus, when we have such an inflation/deflation, this affects the value of nominal contracts in relation to the value of the commodity basket as a whole; thus, in the terms of Quantity Theory, we have:

$$P = \frac{M \cdot V}{Y}$$

Consequently, given physical production changes in the money supply (M) and/ or the velocity of circulation of money (V), the price level will change. But the complicating factor according to Thornton's specification of legal money and PCC is that different market segments will be directly affected in the first instant, dependent on which type of money circulation is changed.

The other type of inflation refers to changes in relative prices. Some commodities like energy are basic commodities in all production, thus a price change will affect most other prices in such a way that the general price level increases due to especially important commodities becoming scarcer; thus we have a deflation but that is not nominal per se but real. Adding a set of commodities and services or increasing taxes on some existing commodities in order to fight a problem like global warming also increases the scarceness of other commodities and is a real form of deflation. Thus, the inflation caused by such matters is not inflation; although it might appear as inflation, it is real deflation.

Let us now go back to money matters. We have the two kinds of money, legal money and PCC. Legal money has to be regulated due to its fundamental role as denoting monetary values of commodities, assets and liability, but that makes such money inert. PCC is from that point of view flexible, more risky but also more practical, not to say profitable. But that means that all PCC are also due to nominal pricing when they are intertemporal. Consequently, they are more sensitive to nominal inflation than real inflation. Since real inflation is a market price phenomena, it could be dealt with in taking subsequent real positions.

Thus, the two market segments we discuss in relation to legal money and PCC have almost contradictory reaction schemes. The real inflation, as we have described it, in the first instance hits ordinary people by lowering demand and supply. The nominal inflation, as we have described it, in the first instance hits PCC by lowering their values vis-à-vis real commodities. We can argue that the PCC market must be divided into assets and liabilities, and that is correct. But if we have a technology where assets are the real securities for liabilities which you can use as securities in turn, like portfolios of financial papers, which of course lowers the risk of the individual investor but increases the systemic risk, we will soon get an overburdened liability side which increases the vulnerability of nominal inflation while real deflation will decrease the commodity prices, thus increasing the real values of nominal contracts.

This means that so-called "austerity policy" can be a very useful instrument to reshuffle wealth and incomes from one market sector to another. Austerity policy as it has worked in Europe has as its fundamental target maintaining or increasing the value of nominal contracts, thus sacrificing eventual distributional goals as well as eventual growth goals.

For countries where the financial industry constitutes a major part of the total industry, we have a funny effect of PCC. When we move a stock of value from somebody to another within a country, nothing happens to GDP, but the transaction per se costs resources, labour and capital, so this will add to GDP. But that means that the increase in PCC and the speed of circulation will increase GDP per se. So, moving values implies an addition to GDP, although no value is produced in ordinary sense. This means that increasing the circulation speed towards infinity with the help of computers may increase the GDP towards infinity. This is in the first instance nominal money, but through the demand for those benefiting from the transactions, it becomes real demand. But if we think of two market segments, which are different in consumption habits/needs, the austerity policy will have consequences both for distribution and allocation.

The structural changes of the financial market

We mentioned earlier that now, in the last decades, we are going through a structural change of the international financial market. It is not an administered change but more an organic change due to globalization, and it is not straightforward, though many countries and the EU are trying to come back into control of the financial market. Thus we have a mixture of systems and different ways that public authorities operate some form of control; the main international agreements are the Bale I–IV agreements completed recently with the new rules of capital requirements for banks.

The Real Bill system was ruling entirely in England until 1810, when it was heavily criticized, most of all by Henry Thornton and David Ricardo. Measures were taken to control the system, and the Bank of England increasingly served as a kind of central bank. Thornton died in 1815 but Ricardo, then very influential, continued the work to reform the British banking sector and his posthumously published INGOT plan (1826) was the foundation for what became the Bank Charter Act of 1844, where the Bank of England was given the exclusive right to issue bank notes and also the responsibilities following with that, like being a bank of last resort, controlling the money supply and *de facto* the official interest rate. Thus it became a true central bank.

This structural reform was accompanied by hard debates between the Banking School, in favour of the Real Bill principle, and the Currency School, in favour of a central bank system.[4]

To picture the present banking system is almost impossible due to the mixture of principles and control systems, mostly global but with regional and local alterations. We can sketch the fundamental principle of the two extremes; however, we dismiss the gold standard discussions and line out the principles for fiat money.

What is important to understand is that the 20th century kind of monetarism could not exist in a Real Bill system, so practically speaking, monetarism in modern form was formally born with the Bank Charter Act. Some allegations have been made that the friars of Salamanca were monetarists, which is completely wrong since they had no link whatsoever to some kind of equilibria and they discussed both nominal inflation and inflation caused by real demand.

The reason for this is, of course, the problems underlying Propositions 1 and 2 in the prologue.

Let us look at Figures 6.3 and 6.4, which are illustrations of the basic forms of the two systems. Normally elements from both systems coexist, but we will discuss the systems as in isolation.

Figure 6.3 illustrates the pure monetarist model.

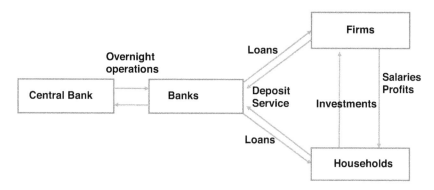

Figure 6.3 Monetarism/Currency School

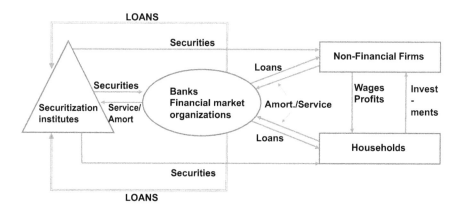

Figure 6.4 Securitization system

The system works for economies with regulated foreign relations, all going through the central banks; the Bretton Woods system is a good example. The central bank controls to a great extent the PCC markets, and the issuance of such papers are to a large extent controlled. This is the proper environment for monetarism. The central bank controls the money supply and thus, given the legal structure of the economy, also controls the velocity of circulation, save for variations in economic activity. We can even admit that, given an intertemporal and thus eternal neoclassical equilibrium with a given price vector, we have solved the whole trick and why we need economists more is beyond my imagination. But of course if we are in an eternal equilibrium, we do not need money in daily meaning; we can use flat stones, as Keynes suggests (beginning of *Treatise on Money*, Part 1), thus we can wipe out the whole Figure 6.3.

When we come to Figure 6.4, we see that the Real Bill principle of security in gold for banks is now replaced by a broader definition of primary security, which the banks have to do, but then they send the loans further and convert them into bonds which are sold at the open market as securities. The financial debacle in 2008 was to a large degree due to the lack of primary control of the payment ability and the securities of the original customer. But such a mechanism is in fact built into the system, since the banks in this system do not particularly earn much on the interest rate differences between lending and borrowing but do earn money on the volume of transactions and the speed of turnover.

As we see from Figure 6.4, there is no other fundamental form of security than that which the lenders come up with, and that is of two kinds: marketable securities, houses, bonds and equities and ability to pay.

Without a doubt, the system of Figure 6.4 is more market-friendly, but on the other hand we may suspect that larger industries are preferred over smaller businesses and richer people to middle-class people.

Obviously, however, the system in Figure 6.4 requires different kinds of control systems and is probably more difficult to control. The debacle in 2008 tells us clearly of the problems. We cannot postulate that everybody within the financial business is a morally superior person.

Particularly not since the bulk of banks' profits lies in the actual turnover volume and too-meticulous controls have a tendency to negatively affect the turnover volume.

As we said above, none of these systems exists in its pure form, and that is a consequence of globalization and deregulation. There are many complaints of deregulation in different countries, but that was more or less a necessity since the rules became obsolete and inefficient.

The reasons for this kind of market development from Figure 6.3 to 6.4 and the different role of inflation are to be found in the development of the economic structure in the aftermath of WWII. The problem of inflation was linked to the Bretton Woods system and the necessity of balancing trade to have a stable system. After the breakdown of Bretton Woods, there was a period in which many countries formed different kinds of policies, multilateral, bilateral as well as unilateral in the form of currency baskets. Such policies led to the same attitude to inflation as before.

However, in the 1970s and 1980s, when markets became more globalized, practical reasons made companies raise money on the very place of investments, which mainly followed the demand structure. As the internationalization proceeded, differences in taxes, labour market rules, laws affecting production and so on came to direct the real investment flows and thus the corresponding money flows. In the 1980s and 1990s, the efforts by the states to make the international financial flows more smooth and secure released the financial flows from the real flows. This was also accompanied by decisions by the Bank of England and the Federal Reserve, other central banks following, to accept the banks' market valuations and rely on controlling the soundness of the valuation principles.

All this implied a refinement of the "financial engineering", and we arrived at an international system where the banking/financial sector was actually defining the concept of money with respect to what Thornton calls "papers capable of circulation".

The inflation problem is to be seen from this perspective. Inflation differences and, more precisely, inflation expectation differences will now directly affect the valuation of securities. As we see from Figure 6.4, this will primarily affect not only the banks but the whole body of assets and liabilities irrespective of holders. Thus, the money system and monetary policy is, with respect to Figure 6.4, in principle endogenous to the real transactions and it is here that the imprecision of the inflation concept hits the economy.

As we have mentioned, it is rather bizarre to see that the attitudes to the problem of inflation and growth have changed 180 degrees rather recently, when Europe is on the brink of social unease and low inflation as a grant for high growth has been changed to increasing inflation to foster growth. The intrinsic uncertainty of the relations between growth and inflation was in fact already discussed by David Hume. It disappeared in the neoclassical model since money as a realistic concept disappeared, and it was revived by Keynes but disappeared again in the IS-LM model only to appear as something called stagflation, which was invented as an answer to irregularities of the Phillips curve which was nothing but a crude statistical relationship where concepts were not even defined in a statistical sense.

Securitizing, uncertainty and trust

The fundamental role of the financial sector is to transform long-run assets into liquid resources. That can concern a single agent who has an abundance of real assets or long-run financial assets but has a current need for liquidity for some reason.

Thus the financial analysis is in most cases asymmetric since it deals with one agent who lowers liquidity at the benefit of someone who increases liquidity. Under the assumptions of a known future or known space of outcome as well as known probability distribution over this space of outcome, the asymmetry is hardly any problem, and the financial sector can in principle be disregarded. To have a meaningful analysis of the financial sector is a necessary but not sufficient condition as the future is *uncertain* in the sense that the space of outcome is not known, and subsequently we cannot attach even a subjective probability distribution. If we assume the existence of inert social structures, we may apply Keynes' expression "sufficient reason", but that is not enough to produce some assumed probability distribution. Thus Keynes divides the "forecast" which an agent may have concerning the future, taking the inertia into consideration, into two steps. First we have the ranking of likelihood of a set of events, and then we have the confidence with which we make the ranking. This is actually rather close to Allais' paradox in his analysis of the expected utility hypothesis.[5]

Keynes' approach to the use of formal probability theory is to a great extent a part of the discussion of atomic and complex facts. In *A Treatise on Probability* (1962[1921]:71), he sketches out the general idea:

> The question to be raised in this chapter is somewhat novel; after much consideration I remain uncertain as to how much importance to attach to it. The magnitude of the probability of an argument, in the sense discussed in Chapter III, depends upon a balance between what may be termed the favourable and the unfavourable evidence; a new piece of evidence which leaves this balance unchanged, also leaves the probability of the argument unchanged. But it seems that there may be another respect in which some kind of quantitative comparison between arguments is possible. This comparison turns upon a balance not between the favourable and the unfavourable evidence, but between the absolute amounts of relevant knowledge and of relevant ignorance respectively.
>
> (Keynes 1962[1921]:71)

In natural sciences the research objects, variables and relations are often very inert; the aspects Keynes raises have little relevance for the research other than when the research concerns universal structures, particularly over considerable times. We know that there are theoretical discrepancies between macroscopic space and time structures and microscopic quantum mechanics, but these are rather well defined and can be avoided in ordinary research. In social sciences where humans are subjects and final causes, this is not the case. Inert periods, even local, are seldom more than the length of a human life and most are considerably shorter; it is enough to look at the political map of Europe during the 20th century to be convinced. Consequently, uncertainty is vital in order to understand the problem of asymmetry in borrowing and lending. But as we said, uncertainty is a necessary but not sufficient condition. The liquidity per se must have a value. The concept of lexicographic preferences was developed for other types of analysis but may be suitable here. Lexicographic preference ordering in the neoclassical theory does not play a particularly important role, and as Arrow and Hahn (1971:405) suggest with respect to bankruptcies, we can have some general insurance system which saves individuals from the negative value effects which cause demand to decrease. But if we look at the financial side and its repercussions, the very issue is valuations and revaluations of real and financial assets, and in principle such revaluation should mirror the changes in pricing of the global commodity basket. But since we cannot assume perfect information of all agents but shattered and asymmetric, which per se induces a possibility of moneymaking outside the assumed "correct" spheres, we will have events leading to results like we illustrate in lexicographic preferences.

Thus, when it comes to the concept of liquidity, this can be treated as lexicographically determined for certain volumes determined by the specific economic activity in question. Keynes discussed three reasons to keep liquidity: for purchases, for security and for speculation. To grant the future purchase of certain commodities, defined by self, the agent needs a certain liquidity. This is a structural condition. But this also goes for the society. When there is a shortage of the medium of exchange for some reason – Hume mentions a lack of physical money, but we may think of distrust in the banking system as in the aftermath of the 2008 debacle – the society in general may go through systemic changes.

Consequently, these matters together with uncertainty imply an asymmetry in the affairs of lending/borrowing.

Arrow and Hahn actually discuss such an asymmetry (ibid.:360–361); however, their discussion is more directed towards the eventual existence of an equilibrium when the debtor goes bankrupt and the creditor has a discontinuous fall in wealth.

From our point of view, however, the asymmetry of liquidity in conjunction with uncertainty, in the sense that the space of outcome is not known, creates the money trade/money exchange. The notion of security is then of course essential. Since there is an asymmetry in the most liquid asset, money of some form, there is a dimension independent from any security that can possibly be obtained. Thus all other physical assets and commodities are bound to be paid in money. The only comparable asset is in fact the future production/salaries of the debtors.

It is however true that a bank craves a physical security which is not comparable to financial borrowing with respect to liquidity but which will hurt the debtor considerably if he fails to pay the debt service. Sometimes, even when it concerns entrepreneur borrowing, the security may not correspond at all to the debt, but we can regard it as a sort of strengthening of moral obligations.

Thus in general when we talk about lending to individual agents, the banks have routines to handle the asymmetry. However, when we consider the macroscopic levels and liquidity slumps, there is no remedy endogenous to the financial system, since the reason for liquidity slump is due to distrust; that is, emotions due to certain events which enlarge the public apprehension of the space of uncertainties. Thus the fundamental problem with the debacle in 2008 was not the events per se but the increased uncertainty of debt defaults, which destroyed the previous apprehensions of risk distributions. Such a change of the general atmosphere cannot be handled by purely intellectual means; it needs actions which at least give an impression of being remedies. So, from a scientific point of view, a general distrust is not only an analytical response but an emotional one, and as such it is more powerful with respect to long-run effects.

As we have discussed earlier, an analytical conviction is due to reasons built on events and processes of the real world while emotions trigger more basic emotions of fear, suspicions, conspiracy theories and so on, some reasonable, some unreasonable. But according to current understandings in neurological research, such emotions will have physiological effects on the brain apart from the intellectual understanding. This is the very central basis of irreversibility of social sciences.

So, if we look at the first decade and a half of the 21st century, it started in Europe with a tight austerity policy to fight inflation, followed by the 2008 debacle which depended on the almost criminal behaviour of banks, and after that an austerity policy because of the reckless bank behaviour allowed by authorities during the first period of austerity policy.[6]

Even non-scientists must ask about the logical consistency of the public policy, and that creates a common emotional climate which is indeed difficult to forecast; current anomalies in international and national politics might be, at least partly, traced back to earlier inconsistencies.

Consequently, the financial sector is necessary for the money economy, and it is also vulnerable due to the discussed asymmetry of lending and borrowing.

However the quote above from Arrow and Hahn hints also at another asymmetry which is a bit more difficult to realize, which is implicit in the inflation/deflation discussion but which has been hidden during most of the 20th century by the sterile discussion of the so-called *real balance effect*. That means that in a deflation, the drop in demand is met by an increase in value of the money balances and thus will stimulate the demand. The real balance theory was developed by Pigou (1943), but Kalecki (1944) pointed out that debts were contracted in nominal prices; why we would expect a sharp increase in real debt values? For the modern financial market, where most debts are transformed into marketed bonds and bills, we would of cause have a huge loss in wealth. Kalecki's critique is fully consistent with the quote from Arrow and Hahn (1971), but then we also have the problem of austerity policy and, more generally, how to pay a debt.

The debt contract has a dual role in that the holder of the contract has an asset for the future. As we said earlier, this is not a problem on the microscopic level where financial discipline is necessary to uphold. But when the financial system creates itself through lax lending and reckless risk analysis, we get a situation where for example austerity policy more or less wipes out real demand and consequently real production. This will have deep-going effects in economic, social and most probably also on political areas. Thus the moral obligations at the microscopic levels which are evident and the good will at the macroscopic levels, if imposed, have structural effects which spread outside the very parties of the lending/borrowing contract. It also raises the question of what are we paying back. A nominal debt is raised according to a certain commodity basket of the society, implying a certain distribution of wealth and income. If the amortization of the debt is changing this commodity basket and distribution, it will certainly lead to a moral dilemma.

We have arrived at a nasty question for economic policy: Shall we protect the future value of paper assets and liabilities at the expense of real growth?

If we answer yes to that question, we must ask what and who we protect. In fact, we then protect financial wealth at the price of a shrinking production system, and we then also create a process of unlimited concentration of economic wealth. Whether this is socially, culturally or ethically sustainable, others than me may answer.

Notes

1 This is a summary of a lengthy conversation I had with a homeless person in Gothenburg, Sweden, in 2005.
2 Sy, Ibrahima, (2013). The Subjective Approach as a Tool for Understanding Poverty: The Case of Senegal, *Procedia Economics and Finance*, Vol. 5, pp. 336–345.
3 https://en.wikipedia.org/wiki/Marginalism
4 In Ekstedt (2013) chapter 2 and Ekstedt (2015:153–168), this debate and other matters are comprehensively discussed.
5 Allais, Maurice, (1953). Le comportement de l'homme rationel devant le risque: Critique des postulates et axiomes de l'ecole amricaine, *Econometrica*, Vol. 21, pp. 503–546. In Ekstedt (2013:203–205) there is a discussion on Allais' paradox.
6 Concerning macroscopic policy, there are no such excuses as "we did not know", "we could not forecast", "we did not have the means".

Bibliography

Allais, M., (1953). Le comportement de l'homme rationel devant le risque: Critique des postulates et axiomes de l'ecole amricaine, *Econometrica*, Vol. 21, pp. 503–546.
Arrow, K.J. and Hahn, F.H., (1971). *General Competitive Analysis*, Holden Day Inc., San Francisco.
Braudel, F., (1992[1979]). *Civilization and Capitalism 15th–18th Century, Vol. II: The Wheels of Commerce*, University of California Press, Berkeley, LA and Los Angeles.
Ekstedt, H., (2013). *Money in Economic Theory*, Routledge, London and New York.
Ekstedt, H., (2015). *Money, Valuation and Growth: Conceptualizations and Contradictions of the Money Economy*, Routledge, London and New York.
Grice-Hutchinson, M., (1952). *The School of Salamanca*, Clarendon Press, Oxford.
Hume, D.A., (1770[1752]). *Essays and Treatises on Several Subjects, Vol. II: Containing Essays, Moral, Political, and Litterary*, Printed for T. Cadell (successor of Mr. Millar) in the Strand; and A. Kincaid and A. Donaldson, at Edinburgh.
Hume, D.A., (2002[1740]). *A Treatise of Human Nature*, Oxford University Press, Oxford.
Kalecki, M., (1944). Professor Pigou on the "Classical Stationary State": A comment, *Economic Journal*, Vol. 54, No. 213, pp. 131–132.
Keynes, J., (1962[1921]). *A Treatise on Probability*, Harper & Row Publishers, New York.
Makarov, V.L. and Rubinov, A.M., (1977). *Economic Dynamics and Equilibria*, Springer Verlag, Heidelberg and Berlin.
Pigou, A.C., (1943). The classical stationary state, *Economic Journal*, Vol. 53, No. 212, pp. 343–351.
Say, J.B., (1834[1803]). *A Treatise on Political Economy; or the Production, Distribution, and Consumption of Wealth*. Grigg & Elliot, 9, North Fourth Street, Philadelphia.
Sy, I., (2013). The Subjective Approach as a Tool for Understanding Poverty: The Case of Senegal, *Procedia Economics and Finance*, Vol. 5, pp. 336–345.
Thornton, H., (1939[1802]). *An Enquiry into the Nature and Effects of the Paper Credit of Great Britain*, George Allen and Unwin, Ltd, London, available at internet http://oll.libertyfund.org/index.php?option=com_staticxt&staticfile=show.php%3Ftitle=2041&layout=html
Wicksell, K., (1936[1893]). *Interest and Prices*, Macmillan and Co. Ltd., London. (The original appeared in German 1893 as *Geldzins und Güterpreise*.)

7 The Other and collective social action

Listen to the truth and grow up

In 1960 in a small Swedish village in a remote area, there was a boy of 14 years. He was at that age when the body's growth is most unbalanced, so although he was rather tall and sturdy, he was dominated by a giant nose and two giant feet. When he entered a room, there first appeared two feet, then a big red nose, and so the rest of the body. But people, relatives and friends told the boy that he was going to become a real Viking. That was obviously something good, so the boy was satisfied to be one of "us", although some doubts of that had earlier popped up now and then.

One day in biology class, the teacher talked about human races and showed pictures of other "races". The teacher, who was very entertaining, characterized the mental characters linked to the pictures. The boy and the other pupils all laughed. Then the teacher told about different tools to measure which "race" a person belonged to. One of the best methods, the teacher said, was to measure the head. The boy thought that was interesting as he was one of "us".

The measurement of the skulls of the pupils was executed. There was one in the class who did not belong to "us", and that was the boy. The teacher leered at him with a sardonic smile and said, "Well, you can also be of some use." The other pupils laughed, probably connecting the measurement to the earlier characterizations.

The boy was stunned. He met his first big crushing defeat. It was proved that he, the alleged Viking, belonged to the Other.

That lesson is the one single lesson from that period the boy, then the man, now the elderly man remembers from that age. He had not had any reason to complain of any problems in that dimension in his life, but when he was 14, during a forty-five minute class, he realized the truth and he aged many years.

Introduction

Nations are collective organizations uniting individuals within a geographical area around some collective goals and purposes. We can see the EU as an intellectual creation to avoid devastating wars in future Europe, but we can also see it as a mainly economic organization. Within the EU there are nations, and nowadays we have strong movements of nationalism while the overall organization is looked upon with scepticism, although the benefits of the union seem to appear after a decision to leave the union. We hear complaints that we do not have an identity as Europeans.

It is often so that people in two neighbouring countries tell rather degrading stories of people of the neighbour country. Mostly this is done as friendly jokes, but there is sometimes a small bite. There is a Danish saying: "Those who take all jokes for jokes and all serious stuff seriously understand little of life".

Macroscopic organizations like nations affect the intrinsic characteristics of their population by differences in law and by demographical and historical differences; patterns differ. Between Sweden and Norway, it is indeed difficult to see any differences between the sides of the national border, except for slight differences in language and in some minor custom and patterns. So, why should there be derogatory stories between those neighbours? Perhaps the stories are not aimed at the other part but for assuring ourselves of some basic national identity, and by historical cherry-picking, we may end up in the conviction that this identity is simply the best. Thus those stories are perhaps a patriotic or nationalistic glue.

A closer look at nations almost always reveals that the internal differences between people are much larger than those detectable on an aggregate level in comparison between the two countries. The national border is not a border between characters of individuals. Perhaps we use these stories to make a difference between *us* and *the others*?

Maybe it is so that during stable and friendly periods, such stories are innocent but in a period of tensions, they become tools to define the others/the enemy. If we look at the UK and the USA today, where both countries define their identities in different ways, we find caricatures of the Other of the same type as we find in innocent friendly stories when the political tension is low. Thus, innocent friendly jokes about *the Other* may be a tool in the national socialization process.

Consequently, when we are considering physical, political and social actions, there is always an *us* as well as a *them*. But a necessary thing is to understand mutual relations, interrelations with respect to potential repercussions. Such questions are not understandable at a simplified aggregate level, which furthermore is underpinned with a broad categorization more based on emotions than on intellect. In our discussions of individual apprehension and actions, we were basically in line with Hume's attitude that passion rules the human being and that the intellect is its humble servant, and we stay with that attitude. But then we must realize that in the social space, the passions create chaos if not understood by the intellect. Consequently, a large part of the socialization process is to bring passions under control by intellectual understanding. But even the most controlled humans must realize at least within themselves that there are moments when emotions become rather powerful and go beyond the control of the intellect; this is both for better and worse. The Portuguese brain researcher Antonio Damasio, whom we have earlier discussed, makes a rather good analogy when he compares feelings/emotions to lighthouses guiding the intellect. Thus when we analyze Kant's and Hume's approaches, we shall not see the passions and intellect as contradictive factors but more that feelings/emotions are the guardians of underlying "axiomatic" personality structures which sometimes are or threaten to be broken by the intellect and send us a sign of danger, support or cautiousness with respect to decisions/actions.

However, when we turn to social action in a democracy, we have to deal with contradictive individual passions. We may normally believe that in a stable social environment the "passion-space" is rather limited and there is a general "live and let live" attitude governing, but that probably depends on what creates stability and how we understand stability. In contrast, we have experiences created by social interactions and the very context of these interactions at the very moment of interaction. As our earlier discussions show, Aristotle and Hume as well as modern neurological and psychiatric research suggest that events, information and experiences are moulded on one hand by momentary emotional reactions and atmosphere and on the other hand by the memory and the intellect. This process is seldom conscious but integrated in the personality.

Collective ethics, the nation and *Fides Punica*[1]

Power, particularly public power, is often regarded as something mystical. In general there are three nodes for this mysticism: the King/Government, the Bureaucracy and the People. But above these nodes there is a mystical sphere, which sometimes is called the world spirit, sometimes evolution and sometimes God, sometimes the people.

With respect to God, we have the principle of "King by the Providence of God" or "to whom the responsibility and power are given, to them God will give wisdom". This deals with the problem of controlling those in power, both for the king and for the bureaucracy, and it is of course those in power who tell the people that they are the legitimate persons to lead and to be in control.

The concept of the people from the mystical, metaphysical point of view is used to unite a population, often in relation to curbed social unease or when there is some form of external pressure. We can see nowadays how nationalism flourishes as a reaction to globalism and how different groups use it to gain power. In Europe during the 19th century, in the aftermath of the Napoleonic wars, nationalism was a means to legitimate a geographical area as being a natural foundation of a state. Belgium is an example where the legitimacy is rather low and thus has a rather complicated constitution, while the Nordic countries have been more successful in claiming their legitimacy.

This often was based on language and cultural similarities, and it is notable that the two great poets Dante Alighieri and Johann von Goethe were initiators of systemizing their respective languages, Italian and German. This meant that the linguistic differences between the ruled and the ruling elite, where the latter produced their documents in Latin and French, were wiped out successively, which was a key factor in the uniting processes of the respective areas, ending in the end of 19th century in Italy and Germany. But the language is in itself extremely complex, and combined with poetry and sagas it easily becomes mystic. During the 17th century, when Sweden reached a position as one of the main powers in Europe and at the same time was, for those times, organized as a modern central power, Swedish had to be regarded as a language as high and valuable as Latin and French, which often were used in the bureaucracy. Olaus Magni, an in many cases interesting thinker, frankly declared (and proved) that the paradise Eden was placed in Sweden. One of the co-researchers of Georg Stiernhielm, Andreas Kempe, who wrote *Die Sprachen des Paradises* (*The Languages of Paradise*), asked the interesting question of what language they spoke in paradise. His answer is significant: God spoke Swedish and Adam, who was not as perfect, spoke Danish, but when these two probably discussed high things, Eve, the weak vessel, spoke with the snake, and the snake seducing her spoke French (Eco 1997:97).

Influenced by romanticism, nationalism during the 19th century was mostly based on the Latin concept *ius sanguinis*, which can be interpreted as birth rights, the rights of the blood, and in Germany concepts like *Blut und Boden* (Blood and Soil) developed which were frequently used during the Nazi era. In Sweden we had similar trends and similar concepts. Nationalism often has racial and ethnic connotations, like the *white man's burden* in the English colonial tradition.

An alternative Latin concept is *ius soli*, the territorial right, where the citizenship was linked to the territory irrespective of ethnic or cultural matters.

In the United States, a country based on rather recent immigration, one expects the latter concept of *ius soli* to be advocated, but here we have the racial problem, or should we perhaps say obsession, which emanates from the times of slavery. There are also two remarkable periods where the *ius sanguinis* principle has been frequently used by the political elite: the early 1950s with Joseph McCarthy and nowadays, culminating in the election of Donald Trump. During these periods *ius sanguinis* seems to be a main path of argumentation. These periods are in some sense similar.

American participation in the two world wars was based more on supporting allies than having a direct enemy. In WWII the USA was attacked by Japan, allied with Germany and Italy, but that was more as a consequence of its position as a supporter of England most of all, and the attack came after Germany's attack on the Soviet Union.

After WWII and the war in Korea, the USA became the leading Western nation and of NATO and was consequently in much more direct opposition to the other victorious nation in WWII, the Soviet Union, which had substantially increased its influence. Thus the USA was in a situation of much harder exogenous pressure than before WWII, so some groups felt a need to merge the population under common nationalistic goals. Consequently Americanism and anti-Americanism were key political concepts. The situation was further accentuated by the Korean War and the ideological conflict between so-called "American capitalism" and communism, which enlarged ordinary nationalism to cover modes and patterns of living.

The situation now is that for the first time since the aftermath of the WWII, the workforce of the USA directly perceives globalism and the global competition to a substantial degree in form of unemployment, outsourcing and technological inferiority in some sectors. It is therefore no surprise that President Trump's rather crude not to say brutal language and politics gain support from the working class and the middle class, while the intellectual class generally dismisses him. We must also point out that the competitive situation of the USA as an industry nation has considerably deteriorated compared with the 1960s and 1970s.

Another element of more long-run character, which might foster racism and fascism, which seem to be present in the so-called Tea Party movement and recent demonstrations (as of autumn 2017) with explicit slogans of Blood and Soil, is the decreasing ratio of non-Hispanic whites. According to the US Census Bureau, the white non–Hispanic ratio of the population will decrease from 63% in 2012 to 46.6% in 2050.[2] Thus the actual economic situation might trigger also long-run fears. The current President Trump promised to build a wall between Mexico and the USA to stop illegal immigration, and he has furthermore tried to initiate draconic visa rules with respect to Arabic countries and non–whites, which is clearly in line with demographic forecasts.

Thus the *ius sanguinis* principle introduces the concepts of *the Other* and *Fides Punica*, both at the individual level and the national level. Consequently, within a nation we have the problem of *the Other* while between nations we will have the problem of *Fides Punica*. Racism and xenophobia is thus a natural outcome, internally to the country and externally. Currently we have heard one of the world leaders actually call some appointed nations "shithole countries", which probably must be sorted under some form of racism.

Fides Punica became a signification for all cultural expressions which were strange and possibly also hostile to Roman life, culture and power. The ethnic aspect per se was perhaps not as important as the cultural. Rome was a wide empire; the ethnic aspect was subordinated to the cultural aspect and the Roman jurisdiction, although there were some ethnic considerations, but these were not always in favour of Rome, as with respect to Tacitus' *Germania*. In many dimensions, particularly moral, Tacitus held the German tribes as a better and more natural society compared to the decadent Rome.

People from all over the empire were able to become Roman citizens, and thus they belonged to *us*.

In the ancient Mediterranean societies, there was generally no nationalism in the modern sense. There were local and regional differences, but these varied with the actual ruler. Earlier we discussed modes of government in relation to Otanes, Megabyzos and Darios. Concerning Herodotus himself, it is remarkable how he succeeded in being objective in his historical writing in the sense that he reports factual events and when he describes persons, he both discusses vices and virtues in a seemingly similar way, be they Athenians or enemies of Athens. He even finds governance structures and persons in Persia who he sees as example for Athens and Athenians. So, although Herodotus was from Athens, he does not look down on people and life in other parts of the Mediterranean world, particularly Persia, with which Athens was in an almost never-ending conflict, but he is convinced that the democracy of Athens is a superior constitution and is proud of that, even if he may criticize the character of singular persons. He tells about factual circumstances, actions and structures, does not use derogative expressions to describe people because they were living in an enemy state and judges persons with respect to personal characteristics, irrespective of origin.

This, by the way, is also the case when we read Thucydides' *History of the Peloponnesian War*, 208 BC, some fifty years after Herodotus. Although he was an Athenian general, Thucydides treats the Spartans and the Athenians with the same kind of respect and objectivity. Nevertheless, both Herodotus and Thucydides had scientific minds, but it is important to mention them since we, particularly in the 19th century, got a historical science which almost lasted to our days where patriotism, nationalism and racism were important ingredients in creating national states and uniting national values.

First traces, to my knowledge, of a clear singling out of *us* and *them* was during the Athenian republic and democracy, which was regarded as superior to other states. With our eyes, however, this democracy was limited to *men* of wealth, education and social position such that we perhaps would like to call it a sort of oligarchy. Nevertheless, the Athenians were proud of their freedom, which free men possessed. It had nothing per se to do with racism or xenophobia but was limited to systemic features, thus based on the *ius soli* principle.

The same can be said about *Fides Punica*, which originally related to Carthage and its way of living and structuring the society, although we know at the bottom economic matters were hovering since both powers had aspirations to control the fertile North African area, which Rome saw as its granary, and the Mediterranean trade. From the beginning it was to be regarded as a parallel to Clausewitz's "rational" wars in so far that mutual coexistence and compromise were impossible, because both states demanded absolute power over an area on trade and production, with few racial or xenophobic overtones.

This attitude changed however as the Punic wars proceeded and Carthage came to be a real threat even to Italy itself and Cato's insistence on the total destruction of Carthage, "*Ceterum censeo Carthaginem esse delendam*", got a deeper and more sinister implication.

Thus Blood and Soil may trace its roots back to Roman times, when those who opposed Rome were characterized by *Fides Punica*, unreliable and of a lower human standard than the Romans. *Fides Punica* means that a person is of a Carthaginian character, which means that his character is destructive and he is unable to build up an ordered society.[3] Those who do not accept the Roman civilization should be extinguished.

Ethnicity: racism and "untermenschen"

The ethnic aspects of *us* and *them* appeared mainly in the acceptance of a culture, a mode of governing a state, jurisdiction and so on. *Us* and *them* were very seldom defined in ethnic views. In Tacitus' *Germania* and Caesar's *Bello Gallico*, we see that both authors had a rather sensitive analysis with respect to the German people as well as their societies, although they were a bit backwards. They both compared with Rome and observed dimensions where Germans were superior and could serve as good examples for the Romans. With respect to black people, that means people from North Africa and Ethiopia, the governing opinion in antiquity was that blackness was a consequence of the sun and there were no other principal differences, and relations which were created between Greeks and Romans with societies of black population worked on equal terms between equals.

The blackness problem seems to originate from European colonization and particularly slavery, when "negroes" were dehumanized and made more animal-like, most probably to avoid the ethical aspect, since if they had been principally called humans there would have been a very severe ethical conflict within the church.

This technique, dehumanization, is used in a smaller degree rather often, for example when telling people of the female sex what is suitable and unsuitable for women, what they are good at and what they should stay away from. Thus a female individual's role as a final cause is a matter of discussion. One thing is telling a person "I do not agree with your analysis/opinion" and giving a reason that is exogenous to the person in question. Another thing is to claim that the other person is not able to make a reasonable analysis. If you are quarrelling, it might be understandable but bad; in an intellectual discussion it is an insult and it is fundamental ethical misdoing. These things are also highly relevant with respect to racism in an even more widespread way. Afua Hirsch, a columnist in *The Guardian*, wrote a column 24 January 2018 titled: "I've had enough of white people who try to deny my experience". It starts:

> "The world is wrong," wrote the American poet Claudia Rankine. "You can't put the past behind you. It's buried in you; it's turned your flesh into its own cupboard." To be black, in a society that invented race for the specific purpose of dehumanising people who are black, and then invented an equally formidable system of denial, is to carry the burden of history that others would rather forget.

Obviously such a denial is a sign that the basic sentiment of racism is actually saved, and it is present and lives in the society but takes other forms than it had during the slavery period. Hirsch said later in the article:

> It's fascinating when white people, who invariably have no personal experience of the frequent othering and subtle prejudice that comes from being born or raised in a country that does not recognize your unconditional right to its identity, tell you what you have and have not experienced.
>
> "Life's move on from race," one of my fellow panellists told me on The Pledge [a TV program in the UK; author's note]. "If it's well intentioned, it's not racism," said another. All of this was, very ironically, good evidence of my point: that white fragility operates powerfully against progress; that there are those in our society, including high-profile and influential

people, who prefer defensiveness to a cold, hard analysis of the pattern of prejudice.

Hirsch makes a perfect description of the subtle forms dehumanization may take, and it shows the role of *ius sanguinis* as opposed to *ius soli*. Let us go back to Roman times: A person in illiquid circumstances could in the worst case be sold as a slave to pay the debt, but from that state he could be released by earning enough money to buy his freedom. After a couple of years, he could then become a Roman citizen with full rights. Let us not forget that slavery was terrible and the slaves were subject to the pleasure of the owner. But principally, the slavery was a consequence of circumstances outside the person who became a slave; he could not pay his debt, he was a prisoner of war and so on. But when he became a free citizen, nobody questioned his full humanity.[4] We should also point out that almost anyone in the Roman Empire, mostly except the patricians, could be sold as a slave if circumstances were unlucky. But on the other hand we must remember that one of the most important Caesars, the great Diocletian, whom we have already discussed, was the son of a liberated slave.

Hirsch makes an interesting comment on historical memory, "an equally formidable system of denial . . . to carry the burden of history that others would rather forget", which is interesting comparing with Rome where the public/collective memory was obviously shorter.

The Romans in their execution of power were not troubled with some fancy ethics. When Vespasianus restored law and order within the Prætorian Guard, he surrounded them with elite troops and forced them to undress to be naked. Then he chose every tenth man to be killed. Hardly a way of behaviour we would support. But at the same time "the people are all in all". People were equal per se; being rich or poor, being patrician or being plebeian, your success decided who you were. In principle, the American constitution takes the same view. But there we also have the racial problem, much more visibly so than in Europe. One line of explanation is the Christian ethics. You cannot get around the Christian ethics but through dehumanization in order to ease the ethical aspects. You want slaves to build up your societies, and efficient traders realize that black people in Africa are different from whites, so we can easily build up a case of non-humanity, half-humanity, which means that the Christian ethics does not cover these creatures.[5] During the Greek and Roman times blackness was a character of an origin where the sun was strong, nothing more.

Blood and Soil versus social engineering

The two ways of looking at a particular social organization, *ius sanguinis* and *ius soli*, often have different ethical implications, but not always; the *ius soli* principle may foster a rational political organization which leads to a kind of social engineering where the individuals are just seen as factors of production. That was similar to the approach Romans had towards people. If you by any chance could not pay your debts or you were an enemy soldier or committed a crime, you could be traded as a slave; you could also sell yourself as a slave if you wanted to save your family from starving. In that case you were only seen as a tool of production. Such sentiments exist also today and may lead to slavery-like conditions in certain parts of the world. The ethics of such an approach is difficult; some say it is void of any ethics, on the other hand we may see clear signs of "duty ethics". The extreme case is Hitler's expressed duty ethics for hierarchies with the Führer at the top: full freedom downwards and full responsibility upwards in the hierarchy. This version is of course applicable at social engineering as seen as a line production scheme.

The one extreme starts from a presumption that the organization is carrying some common denominator of the group of which the interactions are doubly directed, some "Spirit" which may develop as the individuals develop, but the individuals are also affected in their attitudes/faith by the common Spirit. "We Swedes think/are/feel . . ." and we may in any country find the same kind of expressions. Normally such expressions are just sayings to tell about some rather common attitudes and lack any deeper significance, but sometimes in the name of patriotism/nationalism, such expressions are both significant and have a uniting role to play, suggesting that our Swedishness, Englishness, Frenchness and so on has an intrinsic spiritual reference which governs the lives/attitudes/behaviour of the individuals within the organization. How immigrants relate to these thoughts is difficult to say, but the present actions of American and British authorities seem to suggest that it is at least a possibility that these thoughts of Spirit of the People or Blood Brotherhood are coming back into the highest circles of power. As a matter of fact, on 11 August 2017 in Charlottesville, Virginia, white nationalists demonstrated under the slogan of Blood and Soil, and in the clash between those demonstrators and anti-Nazi demonstrators, an anti-Nazi woman was murdered by a man driving a car into the anti-Nazi demonstration. The president of the USA seemed to blame both parties equally for what has happened; in fact, according to CNN coverage, the president blamed the alleged illegal anti-Nazi-demonstration for being "very, very violent".

In the British paper The Guardian, columnist Zoe Williams, in a depressed tone, comments on the growing nationalism in Britain parallel to the Brexit process:[6]

> Nationalism has taken a depressing turn, this past year and a half. The suspicion of foreigners and alienation of former allies are the greatest practical threats to the country's wellbeing and prosperity.
>   . . .
>
> A nationalism constantly asserted defines itself against the foreign; a nationalism that goes unstated defines itself from within – its tacit understandings are its connective tissue. It was no accident that we rarely talked about patriotism. But if meaningful patriotism is social – a nationhood based on building collectively within borders, not for geographical reasons but because those are the perimeters of your democratic agency – there was never any shortage of it.

Often, the representatives of racists and nationalism regard democracy and openness as inferior matters compared with the questions concerning Blood and Soil, but one wonders what would happen if their current goals were reached and the society would find a sort of daily routine; what new goals would be set up and what new *Others* they would set forth and how it would all start over again.

The German Protestant priest Martin Niemöller, who in early 1930s supported Hitler but in 1934 joined the Nazi opposition within the Protestant Church led by Karl Barth and Dietrich Bonhoeffer, wrote a poem in the 1950s:

> *First they came for the Socialists, and I did not speak out –*
> *because I was not a Socialist.*
> *Then they came for the Trade Unionists, and I did not speak out –*
> *because I was not a Trade Unionist.*
> *Then they came for the Jews, and I did not speak out –*
> *because I was not a Jew.*
> *Then they came for me – and there was no one left to speak for me.*[7]

The other extreme attitude, social rationalism, is that a country just consists of a bunch of people which we in some sense have to tame and mould into a nation where collective decisions can be made and hopefully be rational. Such attitudes are often implicit in what we call social engineering and build on some kind of political rationality in analysis and action. With respect to the question of *us* and *others*, it is more difficult to single out a clear line of thought, but there are some good examples, as we will see.

Looking at the problem from a strictly logical point of view at the same time as we accept the Aristotelian view, supported by Hume and to a certain degree by modern brain research, we find that even a social rationality attitude has problems. This attitude, which we assume is based upon rationality of a mathematical description, which is more or less identical to the neoclassical axiomatic structure, is just an intellectual tool due to contextual apprehension and perceived restrictions, as we have shown in the prologue; it is a tool given an epistemic cycle. This implies that social engineering is in principle a rather good thing, given that the social, political and cultural environment governs its scopes and limits. Missing that, social engineering may take any direction.

Adolf Eichmann was certainly very efficient in organizing a fundamental part of the Holocaust and he delivered an optimization of goals vis-à-vis existing restrictions and thus fulfilled his given orders, but he did not add or subtract anything from his orders; he was the perfect administrator.[8]

Thus, from a strictly logical point of view, the social engineering approach to society is just a chimera since it basically suggests that once we agree on goals and means, we optimize the problem in a rational way. What is dangerous is when people suggesting this line of action either imagine clear goals for the society which are sometimes parts of a systematic ideology and sometimes disguised, or the other alternative is that they are unaware of or indifferent to the problem *in toto* and are just administrators. When it comes to Eichmann, Hannah Arendt's description sooner suggests the latter, since Eichmann seems rather void of any deeper approaches to the society. He did his duty, that's it. Stretching Kant a bit, this is the basic problem in his paper on enlightenment [*Aufklärung*] with respect to maturity and immaturity.

A further question which we may ask is what happens to those individuals who do not fit into the rationality scheme.

The dark shadows of the 20th century
Swedish debate of racial hygiene

The story told at the beginning is rather ugly, and when we put that into a proper Swedish historical perspective, it becomes somewhat frightening. However, it gives an excellent example of the two extremes we mentioned in the introduction.

In 1922 the Institute for Race Biology was created in Stockholm. It was the first research institute in the world of that kind. The goal was to find the causes of criminality, alcoholism and psychological problems through research in race biology and thus improve the racial hygiene and create a rational population policy. The Institute for Race Biology became a part of the department of medical genetics at the University of Uppsala. The founder of the Institute, Herman Lundborg, received an honorary doctorate in Heidelberg during the Nazi time and died in 1943.[9] The research mainly concerned Sweden, where people from each of the twenty-four counties were investigated, but also included Finland and the Baltic countries, particularly Estonia and Latvia. Even photos of people from Hawaii were represented in the collections and analyzed. The analysis did not only concern physical differences but also alleged intellectual and emotional differences as well as social conditions.

An interesting fact is that with respect to the photos of naked persons comparing the Nordic type with the Sami type, which were regarded as inferior, those persons representing the Nordic type are between 25 and 30 years old while the Sami were between 40 and 50 years old (Broberg 1995:25). Lundborg had contacts all over the world: Denmark, England, France, Germany, Japan and the USA, to name some. It can also be mentioned that Gunnar Myrdal participated in an international seminar arranged by the Institute in 1930 (ibid.:40).

Another notable aspect was that the research was mixed up with cultural and historical aspects of Sweden. Thus in the Stockholm exhibition in 1930, the Institute displayed four mottos: "To Arian blood the cleanest and the oldest", "To a Swede I was consecrated by a friendly Norn", "I am nothing, but my race, my root, my tribe is all", and finally "A people of a good race are the greatest asset of a nation" (ibid.:49) We see here Blood and Soil expressed *in flagrante*. There is much more to tell, but it is rather clear what was the purpose of the Institute for Race Biology.

Lundborg was replaced in 1935 by Gunnar Dahlberg, who was an outspoken anti-Nazi. He stopped the earlier research and introduced studies on twins which still have an important position in genetics research. Unfortunately, however, Lundborg's opinions penetrated the minds not only of racial extremists but of many ordinary people who thought it was science; it may be that some still do.

However, when the Nazi government in Germany needed a model for racial hygiene, there already existed one which they could use, the one from Sweden, and that was developed within the most respectable scientific establishment. Fortunately, Dahlberg succeeded in preventing much of the development of the racist thoughts, at least in scientific circles, and saved Sweden from a worse development into the swamp – although the later development was bad enough, which we will see.

The highly respected couple Gunnar and Alva Myrdal, the former a Nobel laureate in Economics, the latter a minister of the Social Democratic government for many years, wrote in 1934 the book *Kris i befolkningsfrågan* (*Crises in the Population Question*). In this book they lined up principles for social welfare policy, the education system, childcare, the health system, workers' conditions and some other areas. Many of their suggestions were excellent when seen from a 21st-century perspective. We could say that it was a utopia, which was feasible; they also realized that it was built on solidarity, but this solidarity should not be pressed too far. Thus they advocated a "sorting out of useless individuals" through "a merciless sterilization policy", and between 1934 and 1941, the parliament of Sweden decided laws which gave the society the right to sterilize people with alleged unwanted hereditary dispositions.

In a discussion of the new law (1934) on sterilization of mentally disabled persons they write in chapter 7, which dealt with the question of sterilization, page 260:

> What far-reaching effects on the quality of the population this law will have is obviously difficult to forecast. First of all it depends on the rigour of its implementation, that is to say how often the possibility of sterilization is taken advantage of. From a social-pedagogical and a genetic point of view, it is therefore appropriate from the start with the strictest possible implementation of the law. For those cases where legal capacity cannot be denied, in spite of the fact that the conditions for sterilization are appropriate, physicians and social authorities should actively persuade the person in question to voluntarily submit to sterilization. If this pressure, in too many cases, is inefficient, the laws must be made more stringent and the possibilities of sterilization must be increased, to strengthen the legal power for the authorities to sterilize also against the will of the individuals, even those with legal capacity. Furthermore, the sterilization procedure for the whole group of those individuals, which fall outside the possibility of sterilization,

should be completed with efficient and free distribution of contraceptives and when pregnancy still occurs with abortion on eugenic and social indicators.

(author's translation)

As a motive for the draconic laws on sterilization, Alva and Gunnar Myrdal write further down in chapter 7:

> The problem, as we have emphasized several times, concerns all those not fully able individuals, who in the modern society have difficulties maintaining their physical existence, this decile or perhaps quintile of the population, who are at risk to fail in the brutal competition. In the discussion on these wider perspectives we have to remember, and we have emphasized this, the technical development and its implied consequences on the socioeconomic organization of the society perpetually tends to increase the requirements of intelligence and character.
>
> (author's translation)

Observe that they were talking of a group of people of a size of 10–20% of the population, which in principle would be subject to sterilization.

These laws were removed in 1974. So, during the 1950s, when Germany had removed all such reminiscences from the Nazi times, Sweden used them to the same degree as before; in the 1960s, however, the enthusiasm for implementing the laws diminished. In 1974 there were approximately 16,000 persons still living who were sterilized, and many of them had regained their full legal capacity; in 1980 the Swedish state consented to pay substantial damages to those still living.

It is clear that there were links between Myrdal and Herman Lundborg's Institute; however, with respect to Gunnar Myrdal, we may say more, not in defence of the 1934 book but more to show another side of him. In 1942 he published his study *An American Dilemma: The Negro Problem and Modern Democracy*, in which he claims that there is no scientific evidence for the opinion that black people are in any mental, physical or genetic way inferior to white people. He indeed looked at the problem as a very grave moral problem for the USA, and in the author's preface, he writes (p. xix):

> When, in this way, the data on the American Negro problem are marshalled under the high ideals of the American Creed, the fact must be faced that the result is rather dark. Indeed, as it will be pointed out in the first chapter, the Negro problem in America represents a moral lag in the development of the nation and a study of it must record nearly everything which is bad and wrong in America.

Myrdal (1942) actually took for his time a sensible view that differences in social life and the individual behaviour of black people as a group could be explained by the prejudices and discrimination of the white-dominant society, where the black person does not belong to *us* but to *the Other*.

To explain the difference between Alva and Gunnar Myrdal's 1934 book and Gunnar Myrdal's 1942 book, which wrongly seem to be of similar character, we must see it from a social engineering point of view. In the 1934 book, the Myrdals define the ethical valuation of humans with respect to the individual's participation in the collective development of the society. Those who are not able to work shall not eat. In the 1942 book, Myrdal is keen to pursue the idea that, although black people are able to make a contribution equal in value to that of white people, particularly in the WWI and then-current WWII eras, they are discriminated against and lack access to many facilities of the society in which they serve as good citizens. He is then perfectly consistent with this social engineering point of view and with respect to people who are mentally disabled, criminals or indolent and who cannot survive by themselves, much less feed their children.

There has been a lot of confusion about Myrdal's shifting opinions, but he did not change his basic standpoint, which can be explained by the fact that he did not see human beings as a goal per se but as a means of production. This was also the ruling opinion of the Social Democratic party, to which both Alva and Gunnar Myrdal belonged, and implicitly in radical Marxian materialistic philosophy. But with respect to the execution of a policy, the choice between Lundborg and Myrdal is as a choice between Scylla and Charybdis.

Consequently, Sweden has a rather ugly history both with respect to racial questions as well as with respect to the worst kind of social engineering attitudes.

#MeToo

It is interesting to see the recent transnational #MeToo movement in this light. According to Keith Thomas (1988; chapters 1.V and 4.V), animals could have a higher ranking than humans, and it was discussed whether or not women possessed a soul. Anyway, this was some 240 years ago. Women got the rights to vote in the early 20th century, and up to the late 1960s, women engaged in trade unions had to suffer not only phony jokes but also abusive behaviour from employers as well as male fellow union members. Changing cultures and patterns takes time when it comes to power relations, and particularly power relations when mixed with sexual drive. Thus the #MeToo movement is stirring up some feeling of men in power that they are benevolent to women's rights, but they expect that the persons of the *weaker sex* should be a bit grateful and give them some small favours.

Seen in such a perspective, the #MeToo movement is about something more and deeper than the very acts of sexual harassment; it hits straight into the problem of handling asymmetry of power relations and the ethics of such situations, it is also equivalent with Afua Hirsch's analysis with respect to racial matters.

Thus #MeToo touches on the deepest form of ethical baseline in human relations. In this book we treat humans as subjects and consequently final causes.

That means that the subject may act on his or her own pleasure with respect to the environment, which includes other subjects. Consequently, an action which uses some form of power to deny a person his or her very subjectness is the most fundamental unethical action towards an individual. This has nothing to do with punishments of individuals breaking a common law, where the individual has to take the full responsibility for his or her action, but the punishment must be such that the subjectness of the human is never questioned. Thus, a human can never be used as a means without his or her own consent. The latter implies that forcing people who are poor to do bestial things or sell themselves as slaves is the most fundamental ethical wrongdoing towards people.

This is the very ethical complex which the #MeToo movement charges right into, and this is the fundamental human discussion in which it should end up.

In fact, this point of asymmetric power relations is the fundamental key in the relations between the collective government and the individuals. All governance requires different forms of subordination due to a constitution, due to knowledge, due to asymmetric responsibility. We subordinate to people not because of their attitudes, as shown in Picture 5.1, but because they have a particular responsibility to uphold and protect the order of the constitution which we submit to. Furthermore, we subordinate to people who have particular knowledge. If an engineer suggests a certain joist size when we discuss the building of an extra room, we can ask for a second opinion, but in the end we need to follow building code standards. If the fire prevention authorities suggest certain building materials for a block of flats, we are wise to submit to that to minimize the risk of the spread of fire. This is surely not a matter of excessive power but for the protection of people. Refusal to follow such rules in order to save money is reducing the dignity/subjectness of the potential tenants and is an ethical wrongdoing at the very baseline level.

Thus the baseline ethics is not opposed to asymmetric power relations as such, but it deals with their use and purpose. "The people are all in all", Otanes claimed; consequently, a constitution based on that and preventing that implies the necessity of subordination to a common set of rules governing the social life; we may call it a constitution and particulars following from that. This subordination unfortunately tends to increase with the increasing complexification of the society.

What, then, is freedom for the individual? Well, it has to start in the social interaction of people, social responsiveness, and then the fundamental condition must be in a democracy that the people are all in all; that is, from an Aristotelian view, that all individuals irrespective of race, faith and property are subjects and thus final causes. This must be the main element in a constitution as well as in ethics for individuals. This is so to say the basic contractual relation, if we may use such a metaphor. Saving the humanity of humans implies obviously freedom, but that might vary between different dimensions. We have shown for example that the so-called model of liberal economy as it is expressed in the neoclassical theory is neither particularly free nor stable and most of all nonexistent. That of course implies that the market principle may run into conflicts with our baseline ethics and therefore needs corrections. This does not mean that the market principle per se is in any kind unethical, but it is not a universal solution. It also means that collective measures of controlling the market are not per se antagonistic to the market principle but may stabilize it in the long run.

The most difficult problem when we deal with baseline ethics is the development we sketched out in Figure 5.2 of the increasing complexification.

Power, loyalty and responsibility

Duff Cooper (2001) tells in his biography on Talleyrand, Napoleon's foreign minister as well as a diplomat in the restored monarchy who was by many seen as an opportunist and a turncoat, that when he was approaching his death, Talleyrand said: "I have always been loyal to France but not to her rulers". By that he certainly did not mean any metaphysical ideas of France but the French state and the French people.

With respect to the earlier discussion on government forms in Persia in 486 BC the saying points at the most central question: To whom are we loyal? This was also touched on by Keynes commenting on industrial workers and particularly coal miners who got reduced salaries after Britain's return to the gold standard in 1925, against Keynes' advice.

The reaction from the Tories and the liberal party was very harsh.

> The strikers are not red revolutionaries; they are not seeking to overturn the parliament; they are not executing the first movement of a calculated manoeuvre. They are caught in a coil, not entirely of their own weaving in which behaviour, which is futile and may greatly injure themselves and their neighbours, is nevertheless the only way which seems to them to be open for expressing their feelings and sympathy and for maintaining comradeship and keeping faith.[10]
>
> (Keynes (1981[1926])[11]

Thus, to deny some people the rights to react to ruler's decisions is against the democratic principles put forward by Otanes', and is reducing their subjectiveness. Loyalty to a Nation does not imply loyalty to a government representing group interests.

In a dictatorship, loyalty is enforced and it is also the case in wars quite naturally, but in a democracy, what is loyalty? Loyal to the country, to the government, to a party, to an ideology, to a religion – and how do these different macroscopic loyalties relate to the microscopic loyalties to one's family, to one's friends, to one's home town? Probably most of us have been in situations where we are haunted with different kinds of loyalty conflicts.

We have discussed the concepts of *ius sanguinis* and *ius soli*. They require two different types of loyalty; the former is abstract from individuals and requires loyalty towards some alleged metaphysical character of country race or class, irrespective of the current context. The latter requires loyalty to the constitution of the society of a geographical area where the individual lives and where he is also supposed to take part in the development of the society with respect to the current situation in an active way.

The two principles can be enlarged also to ideologies and party member-ship. Those who have metaphysical approaches to ideologies and/or parties as carriers of particular traditions, values, spirit and so on induce a similar prin-ciple as *ius sanguinis* in the sense that their loyalty is relatively independent of current events; instead, current events must be seen in the perspective of more long-term or eternal values. An example is the classical communist classifica-tion of ideological enemies into tactical and strategic enemies, a classification which was disastrous with respect to the situation in Germany during the 1920s and 1930s.

In elections, there are questions of practical current matters, but there is also the heavy ideological artillery: "Where do you belong, to us or to them?" "Are you a traitor to the ideas and/or your class?" The *ius soli* principle applied to ideologies and parties implies that you judge the party with respect to its actions and declarations with respect to the current situation. Sometimes this behav-iour is called wallet-voting. The behaviour however does not necessarily show a lack of principles but disagreement with the interpretation of the application of certain principles in relation to a specific context and here we come, most probably, close to Talleyrand's claim. Keynes' (1925) "Am I a liberal" expressed similar thoughts as Talleyrand:

> Not to belong to a party; cold and lonely and futile it is. If your party is strong, and its programme and its philosophy sympathetic, satisfying the gregarious, practical, and intellectual instincts all at the same time, how very agreeable that must be! – worth a large subscription and all one's spare time; – that is, if you are a political animal. So the political animal who cannot bring himself to utter the contemptible words, "I am no party man," would almost rather belong to any party than to none. If he can-not find a home by the principle of attraction, he must find one by the principle of repulsion and go to those whom he dislikes least, rather than stay out in the cold.

The latter principle is fully consistent with our attitude that collective organiza-tions are formed by individuals and that the composition of individuals creates the collective attitude; thus we reject any exogenous spirits or other forms of metaphysical constructions. The problem with the latter is that it requires much and relevant information with respect to the important dimensions of the cur-rent situation and structure. Simple formulations of who gains in economic terms of different kinds of politics are much easier than explaining probable long- and short-run structural impacts which may be as wrong as the simple messages but at least show the complexities. In the Brexit referendum, it was said that not paying the fee to the EU could be transformed to increased financial resources for the health care of Britain. Now in the beginning of 2018, it seems as if that aspect is more seldom used or does not play an important role in the Brexit strategy.

If we go back to Otanes, who advocated democracy on the grounds that it implied transparency and free speech, we can add that the structural composition of a society will change and we more or less automatically arrive at an attitude that loyalty must basically refer to the "living city", not the dead city, if we allude to the earlier quote from Luigi Amoroso. My duty as an individual is to take care of my life and my offspring, and as we discussed according to Aristotle, that also includes my social environment by using ethical principles to reach social cohesion. But for the collective bodies, that means that an attitude like "We want to live as we always have done", or even worse, "We want to go back to our great past" is at best meaningless. We discussed in the preceding chapter the principles of saturation and anomie, and furthermore we discussed the human being not only as a social being but a social responsive being. These aspects are not exogenous to the individuals but intrinsic to psychological constitutions and to human interaction. Thus, irrespective of whether we treat ethics as something that God has given to humans or we think that ethics is a human ability received by different socialization processes, the principle is that ethics must first of all be a feature of social behaviour from a pure existential reason, since humans are subjects and temporal and local final causes and consequently induce the highest form of uncertainty to themselves. If we maintain such a view, which is as it seems the most rational, we end up in a sort of application of the *ius soli* principle.

To claim that others should be loyal is easy if it is not linked to responsibility and the risk of punishment of some kind. We have claimed that the most fundamental unethical action is to deprive a subject of its subjectness and its status as a final cause. Claiming that others should be loyal is equivalent to subordination and an enforced or accepted limitation of subjectness. Thus, if we have a situation of dictatorship, the individuals are forced and there is not much to say other than that revolutionary actions are to be judged according to the same ethical norms as enforced dictatorship. In a democracy, however, it is difficult to see the use of loyalty as an argument without a correspondent responsibility.

But that can never concern historical actions, structures and purposes without having a bearing on the current future socio-economic development. In such a case, the attachment to historical structures has consequences for the development, like any other political approach. In saying that we want to restore traditional values, there must be proper explanation of how these values are going be interpreted in the current society, and if they are not valid, how they are to be implemented. A good exercise is to contemplate the saying of Giuseppe Tomasi di Lampedusa (Il Gattapardo) when he joined Garibaldi's revolutionary forces in Italy in the late 19th century: "To let it be as it was, we have to change everything."

From a political and ideological point of view, loyalty implies that we are loyal to a hope for the future. The hope can be a sort of utopia, or it can take realistic forms as social and economic goals. Nevertheless, this implies that believing such a hope implies an almost constant revision of the means to achieve the hope with respect to the society's current structural composition. To separate actions into revolutionary or revisionist is hardly of any use if we do not specify the current structures. Actions are means of achieving a hope and must be judged by efficiency matters and collateral effects; otherwise they are at best poetical whims. The ethical question is of course if humans are a goal per se or a means. If someone claims the latter to be the case, also the one claiming this can be disposed of as a means.

Conflicting loyalties in a collective will obviously be transferred into goal conflicts. In economics, goal conflicts are much discussed, particularly at the macroscopic level. Goal conflicts appear when we have antagonistic goals between groups; that is, the goals per se can be the same but the fulfilment may be contradictory. Such conflicts are mostly due to distribution and/or allocation aspects. In the deepest sense, such conflicts have nothing to do with economic analysis in a narrow sense but are a part of the social and cultural analysis. Then we have indirect conflicts due to conflicting conceptualization and economic means. The most obvious example is inflation and unemployment. To solve these problems, it is claimed that we have to use means which are conflicting, so means to solve inflation must affect unemployment negatively. What we can say is that solving problems defined on the macroscopic levels without a precise structural and conceptual analysis of social and cultural implications in principle disqualifies any solution as relevant.

When we deal with science and its use in practical, political, physical and medical questions, it is of course unavoidable that scientific results have a guiding role in the society even if the results are often heavily criticized from groups which are hit by them, which is normal. A meaningful scientific result concerning some part of reality must affect physical, medical or social reality in an asymmetric way. But what is the responsibility of the scientists in such a case? Why should anyone outside science care about any scientific results whatsoever?

We know by experience and by reasoning that we cannot find any final truth, but that is not important. We know on the other hand that the reality consists of interfering structures of higher or lower complexity and by careful conceptualization and measurement. We are then right to assume that we can approach local and temporal truths which have underpinned historical development of knowledge. But such a development requires constant control of conceptualizations, axiomatic structures, measurement methods and observation techniques. With respect to this, we know and understand that natural sciences are a bit different from social sciences: the object/subject aspect is one difference, and differences in inertia of structures are another. If we look at the social, economic and cultural development after WWII, there are few physical, electrochemical and physiological structures which show more violent dynamics. It is obvious that respective sciences have to adapt to such conditions. But when we find a so-called science, economics, which in its basic analysis uses an a priori axiomatic foundation which concerns a barter economy where such concepts as money, state, monopoly, oligopoly, financial contracts, inflation are not even defined, and it claims that this can mirror the essential features of the modern economy, the question is if any attention at all should be paid to such a science in its practical recommendation. We do not question that many economists are very good in practical policy analysis, but the science per se must get rid of the kind of thinking which is represented by the neoclassical theory and admit that economics is *one of* the social sciences, and more specifically a sub-science within sociology and why not anthropology? The ideological character of economics is embarrassing, and to the author it seems that hardly any policy based on suggestions from economic scientists can be trusted in the same sense as natural sciences and also other social sciences which are undeveloped in their methodology, but at least they are aware of it.

From an ethical point of view, concepts like loyalty, trust and cooperation require mutual responsibility. Cheating, which is often looked upon as some kind of smart behaviour, must by mature individuals – mature in Kant's sense – be regarded as a structural threat to the society. But how do we express such thoughts in economic science, which deals with the economic system which more than anything else needs trust and loyalty to function even if the neoclassical foundation is void of any ethical values of that dignity?

Ethics, the state and the market

It is sometimes instructive to go back in the near history to read comments of academics in close relation to some important events in the world. The last four decades have been extremely turbulent. The 1990s included the breakdown of the Soviet Union, the devastating Balkan war, the genocide in Rwanda, the Gulf war and the steady increase of terrorism. The first decade of the new millennium started with the dot-com bubble collapse, closely followed by the terrorist attack on the Twin Towers in New York, continuing with the Iraq war and the financial collapse of 2008, followed by a worldwide recession. Now in the second decade, we have witnessed the gruesome civil war in Syria followed by increased xenophobia and racism in Europe and the USA, resulting in a blind nationalism prepared to tear down all arduously built links of trust and cooperation just because of the question about what system is the best to protect us from fear, particularly.

Thus for the moment it seems like chaotic trends are overwhelming. The main driving force for this seems to be fear together with short-sightedness and an overestimation of the protection wealth and guns can give. But it is also something deeper, and that is the belief in what in financial analysis is called technical analysis, which means that history can be extrapolated into the future. Our main effort in this book has been to show that modelling is like photos; we arrange or choose a certain motive, and then we ask with respect to the picture what happens if we edit it and change some details or even delete them. In reality, we must speak about inertia, dissipative and inert structures and the robustness of structural changes. We must realize that a structural change may alter the conditions and the possible logic completely and that space-time is neither continuous nor stable with respect to dimensions, due mainly to the fact that humans are subjects. The key to understanding ethics is the recognition of this basic uncertainty.

Robert Kaplan (2002) makes an interesting historical projection from a British mission in the late 19th century in Soudan, the Mahdist war, which is described by Churchill in the *River War* (1902). Kaplan writes about the present context (2002) and claims that:

> Today, unlike in the late 1930s, we face no threat on the scale of Hitler. The bipolar nature of World War II and Cold War alliances is no longer evident. Our situation is more similar to that of the late Victorians, who had to deal with nasty little wars in anarchic corners of the globe, such as Sudan. Is it too far-fetched to imagine our own expedition through similar desert wastes to apprehend another Mahdi-like figure, Osama bin Laden?
>
> (Kaplan 2002:27)

We know that the US security finally got Osama bin Laden, but what that meant besides blazing placards, few know. Hitler, WWII and the Cold War are historical eras and events. They were created by unique structures which have broken down and been replaced by others. In 2018, the changes and the uncertainty of policy which followed the 2016 presidential election in the USA and the Brexit referendum in 2016 have the potential to create substantial structural reorganization in the world. What really comes out of it, nobody can say, but it cannot be solved by means used in the 20th century. From a historical point of view, the current situation seems like we have to merge Nero becoming an emperor in Rome with some of the involved victorious powers breaking the Westphalian Peace, and that is surely a challenging task for even the best historians. To guess the future is impossible since we cannot rule out the appearance of complete unpredictable events in the present atmosphere of fear of declination in the rich countries.

In his book *War Politics: Why Leadership Demands a Pagan Ethics*, Kaplan makes many good observations of the structural social and economic problems in the global society as they could be seen in 2002, and the book is written in an effort to show how the USA and its values should be preserved. He then comes to the conclusion that the USA must navigate by itself and the ethics used must be pagan, particularly that of Athens according to Thucydides, implying that no attention should be paid neither to the other states in question nor to democracy and its spread. Furthermore, his use of the concept *pagan ethics* implies that he regards ethics in a different way compared to Aristotle. For Aristotle, ethics is something integrated in humans, based on the fact that humans unlike animals have an ability of ethical reaction. Animals react more or less directly instinctively on observation. Humans have a space of apprehension, comprehension and speculation between the observation and the action, where ethics is the emotional and intellectual judgement of the context to achieve the highest good, but that is under the condition that *the other's* answer to my reaction affects me. For Kaplan, ethics is like a coat we take on: Christian ethics, pagan ethics or whatever, and furthermore ethics seems to be linked to metaphysics and is independent of the context. Kaplan ends his book in an interesting way, which clearly indicates a *Fides Punica* view with respect to international politics, although not necessarily an *ius sanguinis* attitude:

> At the beginning of the twenty-first century, the world media shows little sympathy for the challenges and awful ironies facing those who wield power; it upholds the safer virtue of sympathizing only with the powerless. Yet our greatest presidents knew that the wise employment of force was the surest guide to progress. In the Roosevelt Room of the White House's West Wing, where important staff meetings are held, there is a relief carving of Teddy Roosevelt with these words of the twenty-sixth president – words that might have been written by Machiavelli, Thucydides, or Churchill: "Aggressive fighting for the right is the noblest sport the world affords."
>
> (ibid.:154)

About Machiavelli and Thucydides, I find it hard to believe that these two analysts would have expressed it like that; Churchill, maybe. The two former were well aware of the possibility of warfare, but they regarded it as a last resort of conflict resolution. Particularly Thucydides, who was an Athenian general, realized the uncertain prospects of war. In his history he praises the wisdom of Nikias in his opposition to Alcibiades, who was the proponent for the Sicilian expedition which became a disaster for Athens (Thucydides 1978[408 BC]:83). Alcibiades, however, might well have uttered the words attributed to Theodore Roosevelt.

Kaplan ends his book very interestingly:

> The United States is nothing without its democracy; rather, it is the homeland of freedom rather than of blood. But to deposit judiciously its democratic seeds in a wider world that is closer and more dangerous than ever before, it will be compelled to apply ideals that while not necessarily democratic, are worthy nonetheless. The more respect we have for the truths of the past, the more certain our journey away from it.
>
> (Kaplan 2002:155)

He notes the basic character of the USA as it appears both in its constitution and in the history of its creation, namely that the USA originally builds on the *ius soli* principle, not *ius sanguinis*. The conclusion, however, that the USA could manoeuvre independently in this increasingly dangerous world is a bit remarkable. Our discussion earlier with respect to Cécile Laborde and Isensee and Schmidt, completed with our discussion of saturation processes and anomie, shows that its internal structural complexity might well be higher than the structural complexity between regions and countries. An independent foreign policy of a nation, built as Kaplan indicates on sheer physical power, is only possible if the nation in question is also independent in social, cultural and economic dimensions. Thus the foreign policy is not something independent of any other political dimensions in a nation but has to be integrated with respect to trade and other economic links as well as social and cultural dimensions. We said above that we can only be loyal to the future, not to history, but we know from our philosophic discussions on Aristotle, Hume, Kant and others, our imagination of the future is created by our current apprehensions, memories, social and cultural structures; thus loyalty to a nation cannot be just to fight the right cause and engage in a noble sport. It has also to contain General Thucydides' resistance to venture into such a noble sport.

Kaplan's analysis, seen in retrospect from early 2018, is interesting since recently the *ius sanguinis* principle seems to have gained ground in the USA. Thus the multitude of ethnicity, culture and social structures was not earlier a feature of the nation as a whole, but the nation obviously contained antagonistic structures which were hidden by a superficial aggregate interpretation, as Laborde discusses. From this perspective, one may suspect that the last quote from Kaplan advocates some sort of ethnic, cultural and social unity to fight the surrounding mean world, which is perhaps the oldest form of the use of *Fides Punica*. At the moment, it seems as if the gap between ethnic, cultural and different types of other social groups are widening. Although the current foreign policy of the USA seems more aggressive than it has been for decades in breaking up international agreements and distancing itself from traditional allies without gaining new allies, we note that the industrial capacity of the USA is far weaker than during the 1960s, when the USA was close to its allies and took a leading position. Furthermore the financial markets, earlier dominated by US actors, are becoming more pluralistic and unstable.

Thus an analysis such as Kaplan's focussing on a rather superficial development of war policy with historical parallels, which are poor parallels since they lack a structural environment, becomes rather dangerous since no attention is paid to structural tensions which do not necessarily have anything to do with national borders. Kaplan's concerns about paying too much attention to poor people is difficult to understand from an ethical point of view, since the question of poor people is one of the most important structural questions we currently experience and which threatens stability to a very high degree.

The breakdown of nations?

It is apparent to many people today, as it seems from ordinary conversations, that the national governments have less control of the public dimensions in the nation. Even when considering decisions/actions by the government, the effects seem to be much more uncertain than some decades ago. People in general often have a feeling that the power of the government is deteriorating and surrounding nations, financial agents and other factors affect our lives more. Much of the current nationalistic groups, actions and beliefs come from such feelings, and the reaction is not difficult to understand: "We want to be a sovereign people", whatever that may mean.

Perhaps the word *breakdown* is an exaggeration of the situation, but the global development and integration does require a different attitude to the concept of nations. During such times of transition, like we have now, it is quite natural that we stick to what is well-known and what seems secure, although these matters perhaps are the most unsecure and isolationism in different forms is not an unnatural reaction. If we look at this reaction, we may think of rather instinctive reactions of herds closing to defend themselves against an aggressor.

However, the problem with human society is that in these days, it seldom can be regarded as a herd, a flock of animals, although both the *ius sanguinis* and the *ius soli* principles can include such a consideration, even if the *ius soli* principle is then to be regarded as a collection of animals of different kinds, not a herd as commonly understood.

We thus start in the *ius soli* principle, and we also can go back to David Hume's enthusiasm for money and the cultural and social benefits it brought to the humanity.

A social and cultural development is never symmetric. If we take the Italian Renaissance, it started with increased trade with the Middle East during the 12th and 13th centuries, creating new demand and new fashion, and on top of that Greece was rediscovered in art and in philosophy. Plato had been known earlier, and now Aristotle was presented by the Muslim Averroes to the western parts of the Mediterranean population. Arabic mathematics was introduced to the Europeans and so on. Obviously it was a relatively small group of fairly wealthy and culturally curious people who could anticipate the news, but they affected the local and regional power elite, such as the Medici family, which obviously affected art, music and literature. Homer was also rediscovered. Artists like Dante and Mantegna appeared. This spread all over Europe but slowly, so the renaissance of Northern France, Flanders and Southern Germany started some fifty or a hundred years later. In Sweden, traces of the Italian Renaissance appeared some 250 years later.

New thoughts penetrated a society asymmetrically with respect to social and economic classes and also with respect to characteristics of the cultural structure.

Consequently the new thoughts and the new structures have a differentiated effect on a society where increasing cultural and social distances become a rather typical feature. This is also in line with the analysis of Johan Asplund, which we related in Chapter 6. But at the same time we get a reaction of adaption and integration which implies that the old concepts undergo changes to meet the new dimensions.

We can see some interesting features in the current debate in the EU. Some people regard the EU as a revised border of the European Nations in the meaning that we protect European civilization against the surrounding world. Others look at the EU as a kind of start to internationalization to get away from the narrow nationalism. Still others regard the EU as a creation of an economic and further a military power which may set or at least affect the global agenda to a higher degree. At the same time, however, we know that the global problems require new solutions which at the moment are unknown or parts of ideas in some rather confused minds.

The same year as Kaplan's book appeared, 2002, there appeared another book written by Philip Bobbitt: *The Shield of Achilles: War, Peace and the Course of History.* The interesting thing is that he had basically the same attitude as Kaplan in analyzing the development and maintenance of the USA from a rather patriotic perspective. Bobbitt has a history as political and military advisor to the American government in both Democratic and Republican administrations.

Bobbitt starts with a very comprehensive historical exposé where, at variance with Kaplan, he tries to isolate the development of trends which might be of later importance. He is aware of non-linearity and structural breakdowns:

> To say this is to contrast "strategic planning" with "scenario planning." Both rely on intelligence estimates that are based on the careful analysis of immense amounts of information, sorting out the true from the false, assigning probabilities to information that might be either true or false, guessing what the future would be like if all the relevant facts were available to the analyst. The problem for estimative intelligence in the current environment is that it depends upon a relatively stable world from which to extrapolate. No one has grasped this better than Joseph Nye, the former head of the National Intelligence Council at the CIA, who wrote:
>
>> Greater complexities in the structure of power means greater uncertainty in estimating the future. Politics often undergo nonlinear change, but such changes have become much more frequent than during the Cold War. . . . Similarly, if one were to estimate today how many nuclear weapons a country with no nuclear facilities might have in five years, the linear answer would be zero. But that would change if the country were able to purchase stolen nuclear weapons on the transnational black market.
>
> (Bobbitt 2002:717)

Thus we live in a world where structures in some sense become more inert due to complexities. An example is the climate problem, which requires means to solve which are known but which imply deep-going political, social, demographic and infrastructural problems. Overlooking such inertia increases the risks of social backlashes, which delays possible solutions considerably. On the other hand, the appearances of new dimensions, like in the example from the quote with respect to nuclear weapons, some structures will also become more dissipative. In the latter example, triggering fear may cause certain social structures to break down due to fear alone, through processes of anomie, *Fides Punica* and similar.

A thing like democracy is perishable and has to be regained in the minds of people every day. All kinds of simple analysis point to the fact that democracy is disposable, naïve and inefficient; it is only after the second or sometimes even the third thought we realizes its benefits, but then we also need to act less instinctively to fear.

We mentioned Kaplan above who recommended a higher degree of isolationism for the USA to defend it efficiently from a principle point of view, but only when it was suitable with respect to international affairs and problems like poverty. Bobbitt gives certainly another picture in the quote above which also includes the USA, and he arrives at a conclusion which is quite different from Kaplan's, written in the shadow of 11 September 2001:

> The world community faces its own historic challenge in creating a constitution for the international order that will emerge from this war [on terrorism]. Will that community – the society of states – use the discredited multilateral institutions of the nation-state as a way of frustrating action in order to control acts of its strongest member, the United States? Or will that society simply expect every state to defend itself as best it can, spiraling into a chaos of self-help, ad hoc interventions, and sabotage? Or will that community consist of islands of authoritarianism, whose institutions focus only inward in an attempt to prevent violence by harsh police methods? Or can we learn to produce *collective goods* – like shared intelligence and shared surveillance information from shared nanosensors and shared missile and cyber defenses? Indeed the production and distribution of collective goods – such as the coalition against international terrorism itself – may be the only way for a market-state to forestall peer competition and defeat international terrorism at the same time.
>
> (original emphasis; ibid.:821)

How can these two analysts, who describe the military situation of 2002 in a fairly similar way and also see the need for a new type of defence strategy, arrive at such different conclusions?

The answer to that is that Kaplan just looks at the military situation. He has obviously not understood Clausewitz's words that war is the continuation of politics, which implies that we can win all the battles but still lose the peace.

Bobbitt makes two remarks at the beginning of chapter 9 which are central to explain the difference and also why in the next chapter in this book, we deal with war.

Bobbitt writes:

> Open any textbook on constitutional law and you will find discussions of the regulation of commerce and the power of taxation, religious and racial accommodation, class and wealth conflicts, labor turmoil and free speech, but little or nothing on war. . . .
>
> Open any textbook on war and you will find chapters on strategy, the causes of wars, limited war, nuclear weapons, even the ethics of war, but nothing on the constitutions of societies that make war – nothing, that is, on what people are fighting to protect to assert, to aggrandize. A constitution

is not merely the *document* that manifests the ways in which a society recognizes the rights of family, of property, of land and personal security, of
commerce, of ethnicity and religious commitment, and of government itself:
rather a constitution *is* these ways.

(original emphasis; ibid.:205–6)

Bobbitt works very near those principles which Clausewitz draws up, and we
will comment on them in the next chapter.

However, in his analysis, Bobbitt looks at the military questions from a
broad social point of view. We can only give just a very rude picture of Bobbitt's analysis, but he claims that globalization, with respect to economic links,
commercial structures, scientific and technological structures as well as social
and cultural structures, has become so intertwined and complex that general
wars such as WWI and WWII are from an intellectual point of view almost
impossible to start for the leading central state as they will more or less lead to
self-destruction. However, due to social friction in a broad meaning there are
always groups, even countries, which may disturb the order of the central states;
that may well be intrinsic to the states in question at the start but also as covert
actions, terrorism and cyberattacks from states and from extremist groups. Such
actions may have roots in inequalities, economic or social, but they may also have
their roots in religious or ideological fanaticism. Seen from such a perspective,
the complexity of our world in different dimensions, as we tried to show in
Figure 5.2, makes our world much more vulnerable, irrespective of where we
live. Bobbitt tries to work out a scheme for the market-state based on the fact
that our technological and economic development may give possibilities for the
individual never experienced before and which cannot be distributed by the
central state. He thus suggests that the central state move a higher degree of its
policy towards matters of central stability and leave to the market a higher degree
of the traditional welfare policy.

To a certain extent, we agree with Bobbitt about the central state, whether it is
a multinational body like the EU or a nation-state. This necessitates a deregulation of trans-border relations, but it also means that the states have to subordinate
to transnational judicial and regulatory bodies, and the Brexit process shows
the difficulty. Furthermore, the instability of the financial market as well as the
monopolization process requires transnational agreements and supervising bodies. Thus Bobbitt's version of the modern market-state is indeed a radical form of
globalism. A consequence of course is that we pay attention to the very sources
of social unease. Inequalities of people are the main source of social unease, and
it takes many forms which superficially point towards something else. Religious
fanaticism is one example, but also other forms of fanaticism: racism, xenophobia, nationalism and so on.

Thus Kaplan and Bobbitt arrive at different answers regarding war and security depending on their different perspectives of the society and the role and
outcomes of wars. Kaplan claims that in order to defend our way of living, we
have to sacrifice Christian ethics and replace it with pagan ethics. Bobbitt on

the other hand claims a rather traditional Aristotelian view (although he does not mention Aristotle) that ethics is an implicit factor in humans and that ethical judgements must be used as a means to achieve the highest good, which also includes our social relations both as individuals and as states.

No man is an island, and that also goes for nations.

Notes

1 This chapter was inspired by Gruen, Erich S., (2011). *Rethinking the Other in Antiquity*, Princeton University Press, Princeton, NJ, and Oxford.
2 2012 National Population Projections: Summary Tables – People and Households. Table 6: Percent Distribution of the Projected Population by Race and Hispanic Origin for the United States: 2015 to 2060.
  The projected figure for 2015 was 61.8%, while the actual figure for 2016, according to statistics released in July 2016, was 61.3%.
3 Källa: The Other in Ancient History.
4 There is a famous and amusing story by Petronius Arbiter (27–66 AD) of an enormous banquet arranged by a former slave, Trimalchio, who had become a Roman citizen.
5 Before slavery, Africa had a flourishing culture as in present Congo, Mali and Ghana, to mention a few. These were destroyed by slavery and colonialism. The dehumanization in Europe was not limited but the patrician classes looked upon lower classes as almost animals (Thomas 1988[1983]).
6 Williams, Zoe, (2017). Irony Used to Define the English: In Brexit Britain, It's Self-Importance, *The Guardian*, October 30th.
7 https://en.wikipedia.org/wiki/First_they_came_. . .
8 The famous philosopher Hannah Arendt gives a fascinating portrait of Eichmann in her book *Eichmann in Jerusalem: A Report on the Banality of Evil*.
9 The facts are taken from Broberg, Gunnar, (1995). *Statlig Rasforskning: En historik över rasbiologiska institutet* [Public Racial Research: An Historical Exposé of the Institute for Race Biology]. Ugglan 4, 2nd ed., Lund Studies in the History of Science and Ideas.
10 Keynes here seems to be a rather keen follower of the *ius soli* principle.
11 Keynes, J.M., (1981[1926]), *Reflections on the Strike The Collected Writings of John Maynard Keynes* (ed) Donald Moggeridge. Vol. XIX Activities 1922–1929. *The Return to Gold and Industrial Policy*. Part II, pp. 531–532. MacMillan, Cambridge University Press, London and Cambridge.

Bibliography

Amoroso, L., (1938). Vilfredo Pareto, *Econometrica*, Vol. 6, No. 1.
Arendt, H., (1996[1963]). *Den banala ondskan* (A Report on the Banality of Evil), Daidalos, Göteborg.
Asplund, J., (1967). *Mättnadsprocesser* (Saturation Processes), Argos Förlag AB, Uppsala.
Bobbitt, P., (2002). *The Shield of Achilles: War, Peace and the Course of History*, Allen Lane The Penguin Press, London.
Broberg, G., (1995). *Statlig rasforskning: En historik över rasbiologiska institutet* (Public Racial Research: An Historical Exposé of the Institute for Race Biology). Ugglan 4, 2nd ed., Lund Studies in the History of Science and Ideas.
Churchill, W.S., (1902). *The River War*, The Project Gutenberg EBook of *The River War* by Winston S. Churchill, available at internet https://www.gutenberg.org/files/4943/4943-h/4943-h.htm
Cooper, D., (2001). *Talleyrand*, Grove Press, New York.
Di Lampedusa, G.T., (1960[1959]). *Leoparden* (Il Gattopardo), Bonniers, Stockholm.

Eco, U., (1997). *The Search for the Perfect Language*, Fontana Press, London.

Gruen, E.S., (2011). *Rethinking the Other in Antiquity*, Princeton University Press, Princeton, NJ, and Oxford.

Herodotus: The History of Herodotus. Trans. George Rawlinson. The English translation is provided by The Internet Classics Archive, available at internet http://classics.mit.edu//Herodotus/history.html

Kaplan, R.D., (2002). *Warrior Politics*, Random House, New York.

Keynes, J.M., (1931). *Am I a Liberal: Essays in Persuasion, Part IV* (chapter 3) (first published 1925), McMillan and Co., Ltd., London, available at internet https://gutenberg.ca/ebooks/keynes-essaysinpersuasion/keynes-essaysinpersuasion-00-h.html#Am_Liberal

Laborde, C., (2001). The Culture(s) of the Republic: Nationalism and Multiculturalism in French Republican Thought, *Political Theory*, Vol. 29, No 5, October, pp. 708–727.

Myrdal, A. and Myrdal, G., (1935). *Kris i befolkningsfrågan* (Crises in the Population Question), Bonniers, Stockholm.

Myrdal, G., (1942). *An American Dilemma: The Negro Problem and Modern Democracy*, available at internet https://archive.org/stream/AmericanDilemmaTheNegroProblemAndModern Democracy/AmericanDelemmaVersion2_djvu.txt

Thomas, K., (1988[1983]). *Människan och Naturen* (Man and the Natural World), Ordfronts Förlag, Stockholm (Translated from English).

Thucydides, (1978[408 BC]). *Kriget mellan Sparta och Athen II* (History of the Peloponesian War), Forum, Uddevalla.

8 War

Introduction

We have now come to the most devastating moment in the interaction with *the Other* and its collective correspondence, *Fides Punica*: war.

Many people believe that war is the final breakdown of ethics, and we have seen how Robert Kaplan advocates a pagan ethics for *the Other*, thus Christian ethics is reserved for *us*.

Obviously war and the actions of war may contain the worst form of bestialities, genocide and similar cruelties which are actions in blind hate. But to think of war as an action of blind hate is probably the worst kind of myth in preserving humans as only driven by blind instinct. Like a conflict between two individuals, it can be controlled by intrinsic emotional and intellectual limitations. The war as an armed conflict between two collective organizations is performed by individuals. If we had homogenous feelings of blind hate from the single individual up to the most aggregate body of the country in war, nothing could save human beings from extinction. Fortunately, there are people who have a more complex view of loyalty.

On the other hand, we have civil wars where the leading bodies of the two sides are competing for the same ultimate power, which makes civil war more brutal.

As a basic ground for our discussions on war between nations, we have chosen *On War* by Carl von Clausewitz. It was published posthumously 1832 by Clausewitz's wife, who organized the more or less ready texts and notes on revisions. Clausewitz was a colonel in the Prussian army and his main goal was to fight Napoleon, so when Prussia in 1812 subordinated to Napoleon in the Russian war, Clausewitz became a Russian advisor. After Napoleon was defeated, Clausewitz returned to Prussia, where he became a major general. His book *Vom Kriege* (*On War*) is generally thought of as one of the fundamental analyses of war, its links to policy, its logic and its unpredictability.

Let us look at his view of war as a kind of alternative to Theodore Roosevelt's words which, according to Robert Kaplan (2002:154), are canonized in the White House.[1] From chapter I.I.28 we read:

> War is, therefore, not only chameleon-like in character, because it changes its colour in some degree in each particular case, but it is also, as a whole, in

relation to the predominant tendencies which are in it, a wonderful trinity, composed of the original violence of its elements, hatred and animosity, which may be looked upon as blind instinct; of the play of probabilities and chance, which make it a free activity of the soul; and of the subordinate nature of a political instrument, by which it belongs purely to the reason.

The first of these three phases concerns more the people the second, more the General and his Army; the third, more the Government. The passions which break forth in War must already have a latent existence in the peoples. The range which the display of courage and talents shall get in the realm of probabilities and of chance depends on the particular characteristics of the General and his Army, but the political objects belong to the Government alone.

These three tendencies, which appear like so many different law-givers, are deeply rooted in the nature of the subject, and at the same time variable in degree. A theory which would leave any one of them out of account, or set up any arbitrary relation between them, would immediately become involved in such a contradiction with the reality, that it might be regarded as destroyed at once by that alone.

The problem is, therefore, that theory shall keep itself poised in a manner between these three tendencies, as between three points of attraction.

The way in which alone this difficult problem can be solved we shall examine in the book on the "Theory of War." In every case the conception of War, as here defined, will be the first ray of light which shows us the true foundation of theory, and which first separates the great masses and allows us to distinguish them from one another.

Consequently, when we discuss wars between organized central states, actions of "blind hatred" are more a trouble to the central command than of any benefit. A vast part of the military training in the organized central state is therefore to learn how to control the blind instincts, but as we all know, success sometimes seems to be limited.

The declaration "Peace for our time" was made by the British prime minister Neville Chamberlain in a speech to the British people less than one year before the outbreak of WWII. Today, nobody even thinks of such a claim since it seems a contradiction in terms with the global environment of climate crises, energy crises, poverty crises and the huge amount of regional war. On top of that there are world leaders who seem to behave like medieval princes, who were prepared to start a war in order to show their virility. One feels that Clausewitz's words in I.I.23 are indeed relevant:

> Such is War; such the Commander who conducts it; such the theory which rules it. But War is no pastime; no mere passion for venturing and winning; no work of a free enthusiasm; it is a serious means for a serious object. All that appearance which it wears from the varying hues of fortune, all that it assimilates into itself of the oscillations of passion, of courage, of imagination, of enthusiasm, are only particular properties of this means.

Since Clausewitz's time, there has been some development of three particular dimensions: the development of means of mass destruction, the increase of the relative involvement of civil population in the war, and finally the different dimensions of global integration. We will partially follow a systematics developed by Colonels William S. Lind and John Boyd, analysts at the Pentagon, on different "generations" of warfare. Their systematics is more limited than Clausewitz's and broadly deals with the character of war per se and also the degree of mobilization of other sectors in the society, but as a complement to Clausewitz it works.

Breakdown of ethics

As long as we associate ethics only with not inflicting bodily pain and death as the ultimate goal, the outbreak of war will be seen as the breakdown of ethics. But if we consider that humans are subjects and thus final causes and we claim a baseline ethics, namely that we always have to respect the subjectness of people, we can still come to situations where the desires of the subjects are contradictory and even contrary. In such a case, if compromises are impossible violence is within the probable space of outcome. Here it is important to understand Clausewitz's basic condition, namely that we do not question our opponent per se, but we consider a conflict of goals. Thus our opponent has the same subjectness as we, but we seriously disagree. That excludes a discourse like the Nazis' categorization of Arians and "untermenschen", and also the colonial attitude like "the white man's burden". The earlier discussed book on pagan ethics by Robert Kaplan is quite interesting since he expresses admiration for many of the colonial purposes and attitudes. One reason why Clausewitz refrains from such attitudes is that when it comes to war, the victorious side writes both the history and the norms.

In the above quote from Clausewitz, he also mentions states of mind which basically prevent any ethical discussion such as blind passion, hatred and animosity. He places these feelings among the general uninformed people. For those who really have to decide the outbreak of war, such as the government of a nation, the mind must "subordinate nature of a political instrument, by which it belongs purely to the reason" (Clausewitz 1943[1832]:I.I.28). Since we regard the concept of ethics in the Aristotelian way as a merely intellectual process of controlling instincts, we see from Clausewitz's description that war covers the whole scale from animal instincts to intellectual analysis, and it is the duty of the leadership to curb the blind passions to a certain degree. When we put Clausewitz's description in relation to our Proposition 1, it is no surprise that we achieve a difference between the macroscopic and the microscopic bodies, it is to be expected, but the interesting thing is that he seems to dismiss any intellectual process of any significance at all at the microscopic level. In Clausewitz's time, the general information on why a state should go to war was limited to a rather small group of people, and the information spread to the general troops was mostly aimed at keeping up morale.

When the author entered the Swedish military forces in 1967 as a conscript officer, the same day as the Arab-Israeli Six-Day War started, the general political situation was such that Sweden mobilized to the fourth level of the five-degree scale. Thus we were informed by the colonel about political, strategic and organizational aspects while the general information was given by the platoon leader. The author listened to both, and the general information was generally based on that: "We are prepared, we have a good organization and we can defend ourselves. So, lads, if things go for the worst, go out and fight; we are defending the right cause." In Clausewitz's time the general information was maybe not so comprehensive but just said, "We are prepared to give our lives for the king and the motherland. Kill the bastards". Furthermore, in 1967 we had a great amount of other information than the military one, given by the colonel or the platoon leader.

In our society, however, the broad information is to a minor degree analytic and to a higher degree emotional. That is, information in the media of our day is both abundant with respect to dimensions and quick with reaction to different events. We may then apply Hume's discussion of perception, where he claims that perceptions which create immediate relations to earlier experiences, particularly of a strong emotional character, are easier for the individual to notice and to order with respect to current information as well as to the memory of earlier experiences. This also seems to be in line with modern brain research, where the emotions are regarded as lighthouses to tell us the suitable route with respect to traditions, commitments, moral and other fundamental aspects which form our actions together with rational analysis.

That means that if we want to convey structural analytic information and are aware of such psycho-social conditions, we have to wrap it up in an emotional form which often is linked to ethical values. The more consequential aspects of an action are buried in ethical opinions, but since most of the conscious opinion-makers are aware of these aspects, we tend to land in a rather foggy ethical landscape where strong lighthouses are pointing in contradictory directions. The intellectual aspects seldom have any strong defender in the end, even if those who convey information would like to present it in its intellectual form.

Consequently, the intellectual discussion and analysis mostly concerns an audience who is prepared through education and who is actually personally involved with more aggregated affairs of the society. Thus the analytic information has by its very character a small audience.

So, then, we turn to the small group of people who should be able, adapted and responsible to make the intellectual analysis of warfare, welfare and stability. We remember then our earlier analysis of government, collective ethics and similar matters. But before we can do so, we have to regard the changing character of basic information to be conveyed, and since we start from Clausewitz's writings, one or two things have happened in conditions, methods and consequences of war which are of importance for the consequences for the aftermath and peace.

The lessons from Clausewitz

First of all, Clausewitz fought an ideological and national war. The latter can be seen as somewhat strange in the light of the fact that he was on his way to join the Austrian troops and later he actually joined the Russian troops. But that was logical with respect to his opposition against Napoleon's universal claims. Clausewitz's opposition towards Napoleon was based both on nationalistic reasons, as he was a Prussian citizen, and on ideological reasons, since he opposed Napoleon and the French revolutionary classless ideology. Clausewitz was born in the upper middle class but advanced socially through his talents as an officer and his marriage to Countess Maria Brühl, whose family was extremely influential and owned vast territories in eastern Germany, Poland, the Baltic states and also in Sweden. Maria and Carl (baptized Karl) belonged to the absolute top of the social elite. Maria, his wife, Mistress of the Robes to Her Royal Highness Princess Wilhelmina, was intellectually Carl's equal and helped him during all his work with his magnum opus, and at the end she organized and edited the book so Carl's ideological resistance against the vulgar usurper Napoleon was not particularly astonishing.

However, irrespective of social class motives, Clausewitz's resistance of Napoleon was also based on broader nationalistic and power balance motives, which to a great extent had been rather insignificant before the Napoleonic wars. He was also undoubtedly unique in incarnating genuine knowledge of war theory and practice with broader philosophical contemplations. It is said that he was a keen student of Immanuel Kant.

> *Clausewitz's definition* (I.I.2): "War therefore is an act of violence intended to compel our opponent to fulfil our will."

The Swedish edition of *Vom Kriege* (*Om Kriget*) is 670 pages, so there are many other learnings, but this single sentence is so simple, so basic and so important that it is almost always forgotten or not understood. However, Clausewitz starts with that and he refers to it again and again, so we shall look at the sentence more closely in Clausewitz's spirit.

First of all, we take a closer look at the words *our will*. The emanation of war cannot be a desire for war per se; it has to be related to conflicting goals between the involved states.[2]

That thought is essential and underlies the famous expression that war is a continuation of politics, but with other means. It also normally implies that it is not the enemy which shall be annihilated, but it is the means of resistance. Thus, as Clausewitz saw it, it is not the opponent state as such which is the target, but its means of resistance *with respect to* the goals of the war, and he says in I.I.24:

> We see, therefore, that War is not merely a political act, but also a real political instrument, a continuation of political commerce, a carrying out of the same by other means. All beyond this which is strictly peculiar to War relates

merely to the peculiar nature of the means which it uses. That the tendencies and views of policy shall not be incompatible with these means, the Art of War in general and the Commander in each particular case may demand, and this claim is truly not a trifling one. But however powerfully this may react on political views in particular cases, still it must always be regarded as only a modification of them; for the political view is the object, War is the means, and the means must always include the object in our conception.

Thus Clausewitz discusses wars between civilized countries, as he also repeats on several occasions, and he follows the ancient tradition of regarding the opponents as enemies without dehumanizing them, still regarding them as subjects and thus local and temporal final causes.

We have to keep this in mind since that thought may be questioned, as we saw for example when we discussed Robert Kaplan's attitude in his book *Why Leadership Demands a Pagan Ethics*.

Thus we cannot discuss war, particularly when we start from Clausewitz, without understanding this general assumption of his analysis. We are going to question this assumption, but that is just further emphasizing Clausewitz's greatness as an analyst.

Consequently, we must not commit the mistake of thinking that he meant an annihilation of the enemy; quite the contrary, he meant that wars should be strictly rational in the sense that they are subordinated to political goals and also that it is possible to win a war but lose the peace, of which the rather recent Iraqi war is an excellent example. But it also has deeper consequences. First, a war can be started when we have a reasonable chance to fulfil our political goals, and that means that the dimensionality of current possible warfare has to be scrutinized with utmost care. That will change over time and is also the reason why we speak of different generations of war. Second, the end of the war is not only due to the lucky or unlucky proceedings of the war but has to be examined with respect to the entire economic, social and cultural evolution; thus common political factors should always be the prime causes of ending a war.

Third, when starting a war or provoking an attack on a state, we must sooner or later return to a non–war situation, and in advance we have ask ourselves who we then have to talk with. That might be the same group of politicians as we started the war against, but the logic of the situation, the epistemic cycles at the start and the end of the war, are most probably different and thus the logic of diplomacy is completely changed.

Fourth, to start or provoke a war and then fight it will most probably be a heavy economic, social and cultural effort. Furthermore, it will affect the state's structural position in the global community, and such an aspect must be taken into consideration.[3]

The complexity of war in its internal and external effects is such that no leader of a civilized state should consider war but for extreme situations. Having said this, we must realize that those conflicts between states which most probably will occur must be possible to negotiate diplomatically, which means that the means of diplomacy must be constantly developed, as wars, according to the most current technology and socio-politico knowledge.

Let us take a small example on a less dramatic level but still rather serious. Sweden has been at peace for circa 200 years. After WWII, it has been regarded as a prosperous, stable and sleepy little country. Such things as water cannons to use for violent demonstrations were not even thinkable in Sweden. At the EU summit in 2001, things were a bit unstable and demonstrations were to be expected, but the current prime minister assured everyone that the police would have full control. The following demonstrations were indeed violent and turned into riots and meaningless destruction. The police were on one hand taken by surprise by the violence, and on the other hand they lacked relevant equipment to fight a mass of people, which implied that from pure self-defence and fear they opened sharp gunfire and people were wounded.

This is a classic example of bad planning; you must look upon such events as a staircase where the rioters may take a further step in escalation that must be followed by measures which are adequate but do not escalate the violence. Thus the "defending" side must never escalate an escalation from the attacking side but still use adequate means of defence, which implies that you must have a great variety of means at your disposal, which should be taken into consideration beforehand in planning the defence against violent riots. For civilized countries, riots may occur, but increasing escalation from the society can easily throw the whole thing out of control.

It is the same relation between using warfare and diplomacy. The untrained mind often reacts emotionally and vengefully, and in such a state, the sensitiveness of choosing adequate means is perhaps not the best.

You may of course have as a goal to exterminate the opponent like Cato, "*Ceterum censeo Carthaginem esse delendam*", but then we have defined the opponent as *Fides Punica* as we earlier discussed and are probably in for huge trouble. This was the case in WWII, since Hitler refused any negotiations irrespective of losses.[4]

So we need diplomatic means from what is called *frank discussions*, which means a big bust-up, to heavy economic and political sanctions. Even some military means can be considered, such as physical blockades and emptying the air territory, but that is obviously only under military superiority and total control of land border and air space. The richness of alternatives in between, though, is essential.

However, we must even with respect to diplomatic means, be careful. First of all, it is obvious that all kinds of repressive means vary in their effects due to the contextual composition; what is efficient at one occasion is not so at another. Furthermore, there are means which are damaging and may create, or might be utilized to create, strong adverse feelings which makes the means in question inefficient and sometimes even counterproductive. Generally, these are economic measures which hit large parts of the population and mainly ordinary and poor people. There is with respect to this kind of problem a development which we will later discuss.

So, as we see, the intellectual analysis based on Clausewitz implies what he later claims, namely that the supreme leadership in wars should not be entrusted to officers who have made their careers as brave, enterprising and experienced troop officers. Instead, the leaders should be those who on one hand can embrace the political, economic and social complexity of a war at the macroscopic level and also understand the necessity of determination, physical and mental courage and the ability to endure uncertainty, changes of luck and the terrible friction/inertia. In all, we need a military genius who combines the experience of a brave and skilled troop officer with the gifts and the ability of intellectual analysis of a philosopher, economist, political scientist and psychologist.

Consequently, when we discuss both diplomatic means and warfare, we have to be absolutely clear on what our goals are. Choosing the wrong means may put us in a worse situation. When we chose the classifications of Colonels Boyd and Williams with respect to generations of war, we are well aware that this classification is not undisputed, but it is one type of possible classification with respect to strategic shifts in how a military organization regards warfare in relation to technological, socio-politico, economic and cultural developments. We will use it but both enlarge it and modify their classification.

Two examples from Sweden[5]

We have said some words on the Westphalian Peace where Sweden was deeply involved. Let us finish this chapter on war with the choice of route of two Swedish kings, Gustavo II and Charles XII. Both were eminent field commanders, the latter much admired; Voltaire wrote a devout book titled *Charles XII*. They both stood in front of a decision of greatest importance for Sweden: Gustavo II in Leipzig in 1632 and Charles XII in Altranstädt, not far from Leipzig, in 1706. Gustavo II and his generals had crushed all the relevant troops of the emperor, the road to Wien was open and there seemed to be no obstacles to taking Wien. After a discussion with his advisor Axel Oxenstierna, he came out red in the face and, most probably against the advice of Oxenstierna, he decided to stick to his original goals and secure the control of vital areas in Northern Germany.

Charles XII reached a very lucrative peace with Poland and some princedoms in eastern Germany in Altranstädt, which fulfilled the main goals of his mission. But inspired by his success and the surprising victory over the Russians in the Battle of Narva in Estonia, he decided to clear things once and for all with the young Tsar Peter. He went for Russia and lost not only the battles, mainly due to long service and support lines, but also everything which had earlier been achieved by him and also by Gustavo II.

Gustavo II understood war; Charles XII at best understood how to fight. Gustavo II went to war in the spirit of Clausewitz's analysis, while Charles XII was more in the line of President Theodore Roosevelt's saying, according to Robert Kaplan, which we quoted in Chapter 7.

Four generations of war

To simplify we start from the classification given by Wikipedia.

First generation: The original analysis by William S. Lind (2004) starts with the Westphalian Peace in 1648, thus ending the Thirty Years' War in Europe. The emphasis in this era was on troops in lines and columns, organized to endure long marches and to quickly form lines for gunfire and for bayonet fights. The increasing improvement of cannons and mortars was mainly for siege, but during the Thirty Years' War, cannons were used in a higher degree in the beginning of the battles in order to disturb the deployment of enemy troops. This led to tactical changes of the role of the cavalry.

Generally, the Thirty Years' War in Europe led to the victory of the two most centralized states, France and Sweden, which both had centralized governments and centralized war leadership and thus could more efficiently provide decisions and implementation of necessary resources.

Second generation: The increased efficiency of firepower of different kinds made the old reliance on army troops in columns and lines supported by cavalry obsolete. There was a further development of fire enlarged to indirect targets such as service areas and deployment areas, since the firing range of the cannon and mortars increased, as did the use of aircrafts and bombing. The development of armoured vehicles was decisive for the design of the battles. These inventions and improvements of aircrafts, armoured vehicles, bombs and cannons emphasized the necessity of total mobilization of a country with respect to both military education and training in order to have coherent cooperation between the different branches of the military organization, but also a mobilization of the civilian society with respect to production and infrastructure. Thus the importance of national identity became necessary for total mobilization.

Third generation: The mechanization of troops was first utilized by the Germans in WWII, when they used armoured troops to make a breach which then was used to spread behind the enemy troops. One of the first on the Allied side to realize this tactics was actually the French colonel and later general Charles de Gaulle, but unfortunately he and his ideas were dismissed as a sort of phantasy by military theorists. WWII became a total war where actions were directed towards the civilian population in order to break support lines, the common determination of resistance and reducing living standard. It was at the same time an ideological war, containing Cato's radical form of *Fides Punica* as well as dehumanizations. In one sense it was a peak of the nationalistic forces and gave birth to internationalism. In the Vietnam War, the US with conventional forces met a guerrilla army which was difficult to separate from the ordinary villagers; thus the war tended to look like a war against civilians. This was the key factor why the United States' armed forces, superior to the North Vietnamese forces and the South Vietnamese guerrillas, still had to withdraw since the legitimacy of US warfare disappeared. This war was perhaps the first war where the home press of the USA was divided in its positions with respect to the war and journalism was thus relatively independent.

Fourth generation: In Wikipedia there is a list of elements occurring in fourth-generation warfare and which is relatively comprehensive:

1   Are complex and long-term
2   Terrorism (tactic)
3   A non-national or transnational base – highly decentralized
4   A direct attack on the enemy's culture, including genocidal acts against civilians
5   Highly sophisticated psychological warfare, especially through media manipulation and lawfare
6   All available pressures are used – political, economic, social and military
7   Occurs in low intensity conflict, involving actors from all networks
8   Non-combatants are tactical dilemmas
9   Lack of hierarchy
10   Small in size, spread out network of communication and financial support
11   Use of insurgency tactics as subversion, terrorism and guerrilla tactics.[6]

With respect to the fifth and sixth points, we are noticing the increased and systematic use of rape of women as a means to destroy cultural patterns of families. The rapes create a link from microscopic actions to widespread macroscopic effects due to the fact that most cultural expressions start with the family, and thus rape creates anomie, fears and gender hostility. The tactic of raping women as an act of war is not only dehumanizing; it destroys socio-cultural links within a population and is a savage expression for a most primitive animalism.

Nations, in the meaning of social organizations of people, have little or no information of who are the parties of such a war. The very executors of the warfare have often an agenda of their own, which is used by other powers since it is at least temporary; it is parallel to their own agenda. An example is the Taliban and Al Qaeda, which have been supported by both of the superpowers at different periods when the respective power saw some parallelism.

Generally, however, it has been learnt by military strategists that being dependent on such local and reginal groups can open Pandora's box. Furthermore, allying with a regional or local group without deep-going knowledge of regional and local structures is, as we have seen in the latest decades, risky since it will reduce clarity of the goals of the war. The Iraqi war is a brilliant example of a biased and insufficiently contemplated war, which gave the result that the attacking countries won the battles but lost the peace.

Is there a fifth generation of warfare?

First of all, wars today consist of elements from the second to the fourth generations, mostly of course from the fourth; however, many and hopefully most military strategists and responsible politicians have learnt the unpredictability of actively directly or indirectly engage in wars like we exemplify in fourth-generation warfare.

If we look around today, we can see a system, a society of nations who are intertwined in commercial, legal, infrastructural and social networks which are almost impossible to get an overview of. Nobody can identify sensitive areas where structures are destabilized, and nobody can forecast structural break-downs. The reason for this is that structural differences, sensitive structural areas and dimensions are no longer linked to national borders. It is as probable that social and economic unease strikes a country with devastating social, economic and political effects as that an international society of states is hit by structural breakdowns.

A feature of the fifth generation of warfare is that general aggressiveness is not smaller now than it has been, and hatred between people, groups and classes seems to increase. However, this has more to do with the effects of what we tried to picture in Figure 5.2 than with intellectually defined political goals of a nation. Thus, we have come to a situation where the cohesion of the nations is deteriorating and seems not particularly more stable than the societies of nations. It is a parallel to Cécile Laborde's conclusion that the cultural differences within France were bigger than those between France and other Western European countries.

Superficially seen, nationalism seems to increase, but it seems like nationalism is more a way to save a kind of identity in the surrounding society. Discussions with refugees often reveal a sort of nationalism with respect to their home country as it was, but those who succeed in becoming integrated are more focussed on their new home country and reveal a kind of new nationalism based on stability and the possibility of building new social networks. But those groups who do not succeed in integrating often form rootless asocial groups or even join xenophobic groups of the new country, which seems a bit contradictory.

Thus nationalism, religions, ideologies and group idiosyncrasies become a means of unification but not a cause of radicalization and/or anomie.

But where do we have the war factor? Philip Bobbitt mentioned in a quote earlier about a nation with no nuclear arms, that it could in the event of a new government buy nuclear arms on the black market. I come back to the Norwegian mass murderer Breivik and the 16-year-old kid who created chaos among Swedish banks. These two were definitely "under the radar" of the society, and I have difficulties in seeing that a democracy could develop a supervision system that takes such events/persons into consideration. All systems are either dependent on persons or on technology; the latter is deterministic and thus rather simple to get around, while the former is suitable with respect to complex information, but then we are thrown back into structural complexities.

Thus the demarcation lines between peace and war today seem to not follow the border of nations but cut right through the nations in hostilities between radicalized subgroups and the ordered society. Furthermore, the complexity of interactions intrinsic to both the international and the national systems is such that a war between nations is almost impossible to forecast with respect to its structural effects. Moreover, the complexity is such that small groups and even individuals who are radicalized and/or feel excluded from the ordinary society may commit severe damage to the central functions of the society. Supervision and control are traditional means, but intrinsic ethics and inclusion in the social network are probably more efficient. Another factor is the almost conscious fragmentation of the society we have today, when the unsound concentration of wealth and incomes has to be changed into a welfare policy focussing on developing individual abilities to participate in social processes.

So, who do we declare war on, and how do we defend a society for ordinary people who just want to live a decent life? But in defending such values, what about ethics, how are the problems created and how are the problems solved? We can suspect that Robert Kaplan's recipe for pagan ethics, in his definition, may create more problems than it solves. In fact, this is the very problem of today. For those who realize the complexities of the world, a traditional war between states is an anomaly since it is also self-destruction, but at the same time we illustrated the increasing gaps in understanding this in Figure 5.2. Persons who desire power per se, which is more the insignia of power than the responsibilities of power, may rise to power by painting a rosy picture of the future and/or riding on waves of fear and hatred, and they may become an enormous threat to the whole world. There is no defence against this except what Kant prescribes in his paper on enlightenment and personal maturity, combined with Otanes' prescription of transparency and freedom of speech.

Notes

1 All quotes from Clausewitz are taken from www.gutenberg.org/files/1946/1946-h/1946-h.html
   The book is organized in eight books, and for each book chapters are enumerated from I to the final chapter of the book, so we will refer to book and chapter. For the first chapters, the subparts are also enumerated, which we will use since most of our quotes are from Book I, chapter I.
2 We will use the word *states* for simplicity's sake, and it will work in many cases. Currently, the state concept is far too simplistic, and then when it is necessary we will discuss it closer.
3 With *global*, we do not mean global in the current use but the collection of states which are seen as important for the future.
4 To understand the situation at the end of WWII, the German historian Joachim Fest (2004) gives an excellent description in *Inside Hitler's Bunker: The Last Days of the Third Reich*, Macmillan, London and Oxford.
5 The parts concerning the Thirty Years' War are to a large degree from the monumental work by Nils Ahnlund (1940) on the Swedish State Chancellor Axel Oxenstierna, who was King Gustav's closest and virtually only real trustworthy advisor.
6 https://en.wikipedia.org/wiki/Fourth-generation_warfare

Bibliography

Ahnlund, N., (1940). *Axel Oxenstierna*, P.A. Norstedt and Söner Förlag, Stockholm.
Clausewitz, C., (1943[1832]). *On War*, (Jolles translation), available at internet www.clausewitz.com/readings/OnWar1873/BK1ch01.html#a
Lind, W.S., (2004). Understanding the Fourth Generation War, *Military Review*, available at internet www.au.af.mil/au/awc/awcgate/milreview/lind.pdf
Kaplan, R.D., (2002). *Warrior Politics*, Random House, New York.

Conclusions and epilogue

We started this book as a consequence of our earlier studies, which led to the two propositions regarding the barter economy saying that there are no a priori logical links in economics between the microscopic and macroscopic levels. Furthermore, when using money values as representatives of commodities and actions, we lose all logical links to the real economy, other than that which comes from social inertia.

Thus the surrounding economic system in the real world cannot be proved to have any intrinsic stability per se. Any stability originates in socio-economic and political stability.

This is our starting point for including ethics in our discussions and also the concept of power. We noted that Adam Smith was already well aware of power as interlinked with political and economic stability:

> Civil government supposes a certain subordination. But as the necessity of civil government gradually grows up with the acquisition of valuable property, so principal causes which naturally introduce subordination gradually grow up with the growth of that valuable property.
>
> (Smith 1952[1776]:309)

Thus, at variance with the mainstream economic theory and particularly the neoclassical theory, Adam Smith recognizes the necessity of power. But then we arrive almost directly at the concept of ethics.

Conclusions

Not ethics in a metaphysical form, but ethics in the Aristotelian form, namely that ethics is an independent ability intrinsic in the socialization process, and the specific form originates in this process. This ability makes the individual rational in searching for the ultimate good in the social context.

Thus ethics is a part of rational behaviour and makes the individual able to grasp both the effects of the other individuals' actions as well as the macroscopic consequences. With respect to economic theory, we can say that it is a counterpart to Arrow's Impossibility Theorem.

The fundamental argument underlying this discussion is that *the human being is to be seen as a subject and thus a final cause.*

However, interpreting ethics in this way leads to a discussion of how the individual apprehends the social context. The economic theory suggests in the neoclassical axiomatic structure as well as in general modelling that the economic reality is an objective organism perceived and comprehended by all agents. This follows from the assumption that the microscopic and macroscopic levels are logically interrelated due to the underlying assumption that agents as well as marketable items are to be seen as atomic variables, which implies that no structural relationships whatsoever exist in the economic system. Consequently, when we reject this, economic measures as well as economic actions will have asymmetric effects in the society. Subsequently, since the economic system is just a social subsystem, this will trigger social effects.

We thus come to a conclusion that economic development resulting in structural changes will have social effects which are asymmetric and furthermore that almost all collective actions will also have asymmetric effects. But this means that ethics, in the Aristotelian meaning, is necessary to obtain a "good" society on both the microscopic level and the macroscopic level. Unfortunately, our derived propositions imply that ethics at the microscopic level will by necessity be different from ethics at the macroscopic level. Thus, we may have contradictions due to the fact that humans are subjects and thus final causes.

Ethical differences in judgements of events and developments depend only on differences in the basic comprehension of ethical behaviour, but they might be due to different comprehension of the exogenous events. We thus include in the analysis of the rationality of the individual that the individual is rational with respect to the apprehended epistemic cycle, which means the contextual apprehension given the specific emotional and social dispositions of the individual.

Thus, ethical conflicts might appear as individual and collective actions affect other individuals asymmetrically.

When it comes to collective organisms like nations, we discuss different principles of governments, particularly monarchy, oligarchy and democracy, and we find that the "good" society from the collective point of view is due to the very person/persons in the two first government forms. Democracy, given transparency and free speech, is the only government form where the ruled can control the ruler, which implies that it is the only system which can give legitimacy to the ruler without using metaphysical arguments.

However, we then arrive at the question of how to find a kind of social cohesion in a collective without excluding individuals, as in the principle of Blood and Soil, or when it concerns nations, using the *Fides Punica* principle to enhance nationalism with respect to foreign threats, and furthermore to enhance the national identity by declaring other nations to be morally, intellectually and culturally inferior. We here discuss the two principles *ius soli* and *ius sanguinis*.

The ultimate conflicts between nations are wars. Wars can be seen as a breakdown of ethics, but claiming that individuals are subjects and final causes and furthermore that individuals form the nations, we might end up in war as the ultimate political means, following Clausewitz's analysis. However, wars change with technology but also due to social and cultural changes. The globalization process has implied a very complex international interaction between individuals, organizations and states which makes the decisions of the nations less significant. Thus, the complexity of interactions intrinsic to the international as well as the national systems is such that a war between nations is almost impossible to forecast with respect to its structural effects. The very problem of today is that for those who realize the complexities of the world, a traditional war between states is an anomaly since that is also self-destruction, not perhaps in a military sense but with respect to economic, social and cultural structures. But for persons who desire power per se, it is more the insignia of power than the responsibilities of power. Such persons may rise to power by painting rosy pictures of the future and/or riding on waves of fear and hatred and may become an enormous threat to the whole world. There is no defence against this except what Kant prescribes in his paper on enlightenment and personal maturity, combined with Otanes' prescription of transparency and freedom of speech.

The fundamental question in the book, however, is whether there exists some kind of ethical principle which is the same for both the individual level and for the collective(s). We have found that, through all complexities and contradictions, the absolute baseline ethics to be followed is this:

> Since human beings are subjects to be seen as final causes, the worst ethical crime is to deprive the human being of its subjectness and of its rights to be a final cause.

This means that individuals and collectives dehumanizing people are ethically wrong.

Furthermore, human subordination to collective norm systems must imply that the only collective form, which does not need a metaphysical legitimation, is democracy given transparency and free speech, and that is the only system where the rulers can be controlled by the ruled.

Epilogue

Our analysis has touched on metaphysics quite naturally, since metaphysical questions are important in forming norm systems and social cohesion. Our conclusions, however, are to be applied within the physical world, open to logical analysis.

But there are two important metaphysical concepts hovering beneath our analysis and which are fundamental for all human life: forgiveness and reconciliation.[1]

Forgiveness is a concept which is purely metaphysical. It can only be based in hopes and dreams of a future relationship. The basic condition for forgiveness is that the one who asks for forgiveness gets the answer "No." The one who asks for forgiveness has no rights to expect anything but no. How can a man who has abused a child expect anything but no? How can one who has killed for benefits, pleasure, a sense of superiority ever expect anything but no?

Why should the abused person, the family of those who have been killed, ever forgive the perpetrator(s)? There is no rational reason. Why should we ever forgive people who dehumanize ourselves? There is no rational reason.

We return to the myth of Chapter 1. With no forgiveness, there is no rest for the reflective mind; there is no future but in pain, agony and fear. Thus forgiveness concerns the future; a future built on reconciliation and trust. Paul Ricoeur (2004) means that forgiveness belongs to the same category of concepts as hope and song of praise, but on the other hand Desmond Tutu (2015) means that it does not mean forgetting; whatever has been done shall never be repeated.

Thus, the party who is seeking forgiveness is the one who must act in such a way that the forgiving party trusts the will, and for the future, is prepared to act in such a way that the trust is confirmed. Then reconciliation is possible, and then we can together participate in the creation of the new earth.

Note

1 We refer here to Ricoeur, Paul, (2004). *Memory, History, Forgetting*, University of Chicago Press, Chicago; Tutu, Desmond, (2015). *The Book of Forgiving: The Fourfold Path for Healing Ourselves and Our World*, HarperOne, San Francisco.

Bibliography

Ahnlund, N., (1940). *Axel Oxenstierna*, P.A. Norstedt and Söner Förlag, Stockholm.

Alexandroff, P., (1961). *Elementary Concepts of Topology*, Dover Publications, New York.

Allais, M., (1953). Le comportement de l'homme rationel devant le risque: Critique des postulates et axiomes de l'ecole amricaine, *Econometrica*, Vol. 21, pp. 503–546.

Amoroso, L., (1938). Vilfredo Pareto, *Econometrica*, Vol. 6, No. 1.

Andersson, Å., (1975). *Barnmiljö och samhällsekonomi* (Childhood Conditions and Economics), Socialdepartementet (Ministry of Social Affairs), Ds S 1975:11, Stockholm.

Aquinas, T., St., (1998[1271]). What makes actions good or bad? *Summa Theologiæ*, Vol. 1–2, pp. 18–20. In *Selected Writings* (pp. 565–611), Penguin Classics, London.

Arendt, H., (1996[1963]). *Den banala ondskan* (A Report on the Banality of Evil), Daidalos, Göteborg.

Aristotle (1990 [original around 334–324 BC]). Biological Treatises Bno. 486a–789b. In *The Works of Aristotle Vol. II*, Encyclopædia Britannica, Inc., Chicago and London.

Aristotle, (1990 [original around 334–324 BC]). On the Soul Bno. 402ª–435ª. In *The Works of Aristotle Vol. I*, Encyclopædia Britannica, Inc., Chicago and London.

Aristotle, (1990 [original around 334–324 BC]). Metaphysics Bno. 980a–1093b. In *The Works of Aristotle Vol. I*, Encyclopædia Britannica, Inc., Chicago and London.

Aristotle, (1990 [original around 334–324 BC]). Nicomachean Ethics Bno. 1094ª–1179ª. In *The Works of Aristotle Vol. II*, Encyclopædia Britannica, Inc., Chicago and London.

Aristotle, (1990 [original around 334–324 BC]). Politics Bno. 1252ª–1341ᵇ. In *The Works of Aristotle Vol. II* (p. 452), Encyclopædia Britannica, Inc., Chicago and London, Bno. 1258ᵇ.

Arrow, K.J., (1950). A Difficulty in the Concept of Social Welfare, *The Journal of Political Economy*, Vol. 58, No. 4, pp. 328–346.

Arrow, K.J., (1963). Uncertainty and the Welfare Economics of Medical Care, *The American Economic Review*, Vol. 53, No. 5.

Arrow, K.J. and Hahn, F.H., (1971). *General Competitive Analysis*, Holden Day Inc., San Francisco.

Asplund, J., (1967). *Om Mättnadsprocesser* (Saturation Processes), Argos Förlag AB, Uppsala.

Asplund, J., (1991). *Essä om Gemeinschaft och Gesellschaft*, Bokförlaget Korpen, Gothenburg.

Basu, S. and Kimball, M.S., (1997). *Cyclical Productivity with Unobserved Input Variation*, National Bureau of Economic Research, Working Paper 5915.

Becker, G.S., (1976). *A New Economic Approach of Human Behaviour*, University of Chicago Press, Chicago.

Benabud, A., (1957). Psychopathological Aspects of the Cannabis Situation in Morocco, *Bulletin on Narcotics*, Vol. 9, pp. 1–16.

Bergson, H., (1912). *Tiden och den fria viljan* (Time and the Free Will), Wahlström and Widstrand, Stockholm.

Bessette J.M., and Faget, J., (2012). *Approces sociologiques de la delinquance*, available at internet www.leconflit.com/article-approches-sociologiques-de-la-delinquance-2-106819543.html

Bobbitt, P., (2002). *The Shield of Achilles: War, Peace and the Course of History*, Allen Lane The Penguin Press, London.

Braudel, F., (1992[1979]). *Civilization and Capitalism 15th–18th Century, Vol. II: The Wheels of Commerce*, University of California Press, Berkeley, LA and Los Angeles.

Broberg, G., (1995). *Statlig rasforskning: En historik över rasbiologiska institutet* (Public Racial Research: An Historical Exposé of the Institute for Race Biology). Ugglan 4, 2nd ed., Lund Studies in the History of Science and Ideas.

Brody, T., (1994). *The Philosophy Behind Physics*, Springer Verlag, Berlin, Heidelberg, and New York.

Carr, J.D., (1950). *The Bride of Newgate*, Harper and Brothers, New York.

Churchill, W.S., (1902). *The River War*, The Project Gutenberg EBook of The River War by Winston S. Churchill, available at internet https://www.gutenberg.org/files/4943/4943-h/4943-h.htm

Clausewitz, C., (1943[1832]). *On War*, (Jolles translation), available at internet www.clausewitz.com/readings/OnWar1873/BK1ch01.html#a

Cooper, D., (2001). *Talleyrand*, Grove Press, New York.

Damasio, A., (2004). *Looking for Spinoza: Joy, Sorrow and the Feeling Brain*, Vintage, London.

Debreu, G., (1987[1959]). *Theory of Value*, Wiley, New York.

Debreu, G., (1982). Existence of general equilibrium. In K. J. Arrow and M.D. Intrilligator (eds.), *Handbook of Mathematical Economics, Vol. 2*. North-Holland Publishing Company, Amsterdam and New York.

DeLong, H., (1991). *A Refutation of Arrow's Theorem*, University Press of America, Lanham, New York, and London.

Diemer, A., (2005, May). *David Hume et les économistes français*, Hermès, Université de Reims, pp. 1–27.

Di Lampedusa, G.T., (1960[1959]). *Leoparden* (Il Gattopardo), Bonniers, Stockholm.

Douglas, R., (1995). Stochastically branching spacetime topology. In S. Savitt (ed.), *Time's Arrow Today: Recent Physical and Philosophical Work on the Direction of Time* (pp. 173–188), Cambridge University Press, Cambridge.

Eco, U., (1995). *The Search for the Perfect Language*, Fontana Press, London.

Eco, U., (2000). *Kant and the Platypus*, Vintage, London.

Einstein, A., (1964[1945]). *Mozart: Människan och verket*, Bokförlaget Aldus/Bonniers, Stockholm.

Ekstedt, H., (2013). *Money in Economic Theory*, Routledge, London and New York.

Ekstedt, H., (2015). *Money, Valuation and Growth*, Routledge, London and New York.

Ekstedt, H. and Fusari, A., (2010). *Economic Theory and Social Change Problems and Revisions*, Routledge, London and New York.

Ekstedt, H. and Larsson, T., (2008). *Growth, Productivity and Democracy in an Ageing Society*. The Swedish Case. Paper presented at the EAEPE International Conference in Porto.

Ekstedt, H. and Westberg, L., (1991). *Dynamic Models for the Interrelations of Real and Financial Growth*, Chapman and Hall, London and New York.

Elias, N., (1991). *The Civilizing Process, Vol. I: The History of Manners* (Sedernas Historia), Atlantis and Stockholm.

Engström, A., (1965[1901]). *En Bok*, Albert Bonniers Förlag, Stockholm.

Fest, J., (2002). *Inside Hitler's Bunker: The Last Days of the Third Reich*, Macmillan, Basingstoke and Oxford.

Foucault, M., (1983). *Styrandet av sig själv och andra* (Le Gouvernement de soi et des autres) Lectures at Collège de France 1982–1983. Here Lecture January 5th, 1983 is used.

Fusari, A., (2014). *Methodological Misconceptions in the Social Sciences: Rethinking Social Thought and Social Processes*, Springer, Dordrecht, Heidelberg, New York, and London.

Georgescu-Roegen, N., (1971). *The Entropy Law and the Economic Process*, Harvard University Press, Cambridge, MA.

Gibbon, E., (1786). *The History of the Decline and Fall of the Roman Empire*, Vol. 2, Basil, Printed for J.J. Tourneisen, pp. 145–147.

Grice-Hutchinson, M., (1952). *The School of Salamanca*, Clarendon Press, Oxford.

Gruen, E.S., (2011). *Rethinking the Other in Antiquity*, Princeton University Press, Princeton, NJ, and Oxford.

Hausman, D.M., (2012). *Preference, Value, Choice, and Welfare*, Cambridge University Press, Cambridge and New York.

Herodotus: The History of Herodotus. Trans. George Rawlinson. The English translation is provided by The Internet Classics Archive, available at internet http://classics.mit.edu//Herodotus/history.html

Hildesheimer, W., (1980[1977]). *Mozart*, P.A. Norstedt & Söners Förlag, Stockholm.

Hirsch, A., (2018). I've Had Enough of White People Who Try to Deny My Experience, *The Guardian*, January 16th.

Hobbes, T., (1985[1651]). *Leviathan*, Penguin Books, London.

Hume, D.A., (1770[1752]). *Essays and Treatises on Several Subjects, Vol. II: Containing Essays, Moral, Political, and Litterary*, Printed for T. Cadell (successor of Mr. Millar) in the Strand; and A. Kincaid and A. Donaldson, at Edinburgh.

Hume, D.A., (2002[1740]). *A Treatise of Human Nature*, Oxford University Press, Oxford.

Jevons, W.S., (1888[1871]). *The Theory of Political Economy*, Macmillan & Co., London, available at internet www.econlib.org/library/YPDBooks/Jevons/jvnPE3.html#

Kalecki, M., (1944). Professor Pigou on the "Classical Stationary State": A comment, *Economic Journal*, Vol. 54, No. 213, pp. 131–132.

Kant, I., (1784). *What Is Enlightenment* (Beantworten der Frage: Was ist Aufklärung), English translation available at internet www.artofthetheory.com/what-is-enlightenment_immanuel-kant/

Kant, I., (1933). *Critique of Pure Reason*, Macmillan Press Ltd, Houndsmills, Basingstoke, and London.

Kant, I., (2007[1795]). Fundamental Principles of the Metaphysics of Morals. In *Great Books of the Western World*, Encyclopædia Britannica, Chicago and London.

Kaplan, R.D., (2002). *Warrior Politics*, Random House, New York.

Keynes, J.M., (1920). *The Economic Consequences of the Peace*, Macmillan & Co., Ltd, London.

Keynes, J.M., (1938). Letter to Roy Harrod 10th of July, Collected Works of Keynes, available at internet http://economia.unipv.it/harrod/edition/editionstuff/rfh.34a.htm

Keynes, J.M., (1962[1921]). *A Treatise on Probability*, Harper & Row Publishers, New York.

Koestler, A., (1970). *The Act of Creation*, Richard Clay Ltd, Bungay, Suffolk.

Laborde, C., (2001). The Culture(s) of the Republic: Nationalism and Multiculturalism in French Republican Thought, *Political Theory*, Vol. 29, No 5, October, pp. 708–727.

Laidler, D., (1984). Misconceptions about the Real-Bills Doctrine: A Comment (The Real-Bills Doctrine versus the Quantity Theory: A Reconsideration), *Journal of Political Economy, University of Chicago Press*, Vol. 92, No. 1, February, pp. 149–155.

Lind, W.S., (2004). Understanding the Fourth Generation War, *Military Review*, available at internet www.au.af.mil/au/awc/awcgate/milreview/lind.pdf

Lundquist, G., (1970). *Alkoholberoende och alkoholsjukdomar*, Almqvist & Wicksell, Stockholm.

Machiavelli, N., (1971[1517]). *Fursten* (The Prince), Tidens Förlag, Stockholm.

Machiavelli, N., (1983[circa 1524]). *The Discourses*, Penguin Books, London.

Makarov, V.L. and Rubinov, A.M., (1977). *Economic Dynamics and Equilibria*, Springer Verlag, Heidelberg and Berlin.

Marks, S.R., (1974). Durkheim's Theory of Anomie, *American Journal of Sociology*, Vol. 80, No. 2, pp. 329–363.

Merton, R.K., (1938). Social Structure and Anomie, *American Sociological Review*, Vol. 3, No. 5, October, pp. 672–682.

Mill, J.S., (1990[1863]). Utilitarianism. In *Great Books of the Western World No. 40*, Encyclopædia Britannica, Inc., Chicago, London, New Delhi, Paris, Seoul, Taipei, and Tokyo.

Minkowski, H., (1909). *Raum und Zeit* (Space and Time). Vortrag, gehalten auf der 80. Natur-Forscher-Versammlung zu Köln am 21. September 1908, Druck und Verlag von B.G.Teubner, Leipzig und Berlin, available at internet https://de.wikisource.org/wiki/Raum_und_Zeit_(Minkowski)

Moore, G.E., (1993[1903]). *Principia Ethica*, Cambridge University Press, Cambridge.

Myrdal, A. and Myrdal, G., (1935). *Kris i befolkningsfrågan* (Crises in the Population Question), Bonniers, Stockholm.

Myrdal, G., (1942). *An American Dilemma: The Negro Problem and Modern Democracy*, available at internet https://archive.org/stream/AmericanDilemmaTheNegroProblemAndModernDemocracy/AmericanDelemmaVersion2_djvu.txt

Navarro, L. and Soto, R., (2006). Procyclical Productivity in Manufacturing, *Cuadernos de Economia*, Vol. 43, Mayo, pp. 193–220.

Newton, I., (2010[1688]). *The Principia: Mathematical Principles of Natural Philosophy*, Snowball Publishing, available at internet www.snowballpublishicng.com

Pascal, B., (2007[1670]). *Pensées*, Encyclopædia Britannica, Inc., Chicago and London.

Pigou, A.C., (1943). The Classical Stationary State, *Economic Journal*, Vol. 53, No. 212, pp. 343–351.

Reichenbach, H., (1938). *Experience and Prediction*, University of Chicago Press, Chicago.

Reichenbach, H., (1991[1956]). *The Direction of Time*, University of California Press, Berkeley, LA, and Oxford.

Russell, B., (1948). *Human Knowledge: Its Scope and Limits*, George Allen and Unwin Ltd, London.

Russell, B., (1992[1903]). *The Principles of Mathematics*, Routledge, London.

Russell, B., (1996[1946]). *History of Western Philosophy*, Routledge, London.

Russell, B., (2007[1956]). *Logic and Knowledge*, Spokesman, Nottingham.

Samuelson, A.P., (1968). What Classical and Neoclassical Monetary Theory Really Was, *Canadian Journal of Economics*, Vol. 1, No. 1, pp. 1–15, and *Collected Scientific Papers*, 1972, Vol. 3, pp. 529–543.

Sargent, T.J. and Wallace, N., (1982). The Real-Bills Doctrine versus the Quantity Theory: A Reconsideration, *The Journal of Political Economy*, Vol. 90, No. 6, pp. 1212–1236.

Say, J.B., (1834[1803]). *A Treatise on Political Economy; or the Production, Distribution, and Consumption of Wealth*. Grigg & Elliot, 9, North Fourth Street, Philadelphia.

Sen, A., (2002). *Rationality and Freedom*, The Belknap Press, Cambridge, MA, and London.

Smith, A., (1952[1776]). *An Inquiry into the Nature and Causes of the Wealth of Nations*, Encyclopedia Britannica Inc., Chicago, London, and Toronto.

Sproul, M.F., (2000). *Three False Critiques of the Real Bills Doctrine*, Department of Economics, California State University, Northridge, available at internet www.csun.edu/~hceco008/critique.htm

Stigler, G.T. and Becker, G.S., (1977). De Gustibus Non Est Disputandum, *American Economic Review*, Vol. 67, No. 2, pp. 76–90.

Stirk, P.M.R., (2010). Multiculturalism and the concept of the state. In Maria Dimova-Cookson and Peter M.R. Stirk (eds.), *Multiculturalism and Moral Conflict*, Routledge, London and New York.

Sy, I., (2013). The Subjective Approach as a Tool for Understanding Poverty: The Case of Senegal, *Procedia Economics and Finance*, Vol. 5, pp. 336–345.

Tarski, A., (1983[1955]). *Logic, Semantic, Metamathematics*, Hackett Publishing Company, Indianapolis.

Theil, H., (1967). *Economics and Information Theory*, North-Holland, Amsterdam.

Thom, R., (1975). *Structural Stability and Morphogenesis: An Outline of a General Theory of Models*, Addison-Wesley, New York.

Thomas, K., (1988[1983]). *Människan och Naturen* (Man and the Natural World), Ordfronts Förlag, Stockholm (Translated from English).

Thompson, D.W., (1992[1942]). *On Growth and Form*, Cambridge University Press, Cambridge.

Thornton, H., (1939[1802]). *An Enquiry into the Nature and Effects of the Paper Credit of Great Britain*, George Allen & Unwin, London, available at internet http://oll.libertyfund.org/index.php?option=com_staticxt&staticfile=show.php%3Ftitle=2041&layout=html

Thucydides, (1978[408 BC]). *Kriget mellan Sparta och Athen II* (History of the Peloponnesian War), Forum, Uddevalla.

Unruh, W., (1995). *Time, Gravity and Quantum Mechanics: In Times Arrow Today: Recent Physical and Philosophical Work on the Direction of Time*. Ed. Steven F. Savitt, Cambridge University Press, Cambridge.

Varian, H., (2006). *Intermediate Microeconomics: A Modern Approach: 7th Edition, International Student Edition*. W.W. Norton, New York and London.

Weissein, E.W., (2000). *CRC Concise Encyclopedia of Mathematics*, Chapman and Hall/CRC, London.

Wicksell, K., (1936[1893]). *Interest and Prices*, Macmillan and Co. Ltd., London.

Williams, Z., (2017). Irony Used to Define the English: In Brexit Britain, It's Self-Importance, *The Guardian*, October 30th.

Wittgenstein, L., (1974[1921]). *Tractatus Logico-Philosophicus*, Routledge and Kegan Paul, London.

Index

For Product Safety Concerns and Information please contact our EU
representative GPSR@taylorandfrancis.com
Taylor & Francis Verlag GmbH, Kaufingerstraße 24, 80331 München, Germany